Hexagonal Variations
Diversity, Plurality and Reinvention
in Contemporary France

FAUX TITRE

359

Etudes de langue et littérature françaises
publiées sous la direction de

Keith Busby, †M.J. Freeman,
Sjef Houppermans et Paul Pelckmans

Hexagonal Variations
Diversity, Plurality and Reinvention in Contemporary France

Edited by
Jo McCormack, Murray Pratt, and Alistair Rolls

AMSTERDAM - NEW YORK, NY 2011

Cover image: 'Winter Satellite View, Charles de Gaulle Airport' and 'Salvia Bed, France Garden, Kunming', both by Murray Pratt, and an untitled photograph by Keith B. Herbert. The photographs of plural Paris in Katherine Gantz's chapter are also reproduced here courtesy of Keith B. Herbert.

Cover design: Pier Post.

ISBN: 978-90-420-3245-3
E-Book ISBN: 978-90-420-3246-0
© Editions Rodopi B.V., Amsterdam - New York, NY 2011
Printed in The Netherlands

Table of Contents

Acknowledgements

This volume has been a collaborative enterprise from the outset. From its conception as a project that first shaped the XXth annual conference of the Australian Society for French Studies (ASFS), 'La France au pluriel' (University of Technology, Sydney, 2007), later informed the continuing research of the editors and contributors, and finally resulted in the completed collection of essays, many people have been involved, and without them, the journey would have been more onerous, and significantly less enjoyable. The editors therefore wish to thank and acknowledge all those whose insights and dedication contributed to the mapping of hexagonal France. In particular, we wish to record our gratitude to those who helped plan and organise the initial conference and whose enthusiasm has carried the project along ever since: Angela Giovanangeli, Kiran Grewal, Finola Methven and Marie-Laure Vuaille-Barcan. We also acknowledge the support of the Australian Society for French Studies, and of the University of Newcastle (New South Wales) and the University of Technology, Sydney, in particular Stephanie Hemelryk Donald, David Goodman, Lyn Shoemark and all those who made the late, lamented Institute for International Studies (IIS) a stimulating and supportive environment for all three of the editors.

In addition to colleagues from their former and current workplaces (Alistair has continued to enjoy the support of the University of Newcastle) Jo and Murray also wish to thank colleagues from their current institutions, the University of Sunderland and Nottingham Trent University respectively, and all four of the in-stitutions named above for providing conditions that have enabled them to complete the project.

The collection itself owes a great deal to the dialogues, conversations and encounters that have informed the work of each its contributors. In this respect, the editors note their appreciation for the encouragement, warmth and intellectual richness that characterise French Studies communities in Australia, Europe and North America and that inform debate and investigation in contemporary French society and culture. Each of the editors wishes to thank their family and friends for the personal support they have received during the preparation of this volume; each of the contributors for their patience, helpfulness and professionalism; and all those at Rodopi who have been a part of the project, in particular our editor, Christa Stevens. Trevor Pull's invaluable technical advice and contribution is gratefully acknowledged, as is Jane Haddon's assistance to Murray in the final stages of editing.

Martine Fernandes's chapter originally appeared in *PORTAL Journal of Multidisciplinary International Studies*, and we thank the editor, Paul Allatson, for his permission to publish a translated version and for his personal support for this project.

Finally, the additional support and intellectual contribution of the following close colleagues of the editors is warmly acknowledged: Jean-Pierre Boulé and the French Studies group at Nottingham Trent University, as well as Catriona Elder, Maja Mikula, Ann Miller and Denis Provencher. Larry Schehr's guidance and mentorship has also been essential to the successful completion of the project and is warmly acknowledged.

This book is dedicated to the memory of our former colleague at IIS, Cajetan Mula, in celebration of his generosity and wisdom, spirit of fun and engagement with global learning.

Towards a Preface

Jo McCormack, Murray Pratt and Alistair Rolls

From its inception this book was designed to consider as wide a range of subjects and positions as possible within a French cultural context. Our aim was to take these views, to arrange them and to see how they reflected this overarching system that we call French culture. In this respect, we could suggest that our approach responds to a certain type of poetics; more precisely, we might invoke Charles Baudelaire's iconoclastic pulling of poetic Ideals into the city streets. There, stranded beneath their blue skies, verse motifs were suddenly seen for what they were *in real terms*, that is to say in terms of the way they are present to us, not as we represent them from our objective point of view (from within and outside the framework of French culture). This new (mid-nineteenth-century) prose poetics offers us a way of looking at culture that is especially French. Indeed, it is especially Parisian, and thereby functions metonymically, if also, no doubt, evanescently, as the capital of Frenchness. Evidenced, since 1980, by the concretisation of the Baudelairean concept on Quai Saint-Bernard, in the form of 'Le Musée de la Sculpture en plein air', poetic ideas and ideals jostle for prominence and vie for the attention of tourists and Parisians alike, alongside as eclectic a collection of street sites as Paris, France can muster: poetic idealism, open to the elements, in one shape or another, it might be said, is what links L'Institut du Monde Arabe with Le Jardin des Plantes.

In *Hexagonal Variations: Difference, Plurality and Cultural Change in Contemporary France*, we hope to respond to the satanic pull of the ultra-urban and symbolically saturated, and head streetwards. Our intention will thus be double: to present a cultural artefact (a film or films, a novel or novels, a *quartier* or the map of France itself) and to seek to understand its representations. But it is this emphasis on presentation, this putting of 'things in France' before their Frenchness, that defines our project and which extends, updates and differentiates the present study from those introductions to French cultures, indispensable to researchers, teachers and students, which have come before.[1]

The perspective that we have chosen here can perhaps best be summed up through a very brief analysis of a text by a writer of the OuLiPo school, Jacques Jouet: *Le point de vue de l'escargot*. This slender volume is a collection of Jouet's "nouvelles du mercredi", which were first published as such in the newspaper *L'Alsace* before being collected into an anthology by Strasbourgeois publishing house Le Verger. A simple explanation of Jouet's title, his snail's viewpoint, is immediately offered by this Alsatian connection. Indeed, in culinary terms at least, the typical fare on offer in an Alsatian Winstub, if we put aside the more obviously 'regional' Choucroute garnie and Flammekueche, is the very expression of Frenchness: snails and frog's legs. If not a frog, Jouet announces himself as a snail. Here, then, is our double movement: synecdochically, the snail (and Alsace) 'represents' France while at the same time offering a ground-level perspective that necessarily forces us to gaze on it through individual snapshots or 'presentations'. The story that opens the book, "Chambre vide et ventre plein", takes us into a Winstub, which Jouet calls, simply if not innocently, a "restaurant".[2]

---

[1] Including Jill Forbes and Michael Kelly (eds), *French Cultural Studies: An Introduction* (Oxford: Oxford University Press, 1995); Alec G. Hargreaves and Mark McKinney (eds) *Post-Colonial Cultures in France* (London: Routledge, 1997); William Kidd and Siân Reynolds (eds), *Contemporary French Cultural Studies* (London: Arnold, 2000); and Hugh Dauncey (ed), *French Popular Culture: An Introduction* (London: Arnold, 2003).
[2] Jacques Jouet, "Chambre vide et ventre plein" in *Le point de vue de l'escargot* (Strasbourg: *L'Alsace*; Le Verger, 1994), pp. 9-17.

Typically of Oulipian writing, the constraints of geographical location give way immediately to mathematical ones. The story's opening line dislocates narrator and reader while drawing attention not only to the means but, more importantly, the number of transport— *one* train: "Je suis arrivé hier en ville par un train du soir."[3] We are pulled into Jouet's singular story on this singular train. His use of tenses operates a similar, and similarly perverse, displacement *and* intimacy: here the *passé composé*, typically used to conjoin the acts of reading and writing in the narrative present, sets up the conditions of a story that takes place subsequently (i.e., as we read forwards) and yet in the tense of the narrative past, *le passé simple*. The story both is and is not therefore the one we are reading; or, in other words, it is both present to us and represented for us.

The use of the key number—one—also plays a double, and increasingly plural, role in the story: in room one there is one coat-hanger in the one wardrobe. And also one bed (but as luck would have it, it is "à deux places", which suggests that we readers have fallen for the oldest forced-intimacy trap in the book). Jouet calls this series of singulars "une [telle] provocation au dénuement"; it is for him the very spirit of travel, an emptying experience.[4] Playing on the double, or doubly double, space of the text (as he empties himself of his tale, the reader, whose stay is in his story, fills herself with his tale; and he fills himself with meaning even as her reading empties the tale of his controlling presence), the story gradually moves into an absurd meal, one in which the solitary traveller becomes a solitary diner who orders the one snail on the menu (*schnecke* is translated for us as "des escargots à l'alsatienne"); this he follows with one slice of *tarte à l'oignon* and, to finish, one goose stuffed *à la Martinsgans* (accompanied with, amongst other things, one chestnut). As the traveller finishes his extravagant dinner the conversation with the *patron* becomes confusing, as if the two are talking at cross-purposes. The explanation arrives in the form of another man who is described as being "une caricature de cadre dynamique porteur d'une malette dite attaché-case".[5] The word *attaché-case* is clearly a double

---

[3] Jouet, p. 9.
[4] Jouet, p. 9-10.
[5] Jouet, p. 16.

entendre: its French resonance in English gives it both a French and English resonance in this Alsatian setting. The man's abrupt arrival marks not only the end of the dinner but also the end of the restaurant, which he has bought in order to turn it into burger joint. The word *hamburger* is used sneeringly to set up a dichotomy between an Americanized future and a disappearing local tradition of *produits du terroir*.

We find ourselves in a Benjaminian space where a restaur-ateur's experience (*Erfahrung*) can no longer compete with the market-driven need for quick experiences (*Erlebnis*). And yet, the new man is not American but French. The forces of homogenization, we are reminded, are those of a national, as well as international, culture. For, Jouet has shown himself to be French in its most universal and universalizing sense; and so too, in his wake, has his reader, his double. The necessarily double dynamics of reading are thus mapped onto those of travelling and eating. We consume culture doubly too, therefore, bringing our experience to the table (explaining away its individuality) and digesting its constituent parts into ourselves. This is, then, a cautionary, as well as a culinary tale. This single space, which is so very typical of France (when seen objectively), is seen as being at the same time richly plural but exposed and vulnerable. Jouet's call is for us to take the position of the snail, to consume locally and avoid the glibly global perspective. In so doing, we can, like the traveller, grow fat with experience(s), enormously so.

Another culinary take on contemporary French debates concerning what is often perceived as a dangerous drift towards communitarianism can be detected as central to the thesis advanced by author and *Le Figaro* columnist Eric Zemmour. As outlined in a review of his *Mélancolie Française*,[6]

> the thesis that lands Zemmour in the hottest water is his belief that France sealed its fate when it abandoned its tradition of assimilating immigrants, for the concept of ethnic diversity. "French culture is not Mohammed", he says. "It is Francois (sic), it is Christian."
>
> The result is a new "barbarism" with the emergence of Muslim ghettos that have broken away from society, he argues in his book. He quotes Charles de

---

[6] Éric Zemmour, *Mélancolie Française* (Paris: Fayard, 2010).

Gaulle as saying mixing Muslims and French Christians was "like blending oil and vinegar".[7]

Much could be said about the veracity Zemmour's claims that France is experiencing a new form of multiculturalism, about his attribution of a key role for the state in promoting this, and, indeed, about how he configures society in such a way that it is absolved from any part in constructing its abject others. What emerges as central to his position, however, is a belief that the classic formula for French dressing, or vinaigrette, requires sticking to the recipe that has served the country over the years, one whereby the added components are successfully 'blended' into the existing mixture rather than allowed to retain their own characteristics.

In recent years, this distaste for discernible plurality has arguably led to less metaphorical, more violent culture clashes, with the 2005 riots in the French *banlieues*, becoming a reference point that traces a series of disfunctionalities within the established Republican order. To take just one, example, sociologist Isabelle Rigoni has contextualised the images of burnt-out cars, torched community centres and schools, and crowds of young French citizens with little or nothing binding them to civic structures that became associated with this moment of revolt, by contrasting them with the symbolic weight of a state that presented itself as unique and indivisible. The questions Rigoni asked, in particular her anxiety about how French Republicanism can accommodate, account for, include and embrace its minorities, are among the most urgent facing the nation. Her contestation is that the generous-sounding principles governing the Republic mask those differences and conditions that would enable a politics of inclusivity, and play themselves out in the national symbolism of the French media on a daily basis.[8]

Contributors to Rigoni's volume point to systemic racisms and sexisms persisting in the national consciousness. They describe,

---

[7] Charles Bremner, "Eric Zemmour provokes France's elite with claims of national decline", *The Times*, 4 June 2010. Available online at: http://www.timesonline.co.uk/-tol/news/world/europe/article7143840.ece. Accessed 21 June 2010.

[8] Isabelle Rigoni (ed), *Qui a peur de la télévision en couleurs?* (Paris: Aux lieux d'être, 2007), p.11.

on the one hand, the tardiness, superficiality and, until well into the 2000s, lack of black representation in authoritative roles (the first black newsreader to appear on national French television is documented as Harry Roselmack, who read TF1's *Journal Télévisé de 20H* on 17 July 2006)[9]; and on the other hand to the regimes of the stereotype or counter-hegemonic niche that defuse, or as Nacira Guénif-Souilamas (drawing on Roland Barthes) explains,[10] 'vaccinate against', any sense that '*white* and white television' and by extension daily life is anything other than norm. These debates are far from over, yet a useful new approach seems to be emerging in recent interventions that attempt to tackle French dilemmas, not in isolation, but within broader international contexts. Elisa Camiscioli, for example, rather than situating France's policies of integration and assimilation solely within Republican terms, asks whether it is possible to co-locate the country's race consciousness alongside transnational systems, whereby doctrines of nationalism and racism "fused" in accordance with world ideologies that crossed, at the same time as they helped establish, national boundaries.[11]

The 2005 riots in the French banlieues led to the creation of the Mouvement des Indigènes de la République (MIR), which Kiran Grewal analyses in this volume. That movement has focused reflection, political activism and media attention on two phenomena which are at the heart of many of the chapters in this book, as well as at the centre of public debate in contemporary France: ethnicity, and historical, social or cultural memory. The MIR has linked current race relations in France to France's colonial history, its legacy and its representation. Commemoration is one way that social memories are generated, and another example of plurality in contemporary France. Social memories, as scholars working in this area have shown, are

---

[9] Cholé Breen, 'Vous aimez tous la télévision… en couleurs!', *Pure People*, 17 February 2009. Available at www.purepeople.com/article/vous-aimez-tous-la-television-en-couleur_a24797/1. Accessed 4 July 2010.

[10] Nacira Guénif-Souilamas, 'L'iconographie républicaine des Marianne "multicolores"', in Rigoni, pp. 85-107.

[11] Elisa Camiscioli, 'Race Making and Race Mixing in the Early Twentieth Century Immigration Debate', in Hafid Gafaïti, Patricia Lorcin and David Troyansky (eds), *Transnational Spaces and Identities in the Francophone World* (Lincoln: University of Nebraska Press, 2009), pp.53-72, p.56.

plural, since people's focus on the past changes less as a function of distance from the event than as how that event ties into concerns in the present. Gérard Namer, discussing Maurice Halbwach's seminal work on social memory *The Social Frames of Memory* states: "[...] se souvenir pour un individu c'est reconstruire son passé en partant des cadres sociaux présents de son groupe".[12] David Thelen agrees:

> The starting place for the construction of an individual recollection is a present need or circumstance [...]. Since an individual's starting points change as the person grows and changes, people reshape their recollections of the past to fit their present needs [...] and select from the present material that supports deeply held interpretations from the past.[13]

Matthew Graves and Elizabeth Rechniewski, in 2010 issue of *Portal* on "Fields of Remembrance", speak of "the need to recognise the fractured and conflictual nature of memory within and across state borders". Plurality is also present since "the 'same' events are constantly being represented and commented from different points of view, exposing the relativity of national perspectives" and "[I]t is increasingly clear that the responses to official commemoration and memorialism vary widely according to cultural difference, ethnic identification, generation, class and gender."[14]

Recent years have seen a myriad of commemorative initiatives in France: 2004 was the sixtieth anniversary of the Liberation, 2005 the liberation of the death camps; 2006 the seventieth anniversary of the Popular Front, 2008 celebrated important anniversaries of the May 1968 events and the Great War. In keeping with this pattern, 2010 has seen an avalanche of publications,

---

[12] Gérard Namer, in the postface to Maurice Halbwachs, *Les Cadres sociaux de la mémoire* (Paris: Albin Michel, 1994), p. 321.

[13] David Thelen, "Memory and American History", *The Journal of American History*, vol. 75, no. 4, (March 1989), p. 1121.

[14] Matthew Graves and Elizabeth Rechniewski, "From Collective Memory to Transcultural Remembrance", *Portal: Journal of Multidisciplinary International Studies*, vol. 7, no. 1, (2010).

television shows, films and commemorations celebrating 1940, at the heart of which has been de Gaulle's "Appel du 18 juin" (seventieth anniversary). President Sarkozy chose 2010 to pay homage on May 8 to the "malgré nous", soldiers from Alsace who were forced to enrol in the German army. Postcolonial issues however remain less consensual. The commemoration of the abolition of slavery, on May 10, passed largely unnoticed. And Rachid Bouchareb's film *Hors-la-loi*, also examining troubling postcolonial questions, generated controversy at the 2010 Cannes film festival... As Matthew Graves and Elisabeth Rechniewski state, "These often acrimonious con-frontations demonstrate just how much is at stake in conflicting narratives of national history; memory, history and individual and collective identity are inseparably bound together."

The focus of this volume, then, is on the plural, on the multiplicities that contextualise the singularities, and the felicities and infelicities of transcultural encounter. It is as much about not-France as it is about France (for there are perhaps only one set of questions, howsoever double in nature), more concerned with discerning innovations and interrogating tensions than with paying homage to traditions. Mapping the Hexagon kaleidoscopically, the essays take the pulse of change and evolution, whether linguistic or gastronomical, cinematic, textual, mediatic, cyber or visual, and texture contemporary France as, now beyond the double question, a set of variations that far exceeds categorisation according to tired Republican themes alone.

The process of editing this volume has, in many ways, reproduced the double dynamics of reading France anew, digesting what the contributors have to say about its ever-inventive auto-differentiation. It has been refreshing and appetising, though, rather than familiar or gluttonous. More than replicating the sauntering itineraries of the *flâneur,* it has given the editors and contributors a chance to meander, encountering all of France, the byways and alleys as well as the boulevards and highways, and always accompanied by knowledgeable and erudite guides—but also to try out some textual parkour, seeing the urban, suburban and rural from unusual angles as essayists improvise new and, at times, risky manoeuvres. The structure of the volume reflects this journey: while organised loosely within a structured rationale, the essays defy any single attempt to impose unity on their multiple and often surprising logics. Context is all, and the essays in this volume, howsoever they differ in style, focus or substance, return to and revolve around the same moments and monuments—the symbols, sounds, enigmas, tracks, trails and texts, and chance encounters that permit a sensing of France, whether this be in analysis or reference, commemoration or celebration, or in anticipation of future Frances whose varied cartographies are yet to be mapped.

Variations on the Hexagon: Getting the Measure of Culture Change in Contemporary France

Murray Pratt and Alistair Rolls

Perhaps more than any other nation, modern France is an entity which has been understood through symbolism. While it is commonplace for countries and empires, states and federations, to espouse myth or allegory as they reach for self-definition, and, as often as not, self-justification, the trimmings and trappings of French statehood have been frequently deployed, reaccentuating the national mission with each new Republic. From Marianne to 'la Marseillaise', the 'tricolore' to the tripartite motto *Liberté, Egalité, Fraternité*, symbols of French national belonging or statehood abound. Listed on the official website of the French Presidency (www.elysee.fr) alongside Bastille Day itself and the Seal (redesigned in 1792), each of them resurrects an association with the French Revolution of 1789, howsoever faint the relevance, and memory, of this foundational moment may be becoming as the sole point of reference and measure for the plural, multi-ethnic, and cannily branded player and product that is contemporary France. Three of the symbols mentioned above are combined in the French Government logo, inaugurated pre-millenially by the government of Lionel Jospin in late 1999, and depicting the three words of the motto beneath a stylized French flag, with Marianne's silhouette looking to the right, no doubt the future, and occupying the white strip. Branding places, and by extension national place, requires "historical depth".[1] As John Gammack and Stephanie Hemelryck Donald point out:

> Places are differentiated not only by their physical forms and architectures, but also by the contexts of their construction and development, by the known experiences of usage, and by the currency of the memories, which attach to them. Arguably, the maintenance of cultural memory will sustain and transfigure the tests of the present by re-appropriating the spaces created...

Importantly, the depth of history and the work of cultural memory, for Gammack and Donald, in addition to supporting and legitimizing brands also enables their reinvention. Like all logos, even this official state identifier will one day meet its expiry date. Equally, rather than fixed and constant stars, the symbols of France and its revolutionary, Republican *raison d'être*, are themselves subject to processes of flux.

(R)evolutionary iconography

As individual components, the import of the symbols themselves is variable—differential, if never entirely arbitrary. Fraternity, for instance, even at its post-revolutionary outset, was obliged to commit serial fratricide in seeing off competing contenders for the third spot in the trilogy of national absolutes.[2] The models chosen for the statues of Marianne delivered to the local *mairie* have famously evolved in line with national taste from Bardot, via Deneuve, and ever onwards, although not without controversy, as the Association of the Mayors of France juggles tradition with innovation. In 2003, while this august body was plumping for Evelyne Thomas, who hosted a populist television talk show appropriately entitled "C'est mon choix", as the chosen iconic (individual yet official) face of the Republic, posters of

---

[1] John Gammack and Stephanie Hemelryk Donald, "Branding Cities: a Case Study of Collaborative Methodologies in Cultural, Film, and Marketing Research", in Mark Gibson, Debbie Rodan, Felicity Newman, Ron Blaber, Wendy Parkins, Geoffrey Craig and Christina Gordon (eds), *Cultural Studies Association of Australasia (CSAA) 2004 Annual Conference, Online Proceedings*, p.7. http://wwwmcc.murdoch.edu.au-/cfel/csaa_proceedings.htm. All internet sources quoted in this chapter accessed 23 July 2008.
[2] Mona Ozouf, "Liberté, égalité, fraternité", in Pierre Nora (ed), *Lieux de Mémoire*, tome III, Quarto (Paris: Gallimard, 1997), pp. 4353-4389. (For an abridged translation, see *Realms of Memory*, Columbia University Press, 1996–1998).

fourteen alternative Mariannes were displayed on the columns of the French National Assembly, as part of a campaign organized by the associative activist group, formed earlier that year to represent the (unheard) voices of women from the troubled suburbs, or banlieues, and known as *Ni Putes, Ni Soumises* (NPNS).[3] This instance of pluralization—the faces were selected to embrace different ethnicities—rather than diluting the allegorical import of Marianne, can be considered, paradoxically, as strengthening the symbol's association with Republican values through demonstrating its flexibility. As Emily Kenney and Hélène David point out, "NPNS strongly supports the traditional French republican values, helping to align them more closely with the national political powers and government officials".[4] To the extent that Marianne's national potency is gendered and sexualized, the allegory's variability enables its mobilization within key national debates such as those concerning sexual violence, parity, and the PaCS (*pacte civil de solidarité*), such that the figurehead adapts her Phrygian headwear to the winds of cultural change.

As with Marianne, the other symbols associated with France have shown a tendency to evolve with the times. That they are not immutable is perhaps appropriate given their revolutionary heritage.[5]

---

[3] See Grewal for a fuller account of the group and criticisms made of their aims and methods. Kiran Grewal, "The Threat from Within: Representations of the Banlieue in French Popular Discourse", in Matt Killingsworth (ed), *Europe: New Voices, New Perspectives* (Contemporary Europe Research Centre: University of Melbourne, 2007), Chapter 3. http://www.cerc.unimelb.edu.au/publications/europe-new-voices.-html.

[4] Emily Kenney and Hélène David, "Taking a Stand: Women's Voices in the Suburbs", in *Humanity in Action Reports, French Program*, 2006, p.3. http://www.-humanityinaction.org/index.php?option=content&task=view&id=345.

[5] One of the most radical examples of this (r)evolutionary aspect to mark the twentieth century was the erasure of 'traditional' republican iconography during the Nazi Occupation, during which *Travail, Patrie, Famille* was the new logo and busts of Marianne were forcibly removed or stored away by mayors. One cannot but help sense in this trauma inflicted on the national psyche an echo of the mythology of loss that marked the poets of the mid-nineteenth century as a direct result of Haussmannization. The gesture, by certain mayors, of putting Marianne away for safekeeping, itself suggests a sense of nation that is both enduring and cyclical, Frenchness forever lost and recaptured. Not only are so-called 'essential' traits the cause of social change; but they are also changed by events. For a more extensive

Not only were the tricolour shades of *bleu, blanc, rouge* perceptibly brightened in recent times, and the central white band used as competing backdrops for competing factions during the Second World War, but more recently the primacy of this colour scheme has been challenged, at least in the popular mind, by the combination of 'black, blanc, beur', denoting the many heritages of France's successful 1998 World Cup winning soccer team. A cause for controversy at the time, the collocation has persisted in the public domain as a shorthand reference for ethnic diversity in France, and continues to embroil commentators such as extreme right-wing politician Jean-Marie Le Pen and philosopher Alain Finkielkraut in debates about representations of Frenchness and the values they incarnate. For some, such as the footballer Lilian Thuram, Le Pen's colour-blindness relegates his interventions to a virtualized version of France, devoid of racial diversity, "not the real one".[6] Meanwhile, back in the real France, the hybrid cultures emerging from across and beyond suburban encounters are globally recognized for their innovation and inclusivity in youth-oriented art forms such as rap, hip-hop, slam poetry, tagging, parkour, and are increasingly storming the barricades of more conventional arts establishments.[7] Subject to competing processes of marginalization and co-option, cultural difference and innovation in France is at the same time corralled off from imaginary national norms, and brought into the Elysian board rooms on an 'as required' basis. A film such as Matthieu Kassovitz's *La Haine* (1995), for example, simultaneously performs an othering of those ultimately not so unfamiliar lives lived beyond *le périphérique*, and their revitalizing recuperation within national standards of humour, philosophy, cinematography and, most potently, fraternity. Alternatively, Serge Gainsbourg's irreverent rendition of *La Marseillaise* as a reggae anthem replaced the national strapline with the tag 'Aux armes, et cætera' and challenged the legitimacy of state symbolism itself. And

---

analysis of the changing nature of Marianne, see Maurice Agulhon and Pierre Bonte, *Marianne : Les visages de la République* (Paris: Gallimard, 1992).
[6] Lilian Thuram, quoted in John Ward Anderson, "A Multi-Hued National Team Thrills Racially Uneasy France", *Washington Post*, 7 July 2006. http://www.-washingtonpost.com/wp-dyn/content/article/2006/07/06/AR2006070601742.html.
[7] See Alain-Phillipe Durand, *Black, Blanc, Beur: Rap Music and Hip-Hop Culture in the Francophone World* (Lanham, MD: The Scarecrow Press, 2002).

Gainsbourg himself is now celebrated and petrified as a must-visit tomb in Montparnasse cemetery.

Hexagonality as always already plural

To the extent that the official indices of French belonging perform a work of ideological colonization, their veneer of permanence covers a secondary characteristic, an equal measure of infinite adaptability that permits the nation to refashion its image, enacting that liminal space of hybrid cultural imagining that Homi Bhabha describes in *The Location of Culture*,[8] and, in the process, stigmatizing those identities it relegates to secondary. And yet, as this brief purview of some of the fault lines that marble French state symbols shows, the official markers of national identity are *always already* other than themselves: like the original complexity of Derrida's trace,[9] the symbols and allegories of France conceal, defer and differ from, substitute for and delay a series of Frances, of 'not-France'. It is this foundational plurality, this structuring diversity, which we define, drawing on a fur-ther but often occluded representation of France, as the 'hexagonality' of contemporary French culture.

The historian Nathaniel B. Smith, tracking the many polygonal models used to understand France's geospatial formation, recalls in detail the varied deployments of the hexagon over time.[10] From ousting earlier circular, pentagonal and octagonal models, the hexagon has established itself as "completely standard", the perfect and harmonious mean that demonstrates, as if by the magic of the natural, to pupils in their equally harmonized curricula, "that France is regular, drawable, logical, desirable to inhabit, unique".[11] As Smith's depiction and account of hexagonal France demonstrate, however, far from a natural formation, the chosen polygon is, like all national symbols,

---

[8] Homi Bhabha, *The Location of Culture* (London: Routledge, 2004).

[9] Jacques Derrida, "Difference" in *Speech and Phenomena, and Other Essays on Husserl's Theory of Signs*. Trans. David B. Allison. Preface by Newton Garver. (Evanston, IL: Northwestern University Press, 1973).

[10] Throughout this chapter 'hexagon' will be spelt with a lower-case 'h' when used to refer to the polygonal shape of France or of concepts based on it; an upper-case 'H' will be used when 'Hexagon' is used, as it traditionally is, as a synonym for France.

[11] Nathaniel Smith, "The Idea of the French Hexagon", *French Historical Studies*, 6:2 (1969), 139-155 (149, 152).

strategic and convenient, contestable and only sketchily accurate.[12] Not only does the hexagon prove only a partial map for the territory (missing coasts, annexing neighbouring lands, and excluding the geographical anomalies of the *outre-mer* and even Corsica), its mobilization is also shown to be politically determined, such as, for example, when the 1962 Gaullist party adopted it as their own symbol in a bid to define the parameters of "renewed nationalism",[13] shaking off the legacy of the Algerian War and confronting newer European permutations. Hexagonality, however, as a process of understanding contemporary French cultural change, more than simply "represent[ing] the sense of belonging that the Republic has always sought to instil in its citizens",[14] highlights the arbitrary, situated and ideological nature of symbolization itself.

Just as France's perceived geometrical form has been subject to change, from circle to various polygons, its symbolic value has also been subject to constant variation. Indeed, the history of the polygon has, as Smith has shown, reflected not only the loss and recuperation of national borders as a result of war, notably with neighbouring Germany, but also, and more importantly, the aspirations of the French. As such, "[t]he idea that a natural right attaches the lost territories to France is here and henceforth [post-1871] implicit in any description of the hexagon as of the octagon."[15] It is noteworthy here that the geographers of France seem just as steeped in regret as those poets, such as Charles Baudelaire, for whom it stood at the centre of their artistic expression. The mid-nineteenth century thus sees a cartography as well as a poetry of mourning for a lost time. It is interesting, too, that what may have appeared to be a regret for a lost city, according to which pre-Haussmannian Paris evolves into a Utopia in the popular imaginary via Baudelairian poetics, is also repeated nationwide in the ongoing (re)configurations of France itself. And as France undergoes successive periods of instability, Baudelairian resonances are repeatedly perceptible in the art that accompanies the various instances of social change. We might think, for example, of Léo Malet's novels of the Occupation-Liberation era,

---

[12] Smith, p. 140, Figure 1.
[13] Smith, p. 150.
[14] Smith, p. 152.
[15] Smith, p. 147.

which draw on images of *Les Petits Poèmes en prose*.[16] More recent examples of intertextuality that seemingly both symbolize and usher in the melancholy of urban change include the bulldozing of historic Paris that stands as the backdrop to Cédric Klapisch's 1996 film *Chacun cherche son chat*. Whereas Malet's referencing stands as a Baudelairian centenary, Klapisch's film, with its remodelling of "Le Cygne", proves the poet's ongoing relevance at the turn of the millennium. That is to say that the loss of old Paris is now, just as it was when Baudelaire configured it as a line both punctuated and infinite, a series of events situated in history and made timeless by their dilution into the intertext.

In this way Paris today continues to take its stand as capital of cosmopolitanism, as it did as the capital of modernity, indeed of the modern world in the nineteenth century;[17] but it stands also and equally as a metonym for a new nation. And this new nation is, just as its capital, forged on mythology and the symbol, such that "tout pour moi devient allégorie".[18] This "geometrical conception of French unity", which Smith locates as already well established by the end of the nineteenth century, is an exquisite piece of engineering:[19] no mere Janus, France will construct its national unity polygonally, in and through many faces.

This concept of the hexagon, what Smith calls "an essentially French idea" inasmuch as it seems to capture the spirit of the Third Republic,[20] will continue to focus concepts and issues of Frenchness around this theme of fluctuating borders. The Hexagon will move from being French as opposed to German to being French differently from and in opposition to all that which lies beyond its boundaries, excluding at times, not unproblematically, permutations that extend to

---

[16] See Alistair Rolls, "Spleen Noir: Images de Marianne dans les petits poèmes en prose de Léo Mallet et Frédéric Cathala" in Sue Ryan-Fazilleau and Serge Linkès (eds), *France and Australia Face to Face. Australie/France : regards croisés* (Paris: Les Indes savants, 2008), pp. 143-160.

[17] See, for example, David Harvey, *Paris, Capital of Modernity* (New York; London: Routledge, 2003) and Patrice Higonnet, *Paris, capitale du monde* (Paris: Tallandier, 2005).

[18] Charles Baudelaire, "Le Cygne" first published in *Les Fleurs du mal* in Paris in 1861.

[19] Smith, p. 148.

[20] Smith, p. 148.

its overseas departments, territories and that space now referred to as Francophone.[21] For the sides offered by the hexagon are themselves perverse in the way that they delimit France, neatly packaging it, Ikea-like,[22] as a form ideal for tidy storage of and within itself, and into a (European) space beyond,[23] whilst also extending beyond its natural boundaries, reaching out virtually over land and sea. France, then, as a hexagon, is both inside and outside itself, a readymade, pre-packaged symbol of inclusivity and exclusivity. For, if borders are most often considered to demarcate and contain, they are also the zones that are used, as Gloria Anzaldúa has demonstrated in the context of the Mexico-USA border,[24] to cross, pass, contact, connect and contest the notional integrities of the nation. France's hexagonality is such that, for better or worse, each side aligns the nation within the cultural and physical contexts of its geography while suggesting its historical spheres of influence and its future lines of flight. The regularization of the hexagon, and let us not forget that hexagons can permissibly be irregular too, defines these as the Channel, the Atlantic, the Pyrenees, the Mediterranean, the Alps and the fields of Flanders, each bringing to bear a not-France that permeates and disrupts the symbol's continuity. The six 120-degree angles themselves (Brittany, the Basque country, Catalonia, Monaco, Alsace and Dunkerque) form niches of differentiation, recall narratives of conflict and pinpoint contestations to come.

The ramifications of such complex hexagonality are neatly illustrated by Danielle Marx-Scouras's study of French group Zebda, according to which "[r]acist fears continue to keep the dream of a *coloré, métissé, nuancé* French society […] an aspiration, not a

---

[21] For further discussion of the problematics of inclusivity and exclusivity of France and its relation to the Francophone world, see Alistair Rolls and Jo McCormack, "Introduction to Voices from Africa", *Australian Journal of French Studies*, 45:2 (2008): 101-109.

[22] For an extensive analysis of the phenomenon of Ikeaization and its ramifications for 'French' culture, see Tod Hartman, "On the Ikeaization of France", *Public Culture*, 19:3 (2007), 483-498.

[23] The physical properties of the hexagon as strong and efficiently fitted into small spaces is not lost on Smith who also reminds us how France has traditionally been marketed to its own schoolchildren as just the right size and shape.

[24] Gloria Anzaldúa, *Borderlands/La Frontera: The New Mestiza* (San Francisco, CA: Spinsters/Aunt Lute, 1987).

reality".[25] For Marx-Scouras, Zebda's success in 'rocking the Hexagon' lies not so much in their political role—she explains how the group affiliated themselves with the Motivé-e-s ticket during municipal elections in Toulouse in March 2001—as in the way that their popularity as musicians has highlighted this tense and paradoxical French relationship with inclusivity and exclusivity. Their musical diversity has meant that Zebda continue to eschew generic definition (they cannot be ghettoized as rappers, for example, Marx-Scouras reminds us); their background is, similarly, far from uniform (not all members, for example, can properly be categorized as Beur). Ultimately, the solution to this conundrum is as poetic as their music: "Zebda [have] succeeded in moving beyond [such] compart-mentalization: their cds are simply under the rubric of 'French music' (*variétés françaises*) or, more recently, French rock".[26] Marx-Scouras's point is, of course, that the only logical category into which Zebda can be put is that of French music; their success is to have ceased being seen as a heterogeneous group and to have been integrated into the mainstream. The term *variétés françaises* is, thus, an interesting one, which suggests homogenization but which is built on a fundamental plurality and 'variety'. The very term for French music necessarily contains within itself that which is not (uniformly) French. The capacity of the term French to encapsulate plurality is perhaps reinforced by the increasing tendency for *variété française* to be written in the singular, both as an invariable adjective (*la musique variété française*) and as the noun used to categorize music in French shops.

The intentional and haunted hexagon

Clearly, the concept of the singular as always already plural has been central to much that has become synonymous with the French. We might think, for example, of Sartrean Existentialism, so often the point of entry for students into twentieth-century French thought. Sartre's model of consciousness is one that is situated and grounded in the reality of our sensory perception. According to this model, conscious-

---

[25] Danielle Marx-Scouras, "Rock the Hexagon", *Contemporary French and Francophone Studies*, 8:1 (2004), 51-61 (53).
[26] Marx-Scouras, p. 53-54.

ness is never entirely abstracted from its surroundings: it cannot 'be' or 'be, full stop'; instead, it exists, or 'is in the world' (as Sartre describes it, we are always conscious(ness) *of* something). As such, its borders with the world are highly problematic. On the one hand, they serve to form a barrier between our consciousness and the world around us; and on the other hand, they promote continuity between consciousness and the world, always signalling to consciousness the way in which its very existence depends on this inescapable relationship. These borders are, in addition, permeable, and consciousness pours continuously beyond them. This tendency for consciousness to be always already beyond itself, other than where and what it is, is known as intentionality. And it is perhaps this way of tending beyond borders that best describes France's being-in-the-world. In this way, the virtual borders of the Hexagon, which putatively join Dunkerque to Strasbourg to Nice to Perpignan to Bayonne to Ouessant and back to Dunkerque, circumscribe an area that is, almost entirely (the stretch from Perpignan to Bayonne is an exception as it lies inside French national borders), beyond the limits of France's physical geography. Hexagonal space suggests, longs for and aspires to; it is a virtual France, one that is always already tending beyond geographical reality. But, insofar as it is, as is Sartrean consciousness, always already recaptured by physical borders, hexagonal space is also actual. The key to the plurality of the Hexagon is that it is both: virtual and actual.

This way of being forever simultaneously in flight from oneself and recoiled into oneself leaves us humans in a perverse condition: our consciousness is forever being torn (I and me are separate) and perpetually being reconstituted (the distance between I and me is nothingness). And so the void, the negating strip that divides us from the world, is both almost tangibly present and infinitesimally thin, to the point of not being there at all; it both maintains our identity (as separate from the world and unique) and situates it in the world of our sensory perception (from which we can never escape, and in the absence of which we can have no existence). In this way, the human condition is one of constant movement along a line between two poles (the situatedness of our physical, visceral reality and the flight of our intentional consciousness). We are always both, and as a result we are never fully ourselves; we cannot coincide with ourselves or constitute the reason for our own existence.

France's being-in-the-world, its hexagonality, is comparable to and yet different from the being for-itself. For France, too, there is a way in which it is not what it is. That is to say that France's existential reality (France as it is experienced in the present) coincides with any number of external perceptions that we have of it without being reduced to or justified by these. And yet, whereas we can add, in our description of the human condition, that we are what we are not (inasmuch as we tend forever towards the future potential of our chosen projects, and thus away from the confines of our present situation), there is a way in which France's intentionality actually alights on or coincides with an essence. There is a way in which France, in addition to being other than it is, also is what it is: France does, in a certain way, coincide with Frenchness. Frenchness is an ideal, which may well always fail to be fully satisfied by real time spent in France, but which is always there shaping our understanding of how it ought to be. (This is also the case for humans, of course, insofar as we create laws and ideas of behaviour for humans to follow, and we can also describe more or less well what it means to be human; this remains, however, a much more subjective exercise, precisely because of the nature of human consciousness. A country is not conscious(ness), but it has a certain life force nonetheless, and its imaginary is created by its past and continually renewed and (re)negotiated by its inhabitants and those who have an understanding of it.)

Let us say, then, that France's existential crisis is also about being constantly torn between two sides of a binary opposition. The difference between Sartre's model of the being for-itself and this model of France, or Frenchness, is that the oscillation is between essence and existence themselves. The importance of the hexagon is that it demonstrates and maps France both as it is in the world and as it *is*, its physical existence and its essence. Inasmuch as this projection beyond geographical boundaries is both an aspiration forwards and a longing for the past, hexagonality recalls the description of the urban condition given by Ross Chambers in his work on the loiterly. For Chambers a modern metropolis is "haunted"; the city as we live it in the present, walking through its streets, is always accompanied by the

ghosts of its past.[27] The city we see is both the same and different
from the city we remember. What grieves Chambers, very much as it
did Walter Benjamin, is that the ever-increasing speed of the modern
world causes us to live very much in the world 'as it exists'; to see the
world 'as it is not', either as it was or as we would that it had been,
requires a loiterly stance. The loiterly individual, who sees the ghost
in the existential world, is described by Chambers as being belated, or
somehow out of step. And the most familiar trope of belatedness, at
least to the reader familiar with France and modernity, is the flâneur.
For Michel Covin the flâneur is both out of step and in step with the
world. His encapsulation of both positions in a binary opposition
makes him the perfect metaphor for Paris, his *lieu privilégié*, and by
extension for hexagonality: he reads the world (Paris and/or France)
both as he experiences it, in real time, and, at the same time, as he
understands it, with all the objectivity and distance (usually both
spatial and temporal for the poet or artist in his lofty garret, but here
more conceptual) of belatedness. To use Covin's terms, he lives the
city as it is present to him *and* as it is re-presented.[28]

Covin's reading of Baudelairian poetics focuses on *Les Petits
Poèmes en prose*, in which the poet simultaneously presents and
represents Paris, thereby bringing the city to life in all the oxymoronic
splendour of modernity at a time when, as we have already mentioned,
Haussmannization was brutally imposing Paris (as we live it now) on
Paris as it had been idealized in Baudelaire's verse poetry. The result
was a mythologization—the creation of a myth of lost Paris—that coexisted with the existential city. Speed of physical change and
permanence of poetic vision were brought together, in the capital of
modernity, to such an extent that Paris became a prose poem (that
non-synthesizable co-existence of poem and prose), that is to say an
oxymoron, both itself and other. This is the plurality of modernity as
incarnated by Paris, and which goes some way to explaining the
problematic nature of Frenchness as an identity in the modern
Hexagon. It explains, for example, why eating a baguette in France
can both be an extremely satisfying experience and, nonetheless, leave

---

[27] Ross Chambers, *Loiterature* (Lincoln; London: University of Nebraska Press,
1999), *passim*.
[28] Michel Covin, *L'Homme de la rue: Essai sur la poétique baudelairienne* (Paris:
L'Harmattan, 2000).

you slightly dissatisfied, as if the myth and the reality interfere with each other (both positively and negatively). It also explains why Zebda are considered somehow to be both French and other than French. Furthermore, it can be read between the lines of the work of such sociologists as Monica Prasad, whose attempts to understand why France is so French continually revert to the ways in which France *is not*—how it is not like Germany and not like America and the UK, for example.[29] But as Roland Barthes wrote of the nature of the text, the most important difference that a text has is not that which differentiates it from other texts but that which differentiates it from itself.[30]

The contemporary politics of plurality

The same might be said to apply to Presidents. If Nicolas Sarkozy is neither Myrkel, Brown nor Bush, there is also a sense in which he is not himself. A generous commentator might disregard the now infamous 'Casse-toi pauvre con' incident at the Salon de l'Agriculture that marked a rude interruption to the rounds of 'Bonjours' and 'Mercis', and perhaps signalled only that the President wasn't himself *that day*. However, Sarkozy's marriage to model and singer Carla Bruni and the couple's subsequent celebrity status suggest a more durable form of auto-differentiation. If politicians and stars are each compelled relentlessly to occupy the public gaze—and if the boundaries between the two often appear blurred—they nonetheless do so in crucially different ways. The dust of celebrity transforms the merely famous or renowned into an archetype, someone who is famous, also, for being famous. The function of a politician, albeit one with star status, at least in principle, requires a certain detachment from the cult of personality such that decisions, legislations, responses and initiatives can be justified with regard for a putative national, rather than mediatic, interest. As Bruni relaunched her pop career with the 2008 release *Comme si de rien n'était*, songs entered the public

---

[29] Monica Prasad, "Why is France so French? Culture, Institutions, and Neoliberalism, 1974-1981", *American Journal of Sociology*, 111:2 (2005), 357-407.

[30] This is eloquently described, for example, by Barbara Johnson in her essay "The Critical Difference" in Diana Knight (ed), *Critical Essays on Roland Barthes* (New York: G.K. Hall & Co., 2000), pp. 174-82.

sphere including lyrics that inevitably attract biographical readings, such as 'Ta tienne', asserting her husband's ownership of her body, soul and chrysanthemum. In part, Bruni's lyrics, like the mediatic spotlight that her relationship with Sarkozy has cast on him, are open to ironization, hexagonable at least in their introduction of a layer of levity, a break from tradition, a nod to the cultural diversity of their own heritage and playful challenge to linguistic supremacism such as in the lines 'Oh oui, je suis ta tienne/Ah ça ne se dit guère je sais mais c'est bon quand même'. Yet it is worth noting that within days of the album's release blogs around the world contained a range of comments, including sexual innuendos, such that any lingering attachment to the notion of a separation of the public and private spheres was left in tatters.

Sarkozy's celebrity is perhaps simply positioned at the vanguard of yet one more brand-conscious global trend in leadership PR. Nonetheless, the President's election campaign speech of 29 April 2007, in which he denounces the legacy of May 1968 for its legitimization of communitarian irresponsibility does a grave disservice to one of the foundational moments of contemporary France. Castigating the leftist inheritors of the revolutionary movement of a generation ago for the destruction of national pride, Sarkozy proposes a rhetorically charged return to traditional French values, worth quoting at length, that goes beyond the symbols of statehood, and sets his agenda for socio-cultural reform:

> Je veux tourner la page de mai 68. Mais il ne faut pas faire semblant. Il ne faut pas se contenter de mettre des drapeaux aux fenêtres le 14 juillet et de chanter la Marseillaise à la place de l'Internationale dans les réunions du Parti Socialiste. Il ne faut pas dire que l'on veut l'ordre et prendre systématiquement parti contre la police. Il ne faut pas crier à l'Etat policier et à la provocation à chaque fois que la police cherche à faire respecter la loi. Il ne faut pas dire que l'on est pour la valeur travail et généraliser les 35 heures, continuer à surtaxer le travail ou encourager l'assistanat. Il ne faut pas dire que l'on veut faire obstacle aux délocalisations et refuser toute expérimentation de la TVA sociale, qui permet de faire financer la protection sociale par les importations. Il ne faut pas se contenter d'afficher de grands principes en se gardant bien de les inscrire dans la réalité. Je propose aux Français de rompre réellement avec l'esprit, avec les comportements, avec les idées de mai 68. Je propose aux Français de rompre réellement avec le cynisme de mai 68. Je propose aux Français de renouer en politique avec la morale, avec l'autorité, avec le travail, avec la nation. Je leur propose de reconstruire un Etat qui fasse réellement son métier et qui par conséquent domine les féodalités, les corporatismes et les intérêts particuliers. Je leur propose de

refaire une République une et indivisible contre tous les communautarismes et tous les séparatismes. Je leur propose de rebâtir une nation qui soit de nouveau fière d'elle-même.[31]

If France is immutable in anything, however, it is in its openness to change, otherness and contestation. By attempting to write the spirit of 1968 out of French history, the nation's ultimate symbol, the President himself, turns away from its ultimate exceptionalism—the hexagonal multi-directedness and openness to possibility that characterizes the best of the nation. The alternative path for French culture is that of isolation and a refusal to engage with those evolutions in cultural diversity and complexity with which it always already brushes its shoulders. If no man is an island, an inward turning hexagon refusing to embrace the traces of its past may well bring about the fixity and nullity that Michel Houellebecq's character, Daniel25, reads in his predecessor's poetic account of the death of desire, an ambivalent verse reproduced in song in Bruni's album, and elucidating the title of the novel in which it originally appears:

Et l'amour, où tout est facile,
Où tout est donné dans l'instant,
Il existe au milieu du temps
La possibilité d'une île.[32]

France and the Other(s)

Such is the nature of hexagonality that it is more often than not impossible to define where auto-differentiation stops and the encounter with (genuine, external) otherness begins. As we have shown, the state of Frenchness and France's situatedness in the world today can be seen to be comparable to Baudelaire's perversely auto-antonymic Paris of the mid-nineteenth century. We have also alluded to a number of significant others, not least of which Germany. Notably in the twentieth century but also before and since, however, the single most important Other—perhaps for the whole world, but especially, it has been often- and long-argued, for France—is the United States of America. In Kristin Ross's seminal study of French culture, for example, France's ambivalent relationship with the United

---

[31] http://www.u-m-p.org/site/index.php/s_informer/discours/nicolas_sarkozy_a_bercy
[32] Michel Houellebecq, *La Possibilité d'une île* (Paris: Fayard, 2005), p. 433.

States is a vehicle for an analysis of a deep-rooted national anxiety permeating all cultural artefacts.[33] Jointly drawn towards the US and repulsed by it, the French seemed, from the beginning of the Cold War into the mid-sixties, only able to express their Frenchness in relation to this Other; the US was always present as France's Other, either explicitly or implicitly, to the extent that Frenchness had become doubly or self-referentially haunted (haunted both by ghosts of itself and America, and unable to rethink itself in other terms). Our own chosen example of this attitude is the elderly couple in Jacques Tati's *Les Vacances de Monsieur Hulot* (1953), whose behaviour can be read as exemplary of singular plurality or hexagonality. Although the couple walk in the same direction, and to all intents and purposes together, they continually face in opposite directions. She looks forwards, with a constantly happy and optimistic appraisal of the world that she finds before her; he, on the other hand, walks behind her, looking forever backwards, rejecting her gifts of the present (he tosses away with the utmost indifference the sea shells that she passes back to him, for example) and finding solace in the anachronistic behaviour of Hulot. Whether one seeks to read this scene in terms of the French love-hate stance towards Americanization or as a culturally non-specific attitude towards modernity, a model of flânerie, the fact of the film's setting in that liminal space that is the coastline makes it ideally hexagonal: it is both itself and other, of its time and out of step.[34] To this day, one cannot be entirely sure whether the bronze statue of Monsieur Hulot is gazing down at the beach at Saint-Marc-sur-Mer, on the coast of Loire-Atlantique, or across the Atlantic towards America.

More recently, predominant attitudes of otherness have been expressed in another direction, despite the President's much-cited infatuation with all things American, Obama included. With one rotation of the hexagon, France looks now to (even as it turns its back on) Europe. Post-millenial France, as outlined by Rémy Herrara, has had to confront three significant moments of revolt in rapid succession: the No vote to the proposed European Constitution; the

---

[33] Kristin Ross, *Fast Cars, Clean Bodies: Decolonization and the Reordering of French Culture* (Cambridge, Massachusetts: The MIT Press, 1996).

[34] David Bellos, for one, is keen to see Hulot as everyman. See David Bellos, *Jacques Tati: His Life and Art* (London: The Harvill Press, 1999).

uprisings in the *cités* of late 2005; and the reconceptualization of, and subsequent mobilization against, laws governing job security less than six months later.[35] For Herrara, this combination of events constituted "a great French upsurge against neoliberalism", the consequences of which are as yet undeterminable.[36] Each of the events he outlines, we would argue, is implicated as much in cultural contestation as in class struggle—indeed, in the context of a contemporary French establishment with a cluey grip on cultural capital as power (witness the government's global use of in-house publication outlets such as *Label France* to corner the brand market), the two are indissociable. From President-to-be Nicolas Sarkozy's intervention in the uprisings (and his now infamous reference to those rioting as *la racaille*) to his imprisonment of protesters against the proposed *contrat de première embauche*, the figurehead's 'tough stance' on social unrest amounts to an assault on cultural contestation that fails to recognize the ways in which the struggles constituted an alternative vision for France. Herrera defines their aim in terms that complicate any easy demarcation between traditional exceptionalism and market-led reform when he writes of their vision of "a France strong and proud of its diversity", where the sacred cow of integration is no longer relevant beyond the discourse of the elite, and where ordinary youths "are building the France of tomorrow, a society of mutual acceptance and cosmopolitanism".[37] The cultural battlefields, despite his optimism, are still open for business, and nowhere are the lines more clearly identifiable than with regard to France's attitude to its position in Europe.

Despite the perception by most commentators that France's May 2005 No vote represented a refusal of global neoliberalism, a strong current of Islamophobia was also apparent in the campaigns, posters and commentaries in the days leading up to the heat-wave of referendum day. While some No campaigners, such as the *Ligue Communiste Révolutionnaire* led with slogans denouncing 'L'Europe des patrons', bigger guns such as Sarkozy's own *Union pour un Mouvement Populaire*, a party which had set its stall against Turkish

---

[35] Rémy Herrera, "Three Moments of the French Revolt", *Monthly Review*, 58:2 (2006), 13-24.

[36] Herrera, p. 24.

[37] Herrera, p. 19.

membership of the European Union, led their ostensible Yes campaign with the slogan 'L'Europe mérite un Oui: Changeons d'Europe pour renforcer la France' and a stylized Euromap ending somewhere just north of Bosnia. The ambivalence of the message consists on the one hand of endorsing a Europe in need of replacement, and, on the other, of conjuring up a France requiring reinforcement. Against what, or whom, one might ask, and among the 55% of voters who rejected the proposed constitution, a good proportion doubtless did. Responding to the vote in *The Turkish Daily News*, Semih Idiz contextualizes the result against what he calls the true clash of civilizations: between secular and fundamentalist visions of Europe.[38] The ironies, paradoxes and hypocrisies of secular France's failure to 'integrate' its Muslim population, most noticeably its anguished nombrilism concerning what women may or may not, should or should not, can or cannot, do or do not wear on their heads, are well documented. If Turkey and the Islamic world are far beyond the Hexagon, the unresolved issues of the place of Europe's Christian heritage surround the country on five of its six sides and inflect, whether explicitly or not, the parameters of cultural change, acceptance and belonging that France confronts.

A popular culture measurement of the extent to which the dilemma of how to be both European and French induces national schizophrenia—the nation's oscillation between the rampantly individual, an openness to renewal, albeit retrospective, and the *chauvin*—can be gauged from the sequence of titles entered as France's recent Eurovision Song Contest entries: 2004, A Chaque Pas; 2005, Chacun pense à soi; 2006, Il était temps; and 2007, L'amour à la française. As if to emphasize the radical uncertainty of France's Eurodirectionality, the video produced for the 2008 entry opens, in quick-fire succession, with a montage of images of heavily bearded singer Sebastien Tellier in various geographical and ethnic contexts, suggesting a character in quest of a performative identity, confonted with situations that oscillate between criminality, religion and luxurious abandon.

---

[38] Semih Idiz, "The French Referendum and All That", *The Turkish Daily News*, 26 May 2005.

Conclusion: the allegorical hexagon

Contemporary French literature also offers examples of hexagonality, which simultaneously allegorize France and eschew attempts to apply such delimiting readings. Whereas France and her visitors are used to images of women in films and novels standing as Marianne figures, we are perhaps less used to attaching allegorical significance to male protagonists or non-human forms.[39] In Marie Darrieussecq's novel of 1996, *Truismes*, the reader is confronted by a female protagonist whose allegorical significance is challenged by her tendency to change into a pig (although it should be noted that it is as a direct result of her porcine features that she is used as a Marianne image by Edgar, the dictator, whose resemblance to Jean-Marie Le Pen, if satirically distended, is unmistakable). As has been noted elsewhere, the protagonist's continual morphing from woman to pig and pig to woman is symptomatic of the novel's paradoxical structure. Like the text itself, the narrative voice continually fluctuates not from state to state but from process to process: the movement is between actualization and virtualization. The text's actualization is the tendency of the narrative voice to write itself into book form, in which case the readerly text is the tale of a woman taking on flesh and gaining solidity (and thus becoming pig); its virtualization is its tendency, actively and blissfully,[40] to cede authorial power to an apocryphal oral tradition—and thus away from the fixed identity of the work towards the multiplicity of the intertext—whereupon the writerly text is (dis)embodied by the desire of the narrative voice to lose weight (and show a human face).[41]

---

[39] This might arguably explain why it is easier to distance Monsieur Hulot from such an allegorical role. While we may readily think of Brigitte Bardot (as actress, singer and model of the bust of Marianne), perhaps the most striking use of Marianne as an allegory of France's ambivalent attitude to the future is Paul Colin's poster of 1944, *Libération*, which has been expertly analysed in Jill Forbes and Michael Kelly (eds), *French Cultural Studies: An Introduction* (Oxford: Oxford University Press, 1995).

[40] We are, of course, deliberately using terms from Roland Barthes's studies of the movement from work to text.

[41] For a more detailed reading of *Truismes* (Paris: POL, 1996) along these lines, see Alistair Rolls and Marie-Laure Vuaille-Barcan, "Une seule ou plusieurs femmes-truies? Une lecture virtualisante de *Truismes* de Marie Darrieussecq", *Australian Journal of French Studies* 46:1 (2009), 31-44.

What interests us more specifically, in the framework of the present volume, about this tendency of *Truismes* to be a text in constant motion, both movement from inside outwards and from outside inwards, is the way in which this can be mapped, allegorically, onto the dual virtualization and actualization of the Hexagon itself. As we have argued, France's relationship to its hexagonal mapping is double: as expression of desire, the hexagon lies beyond France's geographical borders; as a metaphor for France itself, the hexagon coincides with France's existential reality, on the one hand, but also often with strong overtones of exclusivity. In *Truismes* this exclusivity is sublimated; it is everywhere, to the point of diffusion into one ongoing threat that is increasingly meaningless. The characters are thus excluded to the point of overvaluation, such that what they are excluded from is impossible to define. The idea of border as barrier, therefore, is lost. In its place the novel offers a vision of hexagonality based on the permeability of all borders.

The protagonist's status as perpetual movement between states is reflected by *Truismes*'s structure and setting. Not only is the novel's geographical location exaggeratedly liminal (its space covering and moving between the outer limits of central Paris and the nearest towns of the southern *banlieue*), but its diegetic space also creeps beyond its own borders. Indeed, the text of the novel is problematically located inside and outside the parameters of the story proper. Darrieussecq's use of an epigraph clearly provides a subcutaneous layer between the epidermis of the book cover, or paratext, and the narrator's tale. Furthermore, the substance of this subcutaneous text itself reflects the protagonist's status as always already in motion: the epigraph—a quote from Knut Hamsun's *Benoni*, in which a knife is plunged into a pig's flesh—is pointedly *not* the account of a boar's death, but the description of that moment when a boar realizes that death is imminent, that is that it is coming, that it has begun. The death of a boar also offers a neat mirror image of the novel's plot (whose climax is the attempted murder of the sow) as well as picking up its concluding image, in which the protagonist offers up a human face (or expresses that such is her desire), a face that cannot but reflect the reader who, via the mirror-like book that she is holding, sees herself reflected in the text while also becoming an extension of the virtual text or a reflection of the text's capacity to actualize itself beyond its own borders. Mirrors, then, frame the text. And given that the story repeatedly revels in scenes where power is violently disputed—both in a bid for it to be gained and to be lost—the reader is presented with a text that is both linear (the story of the woman turning into a pig) and circular (a pig writing the story of how she became a pig), and self-reflexively both inside itself (within its protective hide) and outside itself (beyond the story proper, located in the action of Hamsun's plunging knife[42]).

As has been mentioned, this example of a simultaneously painful and pleasurable textual process, in which the pain of reading a novel is matched by that of writing one, with both being reflected in a *mise en abyme* that lies just outside the story (the epigraph), provides us with an allegory of hexagonality. As if to confirm this, the story's heart is pierced—as in Hans Christian Andersen's tale of *The Snow Queen*—by fragments of broken glass.[43] This glass is the ruined remains of the pyramid of the Louvre museum, a space only now accessible to the protagonist's lover, Yvan, who is a werewolf. When in wolf form, he can leap across the broken bridge joining (or not quite joining) the island and the pyramid to the rest of Paris. Hence, the novel is built around a pointedly shattered geometrical construction, and this is simultaneously integrated into and distanced from the text by a stylized architectural feature. In classical French gardens a *saut du loup* was a hole in the exterior walls that served to allow people inside to see out (to extend their view of the internal symmetry into the countryside beyond) and to bring the outside in (but only virtually: actual ingress via the hole in the wall was prevented by a ditch as wide as a wolf's bound). In this way, Darieussecq's pyramid represents both the virtualizing and actualizing tendencies of the text. And by allegorical extension, this perverse novel becomes the always already plural, always already changing story of the Hexagon. That Darrieussecq's polygonal focal point should be fragmented only reinforces the dual nature of ruins; as such it testifies both to an

---

[42] The substance of the epigraph—the plunging of the knife through flesh that at first resists then yields—is reworked in the initial pages of the text proper, in which the narrator warns the reader of the dual difficulty that her story initially presents: that of writing (for her) and reading (for us). In this way, the opening of the text itself becomes yet another dermal layer to be fought past by reader and author alike before the linear plot of the young woman's transformation can begin.

[43] The shards of glass come from a shattered mirror in Andersen's fairy tale, and in *Truismes* the act of looking in a mirror is a leitmotiv.

unmaking and to a future remaking. For like a text that is both circular and linear, France's development appears to be one of evolution and revolution. And in this perverse movement, and in the shapes that it takes and resists, lies the Hexagon.

Perspectives on Hexagonality

The Global Nostalgia of a Non-global Language

Rada Iveković

Global Language

Although there are different globalities for different purposes, the one most widespread global language is English. This is not denying the different global outreach (and different publics) of such languages as Mandarin, Arabic, or Spanish. In this chapter, I compare French as a local, and English as a global language in the postcolonial configuration. Having access to a global language does not preclude the local dimension, which has several tracks: the global language in which it is embedded, but with a different public sphere, and its variants in other local languages. But, nostalgia for an imaginary global dimension—supposedly lost—is based on a fantasy of separate and un-communicating languages, on a monolinguistic dream, and on a related imaginary, as well as on a reality of power dimensions in language relations. The global and the local dimensions of a language (and all languages have, to different degrees, aspects of both) do not really impede each other.

There will only be a hint here of the characteristics of a global language, but we need to address these to some extent.[1] English is, of

---

[1] See my other publications on the topic, on which this chapter draws: "Les paradigmes postcoloniaux par la langue", in Marie-Claude Smouts (ed), *La Situation*

course, besides being global, also so many local languages. Different English idioms contribute to the globality of the language, though that in itself, without the historical link to military, political, economic, symbolic power, would not be enough to make it global. But in this one language, local at some, and global at other levels, there are inner connections and interaction. When we use one language for global purposes, and another for local purposes, or when, moreover, we have no access to the global language at all, those two dimensions are separate, and there is much less *translation* between those language dimensions. I want to introduce the notion of *translating* between the local and the global linguistic spheres, which actually constitute a complex and context-dependent continuity. This is very painful for the French language because of French 'regal' national and colonial power nostalgia, but very smooth, for example, for the Swedish language. Swedes are all bilingual: they speak Swedish and English. They do not mix the two idioms at all in the way colonised populations do. Having access to the global language is much less of a class and power issue for them than it is, for example, for colonial populations; which explains why they do not use English in the same sentence as Swedish, and why they assert nothing in speaking it besides what they have to convey. Speaking English is not, for them, a matter of prestige or of status climbing. There are obvious historic reasons for these differences. As I have described in previous publications, contributing to a global (and conditionally, a universal) context amply repays the individual's investment: the redistribution of the universal (global) allows a partaking at the particular level, since particularities (and singularities) are part of the whole. In this way,

---

postcoloniale (Paris: Les Presses de Sciences Po, 2007), pp. 352-357; "Langue coloniale, langue globale, langue locale", in *Rue Descartes*, 58 (2007), 26-36; "Traduire les frontières. Langue maternelle et langue nationale", in *Asylon(s) - La revue des deux asiles*, 4 May 2008, Dossier "Institutionnalisation de la xénophobie en France", eds. l'Observ.i.x, http://terra.rezo.net/article749.html; my book *Les Citoyens manquants*, available at http://www.ciph.org/recherche.php?idDP=27; and an interview I gave to Boris Buden, "Babel for a birthplace. The trap of the belief in a mothertongue": "Born in Babel/ Geboren in Babel", at http://www.turia.at/-zoom/translate3_zoom.html Boris Buden / Stefan Nowotny (Hg.), Übersetzung: Das Versprechen eines Begriffs, Translate/eipcp-Turia + Kant, Vienne 2009, pp. 131-151, http://translate.eipcp.net/transversal/0908/ivekovic-buden/en.

whatever one invests in the global is paid back as a reward, in any case, in one's capacity to belong to the whole.

Historically, the situation of the French language in its relation to English is different from that of Swedish or of high-class Hindi or Bengali (it may, however, be similar for individuals, even in French). For one thing, French did not receive, did not circulate and could not appreciate or take note of post-colonial notions—because, being globalised and diversified, these exceeded the French language and culture. A postcolonial awareness is coming very slowly and painfully to and through the French language, which also befits the historic processes of colonisation and then decolonisation, which were very different for the two language areas. People who have English as a mode of international communication access directly, whether we like it or not, a global and international public sphere; through US, Australian and now also other universities throughout the world (in Singapore, Budapest…), they will access a very considerable crowd of middle-class intellectuals *sans frontières*. For many of these people from different countries, the local and the global language coincide, giving them remarkable latitude. That the global public sphere is limited in many other ways and also irritatingly hegemonic, there is no doubt. But a critique of that is self-understood and also richly documented, and is not our purpose here. People who have only French as a mode of international communication have access to the remnants of the French colonial empire and to an inner world of sorts. Their own regional, local (and however truly universal) experience will not be directly transmitted to the global sphere (English), but will need to be translated from the French. The hegemony and the planetary domination of English take away nothing from the local colours of French, and are not readily translated into French. There is a direct and obvious connection between linguistic hegemony and power hegemony in international relations. That may change if, by the next century, we all learn Chinese.

The Globalisation of Postcolonial Studies?

There is no academic field called 'postcolonial studies' in France, such as exists in the English-speaking space. Postcolonial topics are distributed, in the French cultural configuration, across so many disciplines. There is also no corresponding semantic field as yet; or rather, it is only being constituted at present and probably since the suburban riots in 2005 in France. The denomination itself is new, sounds awkward, sounds like a neologism (the French language dislikes these) and is only reluctantly accepted. It is a fact, not a value judgement or matter for surprise. It is rather perceived as an 'importation of theories' in France. Painting it as importing 'foreign' and 'inadequate' theories prevents the French from grasping the enriching side of postcolonial investigation and benefitting from all that detours, erring, mistakes, misunderstandings and discontinuities in history have fundamentally to contribute. After all, the circulation of knowledge is necessarily made from such 'importing'. Considering that knowledge coming from elsewhere and through other languages is somehow dangerous, prohibits understanding the dynamics of the acquisition of knowledge, since the latter does not only travel along main roads and via recognised channels. Different configurations and tailoring of research disciplines, of knowledge, in different languages are the result of very different histories of knowledge which partly coincide with different languages and cultures. In France, the CNU (*Conseil national des universités*) and, in the final analysis, the will of the state ('une volonté étatique'), defines and delimits academic disciplines, areas of knowledge and scholarship, and maintains them artificially separate despite the inter- and trans-disciplinary efforts of individuals. A highly centralised, severely standardised language (French), historically inculcated through repressive measures of which culture still bears a poignant memory, names, defines, designates, regulates sciences and formalised knowledge. The present reform of universities and of the CNRS (*Centre national de recherche scientifique*) only hammers down the same principle under new conditions, subordinating research, education, sciences and knowledge not only to the market but also to the state administration (bureaucracy). In France, scholars and academics still need to plead for the right to learn from elsewhere, and to allow for knowledge to travel. While, under the conditions of globalisation, and though it may be completely conditioned by the market and the economy, research and education are nowhere any longer merely *national* since they no longer reproduce national elites but produce transnational ones,

French educational, cultural and research politics still reproduce *l'éducation nationale*. About cognitive capitalism, they know nothing.[2]

France will have to recognise sometime soon the non-globalisation of the French language, again, not as a judgement, but for an historical fact. The alternative is limiting itself to provincial-isation through a French particularism, which is usually called universalism.

From Violence in Language to the Violence of Acts[3]

In violence through language, there is usually an anticipation: through a *discourse* on a menace from others (a threat through words), we legitimise and justify in advance our own very real 'response' to the other's presumed, narrated violence, and we are ready to act—that is how we pass from words to *acts*. This is, of course, because violence, as a possibility (though not as a fatality) precedes language and is already there in culture. Both violence and non-violence, as alternatives, are there. We should never think of violence as opposed or contrary to culture. Believing that 'culture' will spare us violence is naïve. There is all the more violence in a language as it is the seat of power. The mother tongue, the national language, praised by poets, loved by its speakers, is the conveyor of violence—as well as of its flipside: the possibility, the choice, to resist it.

Is the *mother tongue* really the *tongue* of the mother (which socially means, in patriarchy, the father's tongue), as we were brought up to believe? Or is it not rather that the myth of the mother tongue, especially inasmuch as it coincides with the national and the state language, has a role in domination and hegemony? Is it—the (father's) language—spoken by the mother and transmitted to the child? We also know of numerous contrary examples, where the mother's and the father's language are not the same and where, depending on the location, command will be transmitted by the language where the parent's tongue—whichever—*coincides* with the politically dominant one. Is the mother tongue 'our' language? Or could the mother tongue

---

[2] Yann Moulier-Boutang, *Capitalisme cognitif* (Paris: Eds. Amsterdam, 2007).
[3] See Rada Iveković (ed), *Translating violence*, http://translate.eipcp.net/transversal/-1107.

be the mother of (all) languages? There is of course a big difference. The first is a myth in the service of power and of maintaining the status quo. But the latter option is more interesting. *A language can be said to be the mother of other languages imbedded in it*. We learn new languages through the one(s) we already have. To say that we have one language at birth does not really describe our language condition: in addition to many people, depending on geographies, having more than one identifiable language at birth or in childhood, rather, we could say with some certainty that we have at birth a complex possibility of acquiring languages (in the plural). Languages help each other, host each other and give birth to each other. In all these languages one feature appears common to all—translation. It is *translation that is the mother of languages*, and therefore our own mother tongue, unethnicisable. As an Indologist, I also know that people have imagined Sanskrit to be the mother of (Indo-European) languages; or that they have imagined a common old Indo-European language, now lost. These are politically idle, though linguistically fruitful, ideas. I have claimed translation as my mother tongue, because translation even precedes language. There would be no language if there were no translation. And the translatability of all languages coexists with, and maybe exists thanks to, untranslatables. Translation comes 'first'; it comes 'before' any language, as a principle inherent to all. A language is not a language if it is not translatable. 'Translatability' is not a mere accidental attribute of language; it is an inherent and fundamental element in it. This is not to say that there are no 'untranslatable' elements in every language, but they coexist with *a principled translatability*. Translatability is the life of languages. Thoroughly untranslatable, they would also be immobile and impermeable to transformation and evolution: we would then have totalitarian language. The untranslatables are absolutely fundamental too, since they are the guarantee of polysemic values. Untranslatables do not prevent translation, they are, on the contrary, its fuel, and we are lucky to have them. We translate thanks to and in spite of the untranslatables. Therefore, we have the context. But fundamentally, you have translation even before you have a language to translate into, because you must translate yourself to the other in communication; you translate inside-out and reciprocally. You also translate social meanings, political codes, institutions, habits, behaviours into language and vice versa, and this is not a solipsistic activity. It is done by all humanity, even beyond one language, and in a complex network that encompasses space and time, but that also reaches beyond. This is how we are both mortal historic beings (as individuals, and untranslatable), as well as transcendent (as a species). And of course, translation is also what is done within one and the same language (if we could define the latter at all—how do we delimit a language from another if not arbitrarily?). But the distinction between 'language' and 'dialect' is a political one (associated with power, at that), and not at all a linguistic one. We might want to use the Tower of Babel as a metaphor for the universe containing so many universes, or as one language containing the seed of all other languages in that it is basically translation. The day when we would have one absolute language and one single translation is the day we would be dead. As Subcomandante Marcos has it, "el mundo que queremos es uno donde quepan muchos mundos".[4] And the same is true of languages: so many languages fit into one language.

There is no language that can say it all, because language is a part of it all. Basically, we feel any language as insufficient and inadequate, and so too is translation. Languages usually have their mono-linguistic dreams. Linked to at least some degree of linguistic purism, you will find at work a feature which is quite characteristic of the French language: a mono-linguistic, mono-semantic paranoia. I of course agree with David Heller-Roazen when he says, "je conteste le fait que toute langue soit une langue, avec sa propre identité",[5] and when he has it that any language points towards, or echoes, another language; or, as I would say, any language is translation. Therefore, any language is inadequate, incomplete, full of 'untranslatables' and yet necessarily *given to translating*, in the manner of a promise and of an unaccomplished project. Not only is Babel confusing; not only is the network of languages mystifying and bewildering; but so is even one language within itself, and within that language any single sentence or even word or sound. We will never have a definitive

---

[4] Marcos, *Cuarta declaracion de la selva lacandona*, http://palabra.ezln.org.mx/-comunicados/1996/1996_01_01_a.htm.
[5] In interview, "La langue, l'écho, l'oubli" in *Le Monde*, 27 April 2007, p. 12; See also David Heller-Roazen, *Echolalies. Essai sur l'oubli des langues* (Paris: Seuil, 2007).

meaning, which is to say that, though in translation, we shall never be thoroughly translated. Luckily so.

As it appears, we need translation because we are immersed in the historical condition.[6] The political consequences in countries speaking one or the other colonial language are huge, both for the metropolis and for the former colonies. Indian intellectuals, whose local language (English, one among their local languages) coincides with the global language, benefit greatly from this situation and go directly to universities in the USA, unlike Algerians for whom there is no equivalent correspondence, since their colonial language is not at the same time global and gives no cosmopolitan access to knowledge. Very convincingly, André Chevrillon argued as early as 1921 that English was more at ease with 'becoming' (*devenir*) and the flow of time, while French was so with 'being' (*être*) as well as with immobile but successive chunks of time.[7] Even today, or today more than ever, the two languages seem to engage in different degrees or intensities of actualisation of the virtual. There are of course continuities and discontinuities between the two at the same time, in the sense in which any language carries in its bosom other languages; and this also has a parallel in *(in)compossible* continuities and discontinuities (i.e. such continuities or discontinuities that are not possible at the same time) between past and present at all times: it all boils down to the present condition of globalisation. The erosion of sovereignties and deregulation has coexisted with new 'assemblages',[8] or maybe rather with Deleuze's *agencements* that, in the interconnectedness of the new cosmo-political *produce new networks and unexpected combinations and connections*. This production—of new ways of life, of politics, of production, of public spheres, of closed spheres, of informal politics, of new sovereignties (including those built on war), of nonlinear developments and unexpected results, of imaginaries, of new meanings and new symbolisations—is also translation. These translations from the global level can even still

---

[6] Vania Baldi, *Appartenenze sconosciute. Politiche della traduzione culturale* (Rome: ER, 2007).
[7] André Chevrillon, *Trois études de la littérature anglaise* (Paris: Plon 1921).
[8] Aihwa Ong, *Neoliberalism as Exception. Mutations in Citizenship and Sovereignty* (Durham, North Carolina: Duke University Press, 2006); Saskia Sassen, *Territory, Authority, Rights: From Medieval to Global Assemblages* (Princeton: Princeton University Press, 2006).

trickle down into the national level: it is still possible to translate from the national state level to the global level[9] as well as to the personal level, and vice versa, with some misgivings, some misfirings sometimes, and many diversions and gaps to be filled with other unexpected elements. Not only do texts change but so too do *contexts*, and these also need translations, and the phenomenology of politics too calls for translation. Indeed, the context is as important as the text in translation, if not more so. This is particularly clear if we study the way translation is understood historically in Greater China, Korea, Japan (and maybe in other parts of the world), as opposed to the western and European idea of fidelity in translation. There, especially if translating from a distant language, fidelity is observed to the context, not to the text. But the context cannot be translated; it must be transposed, and is thereby shifted and transformed. The result is that the translator interprets the text with the context, improvises the context (with a lot of guesswork), and says what he thinks that the author might have meant, more often than not even disagreeing with him/her.

This poses the question of what may be universal and universalisable: do we need universals or can we do without them? It is clear that we cannot come to terms with the world as it is with the sole claim of the universal, or the sole claim of the particular. Resistance movements, women, have claimed both—neither was sufficient. In reframing the relation that universality signifies, we may want to investigate universal singularity. Balibar has worked on this, and so have, in very different ways, Jean-Luc Nancy,[10] Jacques Rancière,[11] Alain Badiou[12] and others.[13] How does one overcome

---

[9] Sassen.

[10] Jean-Luc Nancy, *Vérité de la démocratie* (Paris: Galilée, 2008); *Juste impossible* (Paris: Bayard Centurion, 2007); *La Communauté désoeuvrée* (Paris: Christian Bourgois, 2004).

[11] Jacques Rancière, *La Mésentente* (Paris: Galilée, 1995); *Aux bords du politique* (Paris: Gallimard, 2004).

[12] Alain Badiou, *Saint Paul, La Fondation de l'universalisme* (Paris: PUF, 1998).

[13] Etienne Balibar, *La Crainte des masses* (Paris: Galilée, 1997)—see last chapter "Les universels", pp. 419-455; "Sub specie universitatis", *Topoi*, 25 (2006), 3-16 DOI 10.1007/s11245-006-0001-6, ©Springer Science+Business Media B.V. 2006; "On Universalism. In Debate with Alain Badiou", http://translate.eipcp.net/transversal/-0607/balibar/en

closure of public, social, political spaces? One of the main questions today is how to understand *migrations* politically, and what to do with them *politically*;[14] and also, how to disconnect, in our perception as well as in analysis, political subjectivity from imaginary identity? I have proposed the concept of the *missing citizen*, to render a class visible: for example, the missing citizens of Europe or of Australia, those who are drowned at sea or are *refoulés,* this latter term to be understood positively as a category (those who could have contributed to our collectivities but who have not, through our stupidity and short-sightedness).

Language is the medium of constructing identities, of producing a consensus of the population, of homogenisation and of negotiating hegemony. Meanwhile, colossal desemanticisation, loss of meaning, and a loss and reshuffling of common language is operated too. All technologies of power operate through *language engineering*, especially nowadays in the new topography of the deterritorialisation of terror (now that terror can reach us anywhere) and of the reterritorialisation of hegemonies.

Dictated and monosemic significations are the sign of a universe of absolute sense. A new type of planetary totalitarianism, passing through language or profoundly anchored and induced through it, is slowly making its way and may be one of the options ahead if we are not vigilant. Violence precedes language in that it is already there in memories, narrations and received histories.

Of Political Imagination, of the Other's History

Received history may mask potential alternative histories while at the same time consciousness is belated. Displacement, emigration, being stateless, which have now become a generalised human condition particularly palpable in (post)colonial history, that of partitions and wars, are generally recognised only post-factum. The retrospective

---

[14] Sandro Mezzadra, *Diritto di fuga* (Verona: Ombre corte, originally published, 2002; expanded edition, 2007); *La condizione postcoloniale. Storia e politica nel presente globale* (Verona: Ombre corte, 2008).

narrative is linked to a space and it "translates a space into a place",[15] a *utopia* in a *topos*. The much-needed political imagination requires setting oneself free from the limits of a received narrative, of an identity, of a language, and necessitates opening up to the diversity of languages, narratives and subjectivities.

Colonial Language as a Pivotal Point between Global and Local Language

Globalised language allows for links and connections between levels that the non-globalised language misses, even as the globalisation of language passed through colonial history and through the universalisation of western modernity. The simple comparison of French (regarding Algeria) and English (regarding India) as colonial languages shows that there has been, in the case of English, an important defusing of the violence of colonisation and decolonisation (India), which has not been possible in the case of French (Algeria). Indian anticolonial critical discourse produced, after a time of sedimentation during the eighties, an invited narrative (Subaltern Studies), welcomed and deviated through the neuralgic centres of globalisation: radical United-States university campuses. The intellectuals of that origin have therefore immediately had access to a world-wide public (elitist, certainly), which was possible only because the global and the local language coincided. The global language is 'neutral' and 'universal', in one sense, without it being so in another: its figure is that of the universal (which is always *both* universal and particular, that is indeed what universality is made of!). It derives its planetary force from the coincidence of its global and local aspect. For Algeria and for France, the specular picture does not exist for several hierarchical reasons having to do with the two Mediterranean shores and through the double disjunction of the language: the French colonial language, not being a global language spoken in places of prestige transcending both ends, has simply become, in Algeria, a foreign language. The other language disjunction operated in Algeria

---

[15] Sanjay Chaturvedi, "The Excess of Geopolitics: Partition of 'British India'", in Stefano Bianchini, Sanjay Chaturvedi, Rada Iveković, Ranabir Samaddar (eds), *Partitions. Reshaping States and Minds* (London: Routledge, Frank Cass, 2005).

has been that of Arabisation and of the partial loss, at university, of the French language.[16]

Conclusion

The rejection of the global language when it is other than one's own, as in the case of French, also has to do with some sort of historical envy. It is not the global aspect itself that is rejected, it is global *English*. Global French would not be rejected if, by any chance, it were really globalised. There is in this refusal some sort of nostalgia for other times (colonial, diplomatic) where indeed French had been much more widespread and the world much smaller—nostalgia with an imaginary that, by the way, does not correspond to reality, since it is an ideal. Such nostalgia reveals the eternal inadequacy of any self-identification, including identification with a nation or with a language. It is anachronic nostalgia for a globalisation that never was. That nostalgia, for a globalisation, is after all already *passé*. It is thus one's own place, as it is being constructed in the universe, that needs to be revisited. If we do not position ourselves in the centre, if we relativise our own position, we may be able to overcome the nostalgia of globalisation. Because, after all, what remains is the insufficiency of any language as such, whether global or local, to say it all.

---

[16] I have dealt with this aspect in several texts: Rada Iveković, "Gefärliche Klassen", *Lettre Internationale*, 71 (2005), 120-121; "Le retour du politique oublié par les banlieues", *Lignes*, 19 (2006), 64-89; "Banlieues, sexe et le boomerang colonial", *Multitudes* 24 (2006), 209-221, http://multitudes.samizdat.net/Banlieues-sexes-et-le-boomerang.html; "French Suburbia 2005: The Return of the Political Unrecognised", Available at http://www.mondialisations.org/php/public/art.php?id=21678&lan=EN (17 November, 2005); "French Riots 2005", *Refugee Watch*, 27, June 2006, MCRG, Kolkata, as well as Les Citoyens manquants, see http://www.ciph.org/-direction.php?etAussi=27 (Collège international de philosophie, Paris).

Frenchness in Perspective(s)

Brigitte Jandey

Although the very notion of national identity is disputable and disputed, in France it continues nonetheless to sustain and underlie a class structure that is increasingly unstable. In doing so, it still serves to give the country a unity, colour, flavour and tone that are generally recognized as French. As it becomes ever more remote from the reality of life in France, French identity reveals itself to be, perhaps now more than ever, a notion, a construction. So, how is one to understand Frenchness? We should like to argue that although France is actually made up of a patchwork of different identities, the defining test for being granted French identity, in cultural terms, is whether or not one adopts the traditional values of the Parisian upper class.

Identities

Rogers Brubacker highlights five main aspects of the notion of identity,[1] two of which are particularly relevant here: identity as a collective phenomenon and identity as individual. When identity is a

---

[1] Rogers Brubaker, "Au-delà de l'"identité"", *Actes de la recherche en sciences sociales*. 4.139 (2001), 66-85 (71-2). Available at http://www.cairn.info/article.-php?ID_REVUE=ARSS&ID_NUMPUBLIE=ARSS_139&ID_ARTICLE=ARSS_13 9_0066 (last accessed 26 August 2009).

collective phenomenon, according to Brubacker, it highlights a
fundamental and perceptible similarity between the members of a
group or category. This similarity can be objective or subjective, as it
is felt, sensed or perceived. On the other hand, when identity is
understood to be a central aspect of the individual or a fundamental
condition of the social being, it has to refer to "[q]uelque chose de
supposément profond, fondamental, constant ou fondateur [...]
comme une chose à valoriser, cultiver, encourager, reconnaître et
préserver".[2] Both these aspects underline the fundamental importance
of identity for an individual, which corresponds to the national stakes
that are our focus here.

First, the notion of similarity between the different parts of a
group implies both a list of criteria attesting to this similarity, and
some arbitration to assess them. In the case of national identity, this
whole process is taken over by the country's administrative laws,
which supposedly make the evaluation objective. In this way, national
identity is a fact: to 'be French' is to fulfil a number of administrative
requirements; this is a reality, then, that is established, can be
demonstrated and should be the only criterion for assessment. French
identity also often coincides with the French identity card, a piece of
cardboard or plastic. Indeed for a long time the iconic ID card simply
and clearly established one's belonging to the Republic, but, as recent
events have shown, this is no longer always the case.

Not long ago, for instance, a French sociologist living in
France, Kristian Feigelson, recounted his experience.[3] He discovered,
when renewing his passport, that he was not as French as everyone
else, because his parents, who were French as well, had been born in a
foreign country. In fact, since 1993, the French administration has
refused to renew a passport or ID card automatically when both
parents of the applicant were born outside of France: current
requirements stipulate that the reasons for the initial granting of
French nationality be traced and verification be made that it would

---

[2] Brubaker, p. 72.
[3] Anne Chemin, "Les papiers de vos parents, s'il vous plaît", *Le Monde*, 31 March
2007. http://www.lemonde.fr/politique/article/2007/03/30/les-papiers-de-vos-parents-
s-il-vous-plait_889839_823448.html (accessed 18 June 2009).

still be granted.[4] Therefore, French national identity can now be denied to French people whose parents came originally from former French colonies that are now independent.[5] Being French, therefore, no longer depends on one's own status but also on that of one's ancestors. The implication is that nationality is no longer *jus soli*, a land right, but *jus sanguinis*, a blood right. However, a blood right implies French ethnicity, which per se is nonsense, as will be demonstrated below. Moreover, the truth is that having the right papers is actually not even sufficient for one to be recognized as French. And this touches on the second of Brubaker's points.

In the second part of Brubaker's definition of identity, the alleged 'something' that identity refers to is said to be deep. This implies that it concerns the subjective way in which an individual assesses her own identity according to the emotions attached to her specific situation. This is 'feeling' French, a deep feeling of belonging, either to a group or a value system, as Albert Memmi points out.[6] In both these cases, belonging is culturally referenced and, therefore, exclusive: it assumes an implicit comparison with another group—the non-French, whose own identity may be defined only in terms of this difference. To 'feel' French, therefore, also means to feel that someone else is not, which implies being more conscious of someone else's differences than of their similarities. In this sense, to feel French is undoubtedly one of the contributors of national extremism. Sociologist Nonna Mayer writes as follows on the 'pride' associated with being French: "Si la fierté d'être Français est très largement répandue, elle caractérise plus particulièrement les personnes âgées, les plus démunies socialement et culturellement, les catholiques pratiquants et les électeurs de droite, et va de pair avec des

---

[4] Unionist Gloria Herpin, quoted by Catherine Coroller, in "La 'consonance israélite' réveille le zèle administratif", *Libération*, 7 August 2007. http://www.liberation.fr/-societe/0101108583-la-consonance-israelite-reveille-le-zele-administratif (accessed 18 June 2009).

[5] Michel Tubiana, "La xénophobie informatisée", *Libération*, 10 August 2007, http://www.liberation.fr/tribune/0101108771-la-xenophobie-informatisee, (accessed 18 June 2009).

[6] Albert Memmi, "Les fluctuations de l'identité culturelle", *Esprit*, 1 (1997), 94-106 (94).

attitudes autoritaires, intolérantes et traditionalistes".[7] To feel French is, then, to construct a boundary against both external intrusion and any form of common construction beyond the nation, such as the European Union. This is an active rejection of the other. This rejection in turn prevents the 'other' from identifying with the group, as Richard Alba highlights when he notes "some hesitation in the identification with France on the part of second generation Algerians".[8]

There is a third aspect of French identity. This is the way one is 'perceived' as French. Albert Memmi has worked on this form of identity that calls on the gaze of the other. "Les Français se reconnaissent entre eux, veulent se reconnaître tels",[9] he writes. Indeed, one can 'be' and 'feel' French without being perceived as such. This third aspect is also subjective, but it is rooted in someone else's perceptions and gaze. This might seem simply to be the reverse of one's own gaze. It is not, however, as simple as that. If in both cases there is appreciation, therefore choice, therefore rejection of what is not chosen, 'feeling' French is clearly not the same as 'being perceived as' French. For instance, it is well known that having dark skin increases exponentially the chances of having one's ID checked by the police. As everywhere, difference, be it of colour, religion or culture, generates suspicion.

In order to frame this third aspect of identity in our more specifically French context, we need to consider what it is like when one is born in a country but one is looked on as a migrant. Of course, one is immediately minded of the situation of second-generation North-African migrants. However, the impact of this model of French identity is or has been much more far-reaching.

---

[7] Nonna Mayer, "La fierté d'être français, de l'indépendance algérienne à Maastricht : Nation, nationalisme, citoyenneté", *L'Année sociologique* 46.1 (1996), 151-67 (151).
[8] Richard Alba, "Bright vs. Blurred Boundaries: Second-generation Assimilation and Exclusion in France, Germany, and the United States", *Ethnic and Racial Studies*, 28.1 (2005), 20-49 (29).
[9] Memmi, p. 102.

Prejudices

In a study of the 2005 riots in the Paris suburbs, Laurent Bazin, an ethnologist for the CNRS,[10] quoted Nicolas Sarkozy, then Minister for Internal Affairs: after having announced that the riots were an Islamist plot, Sarkozy declared that their cause was the polygamy of African families. Not only was this irrelevant, but a great majority of the youths implicated in the riots were actually French.[11] It seems that the troublemakers had to be foreigners or of a different culture if they were trying to destroy what were group symbols. Writing on the same prejudiced judgment, Zsuzsanna Fagyal reached a similar conclusion in her own field, linguistics. Her research targeted the speech of suburban youth, who are often regarded as "not having command of the French language"[12] and, as such, creating all sorts of problems in schools and communities. The study was carried out in a disadvantaged working-class suburb of Paris. She quickly realized that although troubled suburbs are chiefly alleged to be multiethnic, and specifically African, more than 80 per cent of the students were actually born in France; that is to say that they had been exposed to the French language from birth.[13] After two years of research, she concluded that the incriminated youths did in fact have a perfectly usual command of French when they wanted to (any linguistic mistakes they made were only the same as those made by most other French students). Often, however, they would display a Northern African accent, even when it was not their own (they often came from French families or other linguistic backgrounds, including Serbia and China). These results, highlighting a linguistic choice as opposed to an impairment, are confirmed by studies such as those by Isabelle Anzorge, for whom:

---

[10] Centre National de Recherche Scientifique, the government's most renowned research centre in France.

[11] Laurent Bazin, "Invoquer l'"identité nationale', comme l'"ivoirité', est un appel à la xénophobie". Interview with Saïd Aït-Hatri published on *Afrik*, Saturday 16 June 2007. Available at http://www.ldh-toulon.net/spip.php?article2098 (accessed 18 June 2009).

[12] Zsuzsanna Fagyal, "La prosodie du français populaire des jeunes: traits héréditaires et novateurs", *Le Français aujourd'hui*, 143 (2003), 47-55 (47).

[13] Likewise, 1999 statistics show that 73% of inhabitants of the difficult suburb La Courneuve are French citizens, most of them born in France.

Ce métissage lexical et syntaxique est avéré par le fait que ces mots ne sont pas seulement utilisés par les jeunes dits 'issus de l'immigration' mais également par ceux qui sont dénommés 'gaulois' [Français de souche]. Il en est de même pour l'accent et la prosodie, notamment l'accentuation des mots ou fin de phrase sur l'avant-dernière syllabe ou le claquement de langue marque l'approbation d'un propos, que l'on observe chez des jeunes qui ne parlent pas arabe et qui n'ont aucun lien géographique ou familial avec le Maghreb.[14]

Again, we see a choice here. Azouz Begag has observed the same thing in young people from a Northern African background. Even if they can use the standard language correctly, they choose to speak in a distorted and playful way: "L'origine maghrébine et africaine des jeunes les conduit souvent à s'exprimer à la maison avec leurs parents dans une langue maternelle différente du français et, partant de là, à déformer, reformer, jouer avec la langue officielle apprise à l'école".[15] He concludes that "l'utilisation de ce code linguistique relève d'une volonté d'affirmer une identité groupale".[16] This may indicate a need to step away from a national identity that does not have much significance for them.

Indeed, in another study, Anzorge notices that most of these young people feel they are in-between two cultures; they remain attached to their family culture without belonging to it.[17] Interestingly, the problem is different when the children come from a European background:

Il est cependant à remarquer que pour les jeunes d'origine italienne, espagnole, ou portugaise [...] le problème d'identification ne se pose pas pour

---

[14] Isabelle Anzorge, "'Du bledos au toubab', de l'influence des langues africaines et des Français d'Afrique dans le parler urbain de jeunes lycéens de Vitry-sur-Seine", *Le Français en Afrique*, 21 (2006), 59-68.
[15] Azouz Begag, "Trafic de mots en banlieue : du 'nique ta mère' au 'plaît-il?'", *Migrants-Formation*, 108 (1997), 33.
[16] Begag, p. 30.
[17] "La plupart ne maîtrisent pas vraiment la langue d'origine des parents, même s'ils affirment qu'ils la parlent à la maison. En réalité, ils la comprennent mais ne la pratiquent que de façon très artisanale, mélangeant français et arabe maghrébin ou français et langue africaine. Il en résulte un problème d'acculturation renforcée par le fait que ces jeunes se définissent eux-mêmes entre deux cultures : la culture française, qu'ils vivent au quotidien au lycée, et l'autre plus confuse, celle de leurs parents, à laquelle ils essaient d'être fidèles tout en ne la comprenant pas toujours". Anzorge, p. 61.

eux dans les mêmes termes. [...] Ces jeunes se sentent avant tout européens et sont, de plus, confortés dans leur légitimation par le fait que la langue des parents soit enseignée comme langue vivante dans la plupart des lycées.[18]

Once more, this clearly outlines the need for at least some identity recognition: having the family language taught at school brings some validation to the family background. However, it is clear that these French youths do not feel they belong to the proposed French model; they need to skip to the European one. They do not 'feel' French and are not perceived as such. European or not, what all these young people have in common is their socio-economic situation. And it is one that does not fit into the model French identity. As such, an entire component of French society is ignored; that is to say that the image, the 'persona', of French society does not correspond to these people's reality.

When these youths are consistently pointed out as failing to use 'standard' French, this refers to the equivalent of the academic written speech that is conveyed by 'standard' French accent and rhythm. This means that teachers expect standard language, but the first thing they perceive is an accent. This prejudice is common and Bernard Conein and Françoise Gadet have demonstrated that the specific accent of those suburbs provokes an immediate feeling of strangeness, negatively labelled.[19]

Whereas Begag promotes the necessity of mastering mainstream language and social cues to use them as social defence-weapons and to access equal opportunities, and ultimately to use them in order to adapt to society,[20] Fagyal suggests that society should officially integrate these lost identities. Anzorge merely raises the question, pointing out that resisting the official language can only prevent social ascension and complete integration for these youths: "Si ce parler des jeunes fonctionne comme une langue intervéhiculaire en réaction contre la langue qui mène à l'ascension sociale ne risque-t-

---

[18] Anzorge, p. 62.

[19] Bernard Conein and Françoise Gadet, "Le 'français populaire' des jeunes de la banlieue parisienne entre permanence et innovation", in Jannis Androutsopoulos and Arno Scholz (eds), *Jugendsprache / Langue des jeunes / Youth language*, (Frankfurt: Peter Lang, 1998), pp. 105-23.

[20] "La meilleure façon de se défendre dans une société où on n'a pas trouvé sa place consiste à acquérir les règles du jeu social et de (sic) les utiliser pour une 'promotion en interne'." Begag, p. 36.

elle pas à terme de devenir pour certains une langue d'enfermement et de refus autodestructeur?" In a catch-22 situation, these youths are refused a national identity that they themselves reject. As Anzorge points out, they claim instead a hybrid culture in line with their hybrid language.[21]

There is a rather prejudiced idea that has a deal of currency in France, according to which true French people can speak French, and do so properly. The feeling of foreignness attached to the suburban youth accent does not come from pronunciation, however; rather, it hinges mainly on a prosody that consists in lengthening the penultimate syllable and simultaneously shortening the last one. 'Standard' French only lengthens the last syllable of a prosodic phrase, either going up or down. However, although Fagyal acknowledges the influence of declarative phrases from occidental varieties of Arabic,[22] she finds a very close equivalence to this prosody in the old popular Parisian accent, *l'accent faubourien* (cinephiles might think of the accent of actors like Arletty or Carette, for instance).[23] Therefore, if this accent is atypical of French people from middle- or upper-class backgrounds, it is in fact in line with the vernacular speech of the Parisian working class. Nevertheless, it is now perceived exclusively as a migrant trait. Again, cultural exclusion stems from one's social background rather than a national one. From this perspective, when these youths are treated like foreigners, they are merely being signalled out as different from the upper class, which is itself a deliberate choice on their part:

> On constate une forte volonté de reconnaissance autour d'une langue commune qui aurait une fonction de contrenorme face au français de la norme représenté par le discours scolaire. S'ajoute une volonté de norme partagée qui

---

[21] Anzorge, p. 64.

[22] Zsuzsanna Fagyal, "La prosodie du français populaire des jeunes: traits héréditaires et novateurs." *Le Français aujourd'hui*, 143, special edition "Français de l'école et langues des élèves : quel statut, quelles pratiques?" (2003): 47-55, http://www.french.uiuc.edu/people/faculty/articles/LFA_2003.pdf (accessed 18 June 2009).

[23] For a full description of the *faubourien* accent *versus* the upper-class Parisian accent, see also Georges Straka, "La prononciation parisienne, ses divers aspects et ses traits généraux", *Bulletin de la faculté des lettres de Strasbourg*, 30.5-6 (1952), 212-53; and Pierre R. Léon, "Réflexions idiomatologiques sur l'accent en tant que métaphore sociolinguistique", *French Review* 46.4 (1973), 783-89.

permettrait de minimiser les conflits interethniques face aux 'toubabs' qui sont représentés dans leur imaginaire par Paris et les banlieues dites 'chics'.[24]

Clearly, for these young people, school represents Paris and the posh suburbs that establish the canon. It is important to remember, however, that this refusal to adopt the standard Parisian accent is a trait shared by many non-Parisian French people: "Parfois la réaction est d'ordre statique comme le prouve la résistance à l'accent du français standard de la part de bien des provinciaux. L'accent devient alors pour le groupe un symbole socio-culturel".[25] It is clear that this choice of pronunciation is a symbolic act.

The French Canon

So, what constitutes 'standard' pronunciation? Maurice Grammont introduces his iconic treatise of 1914 as follows:

> Cet ouvrage est destiné essentiellement aux étrangers et aux provinciaux qui veulent se perfectionner dans la bonne prononciation française ou se ren- seigner sur elle. Toutes les personnes compétentes reconnaissent aujourd'hui que cette prononciation française est celle de la bonne société parisienne, constituée essentiellement par les représentants des vieilles familles de la bourgeoisie.[26]

We should like to highlight a few points in this statement, since they are still relevant today and go some way to filling in the blanks in the discourse around contemporary standard French. First, the right French pronunciation, i.e. the assumed standard for an entire country, is the pronunciation of a tight social group, openly identified as Parisian by Grammont—'old families' in this case means traceable and thus upper-class, of bourgeois descent. But if there is a right, there is also a wrong. This means that a privileged minority in the country is setting the standard and that everyone else is failing to meet it. This is a question of power relations.

Second, the phrase "all competent people acknowledge" is de- limiting and vague enough to imply that if one does not acknowledge

---

[24] Anzorge, p. 64.

[25] Léon, p. 785.

[26] Maurice Grammont, *La Prononciation française, traité pratique* (Paris: Librairie Delagrave, 1914) quoted in Claude Duneton, *Parler croquant* (Paris: Stock, 1973 [1978]), p. 32.

this point then one is not competent. These rules, seemingly so typical of *la vieille France* and outdated, actually still operate. As a matter of fact, Grammont's treatise, written in 1914 and widely distributed throughout provincial schools, was reprinted in 1961 with the same introduction, continuously feeding—and justifying—the cliché that 'good Parisian society' dictates standard values for the rest of the French people. The implied message, here just as in Fayal's study, is that French identity is the privileged possession of a small section of the French upper classes. As Azouz Begag points out, "le jeune qui montrera ses capacités à acquérir les codes standards de la société, celui qui sera capable de ne pas laisser paraître, grâce à une bonne maîtrise du français, son origine (les marques de sa spécificité culturelle) aura plus de chance d'être intégré qu'un autre".[27] That is to say that no matter how long one's family has been French (centuries in the case of provincials or decades in the case of migrant groups) one needs to adopt the standard codes of 'good society' in order to be regarded as genuinely French, and amongst the most obvious of these codes is language. It is very tempting to draw a parallel with contemporary globalization, where all countries are urged to adopt the mainstream neo-liberalism pattern and its counterpart, American English.

Finally, we should like to return to Grammont's quotation and the amalgamation of 'provincials and foreigners'. 'Foreigners' denotes people estranged from a reference group, in this case again, 'good Parisian society': the gaze comes from 'the old bourgeois families'. This is reinforced by the statement that provincials need to increase their knowledge of the right French pronunciation, as is also picked up by Léon. Provincials and foreigners are on the same footing: they are not really French, not sufficiently at least. The gaze consistently comes from this upper class that suburban youths oppose so vigorously, and the standard matches its values. And, of course, this appropriation of French identity is nothing new. The following section isolates a few defining moments of the history of French identity.

---

[27] Begag, p. 36.

History: What Gauls?

"Autrefois notre pays s'appelait la Gaule et ses habitants les Gaulois".[28]

Any French person knows that France was once called Gaul and that his or her French ancestors are Gauls. It is broadly considered an historical fact. In fact, few people know that these words were literally written into the first history lessons of all French primary-school children just over a century ago. And not only in France but also, ironically, in the most remote French colonies. Although begun in the sixteenth century, this myth of the Gauls as the founding fathers of the country was actively taken up for the first time during the Third Republic. In fact, the word *Gallia* initially had nothing to do with a country; it was merely a convenient word used by Caesar to designate a vast, and vaguely defined, territory located between the Atlantic, the Rhine, the Danube and what is now northern Italy.[29] Disparate and motley tribes lived there for six centuries with no administrative or ethnic unity before slowly regrouping through alliances and conquests. This means that from the beginning, the area known today as France was a patchwork of cultures, languages and ethnicities in constant transformation. Just as it is now.

In terms of language, at the end of the fifteenth century France still had a multitude of tongues and dialects that had evolved from this patchwork of tribes. The language of the court, *francien*, was absorbing all sorts of new words, archaisms, neologisms, professional words, other dialects and local vernaculars.[30] In 1634, however, Richelieu, the King's Prime Minister, entrusted Malherbe, a jurist, with 'tidying up' this language, which he considered degenerate. To 'purify' the language Malherbe established a strict doctrine drawing on logic and grammatical rigour. He created the Académie Française, which to this day is in charge of removing 'impurities' from the official vocabulary. In the seventeenth century, this very clearly meant deleting all that did not belong to the language of the court and Parisian high society, which included all regional or professional

---

[28] Emile Lavisse, *Histoire de France illustrée* (Paris: Hachette, 1911).
[29] Suzanne Citron, *Le Mythe national: l'histoire de France en question* (Paris: Les Éditions Ouvrières; Etudes et documentation internationales, 1987).
[30] Duneton. p. 41.

contributions. Even pronunciation was strictly codified. This reframing of language established a radical schism between the upper and lower classes and a linguistic dictatorship. Standard French was spoken nearly exclusively by the French (and some foreign) courts, the aristocracy and upper bourgeoisie. It became a metonym for the aristocracy itself, completely severed from the rest of the country.

Interestingly, this aristocratic method of creating French identity can be contrasted with the bourgeois one: both have imposed an elitist cultural system, but where the aristocracy operated by distancing power from its roots and rejecting input from the lower classes, the bourgeoisie simply ignored other cultures and imposed its own under the cover of gathering forces. Hence, when the bourgeoisie seized power during the French Revolution, the new parliament baptized itself the 'National Assembly'. In so doing, it gathered forces under a common banner, stressing similarities rather than differences (until then the concept of 'nation' referred to a group of people who shared common ancestors, a common language, a common religion and common customs[31]—more or less what we would call a region today, i.e. an ethnic and cultural entity). The nation was proclaimed 'one and indivisible'. In giving a meaningful label to this new collective, which was a kingdom no more, the new Republic for the first time artificially but symbolically blended numbers of radically different cultures under a common identity, thereby setting up the process of imposing its own, Parisian bourgeois, values on the rest of the country. It is easy to imagine how the concept of unity and indivisibility was attributed to this cultural multitude in this period of revolution and promises; equally, one can imagine how challenging it must have been for these multitudes to embrace this new entity.[32] Yet at that stage, local cultures were still different. It was not until a century later that the construction of French identity was systematically organized.

---

[31] Suzanne Citron, "Ecole, histoire de France : construction d'une mémoire nationale, crise de l'identité nationale", *Dialogues Politiques, revue plurielle de science politique*, 2 (2003), http://www.la-science-politique.com/revue/revue2/papier2.htm (accessed 18 June 2009).
[32] Today we have some idea of what it might have been like, given the challenge of creating and enlarging the European community.

Manufacturing French Citizens

After a destabilizing defeat in the war against Prussia, the Third Republic needed more than a purely symbolic national identity to secure power. They would have to break the mould of the culturally different regions if they were to craft a truly unified national identity. Drastic measures were enforced, designed to blend citizens thoroughly and to instil the same cultural foundations in them from childhood.[33] The strategy had three key objectives: reshaping the past, sharing the present and projecting a common future.

The 'Gauls' officially became the fathers of the country as a means of supplying this meaningful and united past.[34] Legendary characters, such as Vercingétorix or Jeanne d'Arc, were called upon. These ideal role models became national symbols: they came from the provinces but had a strong national consciousness; they had not hesitated to die for their country and its values. There was no need to disclose the more obscure aspects of their existence, like Vercingétorix's likely enrolment in the Roman army, for example. After his resurrection in 1850, he became what he would remain forever: the young, rebellious, charismatic and fierce warrior chief of the Gauls. In fact, history itself became a way of instilling into children the respect and admiration of conquerors, the establishment and their glorious ancestors.[35]

In turn, military service became compulsory since France also needed a strongly united present. Besides the obvious benefit of having a reserve army in case of another war, this gigantic human melting pot, where men were systematically removed from their place of origin, meant that in order to communicate, they had to fuse their own tongue into a single French language. Moreover, enduring common hardships created a strong feeling of equality, which endured until the end of the twentieth century when military service was abolished. As a matter of fact, in the beginning of the nineteenth century the nation was still seventy per cent rural, with villages that were self-

---

[33] Citron (2003).
[34] Suzanne Citron, *Le Mythe national : l'histoire de France en question* (Paris: Les Éditions Ouvrières, 1991).
[35] Citron (2003).

sufficient and mainly non-francophone.[36] The working classes in the cities, on the other hand, lived in a different world from the ruling classes. The differences between them were obvious, being at the same time economic, social, cultural and linguistic. But in spite of these widely divergent identities, the founders of the Republic wanted to enforce their idea of a unified nation. They therefore imposed their Parisian bourgeois values on both the multicultural France of the countryside and the acculturated working-class France of the cities. They even rolled out the same principles across the rest of the world: humanity was neatly classified into four main races—white, black, yellow and red, with the white race having the right, indeed the duty, to civilize the others.[37] The bourgeoisie sought nothing less than the civilization of all humanity. In the meantime, it refused to recognize religious, ethnic, cultural or genetic otherness, including other languages (Arab, Yiddish, Occitan, Alsatian, African, English, Polish, Italian, to name but a few). Today, these important components of French identity are still not fully honoured as constitutive parts of the French genetic and cultural heritage.

Next, France needed a politically united future. Schools were assigned the crucial goal of shaping young children's minds and creating new French citizens, patriotic, respectful of the new order and, crucially, French-speaking.[38] In 1881 public primary school education became free; in 1882 it was made compulsory and non-religious. The new religious education was 'civic instruction', a neat curriculum inculcating the religion of a strong Republic.[39]

As early as 1924 Durkheim analyzed the fundamental principle of manipulating school curricula as "[un principe qui] assure la stabilité de la société et le maintien du consensus qui lui permet d'exister".[40] For some thirty years now historians and sociologists have highlighted the socio-political consequences of this manipulation

---

[36] Suzanne Citron, *L'Histoire de France autrement* (Paris: Les Éditions Ouvrières, 1992).

[37] Citron (2003).

[38] Citron (2003).

[39] Writing in a Canadian journal, Morin calls this social manipulation 'the big sting'. See Michel Morin, "La grande arnaque", *Liberté*, 274 (2006), pp. 53-63.

[40] Quoted in Françoise Lantheaume, "Solidité et instabilité du curriculum d'histoire en France: accumulation de ressources et allongement des réseaux", *Education et Sociétés*, 12.2 (2003), 125-42 (126).

of education. Anglo-Saxon studies demonstrated long ago that school curricula reflect the state of power relations in society.[41] For their part, in the 1960s, Bourdieu and Passeron focused on "les savoirs qui contribuent à la légitimation de l'ordre social par l'école".[42] According to Bourdieu,

> tout tend à démontrer au contraire que [le système scolaire] est un des facteurs les plus efficaces de conservation sociale en ce qu'il fournit les apparences d'une légitimation aux inégalités sociales et qu'il donne sa sanction à l'héritage culturel, au don social traité comme don naturel.[43]

Today, it is widely recognized that one of school's essential roles is to solidify the establishment. It is important to bear this in mind when considering the path currently being taken by President Sarkozy, as he aims to reconstruct national identity, which was weakened in the aftermath of May '68 and the Left's rise to power in 1981. In a televised interview, he insisted on his "volonté de refonder le consensus entre l'école et la nation, la première étant solennellement réaffirmée comme le creuset de la seconde".[44] The new curricula therefore are once again a key part of 'civic and moral education', the teaching of which includes "les règles de politesse et de bonne tenue, la connaissance et le respect des valeurs et des emblèmes de la République française: le drapeau tricolore, Marianne, l'hymne national, à l'écoute duquel nos enfants devront se lever".[45] Movement—the act of standing up, as if to attention—is a crucial part of this lesson in respect. This time, however, the strategy is being openly announced as a salutary measure to safeguard the Republic. This is the same scheme of standardizing individuals from birth, with

---

[41] See Basil Bernstein, "On the Classification and Framing of Educational Knowledge", in Michael F. D. Young (ed), *Knowledge and Control: New Directions in the Sociology of Education* (London: Collier Macmillan, 1971), pp. 245-70.

[42] Pierre Bourdieu and Jean-Claude Passeron, *Les Héritiers : les étudiants et la culture* (Paris: Minuit, 1964).

[43] Pierre Bourdieu, "L'Ecole conservatrice : Les inégalités devant l'école et devant la culture", *Revue Française de Sociologie*, 7.3 (1966), 325-47 (325).

[44] Luc Cédelle, " Nicolas Sarkozy et Xavier Darcos font bloc pour réformer l'école primaire", *Le Monde*, 15 February 2008, http://www.lemonde.fr/cgi-bin/ACHATS/-acheter.cgi?offre=ARCHIVES&type_item=ART_ARCH_30J&objet_id=1024856 (accessed 17 June 2009).

[45] Documentary aired on French television network France 2, 15 February 2008.

no regard to their origins, customs and aspirations; French identity is a
uniform, clearly defined and to be worn by all.

Françoise Lantheaume tells the story of a general inspector for
education who, in 2000, reminded teachers that the mission of the
educative system and the teaching of history consisted in "constructing citizens [...] and continuing to produce French nationals",
which is to say, perpetuating the same system.[46] More recently, in
2005, politicians from both the Left and the Right rejected a bill that
aimed at abrogating article 4 of the Law of 23 February 2005, which
pushes school curricula to underline "le rôle positif de la présence
française outremer".[47] Whilst the French dream of colonization is long
since gone, it seems that some vestiges of "le rayonnement de la
France", the radiant French presence beyond its borders, still remain.

Languages of France

The process of *francisation* instigated by the Third Republic has not
been an easy task. As late as 1930, seventeen million French citizens
could speak French only a little or badly, because it was not their
mother tongue. The remaining two thirds spoke dialects or local
languages. In schools, teachers would beat children for not speaking
French and teach them that speaking their own language was a source
of shame.[48] This position mirrored what Rivarol had written five years
before the French Revolution: "A cet égard, la France paraît plus
heureuse : les patois y sont abandonnés aux provinces, et c'est sur eux
que le petit peuple exerce ses caprices, tandis que la langue nationale
est hors de ses atteintes".[49] This also matched the idea behind his other
revealing words:

> En effet, quand l'autorité publique est affermie, que les fortunes sont assurées,
> les privilèges confirmés, les droits éclaircis, les rangs assignés [...], alors on
> commence à distinguer autant de nuances dans le langage que dans la société.

---

[46] See Dominique Borne, "Où en est l'enseignement de l'histoire?" *Le Débat*, 110
(2000), 167-76.
[47] Jean-Pierre Thibaudat, *Libération*, 30 May 2007. Paragraph two of article four was
suppressed on 25 January 2006.
[48] Duneton, chapter 1, *passim*.
[49] Quoted in Duneton, p. 70-1.

[…] Les styles sont classés dans notre langue comme les sujets dans notre monarchie.[50]

Although the monarchy was dead, the idea of a social hierarchy of languages was still alive. As the French language had been crafted out of the categorical refusal of any popular roots,[51] it immediately became a class language. Its logic made it the ideal vehicle for articulating abstract thought—hence its reputation in philosophy— and, its control system, the Académie Française, made it unique in the world and quickly earned it the praise of foreign courts throughout the eighteenth century. It is this court language that the Third Republic later imposed on its peasants and labourers.

A century before globalization, *francisation* was enforced to the same outcries of those who opposed the process. The result is a linguistic caste system, where people who experience difficulties mastering the language are misjudged by those who learnt from birth to articulate all its nuances; where having an accent tends to imply a lack of 'education', because it indicates origins one ought to be ashamed of. It is on this basis that 'good society' claims that subjection to the Académie Française and a century of strong-armed persuasion has finally succeeded in creating a profound love of their language in the French people.

In the same way that provincials were denied their identity and regarded as second-class citizens a century ago, second- and even third-generation French people are looked at as migrants today. It is this situation that prompted a young man, interviewed by a national TV channel during the 2005 riots, to say that what the rioters wanted was to be considered and looked at as fully French, a part of the country where they were born.

Egalité

If all were supposed to receive this same Republican education, in reality equality was only for some: the bourgeoisie was never supposed to fuse with the lower classes, as numerous sociological studies have shown:

---

[50] Quoted in Duneton, p. 70-1.
[51] Duneton, p. 66.

Ainsi, les premières générations ont connu un système éducatif où coexistaient deux ordres scolaires : l'enseignement secondaire réservé à la bourgeoisie et l'enseignement primaire pour les enfants issus du milieu 'populaire'. La distinction sociale se faisait non pas à l'intérieur du système scolaire mais en amont de ce dernier.[52]

It is important to keep in mind this double-barrelled equality. The social elite had and still has its coded reference system and its own schools, from kindergartens through to the most prestigious *Grandes Ecoles*.[53] Not only are they hugely expensive, but these private tertiary schools also still, as they always have, admit students on the basis of their *dossier scolaire*, their individual student files, which trace all their personal and, sometimes, family history. This effectively allows each school to handpick its students. Some of these schools had been created even before the Revolution and were initially known as 'royal' schools. They had no problem surviving the political turmoil and proliferated under the Republic, teaching students how to rule the country, manage the newly established factories, and transmit and perpetuate values and etiquette. This system is still in place. With time they began to take in some lower-class students, but not necessarily as part of a democratizing process: it must be borne in mind that these students had to be exceptionally bright to be granted a scholarship, which in turn served to bolster the school's image as a place of excellence and, of course, democracy. In this way, face was saved. Besides, the percentage of these students has always been very low and still is. Albouy and Wanecq have established that "[u]ne analyse portant sur l'origine sociale des élèves ayant accédé à ces grandes

---

[52] Valérie Albouy and Thomas Wanecq, "Les inégalités sociales d'accès aux grandes écoles" (report by the Institut National de la Statistique et des Études Économiques, 2002), *Economie et statistique,* 361 (2003), p. 34.
[53] See Pierre Bourdieu, *La Noblesse d'État : Grandes écoles et esprit de corps* (Paris: Les Éditions de Minuit, 1989), in which the *Grandes Ecoles*, private selective universities, are presented as the structural heirs of the aristocratic class of the Ancien Régime. See also Bourdieu (1966); Michel Euriat and Claude Thélot, "Le recrutement social de l'élite scolaire en France : Evolution des inégalités de 1950 à 1990", *Revue Française de Sociologie*, 36.3 (1995), 403-38; and Raymond Boudon, *L'Inégalité des chances : la mobilité sociale dans les sociétés industrielles* (Paris: Armand Colin, 1973).

écoles des années 1940 aux années 1980 souligne la permanence d'une sélection sociale et culturelle très marquée".[54]

In 2007, the Sarkozy government imposed a new quota on French high schools, with especial focus being placed on those in sensitive areas: all high schools were now systematically to present five per cent of their best students for admission into the *prépa* system, classes designed to prepare students for the competitive entry examinations for the *Grandes Ecoles*. However, on 25 March 2009,[55] he suppressed the system of ranking students for the *Ecole national d'administration* (ENA), a system that insured that the fifteen highest ranked students could choose their positions within state administration. Removing this grading system opens the door to a return to nepotism, as the overwhelming majority of these important positions are held by members of wealthy families, who are in turn likely to recruit people from amongst their peers. It also protects the existing social hierarchy, thus preventing French identity from including the multiple identities of the French people.

For over a century, the social structure has been protected and shored up by a ruling class proud of its domination in the intellectual, cultural and diplomatic arenas. In fact, the nineteenth-century ruling elite had genuine faith in their construction of the nation. They believed in "la France supérieure comme dogme et comme religion",[56] as Michelet had already written in 1847—a dangerous slogan at all times, as recent history has often shown. This class has continuously nurtured the myth of a homogeneous France, whose identity it designed in its own image. Pierre Nora, in his iconic *Lieux de mémoire*,[57] refers to this methodical construction as a "dispositif de mémoire dont l'essentiel a été mis en place très vite—qui s'est

---

[54] Albouy and Wanecq, p. 27. In fact, Euriat and Thélot show that the percentages of students from working-class backgrounds admitted into the four main Grandes Ecoles covered in their study have dropped over the last forty years: from around 29 per cent in the early 1950s to only nine per cent today (p. 50).

[55] Christian Bonrepaux, "La fin du classement de sortie de l'ENA soumise au conseil des ministres", *Le Monde,* 25 March 2009, http://www.lemonde.fr/societe/article/-2009/03/25/la-fin-du-classement-de-sortie-de-l-ena-soumise-au-conseil-des-ministres_1172373_3224.html (accessed 18 June 2009).

[56] Cited in Citron (2003).

[57] Pierre Nora (ed), *La République*. 7 vols. Vol. 1, *Les Lieux de mémoire* (Paris: Gallimard, 1984).

rapidement fondu dans le capital mémoriel collectif pour en constituer la toile de fond et perdurer, somme toute, jusqu'à nos jours".[58] Then as now, the ideal of *Liberté, Egalité, Fraternité* was in reality completely irrelevant. Just as there were two worlds in the education system, there were two worlds in the social one. Social classes became more separated than ever with the beginning of capitalism. From the beginning, labourers lived in miserable conditions and their world remained parallel to that of the people for whom they worked, with whom they sometimes rubbed shoulders without ever mixing. A century later, in an original field study on the bourgeoisie, Beatrix Le Wita interviews women about their childhood and early adulthood at the beginning of the twentieth century:

> We were completely ignorant of how people lived who were not like us. We had no contact, as children, with working-class children. [...] I didn't know [working men's wives] at all. We only saw country people. I felt a tremendous gulf, discovering those women, in fact I still feel it.[59]

There were indeed two separate Frances, whose identities were quite different in spite of the common national motto.

This methodic construction, which ignores difference, has survived revolutions and all reforms. In May '68, as Perry Anderson points out,[60] the mere spectre of social reorganisation stirred such a panic in the establishment that it was instantly dismissed and provoked violent reactions against all '68 ideas. A comparable reaction was witnessed after the recent riots in the Paris suburbs when politicians from all sides campaigned in one voice for 'unity'. That is to say that for the last presidential elections they again invoked the old discourse of Nation and French identity—at that very moment when it had been proven to be completely irrelevant.

Conclusion

Philosopher Charles Taylor has written that "[a] fragmented society is a society in which the individuals find it harder and harder to identify

---

[58] Nora, p. 651.
[59] Beatrix Le Wita, *French Bourgeois Culture* (Cambridge: Cambridge University Press, 1994), p. 45 (this quotation includes responses from two separate interviewees).
[60] Perry Anderson, *La Pensée tiède : un regard critique sur la culture française* (Paris: Seuil, 2005).

with their political entity as a community. This weak identification may reflect an atomist perspective that leads people to consider society from a strictly instrumental point of view only".[61] Although French identity has been carefully crafted in the image of a social class, for a long time most French people felt they recognized themselves in it because it mirrored what they had learned for generations at school and generally in their day-to-day social interaction. But new generations, specifically of migrant-born children, have not necessarily been spoon-fed the same French bourgeois values and thus do not recognize themselves in the proposed model. Indeed, their use of society tends to be more instrumental. For them, France's historical reality is not the glossy image that the Republic has been successfully exporting over the course of the last century. *Liberté*, *Egalité*, *Fraternité*, the 'universal' republican motto, does not apply to them.

France has always been plural; that is what made it France. But although assimilation has been an ongoing process, it has been a matter of imposing dominant, leading values rather than creating an adapting reality by acknowledging new social input. Indeed, out of a pious wish for unity, French bourgeois identity has denied other classes and origins their existence. As has been shown, this construction has worked for more than a century, which has prompted Albert Memmi to state that "le plus remarquable dans l'identité culturelle n'est pas sa réalité mais son efficacité".[62] And yet, there seems now to be an urgent need for all parts of society to be allowed to identify with the country as a community. Rather than trying to 'integrate' difference, this requires social and cultural means of highlighting this multiplicity as an active component of a real collectivity and as a rightful constituent of the national identity, past and present.

---

[61] Quoted in Jean-François Hersent, "L'identité culturelle de Geneviève Vinsonneau", *Bulletin des Bibliothèques de France*, 48.2 (2003), p. 123.
[62] Albert Memmi, "Les fluctuations de l'identité culturelle", dossier "La fièvre identitaire", *Esprit*, 1 (1997), 94-106 (106).

National Genius and Universal Sociability: The Relevance of the Enlightenment Today

Jean-Marc Kehrès

Translated from the French by Alistair Rolls

In March 2007, even as Nicolas Sarkozy, the UMP candidate for the presidential election, was voicing his support for the creation of a ministry of immigration and national identity, Ségolène Royal, the socialist candidate, was calling on her supporters to sing the Marseillaise at electoral meetings. But the question of the threat posed to a French identity by diversity was already a subject of debate in the eighteenth century and the *Encyclopédie*. Voltaire, for example, seeks to define French identity and the Chevalier Louis de Jaucourt defends the concept of welcoming foreigners in the name of human sociability and economic progress.

Our aim here is to examine the various ways in which the *Philosophes* sought to resolve the tensions opposing 'national character' and various types of diversity, be they provincial or national. How does the 'national genius' fit with the diversity of 'souls', for example? To what extent does a French spirit endure over time? How do the *Philosophes* stand in relation to naturalization? And what are the consequences of defining French identity as the synthesis of its plural origins? The exploration of these issues will reveal the extent to which the 2007 French presidential elections echoed the questions, contradictions and silences that punctuated the discourse of the Enlightenment as presented in the *Encyclopédie*.

Twenty-five years after the first volume of Diderot and d'Alembert's *Dictionnaire raisonné des arts et des sciences* was published in 1751, the *Encyclopédie* already extended to twenty-eight volumes with more than 150 contributors. As Fabienne-Sophie Chauderlot notes, "l'*Encyclopédie* [...] déploie un espace où l'hétérogène est privilégié".[1] This heterogeneity, which springs from the work's structure and the multiplicity of its authors, will be central to our analysis of a group of entries, for the majority of which the Chevalier de Jaucourt was responsible. Indeed, he himself was the author of almost a quarter of the entries that made up the *Encyclopédie*.

If for royalists such as Marchand, author of *La Constitution en vaudevilles* (1792),[2] citizenship was a right for those born on French soil, in revolutionary France it could now be obtained through an oath of allegiance and for the payment of a small sum that represented a remnant of the Ancien Régime *chenage*. The France of the eighteenth century distinguished between those born in the kingdom ('Naturel François ou régnicoles') and those 'aubains ou étrangers' who could only secure the same privileges by obtaining a letter of *naturalité*, which in theory was given by the sovereign.[3] In order to be able to settle in France, foreigners needed to have this letter confirmed for an initial sum of one thousand *livres* plus an annual fee. The entry on *naturalité* states that: "Il y a des lettres de naturalité accordées à des nations entières qui sont alliées de la France, de manière que ceux de ces pays qui viennent s'établir en France y jouissent de tous les privilèges des régnicoles sans avoir besoin d'obtenir des lettres particulières pour eux".[4] In this way, some people were exempted from the 'aubains' category:

---

[1] Fabienne-Sophie Chauderlot, "Encyclopédismes d'hier et d'aujourd'hui: informations ou pensée? Une lecture de l'*Encyclopédie* à la Deleuze", *Studies on Voltaire and the Eighteenth Century*, 5 (2002), 37-62 (42).

[2] Marchand, *La Constitution en vaudevilles* (Libraires royalistes, 1792).

[3] For an analysis of the policies and methods of attributing letters of naturality, see Peter Sahlins, *Unnaturally French: Foreign Citizens in the Old Regime and After* (Ithaca: Cornell University Press, 2004), pp. 8-11.

[4] *Encyclopédie*, Vol. XI, p. 39.

Quelques peuples alliés de la France ne sont point non plus réputés aubains : tels sont les Suisses, les Savoyards, les Ecossais, les Portugais et les Avignonnais ; qui sont réputés naturels et régnicoles, sans avoir besoin de lettres de naturalité. Les Anglais même sont exempts du droit d'aubaine, au moins pour ce qui est mobilier, en vertu de l'art. 13 du traité d'Utrecht.[5]

The prerogatives regarding inheritance, as reserved for the English, were thus accorded quite liberally to foreigners, notably for reasons of foreign policy.[6]

In 1792, hospitality—that great Enlightenment ideal of relations with the other, i.e. the foreigner—seems to find a political application. In his entry entitled *Hospitalité*, the Chevalier de Jaucourt defines hospitality as "la vertu d'une grande âme, qui tient à tout l'univers par les liens de l'humanité".[7] Throughout, Jaucourt is at pains to underline the universal aspect of human sociability, citing the Stoics for whom hospitality was a virtue and something to be extended to all men. In addition to being universal, hospitality was also a natural and exemplary act that had accompanied man from the time of his first travels. And if he recognizes that in the infancy of travel, hospitality relied only on the charity of certain individuals, Jaucourt nevertheless continues to build his list of precedents with examples taken from the Bible, such as Abraham's compassion for foreigners and the Egyptians who, in their belief that gods took the form of travellers to correct man's injustice, held hospitality amongst the most sacred of duties.[8] He goes on to quote the Ethiopians, the Greeks and the Persian kings who benefited greatly from the hospitality that they offered to various peoples.[9] By positing hospitality amongst the most fundamental human rights, Jaucourt is pleading the case for political asylum. Not only does Jaucourt consider that he has proven hospitality to be a praxis accepted universally across the ancient world, he extends his timeline into the annals of modern history: "Les Germains, les Gaulois, les Celtibériens, les peuples Atlantiques, et presque toutes

---

[5] *Encyclopédie*, Vol. I, p. 863.
[6] For an historical and social study of foreigners naturalized between 1660 and 1789, see Sahlins, pp. 135-212.
[7] *Encyclopédie*, Vol. VIII, p. 314.
[8] *Encyclopédie*, Vol. VIII, p. 315.
[9] *Encyclopédie*, Vol. VIII, p. 314.

les nations du monde, observèrent aussi régulièrement les droits de l'hospitalité".[10]

Whereas he previously evoked hospitality in terms of charity, Jaucourt proceeds to discuss it in terms described in the *Encyclopédie* as a form of case law. Hospitality is thus described as a kind of contractual relationship, of the type entered into by the Persians according to Homer, which, by definition, unites two parties, each of whom is free to accept or to refuse the terms of the agreement: "ce qui forme le contrat, c'est le consentement mutuel et réciproque des parties contractantes; d'où il suit que ceux qui ne sont pas en état de donner un consentement libre, ne peuvent pas faire de contrats".[11]

This view of hospitality as a 'contract' is clearly problematic. Unlike the spontaneous act of charity, the contract is an exchange based on common interests. The asylum seeker and his host are in fact on an equal footing insofar as the latter anticipates reciprocal benefits from the former. This personal interest is legitimated because

> [l']amour-propre ou le désir continu du bien-être, l'attachement à notre être, est un effet nécessaire de notre constitution, de notre instinct, de nos sensations, de nos réflexions, un principe qui tendant à notre conservation, et répondant aux vues de la nature, serait plutôt vertueux que vicieux dans l'état de nature.[12]

Conceived of as an advantage or profit in the field of commerce, the benefit here becomes for Jaucourt *"une espèce* de bénéfice".[13] Hospitality is

> [u]ne libéralité exercée envers les étrangers, surtout si on les reçoit dans sa maison : la juste mesure de cette espèce de bénéfice dépend de ce qui contribue le plus à la grande fin que les hommes doivent avoir pour but, savoir aux secours réciproques, à la fidélité, au commerce dans les divers états, à la concorde et aux devoirs des membres d'une même société civile.[14]

Here reciprocity annuls the idea of profit, for human society is based upon mutual assistance.[15]

---

[10] *Encyclopédie*, Vol. VIII, p. 316.
[11] *Encyclopédie*, Vol. IV, p. 122.
[12] *Encyclopédie*, Vol. VIII, p. 818.
[13] Our emphasis.
[14] *Encyclopédie*, Vol. VIII, p. 314.
[15] *Encyclopédie*, Vol. VIII, p. 818.

Jaucourt's definition of liberality differs markedly from the meanings given in dictionaries of and before his time. Nicot, for example, in the *Thrésor de la langue française* published in 1606, associates liberality with abundance and largesse, while the 1694 and 1762 editions of the *Dictionnaire de l'Académie française* suggest an identical connotation: "Grande libéralité, Libéralité Royale [...] Voilà une libéralité extraordinaire".[16] For Jaucourt, this overabundance characterizes generosity, which is to be distinguished from liberality: "une qualité moins admirable que la générosité ; parce que celle-ci ne se borne point aux objets pécuniaires, et qu'elle est en toutes choses une élévation de l'âme".[17] In a semantic shift liberality comes to signify for Jaucourt "une vertu qui consiste à donner à propos, sans intérêt, ni trop, ni trop peu".[18] Here we see the introduction of the idea of an equal relationship: the action is described as *à propos*, i.e. it displays reason (*la raison*) in the strict sense of the Latin *ratio* or proportion. One should give neither too much, so as not to display superiority vis-à-vis the recipient, nor too little, which would constitute an affront or an attempt to gain some advantage.

According to Jaucourt hospitality is not about displays of blind altruism; rather, it should preserve the benefactor's economic integrity. Born of cautiousness, which is not to be confused with rapaciousness, pettiness or prodigality whose blind excess transgresses the requirements of reciprocity, liberality negotiates a path between these two extremes and strengthens social harmony: "En tout cela la juste mesure de la bénéficence, dépend de ce qui contribue le plus aux diverses parties de la grande fin ; savoir aux secours réciproques, au commerce entre les divers états ; au bien des sociétés particulières, au-tant qu'on peut le procurer, sans préjudice des sociétés supérieures".[19]

Amongst the other forms of liberality, Jaucourt includes alms and compassion, which he terms 'practical'. Here he is referring to the tensions inherent in a secular *caritas*, which are attested to by the use of a double—religious and juridical—register, with liberality being defined as a 'contract'. Described as stemming from a natural impulse,

---

[16] See *Dictionnaire de l'Académie française*, First Edition (1694), p. 644, and *Dictionnaire de l'Académie française*, Fourth Edition (1762), p. 32.

[17] *Encyclopédie*, Vol. VII, p. 574.

[18] *Encyclopédie*, Vol. IX, p. 460.

[19] *Encyclopédie*, Vol. IX, p. 461.

the gift does, however, put the beneficiary in the debt of his host. Inasmuch as it embodies the idea of exchange, the contract, by the obligation that it sets up, is a supplement that calls into question the natural origins of the reciprocity. Indeed, Jaucourt states that "le contrat produit l'obligation, et celle-ci produit l'action pour contraindre l'obligé à exécuter son engagement".[20] Benevolence towards the other, therefore, stems from a perverse combination of natural empathy, interests that are clearly understood[21] and a reciprocity that is contractually guaranteed.

For Jaucourt, hospitality's conflicting origins are masked by the antithetical tension in the nature of human relations, which sees sentiment opposed to venality. As a result of this, he considers the decline of hospitality to be directly linked to the development of commerce. After all, the *sine qua non* condition of hospitality is the traveller's vulnerability and lack of material possessions. A new love of objects, for Jaucourt, replaces something natural by which mankind was united.[22] In a conception of history where the age of gold replaces the Golden Age, Jaucourt now paints an idealized vision of ancient hospitality, and this in spite of the limitations that he had initially observed.

By eroding the ties of authentic, unifying humanity, commerce, which introduces the mediating factor of money, contravenes natural law and the ideal of sociability.[23] Man, as an essentially social being, can only survive thanks to his fellow man. Without sociability, Jaucourt considers, there is no human union, and without that no self-preservation and no happiness.[24] In light of this, the question must be raised as to whether this universality of the spirit of sociability, driven by the search for happiness, is not contradicted by the *Encyclopédie*'s

---

[20] *Encyclopédie*, Vol. IV, p. 122.

[21] The reference here is to Rousseau, for whom interests are *bien compris* to the extent that one recognizes the same expectations in the other and sacrifices immediate and selfish gratification to the protection of interests that will ensue at a later stage.

[22] *Encyclopédie*, Vol. VIII, p. 316.

[23] This recalls Montesquieu who, in *L'Esprit des lois*, even as he praises commerce for the peace that it establishes between peoples, denounces its consequences for the relations between people of the same nation. See Montesquieu, *L'Esprit des lois*, Book XX, Chapter II, in *Œuvres de Montesquieu* (Amsterdam; Leipzig: Arkstée et Merkus, 1772), p. 239-40.

[24] *Encyclopédie*, Vol. XV, p. 252.

reflections on the 'national genius' and the theories justifying the determination of beings.

D'Alembert's entry on climate takes up Montesquieu's analysis of the influence of heat and cold in *L'Esprit des lois*.[25] In addition to being a determining factor, physically and mentally, climate produces effects on morals. These effects being negative in the case of hot climates, they require the introduction of legislation to counteract them. D'Alembert quotes Montesquieu's reflections in this regard, noting in particular how Indians, for whom heat produces a weak body and lively imagination, are capable of equal amounts of courage and weakness. This is said to explain their natural laziness and attachment to customs. The role of legislation in such a case, according to Montesquieu, should be to discourage indolence.[26] Oddly, the legislative process is governed by pure reason and unaffected by climate. The legislator who seeks to correct moral excesses brought about by climatic influences on physiology is to impose a universalist ideology predicated on work.[27]

The mark of climate is not indelible, however. Again drawing on *L'Esprit des lois*, d'Alembert points out that "[n]os pères les anciens Germains qui habitaient un climat froid, avaient des lois très-peu sévères sur la pudeur des femmes. Ce fut autre chose quand ils se virent transportés dans le climat chaud d'Espagne".[28] The climate to which the individual is exposed also leaves its mark on the national character and the morals that it 'inspires'.[29] This notion of national genius is taken up in the *Encyclopédie*'s entry on the *Nation*.

---

[25] Montesquieu's physiological explanation of Nordic peoples' greater strength, resilience and self-confidence, which in turn leads to increased political honesty, are found in book XIV, p. 31-32. See also Henry Vyverberg, *Human Nature, Cultural Diversity, and the French Enlightenment* (Oxford; New York: Oxford University Press, 1989), pp. 64-87.

[26] *Encyclopédie*, Vol. III, p. 532.

[27] Montesquieu's ethnocentrism is based on a gendered north-south divide along climatic lines. In this way, peoples of the north are masculine, i.e. vigorous but heavy, and peoples of the south are feminine, i.e. physically delicate but sensitive. *Esprit des lois*, XIV, p. 37.

[28] *Encyclopédie*, Vol. III, p. 533.

[29] Montesquieu states that laws are institutions clearly made by the legislator whereas morals are institutions generally *applicable to* the nation. *Esprit des lois*, Book XIX, Chapter XIV, p. 200.

Defined as "a considerable quantity of people inhabiting a certain area of land, enclosed by certain limits, and which answers to a single government", the nation is distinguished by its unique character.[30] The contradictions that mark these reflections on national character have not been lost on critics. As Robert Morissey writes,

> the two paragraphs contradict one another in at least one aspect. For in the list of nations illustrating various national temperaments some entities figure, such as Italy and Germany, that are not united under a single government [...]. This oversight would seem to imply a kind of automatic assumption that cultural and geographical coherence of nations correspond to political boundaries. In any case, to all appearances this is a hastily written article drawing upon standard material and composed without much thought.[31]

Highlighting that national characters are recognized in the *Encyclopédie* as being stereotypes, Elizabeth Rechniewski notes: "[t]he fact that such ideas are 'une espèce de proverbe' is not apparently cause for deeper reflexion. On the contrary, it seems as though the reference to 'la sagesse des nations' is proof in itself".[32] Does this entry reveal an unreflecting adherence to a *sagesse des nations*? The qualities attributed to the nations quoted in the entry are hardly favourable. The French are characterized by a flightiness that, according to Montesquieu, is due to the balanced climate in which they live. Paradoxically, peoples that enjoy a temperate climate are not characterized by moderation, but by inconstant behaviour.

Under the entry *Caractère des nations*, the very notion of national character becomes increasingly problematic. Not all the French share the national character, for example:

> Le caractère d'une nation consiste dans une certaine disposition habituelle de l'âme, qui est plus commune chez une nation que chez une autre, quoique cette disposition ne se rencontre pas dans tous les membres qui composent la nation : ainsi le caractère des Français est la légèreté, la gaieté, la sociabilité, l'amour de leurs rois et de la monarchie même, etc.

---

[30] The entry notes the following proverbial characters: the French are flighty, the Italians jealous, the Spanish serious, the English malicious, the Scottish proud, the Germans drunken, the Irish lazy and the Greeks two-faced.
[31] Robert Morrissey, "The *Encyclopédie*: Monument for a Nation", *Studies on Voltaire and the Eighteenth Century*, 5 (2002), 143-61 (146-47).
[32] Elizabeth Rechniewski, "References to 'National Character' in the *Encyclopédie*: The Western European Nations", *Studies on Voltaire and the Eighteenth Century*, 12 (2003), 221-37 (228).

And furthermore:

> Il y a grande apparence que le climat influe beaucoup sur le caractère général ; car on ne saurait l'attribuer à la forme du gouvernement qui change toujours au bout d'un certain temps : cependant il ne faut pas croire que la forme du gouvernement lorsqu'elle subsiste longtemps, n'influe aussi à la longue sur le caractère d'une nation. Dans un état despotique, par exemple, le peuple doit devenir bientôt paresseux, vain, et amateur de la frivolité ; le goût du vrai et du beau doivent s'y perdre ; on ne doit ni faire ni penser de grandes choses.[33]

If climate informs the national character, the importance of its role is twice challenged in the extracts quoted above: on the one hand by the ambiguous expression *il y a grande apparence* and on the other by its subordination to the effect of a long-lasting government. This challenge to the existence of a national character allows for the existence of French people who are unmarked by this 'flightiness' and who do not share a love of the monarchy. Indeed, the author of the entry is among their ranks. For, we should bear in mind that the entries *Nation* and *Caractère des nations* are left unsigned. There is every reason to believe that the anonymous authors were hoping to avoid potential political repercussions.[34] The inclusion of examples presented as *espèces de proverbes*, and thus departing from the stereotypes that are given, shows that the long list of national characters is in fact designed to dissimulate, inside a discourse belonging to the doxa, a criticism of a power considered to be absolutist.

This entry concludes with a reference to the entry *Caractère*, which, however, offers no explanation as to the origin of the national characteristics mentioned. Also anonymous, it defines character as a general propensity towards a certain type of behaviour. It is significant that the concluding example used to illustrate the danger of French 'flightiness' is taken from politics, and more particularly the example of a revolt against the established order: "Cela me rappelle cette belle loi de Solon, qui déclarait infâmes tous ceux qui ne prenaient point de parti dans les séditions : il sentait que rien n'était plus à craindre que

---

[33] *Encyclopédie*, Vol. II, p. 666.

[34] The entries devoted to Germany, Italy, Ireland and Greece are signed by Jaucourt. Although he evokes the unity that Germany's emperor conveys, he does not fail to mention Italy's political fragmentation, Ireland's status as belonging to Great Britain and Greece's subjugation to the Ottoman Empire.

les caractères et les hommes non décidés".[35] Made via a critique of indecision in terms of political engagement, this entry's reflections on character initiate a critique of French 'flightiness' and of the autocratic regime that is based upon it.

Recalling this 'flightiness' by its reference to the 'frivolity' that is the mark of peoples subjected to despotism, the entry *Caractère des nations* constitutes a denunciation of the power of the monarchy and of the decadence that it engenders. Commenting on the use of these adjectives, Rechniewski notes that "[t]hese critical observations have a political function: they reflect the views of an intellectual elite which has adopted a critical stance towards the current regime and imply that absolutism leads to weakness and decline in the strength of the national character".[36] These reflections on national character can thus be argued to be a veiled attack on a regime that forbids its people to "faire et de penser les grandes choses", and which above all was attempting to suspend the publication of the *Encyclopédie*.

The French national character and the social and political ideal that it represents crystallize around the figure of the Gaul. The writings of Jaucourt[37] and Voltaire on this figure differ markedly. In the entry *Gaule ou les Gaules*, Jaucourt defines a region that "renfermait le royaume de France, tel qu'il est aujourd'hui, la Savoie, la Suisse, le Piémont, une partie du pays des Grisons, et toute la partie d'Allemagne et des Pays-bas qui sont au couchant du Rhin".[38] *Gaule* was thus occupied by a great number of independent peoples. Jaucourt notes how this demographic and political heterogeneity is accompanied by the absorption of those peoples who took the name of Gauls after being conquered by them in battle. To talk of one original Gaul is thus highly problematic; indeed, Jaucourt himself speaks of 'plural Gauls'. The term 'nation', in this context, is clearly unworkable. Highlighting the near impossibility of knowing anything of Gaul's political and administrative organization, Jaucourt shows the contradictions between the descriptions of Roman historians and Gallic practices, each presented as an irrefutable eye-witness account.

---

[35] *Encyclopédie*, Vol. II, p. 666.
[36] Rechniewski. p. 233.
[37] For example, his entries *Gaule ou les Gaules*, *Gaulois* and *Temple des Gaulois*.
[38] *Encyclopédie*, Vol. VII, p. 527.

In terms of its geography and even the number of Roman provinces that it constituted, ancient Gaul remains an enigma.

The mystery surrounding Gaul and its inhabitants is also evidenced by the entry *Gaulois*, according to which even the etymology of the name itself is unknown. Certainly, no case is made for a Greek, Breton or Cimbrian origin. But the mysterious origin of the name is the tip of iceberg. According to Jaucourt, nothing can be known of the origins of Gaul's peoples, their religion, their customs or their form of government.[39] The meagre knowledge that survives comes via Greek and Roman historians, and is as such of dubious value.

Despite his reluctance to rely on Greek and Roman sources, Jaucourt draws on Livy and Caesar when discussing the Gauls' military expeditions into Italy. Their sacking of Rome, after the Battle of Allia (c.387 BC), was followed by successive defeats, culminating with that inflicted upon them by Caesar. Jaucourt notes with surprise the lack of solidarity and national spirit expressed by the Gauls throughout this period. To this failure to act together in the face of a common enemy, Jaucourt adds the Gauls' own cruelty and superstition, such as human sacrifice, including the burning of men inside wicker statues and the use of entrails for divination. By way of a conclusion to his entry, he writes: "Il faut, comme le dit M. de Voltaire, détourner les yeux de ces temps horribles qui font la honte de la nature".[40]

This critique of Gallic customs allows Jaucourt to denounce superstition and the hold over political power maintained by the clergy. His references to ritual burnings, with their overtones of the inquisition, stand as a condemnation of religious intolerance, as voiced also by Voltaire. Yvon's entry on the *Celtes* presses the same point. Again, in this criticism of the supreme power of the druids we should read a denunciation of the church's tyrannical hold over the monarchy and the wealth and superstition on which its power was based. For Yvon, however, the Gauls stand out from other Celtic peoples on the grounds of their civility:

---

[39] *Encyclopédie*, Vol. VII, p. 528.
[40] *Encyclopédie*, Vol. VII, p. 529.

> Par exemple, du temps de César et de Tacite, les Gaulois différaient beaucoup des Germains, quoiqu'ils eussent une même origine. Les Germains étaient extrêmement grossiers en comparaison des Gaulois, qui, au rapport de Justin, avaient adouci leurs mœurs par le commerce des Grecs, qui étoient venus s'établir à Marseille, et avaient puisé chez eux quelque teinture de cette politesse qui leur était comme naturelle.[41]

For Voltaire, this civility will be the cardinal virtue of the Gauls as ancestors of the French. For, unlike Jaucourt, Voltaire appears to believe in a perennial national character. In his entry on the *Français* we read: "On ne connut guère le nom de François, que vers le dixième siècle. Le fond de la nation est de familles gauloises, et le caractère des anciens Gaulois a toujours subsisté".[42] Voltaire next establishes a dialectic allowing the integration of newcomers, according to which the origins of this genius lies in the synthesis of climate (nature) and customs (habit). National genius is thus a common denominator arising from regional diversity. In this way: "Les peuples de la Guyenne et ceux de la Normandie diffèrent beaucoup: cependant on reconnaît en eux le génie français, qui forme une nation de ces différentes provinces, et qui les distingue au premier coup d'œil, des Italiens et des Allemands".[43]

This tendency for national genius to outweigh regional characteristics extends to art. Indeed, French art is emblematic of a French identity forged out of diversity; it too synthesizes and smoothes away the plurality of foreign origins:

> S'il cultive aujourd'hui tous les arts dont il fut privé si longtemps, ce n'est pas qu'il ait un autre esprit, puisqu'il n'a point d'autres organes, mais c'est qu'il a eu plus de secours ; et ces secours il ne se les est pas donnés lui-même, comme les Grecs et les Florentins, chez qui les Arts sont nés, comme des fruits naturels de leur terroir ; le François les a reçus d'ailleurs : mais il a cultivé heureusement ces plantes étrangères ; et ayant tout adopté chez lui, il a presque tout perfectionné.[44]

---

[41] *Encyclopédie*, Vol. II, p. 808.

[42] *Encyclopédie*, Vol. VII, p. 284.

[43] *Encyclopédie*, Vol. VII, p. 284.

[44] *Encyclopédie*, Vol. VII, p. 285. For a more detailed analysis of Voltaire's conception of physiological inscription of taste, see Jean-Marc Kehrès, "Libertine Anatomies: Figures of Monstrosity in Sade's *Justine ou les malheurs de la vertu*", *Eighteenth-Century Life*, 21 (1997), 104-05.

Voltaire goes on to describe how the natural world has an unchanging effect on men, whilst the determining effects of culture (government, religion, education) are subject to variation. It is this nexus that, for Voltaire, explains how certain elements of the ancient character are retained and others lost. This plural vision of the French national character—previously described as the common denominator of provincial characters—is replaced, however, by the concept of Gallic immutability: "Le fond du Français est tel aujourd'hui, que César a peint le Gaulois, prompt à se résoudre, ardent à combattre, impétueux dans l'attaque, se rebutant aisément. César, Agatias, et d'autres, disent que de tous les barbares le Gaulois était le plus poli : il est encore dans le temps le plus civilisé, le modèle de la politesse de ses voisins."[45]

This exaggerated picture of Gallic sociability is presented as the universal example of civilization. Voltaire moves seamlessly from a description of the Gaul, as offered by Caesar, to the Parisian, as described by the Emperor Julian and Marcus Aurelius:

> Mais comment concilier le caractère des Parisiens de nos jours, avec celui que l'empereur Julien, le premier des princes et des hommes après Marc-Aurèle, donne aux Parisiens de son temps? J'aime ce peuple, dit-il dans son Misopogon, parce qu'il est sérieux et sévère comme moi. Ce sérieux qui semble banni aujourd'hui d'une ville immense, devenue le centre des plaisirs, devait régner dans une ville alors petite, dénuée d'amusements : l'esprit des Parisiens a changé en cela malgré le climat.[46]

Paris is thus described as the centre of pleasure, whose inhabitants are alienated from politics and where political power grows unchecked. It has often been noted how the flightiness of the French character includes two opposed behaviours: a positive type, embodying sociability; and a negative one that shirks political responsibilities. The original inconstancy of the French, their 'flightiness', changes under Voltaire's pen into a 'vivacity' that is itself similarly double:

> Comment expliquer encore par quels degrés ce peuple a passé des fureurs qui le caractérisèrent du temps du roi Jean, de Charles VI de Charles IX, de Henri III et de Henri IV même, à cette douce facilité de mœurs que l'Europe chérit en lui? C'est que les orages du gouvernement et ceux de la religion poussèrent la vivacité des esprits aux emportements de la faction et du fanatisme ; et que cette même vivacité, qui subsistera toujours, n'a aujourd'hui pour objet que

---

[45] *Encyclopédie*, Vol. VII, p. 285.
[46] *Encyclopédie*, Vol. VII, p. 285.

> les agréments de la société. Le Parisien est impétueux dans ses plaisirs, comme il le fut autrefois dans ses fureurs. Le fonds du caractère qu'il tient du climat, est toujours le même.[47]

With this diachronic portrait of the French, Voltaire portrays a being at the mercy of political power, and especially religion and the 'enthusiasm' and intolerance engendered by it.

This sociability of the French, innate and yet to be achieved, recalls what Stéphane Pujol writes on Enlightenment reason: "Pour les hommes des Lumières, la raison est d'abord une donnée originelle : commune à tous les hommes ; elle est même le critère constitutif de l'humanité. Mais elle peut aussi se comprendre comme une conquête historique : il y aurait alors un trajet de la raison vers l'universel".[48] This journey towards a perfected form of sociability which is paradoxically already inherent in the French character is mirrored by the advent of the French national character itself, immutable and sporadic. In Voltaire's mind, the Middle Ages constitute an eclipse— feudalism engenders a diversity of mores and laws, and even the provinces which have remained loyal to the king lose their common features:

> Lorsque la monarchie fut démembrée dans la décadence de la race Carlovingienne ; lorsque le royaume d'Arles s'éleva, et que les provinces furent occupées par des vassaux peu dépendants de la couronne, le nom de François fut plus restreint ; et sous Hugues Capet, Robert, Henri, et Philippe, on n'appela Français que les peuples en-deçà de la Loire. On vit alors une grande diversité dans les mœurs comme dans les lois des provinces demeurées à la couronne de France. Les seigneurs particuliers qui s'étaient rendus les maîtres de ces provinces, introduisirent de nouvelles coutumes dans leurs nouveaux états. Un breton, un habitant de Flandres, ont aujourd'hui quelque conformité, malgré la différence de leur caractère qu'ils tiennent du sol [et] du climat : mais alors ils n'avaient entre eux presque rien de semblable.[49]

We see how Voltaire suppresses the determining role of climate, arguing instead that it is the political regime and culture that shape people. In this way the court, as source of civility, is also the source of

---

[47] *Encyclopédie*, Vol. VII, p. 285.

[48] Stéphane Pujol, "Histoire et philosophie de l'histoire au XVIIième siècle: La critique de l'universalisme chez Voltaire et Herder" in David Bell, Ludmilla Pimenova and Stéphane Pujol (eds), *La Recherche dix-huitièmiste. Raison universelle et culture nationale au siècle des Lumières* (Paris: Champion, 1999), p. 184.

[49] *Encyclopédie*, Vol. VII, p. 285.

the uniformity that characterizes the nation, shining its civilizing light out into the provinces and throughout the world:

> Ce n'est guère que depuis François I que l'on vit quelque uniformité dans les mœurs et dans les usages : la cour ne commença que dans ce temps à servir de modèle aux provinces réunies ; […] La galanterie et la politesse commencèrent à distinguer les Français sous François I, les mœurs devinrent atroces depuis la mort de François II. Cependant au milieu de ces horreurs, il y avait toujours à la cour une politesse que les Allemands et les Anglais s'efforçaient d'imiter. On était déjà jaloux des Français dans le reste de l'Europe, en cherchant à leur ressembler. Un personnage d'une comédie de Shakespeare dit qu'à toute force on ne peut être poli sans avoir été à la cour de France.[50]

As we have seen, this argument is based upon a diachronic contradiction which posits a politeness that was already characteristic of the Gauls and which, at the same time, results from the civilizing work of the court of François I. Furthermore, this contradiction is duplicated at the synchronic level in the assertion of the coexistence of sociability and atrocity.

We must now consider what ramifications this question of national character has on our understanding of the welcoming of foreigners. Does incompatibility of character, for example, affect the question of naturalization? In the same way that national belonging is not defined in racial terms in the entry *Nation*, there is no mention of any potential conflict caused by the inclusion of foreigners within the French nation. Posed in economic terms, the question of naturalization is broached via a consideration of the English situation. The author is again Jaucourt:

> Naturalisation, (Hist. d'Anglet.) acte du parlement qui donne à un étranger, après un certain séjour en Angleterre, les privilèges et les droits des naturels du pays. Comme cet acte coûte une somme considérable que plusieurs étrangers ne seraient pas en état de payer, on agite depuis longtemps dans la Grande-Bretagne la question importante, s'il serait avantageux ou désavantageux à la nation, de passer un acte en parlement qui naturalisât généralement tous les étrangers, c'est-à-dire qui exemptât des formalités et de la dépense d'un bil particulier, ou de lettres patentes de naturalisation, tout étranger qui viendrait s'établir dans le pays, et les protestants par préférence.[51]

---

[50] *Encyclopédie*, Vol. VII, p. 286.
[51] *Encyclopédie*, Vol. XI, p. 39.

This entry allows Jaucourt to advocate naturalization. His first step is to pick up the arguments raised by the opponents of naturalization, including the fear that the native population would lose their work and be thrown into poverty, and that a sudden wave of immigration would usher in, to borrow a phrase from Michel Rocard, 'all the misery of the world'. He then rejects these arguments by quoting the economic advantages of admitting a foreign population:

> Les personnes qui tiennent pour l'affirmative (et ce sont les gens les plus éclairés de la nation) répondent, 1°. que de nouveaux sujets industrieux acquis à l'Angleterre, loin de lui être à charge, augmenteraient ses richesses, en lui apportant de nouvelles connaissances, de manufacture ou de commerce, et en ajoutant leur industrie à celle de la nation. 2°. Qu'il est vraisemblable que parmi les étrangers ceux-là principalement viendraient profiter du bienfait de la loi, qui auraient déjà dans leur fortune ou dans leur industrie des moyens de subsister. 3°. Que quand même dix ou vingt mille autres étrangers pauvres, qu'on naturaliserait, ne retireraient de leur travail que la dépense de leur consommation sans aucun profit, l'état en serait toujours plus fort de douze ou vingt mille hommes. 4°. Que le produit des taxes sur la consommation en augmenterait, en diminution des autres charges de l'état, qui n'augmenteraient aucunement par ces nouveaux habitants. 5°. Que l'Angleterre peut aisément nourrir une moitié en sus de sa population actuelle, si l'on en juge par ses exportations de blé, et l'étendue de ses terres incultes ; que ce royaume est un des plus propres de l'Europe à une grande population par sa fertilité, et par la facilité des communications entre ses différentes provinces, au moyen des trajets de terre ou de mer assez courts qui les produisent. 6°. Que les avantages immenses de la population justifient la nécessité d'inviter les étrangers à venir l'augmenter.[52]

The tension in Jaucourt's argument is between two visions of immigration, which, in the terms of the current French debate, are 'chosen' versus 'endured'. As an advocate of hospitality and political asylum he writes in his entry on *Sujet* that "c'est un droit naturel à tous les peuples libres, que chaque sujet et citoyen a la liberté de se retirer ailleurs, s'il le juge convenable, pour s'y procurer la santé, les nécessités, et les commodités de la vie, qu'il ne trouve pas dans son pays natal".[53]

Having drawn on history to underline the negative consequences of xenophobia, in his entry on *L'Étranger* Jaucourt moves on to praise Alexander who "ne se montra jamais plus digne du nom de grand, que quand il fit déclarer par un édit, que tous les gens de

---

[52] *Encyclopédie*, Vol. XI, p. 39.
[53] *Encyclopédie*, Vol. XV, p. 643.

bien étaient parents les uns des autres, et qu'il n'y avait que les méchants seuls que l'on devait réputer étrangers".[54] In conclusion he returns to the arguments put forward in Great Britain on the matter of naturalization, according to which,

> [a]ujourd'hui que le commerce a lié tout l'univers, que la politique est éclairée sur ses intérêts, que l'humanité s'étend à tous les peuples, il n'est point de souverain en Europe qui ne pense comme Alexandre. On n'agite plus la question, si l'on doit permettre aux étrangers laborieux et industrieux de s'établir dans notre pays, en se soumettant aux lois. Personne n'ignore que rien ne contribue davantage à la grandeur, la puissance et la prospérité d'un état, que l'accès libre qu'il accorde aux étrangers de venir s'y habituer, le soin qu'il prend de les attirer, et de les fixer par tous les moyens les plus propres à y réussir. Les Provinces unies ont fait l'heureuse expérience de cette sage conduite. [...] D'ailleurs on citerait peu d'endroits qui ne soient assez fertiles pour nourrir un plus grand nombre d'habitants que ceux qu'il contient, et assez spacieux pour les loger.[55]

In the mid-eighteenth century this discourse is already marked by a familiar tension: that between immigration open to victims of persecution and those in search of a better life on the one hand, and on the other, immigration limited to hard-working and industrious foreigners who will be an asset to the economy. Familiar indeed, if we consider the the words of then candidate for the presidency, Nicolas Sarkozy on 25 March 2007: "Tout au long de cette campagne, ce qui est important pour moi, c'est [...] de montrer que la maîtrise de l'immigration, c'est possible". He goes on to place the following conditions on family entry and settlement:

> [P]our pouvoir faire venir sa famille il faut un logement, parce que c'est quand même extravagant de faire venir sa famille quand on n'a pas de logement. Ou alors qu'est-ce qu'on veut, des squats? La seconde condition, c'est qu'on ait un revenu, parce que faire venir sa famille si on n'a pas de quoi la nourrir c'est curieux, mais attention, je dis un revenu de son activité, pas le revenu des allocations sociales.[56]

The invitation made to 'hard-working and industrious' immigrants, however, stands in contradiction only moments later to the generosity

---

[54] *Encyclopédie*, Vol. VI, p. 71.
[55] *Encyclopédie*, Vol. VI, p. 71.
[56] "Le grand jury": Interview broadcast on French television network TV5 on 25 March 2007.

of a France styled as the land of human rights. Speaking to Philippe Dessaint on the issue of Darfour, Sarkozy states that "[l]a France des droits universels, la France des droits de l'homme ne peut pas laisser faire le scandale du Darfour. [...] la France qui est la patrie des droits de l'homme doit considérer comme Français tous ceux qui par le monde sont opprimés".[57]

Upon further analysis, the expression "patrie des droits de l'homme" proves to be fraught with ambiguity. Here is Jaucourt's definition of *la patrie*:

> PATRIE, s. f. (Gouvern. politiq.) le rhéteur peu logicien, le géographe qui ne s'occupe que de la position des lieux, et le léxicographe vulgaire, prennent la patrie pour le lieu de la naissance, quel qu'il soit ; mais le philosophe sait que ce mot vient du latin *pater*, qui représente un père et des enfants, et con-séquemment qu'il exprime le sens que nous attachons à celui de famille, de société, d'état libre, dont nous sommes membres, et dont les lois assurent nos libertés et notre bonheur. Il n'est point de patrie sous le joug du despotisme. Dans le siècle passé, Colbert confondit aussi royaume et patrie...[58]

He states further that

> [i]l ne peut point y avoir de patrie dans les états qui sont asservis. Ainsi ceux qui vivent sous le despotisme oriental, où l'on ne connaît d'autre loi que la volonté du souverain, d'autres maximes que l'adoration de ses caprices, d'autres principes de gouvernement que la terreur, où aucune fortune, aucune tête n'est en sûreté ; ceux-là, dis-je, n'ont point de patrie, et n'en connaissent pas même le mot, qui est la véritable expression du bonheur.[59]

The distinction that Jaucourt draws between *royaume* and *patrie* is based on the understanding of the former as a model of political subjugation. His argument is utopian, emerging as it does from an imagination that conceptualizes relations along the same framework as the model that he seeks to denounce, but which invents ways to resolve tensions by neutralizing their negative consequences.[60] The understanding of *patrie* that results from this maintains the familial structure of the monarchy and the father/king figure while positing, at the same time, intersubjective relations freeing the members of this

---

[57] "Le grand jury".
[58] *Encyclopédie*, Vol. XII, p. 178.
[59] *Encyclopédie*, Vol. XII, p. 180.
[60] I am drawing here on Louis Marin's analysis of utopia in his work *Utopiques: Jeux d'espaces* (Paris: Éditions de Minuit, 1973).

'family' from any form of inequality. The tension here, then, is one between, on the one hand, a paternal-style family model, with blood ties, a hierarchy and a dimension of exclusivity, and on the other, a free association of a contractual nature.

A comparable contradiction can be seen at work in the expression *patrie des droits de l'homme* used by Nicolas Sarkozy, for while *patrie* refers to an particular entity born of common ancestors and a shared history, *droits de l'homme* refers to universal principles.

In conclusion, despite acknowledging the existence of regional identities, Enlightenment discourse, under Voltaire's pen, constructs 'national genius', via (linguistic) exclusion and subordination, in order to make Paris the universal emblem of sociability and its language that of reason. The *Encyclopédie* elaborates a dual discourse that posits the existence of a national character handed down from the time of the Gauls, while at the same time arguing for a determinism based on political culture over climate and nature, and allowing for the assimilation of people from outside national borders.

Jaucourt's understanding of hospitality is predicated on a tension between a secular *caritas* and an interestedness springing from a contractual vision of society. This tension is manifested in the con- tradictory arguments justifying immigration: the individual's right to happiness according to natural law *versus* the economic advantages secured by the nation. We have seen how this tension is present in the discourse of Sarkozy the candidate. But in what terms is it addressed in the immigration policy of Sarkozy the President? In an interview given to *Le Parisien* on the sixtieth anniversary of the Universal Declaration of Human rights, French Foreign minister Bernard Kouchner made the following declaration:

> Je pense que j'ai eu tort de demander un secrétariat d'Etat aux Droits de l'homme. C'est une erreur. Car il y a contradiction permanente entre les droits de l'homme et la politique étrangère d'un Etat, même en France. Cette con- tradiction peut être féconde mais fallait-il lui donner un caractère gouvernemental en créant ce secrétariat d'Etat ? Je ne le crois plus et c'est une erreur de ma part de l'avoir proposé au président.[61]

A similar pragmatism seems to rule in matters of immigration, where Human rights take a back seat to utilitarianism. The immigration laws

---

[61] *Le Parisien*, 10 December 2008.

of 26 November 2003 and 24 July 2006 were modified by that of 20 November 2007. The Ministry of Foreign and European Affairs states:

> [l]a loi n°2007-1631 du 20 novembre 2007 relative à la maîtrise de l'immigration, à l'intégration et à l'asile a pour objets de lutter contre l'immigration irrégulière, de limiter les conditions d'entrée et de séjour en France, de maîtriser l'immigration familiale et d'encourager l'immigration pour des raisons professionnelles. En matière d'immigration familiale, la loi a ajouté quatre principes au dispositif existant: atteindre un certain seuil de ressources, fixé par la loi, pour prétendre au regroupement familial; réussir un test de connaissance du français et des valeurs de la République ou, à défaut, avoir suivi une formation suffisante afin de pouvoir rejoindre sa famille en France; veiller à l'intégration des enfants en vertu d'un 'contrat d'accueil et d'intégration pour la famille'; recourir à un examen génétique (test ADN) pour les ressortissants des pays où il existe un doute sérieux sur l'authenticité de l'état-civil, pour les étrangers candidats au regroupement familial, à titre expérimental pendant dix-huit mois.

Regarding political asylum, Patrick Weil points out that "[p]our le moment, l'asile ne semble plus être la cible directe de la politique de Nicolas Sarkozy: la diminution du nombre des demandes, favorisée par la loi de 2003 (52 200 en 2003, 23 800 en 2007) n'a pas entraîné une baisse significative du nombre de statuts accordés (9 790 en 2003, 8 780 en 2007)".[62] However, the priority given to targeted immigration, set to reach 50 per cent of all foreigners granted residency status, the limits placed upon family reunion,[63] the added obstacles in the naturalization process and the government's annual goal of 26,000 deportations of illegal immigrants suggest that France's Enlightenment ideal of universal assistance may no longer be one of President Sarkozy's guiding principles.

---

[62] Patrick Weil, "Politique d'immigration : le dessous des chiffres", *Le Monde*, 14 January 2009.

[63] According to Weil "[l]a cible principale de la loi de 2007 était les conjoints de Français, catégorie principale de l'immigration familiale (50 000 titres de séjour par an). Les contrôles des mariages à l'étranger ont été durcis, mais cela ne suffit pas. Des tests de français ou de connaissance des valeurs de la République permettront de ralentir encore l'attribution de visas et peut-être de décourager les postulants de vivre ensemble".

Expressing Plurality

So Over the Rainbow? The Singular Plurality of Martineau and Ducastel's *Drôle de Félix*

Joe Hardwick

If any film might be particularly well placed to comment on what exactly the concept of a plural France might mean in the new millennium, it is Jacques Martineau and Olivier Ducastel's *Drôle de Félix*, released in 2000. The film tells the story of a journey which traverses, as one review puts it, *la France en diagonale*, from the northern port of Dieppe to the southern port of Marseille from the point of view of a character who counts as marginal in several respects.[1] The Félix of the title is an attractive, vibrant young steward on a Channel cruise liner who has been recently laid off. Félix lives a comfortable middle-class existence with his teacher boyfriend Daniel in Dieppe. After rummaging through photos at his mother's house, he decides to hitchhike to Marseille in search of his father of unspecified North African background whom he has only met once. The film traces Félix's tour of regional France and his interactions with five characters he meets along the way, while all the time maintaining his routine of watching his favourite soap opera and taking his combination therapy drugs, for Félix is HIV+.

---

[1] Yasmine Youssi, "Road movie à la française d'un beur serein", *La Tribune*, 20 April 2000.

Félix, then, we might consider at least three if not four times marginalized, with reviews regularly multiplying identity categories in describing him: the title of the review in *La Tribune* reads "road movie à la français d'un beur serein" and Félix is described variously: by *Libération* as "un jeune Français d'origine arabe, séropositif, chômeur et qui n'a jamais connu son père";[2] by *Humanité* as a "drôle de héros homo, normand et attachant";[3] by *Les Echos* as "beur, chômeur, séduisant, homosexuel, et bien dans sa peau";[4] or most succinctly by *L'Evénement du jeudi* as "Beur homo, séropo et sans boulot".[5] Identity, in fact, is one of the central concerns of the film, and the road movie genre is particularly well suited to posing questions of identity, both at an individual and a cultural level. In the road movie, the road often becomes a metaphor for life itself, and the journey tends typically to be a transformative experience, offering characters the opportunity to find themselves by losing themselves. Alternatively, as Cohen and Hark write in *The Road Movie* book, it may ultimately be more conservative in orientation, with time away allowing characters to discover that there is no place like home.[6]

However, *Drôle de Félix* counts as a strange kind of road movie since from day one, doubts are raised as to the point of Félix's quest, one that will be subverted by the end of the film in any case. Moreover, Félix takes his time in reaching his destination, five days in fact, much longer than had previously been arranged, as Daniel reminds him in Marseille. In other words—as with many road movies—the destination is somewhat of a pretext, the interest lying more in the digression. This pushes *Drôle de Félix* closer to the category of texts Ross Chambers categorizes as loiterly, featuring characters who wander, cruise, tour or loiter with or without specific intent. One of the characteristics of the loiterly text is its time-out function, its digression from a formal structure to which it must nonetheless return.[7] Another aspect of certain loiterly protagonists is

---

[2] Jean-Marc Lalanne, "Œdipe gay et sans complexe", *Libération*, 19 April 2000.
[3] Michaël Mélinard, "Sami Bouajila toujours à l'affut", *L'Humanité*, 19 April 2000.
[4] Annie Coppermann, "Le bonheur est sur les routes", *Les Echos*, 19 April 2000.
[5] Isabelle Danel, "Sida-sol-fam-ré drôle de film", *L'Evénement du jeudi*, 9 April 2000.
[6] See their introduction in Steven Cohen and Ina Rae Hark, *The Road Movie Book* (London and New York: Routledge, 1997), pp. 1-14.
[7] Ross Chambers, *Loiterature* (Lincoln and London: University of Nebraska Press, 1999), p. 32.

that they appear to be, as Chambers puts it, "out of sync with the patterns and rhythms of modernity."[8] This is precisely how some reviews have read Félix in the film. Louis Guichard in *Télérama*, for example, talks of:

> le plaisir communicatif que Félix prend à ses heures de marche solitaire le long des routes de campagne—au point qu'il se met parfois à danser. C'est une invitation implicite à aller au-devant d'autrui, à reconstituer le lien social au gré du hasard, de l'"ici-et-maintenant". Un appel à la frivolité et au jeu quand bien même les jours sont comptés. Un éloge du vagabondage et des chemins de traverse… Autant de "possibles" non tarifés ni rentables que la société marchande passe sous silence, et dont ce petit film suave exalte très exactement les charmes.[9]

There are two aspects in particular which both the road movie and the loiterly text share. The first is their interest in marginal protagonists. The loiterer, Chambers writes, "becomes a socially marginal figure to the extent that social centrality is defined in terms of stability, permanence and closure—the virtues of single-mindedness and discipline that eschew digressivity. Thus, he is always on the cusp of a dominant social context and its other, always on the periphery of things".[10] In other words, the loiterer is a boundary crosser, forever shifting contexts, his or her story structured by encounters with others which bring about transformations in identity, what Chambers calls "changing the subject",[11] an idea relevant in terms of genre as well as character, explaining the loiterly text's generic hybridity. In fact, Félix is associated with a specific mythical boundary crosser: about halfway through the film, a conversation takes place concerning Mercury, the Roman version of Hermes, the Olympian God of roads and travel, inviting us to read Félix as a Hermes figure.

The second characteristic shared by road movies and loiterly texts is that protagonists are often forced to rely on the kindness of strangers in their travels, introducing both hospitality and the negotiation of cultural difference as major themes in both genres. Now, it is the question of Félix's cultural difference, or more precisely of his apparent cultural assimilation, which is the subject of two of the

---

[8] Chambers, p. 56.
[9] Louis Guichard, "*Drôle de Félix*", *Télérama*, 19 April 2000.
[10] Chambers, p. 57.
[11] Chambers, p. 40.

major pieces of academic writing on *Drôle de Félix*. Carrie Tarr, in her, discussion of the movie in *Beur and Banlieue* filmmaking, concentrates mainly on the question of Félix's ethnicity.[12] Murray Pratt's article in the *Australian Journal of French Studies*, on the other hand, focuses principally on Félix's sexuality. Pratt writes that in general:

> reviewers are keen to celebrate a portrayal of an autonomous and relatively empowered gay man living with HIV, whose personality is informed, rather than determined, by his sexuality and immune status. Their reading is one that largely corresponds to contemporary French social discourse that positions lesbian and gay identity according to the right to 'indifference' as opposed to more communitarian demands for differentiation.[13]

So how does such a singular identity as Félix find a place in a France which might be plural but which still places great emphasis on the idea of the *république, une et indivisible?* In the present chapter, I too want to look at how difference—and similarity—manifest themselves in Félix's journey in relation to the characters he meets, though by reading Félix's sexuality and ethnicity together, in the specific context of a Republican, integrated France. In the travel narrative, as Chambers writes, the reaction to otherness has as its extremes the reduction of alterity to sameness, or acts of differentiation that can result in exoticisation.[14] At the same time, however, the loiterly text has the capacity to offer models slightly different from both Republican integration or communitarian assertions of difference. It is this question I will explore in looking in particular at what Chambers refers to as self-alterity, the ability of marginal figures to use their fringe knowledge—of both the centre and the periphery—to recognize the other in the self and the self in the other, and to use this as a bridge in connecting with others and otherness.[15] I want then to link Félix's journey with broader debates concerning the negotiation of similarity and difference at the political

---

[12] Carrie Tarr, *Reframing Difference: Beur and Banlieue Filmmaking in France* (Manchester: Manchester University Press, 2005), pp. 147-150.
[13] Murray Pratt, "Félix and the Light-Hearted Gay Road Movie: Genre, Families, Fathers and the Decolonization of the Homosexual Self", *The Australian Journal of French Studies*, 41:3 (2004), 88-101 (89).
[14] Chambers, p. 30.
[15] Chambers, p. 59.

level, namely in terms of the policies of integration—often read as a form of assimilation—and multiculturalism, which are generally read as the extremes of the spectrum that takes us from sameness to difference.

* * *

From the opening frames of *Drôle de Félix*, two aspects of Félix as Hermes figure are obvious: the first is the travel motif, as we see Félix, a traveller by trade, cycling along the docks of Dieppe, placing him immediately at the boundary of land and sea, as will the closing shot which shows him and Daniel embracing on a boat on the Mediterranean. Hermes is first and foremost the Olympian God of boundaries and those who cross them, having patronage of roads and land travel, recognisable by his herald's staff and winged cap. Hermes is also a translator, bridging the gap between strangers. In both opening and closing sequences, Félix's movements are accompanied by the voice of American jazz singer Blossom Dearie. The multi-skilled Hermes was also mythically associated with music, having invented the pan-pipe and the flute, and this connects with the musicality of the film, part of its generic hybridity, giving the viewer the feeling that the film could easily transform into a musical at any point. This is cited by several reviewers, one seeing the film as "une comédie sans musique mais très musicale"[16] and described by *L'Evénement du Jeudi* as "une balade en forme de ballade".[17] The absent cinematic father-figure for the film is Jacques Demy, with Ducastel having worked on Demy's final film, *Trois Places pour le 26*. Ducastel and Martineau's preceding film *Jeanne et le garçon formidable* (1998) was a musical comedy about AIDS shot very much in the Demy style, with the major male character played by Mathieu Demy, the son of Jacques Demy and Agnès Varda.

While the musical comedy remains an absent presence in the film, the genre which it explicitly subscribes to is that of the road-movie, and there is one road-movie musical in particular which *Drôle de Félix* subtly invokes, this being the camp classic *The Wizard of Oz*

---

[16] Sophie Bonnet, "L'art de la fugue", *Les Inrockuptibles*, 18 April 2000.
[17] Isabelle Danel, "L'*Edj* vous recommande (absolument) *Drôle de Félix*", *L'Evénement du jeudi*, 20 April 2000.

(1939). Although Félix's journey lacks the obstacles which block Dorothy's quest to reconnect with family,[18] it importantly picks up on two metaphorical readings of the film underlined by Pamela Robertson in Steven Cohen and Ina Rae Hark's *The Road Movie Book*. Explaining the popularity of the movie among queer audiences, Robertson writes that:

> Against its own domestic motto, the *Wizard of Oz* offers a narrative about leaving conventional models of domesticity and creating alternate families and alternate homes. Even back in Kansas, Dorothy's family consists of Aunts and Uncles, stereotypically privileged figures in queer iconography. Equally important to a camp reading, I think, is the way *The Wizard of Oz* captures the feeling of being different, out of place, incongruous, not at home.[19]

In alignment with this model, *Drôle de Félix*, is divided into chapters according to the characters Félix meets along the way, these being entitled in order "mon frère", "ma grand-mère", "mon cousin", ma sœur" and finally, "mon père".

The second figural reading of *The Wizard of Oz*, Roberston writes, is:

> about travel and emigration in a multicultural world. In this light, Dorothy is the out-of-towner or the newest immigrant to a culture that already consists of many varied inhabitants. Her trip can be seen in terms of her negotiation of cultural difference both as she encounters new customs and 'persons' and as she is rendered different and strange by her new surroundings.[20]

In this respect, though, *Drôle de Félix* presents itself as a very different kind of yellow brick road movie, since it is largely a monocultural terrain—with regional variations—that Félix traverses. From the outset, it is clear that Félix's quest has nothing to do with his sexuality. Early scenes show Félix in bed hugging and kissing Daniel, and we later see the two kissing—and arguing—with each other at dinner in a local restaurant, to the raised eyebrows of the waiter, though it is unclear whether it is because the couple are gay or because they're simply an overly domestic couple in public that meets with his disapproval. For the most part—and in what many reviewers

---

[18] My thanks to Larry Schehr for pointing out this important difference.
[19] Pamela Robertson, "Home and Away: Friends of Dorothy on the Road in Oz", in Cohen and Hark, pp. 271-286 (p. 274).
[20] Robertson, p. 275.

have read as the utopian aspect of the film—Félix's sexuality is simply not an issue, though perhaps not to the extent that some critics have underlined, a point to which I will return later. On the other hand, Félix's decision to track down his father is intimately bound up with his own perceived difference, with a curiosity as to cultural origins and in this it poses potential questions as to how Félix sees himself. Félix notices one day a little boy eating an ice-cream in front of his mixed race parents, to the extra-diegetic strains of Mozart's *L'Egyptien* which combines both Middle Eastern and European influences.[21] Soon after, we see Félix rummaging through a box of photos in search of the one letter that exists from his father to his mother. When Félix announces his quest, Daniel says to him: "je me demande pourquoi tu veux te jeter dans la gueule du loup?", to which Félix curtly replies: "parce que je ne sais pas quelle gueule il a, le loup".

The question of the *gueule*—the face that one shows the world and the visible marker of Félix's difference—will recur as a leitmotiv throughout the film. This is linked to the theme of hospitality. As Tahar Ben Jelloun points out, citing Derrida on Lévinas: "'l'hos-pitalité est le nom même de ce qui s'ouvre au visage, ce qui accueille l'autre comme visage. L'accueil accueille seulement un visage'. Emmanuel Lévinas définit ainsi le visage : 'La manière dont se pré-sente l'Autre, dépassant l'idée de l'Autre en moi, nous l'appelons visage".[22]

This brings us to another subtle intertext in the film. In stark contrast to the fantasy of Oz stands the other film to which *Drôle de Félix* subtly alludes, Agnès Varda's *Sans toit ni loi*, her gritty 1986 film about the last weeks in the life of Mona, a hitchhiker in rural France. This occurs late in *Drôle de Félix* when his sister-figure Isabelle comments on the disappearance of the plane trees along the sides of the road, the same plane trees which Mona is told in Varda's film are being killed by a parasite. Referring to Michel Serres' theories of parasitism, Chambers in *Loiterature* reads Mona, the

---

[21] For a detailed reading of the role of music in the film, see Thibault Schilt, "Hybrid Strains in Olivier Ducastel and Jacques Martineau's *Drôle de Félix* (2000)", *Contemporary French and Francophone Studies*, 11:3 (2007), 361-368.

[22] Tahar Ben Jelloun, *Hospitalité française : racisme et immigration maghrébine* (Paris: Editions du Seuil, 1984).

rebellious *auto-stoppeuse*, as a parasitic figure and symbolic of society's willingness to accept or reject otherness.[23] Mona, like so many characters on the road, is forced to rely on the generosity of others, with the laws of hospitality determining her interaction with them. Both Chambers and Serres remind us that *hôte* in French can refer to host or guest, and that hospitality and hostility derive from the same latin root.[24] The happy-go-lucky Félix contrasts with the sullen and wild Mona, who eventually dies after being doused with wine in a provincial ritual and freezing in the cold. Though Mona's polar opposite, Félix too will run the full gamut from hostility to hospitality in his travels through provincial France.

His first stop is in Rouen where he will find out all too quickly what the different face he presents to the world can mean. When crossing a bridge, he witnesses the violent beating and murder by racist thugs of a man later described by news reports as Algerian. Félix is chased by one of the attackers who eventually beats him and taunts him about going to the police, saying that "personne ne te croira avec la gueule que tu as". When Félix goes to the station—an *Hôtel de Police* underlining the hospitality theme even further—he sees a young man of Arab appearance in handcuffs in the police station. He can't bring himself to file a complaint, feeling that the hand of hospitality does not extend to people like himself.

Of course, hospitality is a loaded metaphor in the context of France's relationship to its migrant population, and in particular to those from former colonies, as Mireille Rosello has so convincingly argued.[25] Even though Félix is born in France and raised as French, he finds himself nonetheless in a double bind. As Ben Jelloun points out, this is the case of many French children of North African parents: on the one hand, described as second- or third-generation migrants in a way that, for example, the children of Portugese or Italian migrants aren't; on the other, denied at least some of the benefits of the hospitality afforded their parents as migrants.

Now, Félix's inability to go to the police can be read as a function of his self-alterity. Chambers writes that the identity of

---

[23] Chambers, pp. 42-46.
[24] See Chambers, 1999; and Michel Serres, *Le Parasite* (Paris: Grasset, 1980).
[25] Mireille Rosello, *Postcolonial Hospitality: The Immigrant as Guest* (Stanford: Stanford University Press, 2001).

marginal subjects is split "because (socially, historically, geographically) it is peripheral" having a "fraught relation with the representatives of disciplinary power".[26] The narrative thread of the film is not simply about Félix's search for the biological father, but also about Félix's facing up to disciplinary power in general, embodied by the police on the one hand and the figure of the partriarch on the other, as underlined by Pratt.[27] Rather than face up to further threats of racist attacks, Félix changes course, resolving to avoid any cities that voted Front National. The incident in Rouen will be the major *bémol* in Félix's *bal(l)ade*, but it will haunt him like a refrain throughout the rest of the journey. In a way, the scene on the bridge recalls Albert Camus' *La Chute* whose protagonist is also haunted by a death along the Seine in Paris further upstream. Nonetheless, Félix's strategic remapping of France works, for genuine hospitality will dictate the meetings with the other characters he encounters. Hospitality, though, as Serres and Chambers write, has less to do with generosity than implicit contracts, unspoken quid pro quos. This is where that ambiguity with the word *hôte* comes in, for guests can quickly transform into hosts of sorts, with the mutual interaction changing the subject or subjects.

In Félix's encounters with the five characters described as his adoptive family, I want to concentrate on the ways his similarity and/or difference are underlined, on the recurrence of the face motif, and in particular on the different manifestations of self-alterity that arise in his interactions.

It is the interchangeability of the host/guest relation which marks Félix's encounter with the first member of his adoptive family, Jules, referred to as "mon frère" on screen—the teenage boy in *terminale* whom Félix comes across trying to draw a statue on a cathedral, a statue, in fact, of Aristotle, the curious juxtaposition of the secular and the religious being pointed out by Félix. In return, Jules offers Félix his bed to sleep in, with the teenager developing an unrequited crush on him. It is in a conversation with Jules that the conversation concerning Hermes takes place, and there are two particular Hermes-like functions that Félix will perform in his interactions with Jules. The first—like that contradictory combination

---

[26] Chambers, p. 65, 66.
[27] Pratt, pp. 97-101.

of the religious and the secular—concerns Hermes' patronage of both
thieves and shopkeepers, whom as Félix points out, one would
normally expect to be opposed to each other. It is the role of thief that
Félix fulfils. In one of the more unrealistic passages in the film, Félix
temporarily steals a car with Jules. Later in the film, Félix says why he
did this, explaining that "il me prenait comme un caïd". In this, we
might see a particular application of loiterly self-alterity. Being border
crossers, able to travel from the mainstream to the margin, loiterly
figures are fully aware of how they are perceived as other, from the
perspectives of both the centre and the margin. The stereotype of the
caïd is one that Félix reworks for his own purposes, in a kind of
playful performativity, a production of the self as other.

The second Hermes function is that of escort. Félix drives Jules
around the countryside, in the process introducing him to the music of
Cheb Mami and taking Jules to his first gay bar. Fringe communities,
both Félix and Jules learn, have their own forms of discipline as well,
as both are thrown out when it becomes clear that Jules is underage.
The owner comments that they already have enough problems with
the police, the only reference in the film to the marginalisation of
homosexuals as a community.

The question of Félix's sexual identity also arises with his next
two encounters, in very different ways. Mathilde, an elderly woman
described as "ma grand-mère", finds Félix sleeping on a park-bench
and coerces him to help her take her shopping home before assigning
him various domestic duties in exchange for a bed for the night. The
quid pro quo of the hospitality arrangement sees Félix not only keep
Mathilde company, but his presence allows her to enjoy surreptitious-
ly the spectacle of Félix's body, as he catches her gazing on his naked
form, a reminder that the elderly, too, have a sexuality. If Mathilde
might otherwise form part of mainstream French society, we're also
reminded that, as an elderly person, she is marginal as well. The *mise
en scène* of one sequence in particular underlines their similarity, a
medium close up symmetrical image of them both taking their
medication with a glass of water in front of the soap opera that they're
both addicted to. The subject of the *mélo*, in fact, is imperfect families,
this being a reflection of Mathilde's own situation, married for many
years to a man she didn't love, and in many ways estranged from her
son and daughter-in-law. Of Félix's own attempt to reconnect with
family, Mathilde tells him directly, "le père, c'est un prétexte".

Despite her comfort with Félix's presence, Mathilde is nonetheless slightly taken aback when Félix tells her frankly "je suis pédé", the elderly woman initially incredulous as he doesn't fit her image of gay men: "les homos, je les ai connus, mais pas vous". Félix's use of the word *pédé* is ambiguous here, a term that may or may not be pejorative, depending on the context, on the one hand perhaps showing his awareness again of his self-alterity, of how he might be stereotyped again as gay man, on the other perhaps showing that he is comfortable in using the term in her presence. The gay man who seems straight raises again the thematic of the difference between appearance and reality, as well as the careful play of differentiation and indifferentiation that Félix's marginal status requires.

No such qualms, however, in the following encounter as Félix hitches a ride with a *cheminot*, a kindred soul who travels for a living, and who shares Félix's taste for kite-flying. Back in Dieppe, at the start of the journey, Félix had bought a multicoloured kite, the colours reminiscent of the rainbow flag which has become the symbol for LGBTI communities. It is while flying the kite together that the *cheminot* embraces Félix, before the two make love in the open air then continue on their way. It is perhaps in this scene that the film seems at its most celebratory, and its most utopian, the two able to openly show their love. This apparent case of celebrating difference quickly transforms into an instance of happy indifference when they reconnect with the world. The two share an ice-cream together bought from a road-side vendor, with the *cheminot* rubbing Félix's body with vinegar to treat a rash he picked up while making love in the grass, leading to the two hugging and kissing together in public, uncommented on by the others present, the encounter functioning as a joyous time-out within the overall time out structure of Félix's journey.

The final two encounters will see Félix in the world of hetero-sexual family life for the first time, bringing to a conclusion the issue of paternity as well as Félix's relationship with disciplinary power. Félix stops to help Isabelle—"ma sœur" according to the subtitles— whose car has a flat tyre. In return, she offers Félix a ride with her three children in the back who have three different fathers, being *des enfants du Rhône et de la Nationale 7*, as their mother calls them. Just as Félix has been appropriating a family of sorts in his travels, the children have been appropriating fathers, often preferring to spend time with the fathers of their siblings. Félix, too, is temporarily appropriated by one of the children as a father who teaches him a lesson about paternity, chastising him for calling the children's non-biological fathers *faux-pères* and *demi-pères*.

This is not the only way in which Félix's preconceptions regarding authority figures are changed. Isabelle, much to Félix's surprise, is a police officer. The question of the *gueule* and identity arises again, as Isabelle asks him: "est-ce que j'ai une gueule de flic" to which he replies "j'ai une gueule de Normand?" But as much as as Félix would like others to be indifferent to his apparent difference, he is soon reminded that this is not the case when Isabelle is involved in a collision and the enraged driver of the other vehicle hurls abuse at him, calling him "freluquet, enculé", and giving him a black eye, to which Félix responds: "enculé, traitez-moi de sale arabe pendant que vous y êtes". Félix's response shows again his awareness of his self-alterity, an othering of the self related to racial and cultural stereotypes. This comes to the fore shortly after when Félix confides in Isabelle about the incident in Rouen, this coinciding with the arrest of the murderer. Félix explains to her that he couldn't go to the police because he has "une gueule d'Arabe". Nonetheless, through Isabelle, Félix as loiterly figure is able to reconnect with mainstream society, perhaps because this time the representative of disciplinary author-ity—the single or at least unmarried mother of three children—does not show the face that he was expecting.

This sets the scene for a reconciliation with patriarchal authority, with the final character subtitled "mon père". Just outside Marseille, Félix strikes up a conversation with a man fishing in a river, complaining that no one will pick him up, to which the man replies that this is hardly surprising, "vu ton visage", he says. In the course of the conversation, Félix tells the man of the reason for his journey, but the fisherman is unimpressed. The reason he is fishing is precisely to avoid his own family: his reaction to Félix's quest for his father is to ask if he is angry with him. Why otherwise would he want to meet a man who has neglected him for his whole life?

Two small details are worth commenting on here. In the background, we see a large bridge, with Félix's journey being framed by two bridges, the one in Rouen with the racist attack that came to haunt him, and the one in this scene where the father-figure he meets dashes Félix's dreams concerning his father. He finally makes the connection about the meaning—or meaninglessness—of biological paternity in his case. This is linked to the second detail: on the back of the fisherman's chair is the word Merlin, as in the Wizard, recalling again the *Wizard of Oz*. In that film, of course, the Wizard in whom Dorothy had placed so much faith as the font of all knowledge, and whom she hopes holds the key to making it back to Kansas, is all smoke and mirrors: he is simply an old man with no special powers at all.

The end of the yellow brick road for Félix might result in a similar disappointment concerning the father-figure, but he nonetheless has a newfound knowledge concerning the question of patriarchy. In the end, Félix teaches the father-figure how to fly a kite, with this—as Pratt points out—inverting the normal order of patriarchal authority. Pratt reads this as an example of how the film—in terms of sexuality—actually presents itself as a case of differentiation, despite its apparent concordance with a right to indifference. This results in a reading of the film as ultimately one that "contests national scripts, particularly those that seek to uphold the values of patriarchal authority".[28]

In terms of the notion of self-alterity, Félix's journey follows an arc that begins by emphasising the self as other and ends with emphasising the self in the other. The first meeting, the racist attack, sees Félix violently othered in the country of his birth. In the second, with brother-figure Jules, Félix playfully takes on the stereotype that Jules sees him as. His encounter with the grandmother figure allows him to right the elderly woman's preconceptions about gay men. Following his meeting with the *cheminot*, the final two encounters see a switch from how others view Félix to how Félix himself views others, with his own preconceptions about authority figures challenged through the police officer Isabelle and the father-figure at the end whose name we will never know.

Although Pratt is able to read Félix's sexuality as, ultimately, an assertion of differentiation in terms of the renunciation of the quest for the father, it would be easy to see Félix's *bal(l)ade* as a kind of hymn to integration, corresponding to a renunciation of the idea of connecting with his father's North African origins. After all, when

---

[28] Pratt, p. 101.

Félix meets up with his boyfriend in Marseille, the two continue their journey, not to North Africa, but to Corsica, the very limit of Mediterranean France. The film might be read simplistically as saying that identity is where you are, not where you or your family are from, and certainly not both as in the happily hyphenating identity categories of multicultural societies. This is, indeed, how Carrie Tarr has read *Drôle de Félix*, writing that the film: "sets him up as a model of successful assimilation, whilst demonstrating the limits of Ducastel and Martineau's vision of a multicultural France. Not only is Félix not allowed to reclaim his Maghrebi heritage but, as a mixed-race gay man, he is not in a position to establish his own place and his own lineage".[29] Tarr also writes that: "Undoubtedly (and no doubt unintentionally), the film confirms that the most loveable ethnic 'other' is the one who is least culturally different, and that, if Félix wants to be integrated, he should accept that his family is to be found elsewhere".[30] Denis Provencher, in reading Félix as "'good' sexual citizen", is largely in accordance with Tarr, writing that "Félix feels more comfortable and 'at home' in mixed republican spaces that erase signs of ethnic difference and queerness".[31]

Now, while in partial agreement with Tarr and Provencher, I think that such analyses only tell half the story, for three reasons. First, they overlook the very important metaphorical dimension of the specific form of musicality which underlines Félix's character as Hermes figure and which permeates the film. It is through the mechanism of music, Thibault Schilt argues, that *Drôle de Félix* "fully engages in a politically pregnant reconfiguration of hybridity in terms concurrent with recent postcolonial thought".[32] Schilt concentrates on the three major pieces of music in the film, the songs in the opening and closing credit sequences by Blossom Dearie whose American accent remains very prominent in her rendition of the songs *Tout Doucement* and *Plus je t'embrasse*, together with the raï of Algerian singer Cheb Mami and the strains taken from Mozart's *L'Egyptien*

---

[29] Tarr, p. 150.
[30] Tarr, pp. 147-148.
[31] Denis Provencher, "Tracing Sexual Citizenship and Queerness in *Drôle de Félix* (2000) and *Tarik el hob* (2001)", *Contemporary French and Francophone Studies*, 12:1 (2008), 51-61 (52, 55).
[32] Schilt, p. 362.

which recur as a refrain at key moments in the film. All three underline the hybridity of musical forms, though it is true that the extent to which this might be extended to the character of Félix himself is debatable.

Second, the question of assimilation is one that should not even arise with Félix, a character born in France and raised as French. Indeed, one could easily argue that, rather than an anthem to assimilation, the film takes on the loiterly characteristic of carrying "an implied social criticism. It casts serious doubt on the values good citizens hold dear…but it does so in the guise of innocent and, more particularly, insignificant or frivolous entertainment".[33] It is because of the importance of that *gueule*—the face which is welcomed as hospitable or hostile—that assimilation is shown to be an impossibility for Félix, who is still the victim of racist attacks. One of the insistent themes in the film is the difference between appearances and reality— Félix as French but read as *beur* or Arab; Félix who appears straight but is gay; or Isabelle whose demeanour suggests anything other than that of a police officer. But this is not to say that appearances still don't count and can simply be dismissed. This forms part of Félix's marginal self-alterity, being fully aware of the stereotypes that define him.

Third, Tarr's analysis is based on a simplistic distinction between assimilation and multiculturalism. As Rosello points out, the difference between integration or universalism, in which citizens are seen to be best protected "as abstract subjects whose racial, gendered, ethnic or class difference is rendered irrelevant by the …'Law of the Republic'",[34] and a multiculturalism which favours communitarian-based demands for equality is, in many ways, a false distinction. What interests Rosello, as she puts it, are cultural practices rather than cultural identification, where cultural identity is mobilized for specific ends. Rosello calls this tactical universalism, citing the PACS arrangement as an example whereby homosexual unions came to be recognised though under the general heading of solidarity.

---

[33] Chambers, p. 9.

[34] Mireille Rosello, "Tactical Universalism and New Multiculturalist Claims in Postcolonial France", in Charles Forsdick and David Murphy (eds), *Francophone Postcolonial Studies: A Critical Introduction* (London: Arnold, 2003), pp.135-144 (p. 135).

In a way, *Drôle de Félix* mobilises its one kind of *pacte de solidarité*. Ultimately, the film is less about Félix as individual, or about pre-established communities, than about the connections he establishes with those who seem so different from him. It is about familiarity rather than the family, similarity rather than assimilation, and indeed about the the *fil* rather than the *fils*, not so much the ties that bind, not about lineage, but lines of connection. The line, here, recalls the fishing line of his father, and the string of Félix's kite, this being the last in a series of aspects of the *mise en scène* which underline Félix's similarity with the quite different characters he meets, as with the *cheminot* and his kite flying, as with Mathilde and her pill-taking and melodrama-watching. Félix's string, of course, is connected to that multicoloured kite, a rainbow kite, rather than a rainbow flag, which also tells us something about the notion of identity in the film. On the one hand, it is a kite, not a flag, and we might see it symbolic of a somewhat ambiguous, tactical form of identification. Félix can assert his sexuality when needs be—as he does with Mathilde—but he doesn't need to fly his colours all the time. On the other, its multicoloured form doesn't necessarily link it to the rainbow flag, since it might just as easily be associated with the very similar peace flag, therefore not associated with a particular community. Moreover, just as it is not a film about filiation, nor is it about affiliation. If what we mean by gay is membership of a specific community, then in this sense Félix isn't quite gay, but merely *drôle*, which of course, in a sense, is French for queer, and perhaps a very specific French form of queer. In Félix's case, this *drôle* enacts a particular kind of self-alterity, an intermingling of the self and the other with an emphasis on movement and fluidity. For Félix, as Hermes figure, as traveller, home is not a specific locale, but rather where the heart is, in this case with his lover, as Félix repeats his forward movement in the opening frames on his bicycle in the closing frames which see him embracing Daniel on the boat headed for Corsica. The fact that both sequences—tracking shots or *travellings*— are accompanied by the hybrid strains of Blossom Dearie singing in French, remind us as well that hybridity is inscribed in the figure of Hermes himself, his winged cap a reminder of the intermingling of bird and human forms in the same being.

In conclusion, being over the rainbow, in the world of Félix, means moving beyond the need for flag-waving forms of affiliation with a specific community, to work towards more generalised egalitarian goals with other marginal groups. After all, what use is a sexual egalitarianism if an ethnic egalitarianism is not also part of that new won freedom? For all subjects remain ethnicised as well as sexualised in new millennium France, despite Republican assertions of universality. In place of a community defined along strictly sexual or ethnic lines, the film establishes its own pact with other marginal figures, for Félix's adopted family members are all marginal in some way. In its emphasis on the interrelationship between self and other, community—in the form of the adopted family—becomes internalised, and this is the final loiterly aspect of the film I want to stress. In a way, *Drôle de Félix* reworks the loiterly text of the cruising narrative—a listing of sexual encounters. Chambers in *Loiterature* talks of gay male culture as "digressively constituted", writing that "cruising becomes a fundamental practice of gay-community construction, as an act of mutual recognition across barriers of otherness".[35] *Drôle de Félix*, however, replaces recognition of like-minded sexuality with like-minded marginality. This is its general-yet-specific form of self-alterity. As Chambers writes, self-alterity means that the marginal subject nonetheless is able to seek out other marginal subjects, leading to the formation "of a community of the marginalized—a community not of a group of disciplined individuals but of peripheral subjects whose consciousness implies the recognition, not simply of alterity but self-alterity, the inexhaustible community of self".[36]

---

[35] Chambers, p. 64.
[36] Chambers, p. 66.

Youth Speech *au pluriel* in the Written Press

Monique Monville-Burston

Numerous are the domains of artistic and intellectual activity, popular culture, and social life (television, written press, novels, cinema, cartoons, dictionaries, specialised publications, etc.) which are part of what Henri Boyer has called "la nébuleuse du 'parler jeune'",[1] i.e. productions that have taken as a theme the speech of French adolescents. The youth language nebula is still thriving, twenty-five years after Alain Schiffres penned in *Le Nouvel Observateur* his article "Le jeune tel qu'on le parle".[2] This phenomenon has even attracted the attention of sociolinguists.[3] Two reasons have been advanced for the success of *français jeune* in the French media and general population.[4] First the audience/readership is presented with speech forms that are somewhat exotic, but still familiar: nothing in

---

[1] Henri Boyer, "Le jeune tel qu'on en parle", *Langue et Société,* 70 (1994), 85-92.

[2] Alain Schiffres, "Le jeune tel qu'on le parle", *Le Nouvel Observateur,* 143, Decemeber 1982.

[3] For instance, Henri Boyer, "«Nouveau français», «parler jeune» ou «langue des cités»", in Henri Boyer (ed), *Les Mots des jeunes. Observations et hypothèses. Langue Française*, 114 (1997), 6-15; Zsuzanna Fagyal, "Action des médias et interactions entre jeunes dans une banlieue ouvrière de Paris", in Thierry Bulot, *Les Parlers jeunes. Pratiques urbaines et sociales, Cahiers de Sociolinguistique 9* (Rennes: Presses Universitaires de Rennes, 2004), pp. 41-60.

[4] Boyer (1997), pp. 6-15.

them is abstruse enough that it cannot be deciphered. Second, as it is described and discussed,[5] this 'jargon' is kept under control and somehow officialized; its violations of the norm are neutralised. As a result, the unity of the language, a Jacobinic concept still strongly valued in the French mentality, is preserved.

We will concentrate here more specially on representations of adolescents' language found in the written press: youth speech presented as an entertaining topic, as an object claimed to be authentic, but whose essence in reality is contradictory, and as an entity recognized to be multiform but which is in fact normalized. We will show how adolescent speech diversity is in fact lost, since the press concentrates its attention on a particular group, youths from the suburbs (*les jeunes de la cité*), and journalists show a predilection for for one component of the linguistic system, the lexicon.

Youth Language: Fascination and Entertainment for the Readers

While Boyer and Fagyal underscore the media's harnessing of youth language, what they do not stress as much is the benevolence with which this sociolect is treated, although of late an evolution has taken place, to which we will return at the end of the chapter.

'Linguistic journalism' usually endeavours to explain usages and etymologies, often reminding readers/listeners of what the norm is

---

[5] It should be noted that, at the same time, aspects of adolescent speech have been examined in a more scientific fashion by sociolinguists. See, among others, Henriette Walter, "L'innovation lexicale chez les jeunes Parisiens", *La Linguistique,* 20.2 (1984), 69-84; Henri Boyer, "Le *français des jeunes* vécu/vu par les étudiants. Enquêtes à Montpellier, Paris, Lille" *Langage et Société* 95 (2001), 75-87; Cyril Trimaille, "Etudes de parlers de jeunes urbains en France. Éléments pour un état des lieux" in Bulot (2004), pp. 99-132; Dominique Caubet, Jacqueline Billiez, Thierry Bulot, Isabelle Léglise and Catherine Miller (eds), *Parlers jeunes, ici et là-bas* (Paris: L'Harmattan, 2004). Dictionaries and glossaries have also been published. For example, Pierre Merle *Dictionnaire du français branché* (Paris: Seuil, 1986); Pierre Merle, *Dictionnaire du français qui se cause* (Toulouse: Milan, (1998, 2nd ed. 2004); Jean-Pierre Goudailler, *Comment tu tchatches!* (Paris: Maisonneuve & Larose, 1998); Alhassane Sarré *et al.*, *Lexik des cités illustré, précédé d'un dialogue entre Alain Rey et Disiz la Peste* (Paris: Fleuve Noir, 2007).

and encouraging them to follow it.[6] There is however, we believe, a major difference between, on the one hand, newspapers articles on youth language and publications whose authors are journalists or enlightened amateurs and, on the other, general linguistic journalism. The former are never overtly prescriptive or corrective. In addition, they often aim to entertain and inform at the same time. In the introduction to his *Dictionnaire du français branché*, Merle writes: "Outre l'amusement qu'il procurera au simple amateur en mal de curiosité légitime, ce *Dictionnaire du français branché* sera réellement utile à tous ceux qui se sentent un tant soit peu débordés par la florescence [sic] du vocabulaire ambiant."[7] *Le manuel ado/parents—Guide de conversation*[8] takes a light-hearted look at the language of younger speakers: it is laid out like a foreign-language textbook, with rules, exercises and a final exam. By a sort of role reversal, the 'deviant' form of speech becomes the model to be acquired. This indulgent and accommodating attitude towards adolescent language makes the Jacobinic intent to control French, as evoked by Boyer, subliminal (and possibly all the more insidious, since it is relegated to the subconscious of both authors and readers). All these publications therefore appear to adopt a positive attitude towards youth language, and, combined with ethnographic curiosity for an unknown linguistic species, make light and pleasant reading. Furthermore, they highlight the ludic role of youth language in constructing identity.[9] Stigmatization is perhaps implicit, but it is the

---

[6] One may think of Bernard Pivot's dictation contest, or Cerquiglini's television program on TV5 where the history of words and current usages are discussed, or various other linguistic columns in French dailies.

[7] Merle (1986), pp.9-10. See also Boris Seguin and Frédéric Teillard, *Les Céfrans parlent aux Français* (Paris: Calmann-Lévy, 1996), where youth French is said to be funny, vivacious and inventive.

[8] Éliane Girard and Brigitte Kernel, *Le Manuel ado/parent* (Paris: Hors Collection/Presses de la Cité, 1994). The two authors have also written *Le Vrai Langage des jeunes expliqué aux parents (qui n'y entravent plus rien)* (Paris: Albin Michel, 1996).

[9] See also Françoise Gadet, "La variation: le français dans l'espace social, régional et international", in Marina Yaguello (ed), *Le Grand Livre de la langue française* (Paris: Seuil, 2003), pp. 291-152; Didier de Tejedor de Felipe, "A propos de la 'folklorisation' de l'argot des jeunes", in Marie-Madeleine Bertucci and Daniel Delas (eds), *Français des banlieues, français populaire?* (ERTH, Université de Cergy-Pontoise, 2004), pp. 19-31.

fascination for creativity that wins out. This is not innocent of course: these studies are intended to entice adults, and draw on the popularity and marketability of youth culture today.[10]

Authenticity and "Circular Circulation"

Since the purpose of journalistic publications on youth language is not prescriptive or intended to be corrective, one could expect an objective presentation of this sociolect. As we are informed by *Télé 7 Jours*,[11] journalists Eliane Girard's and Brigitte Kermel's dictionary contains neither censorship nor selection. However, regarding selection, one may recall Bourdieu's analysis of information-processing by the media.[12] Youth speak is no exception. What is offered to the reader in the print media is often information on information. Journalists take their information second-hand from experts, be they linguists or lexicographers, who, themselves, can be more or less reliable. Then they select features that look new to them, scoop-like or that will be, according to their judgment, more attractive to the public; this information spreads virally as journalists read one another's articles. It is easy to see how stereotypes get created.[13] Of course, a pinch of authenticity can be added by consulting first-hand speakers of youth language, and college and high-school students are sometimes interviewed. However, such brief interviews can only generate superficial results; it is well known that it is difficult to obtain access to linguistic diversity and heterogeneity as a casual external observer, i.e. if data are not gathered through participating observation.

---

[10] "Il est d'ailleurs bien porté dans le Paris cultivé intello de prouver qu'on connaît le «parler jeune»", *L'Humanité* writes about the affected use of youth language by adults. ("Besides, it is fashionable among educated intellectuals in Paris, to show that one knows youth language.") (François Taillandier, "SMIC", in *L'Humanité,* March 2005).

[11] "Le guide sourire de la génération verlan", *Télé 7 jours,* 4-10 January 1997.

[12] Pierre Bourdieu, *Sur la télévision* (Paris: Raison d'agir, 1996); See also Fagyal, p. 44.

[13] The print media sometimes publish interviews of recognised linguists or lexicographers (Henriette Walter, Jean-Pierre Goudaillier, Thierry Bulot, Louis-Jean Calvet, Alain Rey, for example). In such cases there is a little more depth in the content, yet the limits of a newspaper article do not allow complex or finely shaded expositions.

Youth Speech: a Pluralistic Entity

Under these circumstances, what happens to youth speech diversity? This form of speech is a pluralistic entity. How does the written press handle this plurality? How do non-specialists construct 'youth language', a social object which sociologists and sociolinguists agree is a multi-facetted entity, with changing and uncertain limits?[14]

One may well ask what youth French is? A generational variety? This sounds as a truism: youth French is the French spoken by young people. But what is youth? Sociologists are still debating the question.[15] Age is certainly a useful defining criterion; developmental approaches have shown that by the end of childhood, we are still in the process of refining our awareness of the social importance of linguistic variants and acquiring stylistic variation as well as the standard variety. Adolescence is a time when we begin to build our linguistic identity, which we do, on the one hand, by diverging from adult speech and, on the other, by identifying with the speech of a peer group, which results in the overuse of non-standard forms.

However, the age criterion is not sufficient to define what youth French is. Other factors need to be considered. The youth speech variety is also diastratically structured by the social class to which one belongs and one's level of schooling, while entry into the workforce generally causes the abandonment of 'youth' linguistic forms. Youth speech is also structured diatopically: sociolinguists have shown the existence of fluctuations from region to region, city to city, school to school in adolescent speech.[16] This sociolect also includes a dia-chronic dimension: adolescents' unstable cultural behaviour is man-ifested by neologisms, many of them ephemeral. It is also subject to situational variation since, like their elders, young people adapt their

---

[14] G. Mauger speaks of youth as a "catch-all category with variable geometry" where "vagueness is the rule and definition the exception." See "La catégorie de jeunesse. Essai d'inventaire, de classement et de critique de quelques usages courants ou savants", in *Les Jeunes et les autres* (Vaucresson: Centre de recherche inter-disciplinaire, 1986), pp. 43-63.

[15] The concept of youth refers as much to natural age as to a shared imaginary identity. For sociologists, therefore, youth can be studied from the point of view of inter-generational conflicts or from the point of view of cultural behaviour and practices.

[16] See for example Boyer (2001); Bulot (2004); Caubet et al., pp.7-15.

language to the circumstances of communication. In other words, they do not exclusively use youth speech. Finally, sex cannot be over-looked.[17] In total, there exist a plurality of "young" modes of expression that are inextricably linked.[18]

Designations

When discussing the nature of youth speak, it is methodologically essential to define the population whose speech is being described in order to delineate its characteristics. This is how sociolinguists working in the field proceed. In newspapers, however, this is rarely the case. In addition, in order to designate the linguistic object discussed here, a number of terms are used without rigorous definitions: for example, *le langage des jeunes*, *le français jeune*, *le français branché*, *le djeun(e)*, *la langue des banlieues*, *la sous-langue des banlieues*, *l'idiome né au pied des HLM*, *la langue des exclus*, *le parler urbain*, *la langue des cités*, *le français contemporain des cités*, and *la langue racaille* to name but a few. One will note the number and therefore the fuzziness of these appellations, which are often treated as synonyms. To be noted too is the unifying effect produced by the generic definite article (*le*), and also the frequency of the term language (*langue*), which suggests an independent entity, separate from the standardized language. The fact that these designations are never problematized, never questioned, raises concerns in that they carry social representations that become fixed, stabilized and thus stereotyped in the minds of readers.

An important remark is in order here, concerning the history of these appellations in the press and the media in general (and indeed also in some more scholarly works). Interest in the language of young people began in the early 1980s. As mentioned above, the pioneer was Alain Schiffres in *Le Nouvel Observateur*. From the 1980's until the early 1990's, media references to youth speak denoted an adolescent

---

[17] See Jacqueline Billiez and Patricia Lambert, "La différenciation langagière filles/garçons: vue par des filles et des garçons", in Caubet et al., pp. 173-184.
[18] Sanders's diagram, which combines all the factors involved in socio-situational variation gives a good representation—*mutatis mutandis*—of this complexity. See Carole Sanders, "Sociosituational variation", in Carole Sanders, *French Today: Language in its Social Context* (Cambridge: Cambridge University Press, 1993), p. 52.

form of what was otherwise called *français branché*,[19] which is essentially a variety of French spoken by people with a sense of what is fashionable. In the 1990's a new meaning emerged which is still applicable today: youth language now refers more to forms of French slang spoken in the vicinity of large cities, where immigrant populations are established (*les cités*).[20] Youth speech is thus associated with social schism (*fracture sociale*).[21] Why refer so insistently to this sociolect in preference to others? Probably because forms of speech used in the suburbs, being farther from the norm and more deviant, are seen by journalists as more innovative and as more apt to be exploited by the media; perhaps also because in the 1990's the politically correct ideology was that of communitarianism: the diversity brought by the suburbs to the social landscape is viewed positively and we marvel at the richness, at the linguistic creativity of the young in the suburbs. For example, Pierre-Adolphe *et al.* write:

> Les mots inventés de l'autre côté du périph' ne sont ni le fruit du hasard, ni le résultat d'un quelconque abâtardissement de notre langue. Ils sortent d'un volcan bouillonnant dont la lave est faite de formidables pépites linguistiques. Une alchimie de mots concoctée par des sorciers de la langue et des acrobates de la rhétorique.[22]

To sum up, a synthetic analysis of newspaper articles shows that from the 1990's on, youth language has been presented as a generational sociolect spoken essentially in the suburbs, a form of familiar/popular French full of borrowings from English and the languages of immigrants, and strongly tinged with *verlan*. Linguistic

---

[19] Verdelhan-Bourgade, a linguist, observes that "l'usage du français branché semble être un signe de reconnaissance non d'un groupe restreint et clos, mais de toute une couche de la population : celle qui lit les journaux, va au spectacle, s'intéresse à la mode, à l'actualité […]. Il y a une mouvance large du *branché*." Michèle Verdelhan-Bourgade, "Procédés sémantiques et lexicaux en français branché", *Langue Française*, 90 (1991), 65-79.

[20] It is, as Henriette Walter explains in an interview (without questioning the expression though): "un parler, une variante de français utilisé dans un milieu donné, celui des banlieues, ou encore, si vous préférez de l'usage du français dans les banlieues". ("Quand ils prennent la parole", *Le Nouvel Observateur*)

[21] Nowadays, the prototype of the young in the media is typically a high-school student, who lives in a suburb, is of foreign descent, is normally in difficulty at school and may already have been in trouble with the police.

[22] Philippe Pierre-Adolphe, Max Mamoud and Georges-Olivier Tanoz, *Le Dico de la banlieue*, (Paris: La Sirène, 1995).

practices of other teenagers do not seem worthy of attention—because they allegedly show little creativity—and if they are given a small place in the media, it is only insofar as they copy or imitate the practices of the suburbs.

The Press and the Pluralistic Nature of Youth Speech

We noted above that generalizing designations of *the* language of young people tend to obscure the complexity of the sociolect. That is not to say that youth-speech heterogeneity is not recognized by some journalists. We are told that youth language varies from region to region, from neighbourhood to neighbourhood. But the presentation given by the press of this fluctuation is always anecdotal, limited and unsystematic. For example, readers learn that the term *mia*, is used in Marseille to designate a handsome male, but that it is unknown in Paris. When journalists focus on the hetereogeneity of adolescent speech, it is in such a caricatured fashion that one has the right to be concerned about how an uniformed readership will understand this information. The following excerpt from *Phosphore*—a periodical whose readership is made of teenagers from the middle and upper classes—is a ranking of lexical creativity in youth speech, according to speakers' socio-economic status, a diastratic approach therefore, which aims to demonstrate that capacity for linguistic innovation de-creases as affluence and social influence increase. The classification is established as follows:

> 1) Au bas de l'échelle de la créativité lexicale on a les "Marie-Chantal", des BCBG qui vouvoient encore leurs parents;
> 2) Puis on a les "Ophélie Winter", qui s'approprient une langue siliconée;
> 3) Ensuite viennent les bobos, jeunes Français qui ne vivent pas dans les cités et utilisent seulement une partie de son [sic] vocabulaire, auquel ils mélangent leurs propres inventions;
> 4) Enfin la langue des "lascars" […] est une matrice en perpétuel renouvellement et qui irrigue l'ensemble de la génération.[23]

The artificial character, and even the falsehood, of this presentation, its excesses, its implicit reference to numerically inferior social strata

---

[23] Florence Monteil, "Dix expressions et leurs secrets de fabrication", *Phosphore*, March 2002. *Phosphore* cites as an authority on the matter the sociolinguist Jean-Pierre Goudaillier, author of *Comment tu tchatches!*

(high bourgeoisie, show business, the under-privileged population of Paris and large cities) is disturbing: the *provinces* have been forgotten, as are rural areas, sub-categories of group (3), and women in group (4). One might wonder how the lexical creativity of each stratum is measured: by the quantity of lexical items which are not standard and by the resulting difficulty for the outsider-hearer to make sense of a sentence? If so, compare the following Ophélie-Winter type of sentence (1) with lascar-type sentence (2):

(1) Je ne le trust [borrowing: *to trust*] pas, il ne m'a pas caré [borrowing: *to care*] de la résoi [verlan: *soirée*].[24]
= I don't trust him, he hasn't paid attention to me for the whole evening.

(2) Je kiffe [borrowing: Arabic] pas ces keums [verlan: *mecs*] qui font crari [borrowing: Romany] parce qu'ils ont de la maille [borrowing: 'classical' argot].[25]
= I can't stand these guys who show off because they have big bucks.

Neither of these sentences is immediately understandable to the lay person; in each of them the key lexical items are *verlan* or borrowings. What distinguishes them is solely the source of the borrowed words: English in the Ophélie-Winter variety; Arabic, Romany and *argot* in the *lascar* variety. One could therefore claim that they are equally creative. Furthermore, these two phenomena (verlanisation and borrowing) are not particularly innovative. Verlan is a coded language already attested in the sixteenth century: for example, the lower classes applied syllable metathesis to the name of the royal family and so the Bourbons were called *Bonbours*.[26] We also know that, although not extensively used, verlan was not absent from *argot* in the 1950's.[27] As for borrowing, it is a widespread factor of language change. What is new therefore is a) the lexical items to which the verlanisation process can be applied at a given time (it is a selective coding mechanism which does not affect all French words), and b) the donor

---

[24] From Loïc Prigent, "Elles parlent l'ophélie-winter", *Le Nouvel Observateur* (1998, Oct. 15-21).
[25] From Monteil.
[26] Pierre Merle, *Argot, verlan et tchatches* (Toulouse: Éditions Milan, 2006), p. 48.
[27] Marc Sourdot, "L'argotologie: entre forme et fonction", *La Linguistique*, 38 (2002), 25-39.

languages or varieties from which lexical items are transferred for inclusion in youth language.

Diachronic variation is alluded to, and occasionally mentioned at length, however not from a linguistic perspective, but from a social one. The fact that youth language changes quickly prevents parents from keeping up with it and, as a consequence, guides and glossaries are necessary. When *Télé 7 Jours* puts the spotlight on some examples from Girard and Kermel (parallel sentences to illustrate words that have fallen out of fashion and been replaced), it is obviously more to bridge the generational gap than to discuss linguistic evolution.

Diachronic variation is also dealt with indirectly in relation to the phenomenon of *jeunisme*, the cult of values linked to youth. Advertising companies, television and radio stations, aging adults in search of youth therapy,[28] are lying in wait for new words and changes in the language.

The question of register and situational variation in youth language is never raised in newspapers. However, it is easy to observe that children speak differently to classmates and to teachers. And this is true of middle-class and of less well-to-do teenagers as well. We have evidence from sociolinguist research, concerning the latter, that children of migrant families have a large linguistic repertoire at their disposal: foreign languages or mixed languages for home with parents; mixed languages and forms of French with brothers and sisters; network sociolects with close friends and peers; and speech closer to the standard (*langue bourge*) when they address social workers or teachers. Just as the boundary between dialect and standard in diglossia, or between acrolect and basilect in creoles is never water-tight, the boundaries between youth speech and the common language can never be perfectly clear. It is better to envisage the situation as a multidimensional continuum where varieties do not exist as linguistic entities but are abstract representations at which speakers aim and

---

[28] Today's version (1997): Samedi, à la teuf de Rémi, j'ai linké une go!
1970s version: Samedi, à la fête de Rémi, j'ai branché une nana!
1950s version: Samedi, à la party de Rémi, j ai levé une gonzesse!
[28] Guillaume Malaurie, "Tchatchez-vous céfran? (Parlez-vous français?)", *Le Nouvel Observateur* (1998, 15-21 Oct.).

which they help to reinforce or modify.[29] In the light of all these remarks, we can see that young people move in a pluri-dimensional social and linguistic space, an impression one fails to get when reading the written media.[30]

Language is pluralistic in its social dimension, as we have seen, but it is also pluralistic as a system. In this second perspective, youth language is again presented narrowly and selectively in the press. The phonological dimension is neglected, except for occasional remarks like those by Mazure on two types of rhythms in the speech of teenagers which he calls "gnangnan" (soppy) and "speedé" (accelerated).[31] Gadet, however, writing on the language of the suburbs, notes that the phonology of this sociolect is striking and the the soundtrack of the film *La Haine*, for example, "produit immédiatement un effet d'étrangeté" when one first listens to it.[32] She identifies, in the language of adolescents living in the suburbs, specific phonological features such as the glottalized production of /r/, the affrication of certain stops, a high number of assimilations and a prosody which strongly emphasizes the last syllable in a rhythmic group.[33]

Similarly, journalists do not pay much attention to syntax, and when they do, youth syntax is erroneously confused with the syntax of familiar French. Non-existing divergences from the norm are named, differences with non-'young' forms of the language are overstated. For example, consider the comments made in *Phosphore* on the 'adolescent' sentence: *Comment t'es laid* (the norm would be: *Comme tu es laid*):

---

[29] See Estelle Liogier, "Quelles approches théoriques pour la description du français parlé dans les cités?", *La Linguistique,* 38-1 (2002), 50.

[30] Note that some young people react strongly to reductive views of youth language: "Je ne pense pas pouvoir supporter cette expression «parler jeune» ou «jeune». On a le droit d'être différent et de ne pas faire partie de la masse ou d'un troupeau." Quoted in Boyer (2001), p. 80.

[31] D. Mazure, "Savez-vous parler le jeune?", *L'Echo des savanes*, 128, June 1994.

[32] Françoise Gadet, "Des fortifs aux técis: persistances et discontinuités dans la langue populaire", in Dawn Marley, Marie-Anne Hintze and Gabrielle Parker (eds), *Linguistic Identities and Policies in France and the French-speaking World* (London: CiLT, 1998), pp. 11-26.

[33] See also Françoise Gadet, "«Français populaire»: Un concept douteux pour objet évanescent", *Ville-École-Intégration Enjeux,* 130 (2002) 40-50.

> Cet exemple souligne que le "parler jeune" multiplie les infractions à la
> syntaxe: disparition des négations, pronoms tronqués ou mal utilisés, absence
> de verbe, avec une préférence pour tout ce qui peut abréger ou accélérer le
> langage. Ex: *Ça s'fait pas, comment y m'traite.*[34]

In fact, the features mentioned in the above quotation and illustrated in
the accompanying examples do not violate the rules of syntax. They
are what Blanche-Benveniste calls "des fautes qui n'en sont plus";[35]
rather, they are characteristics of spoken French, differing from the
norm, which everyone—young or old—uses and which no one notices
any more. In the same vein, *Resonances* quotes an excerpt from a
musical written by students in their own way of speaking:

> *Djalil* : Salut les copains, vous parlez de quoi?
> *Les autres* : Ça te regarde pas! Casse-toi, t'es nul! Vas-y, rentre chez toi.
> Retourne dans ton coin! Tu nous fatigues. [36]

The extract is probably regarded as typical or exemplary by the
journalist, since it is presented in a box. But it should be pointed out
that its syntax—and its lexicon—are simply those of familiar spoken
French: omission of *ne* in negative sentences and interrogative
constructions without inversion.

The language component favoured by journalists is the lexicon.
Articles on youth French always contain selected vocabulary items,
more or less structured into categories, accompanied or not by
comments, often extracted from glossaries published by popularizers,
some journalists themselves. The words or phrases that are more
readily collected are those which clearly deviate from the norm.

They are quoted without context along with their equivalent in
the standard language. The press conforms here to the tradition of
'argotography' with words accumulated in lists.[37] Moreover, *Télé 7*

---

[34] Monteil.
[35] Claire Blanche-Benveniste, *Approches de la langue parlée en français* (Paris:
Ophrys, 2000), pp. 38-41.
[36] Nadia Revaz et al., "Le parler des jeunes", *Résonances,* June 2003, 1-18 (12).
[37] See, for example, Roselyne Bosch, "Évolution de la langue française: Le français
qui décoiffe", *Le Point*, 17 November 1986; Walter, where the article is followed by a
list of words considered to be typical; Jean-Pierre Goudaillier, "Les parlers branchés",
Le Nouvel Observateur, 15 June 2000. Bulot criticizes this procedure and adds: "Faire
des dictionnaires du parler jeune ne suffit pas. On doit tenter de comprendre pourquoi

Jours tells us that Girard and Kernel are word collectors.[38] Why this concentration of interest in the lexicon? Perhaps because words are particularly visible items, non-specialists notice them immediately when they compare their way of speaking to that of others. It might be objected that non-standard pronunciation is just as noticeable (it can be used to classify speakers favourably or unfavourably). But journalists do not have the expertise to systematically encode speech in IPA symbols, or their audience the expertise to decode it, whereas spelling is available to all.

In addition, among words used by young people, it is the most formally salient which are selected by journalists: words affected by truncations (for example, for *musique*: with apheresis *zique*, or with apocope *muz*), borrowings from foreign languages (*cool, marave,*[39] *niquer*[40]) or verlanisations. Verlan[41] is at the core of all journalistic descriptions, staged for effect as it were, emblematic, although sociolinguistic studies and teachers' accounts report that this coded language is far from being shared by all of the younger generation. And so, these processes of lexical innovation are overvalued, touted as original experiments which contribute to renewing and revitalizing the French language.[42] According to *Phosphore*, [l]La langue des jeunes est un véritable labo du mot".[43] Actually, highlighted by the media,

---

les jeunes s'expriment ainsi." Thierry Bulot, "Sociolinguistique urbaine: Langue(s). Pourquoi le parler jeune?", Interview for *l'Humanité-Hebdo*, 5 October 2002.

[38] Malaurie remarks that advertising agencies are on the lookout for youth vocabulary and "want just words". It describes as word catchers staff in charge of finding novel words which will be successful with a public characterized by "jeunisme médiatico-industriel".

[39] From Romany: "to hit, to beat up".

[40] From Arabic: "to have sexual intercourse with".

[41] For Monteil, "[l]e verlan est LE procédé". Some articles are entirely dedicated to it, and in others, it occupies a place of honor. See in particular Daniel Garcia and Guillaume Malaurie, "Verlan cherche deuxième souffle", *Le Nouvel Observateur*, 15-21 October 1998; Daniel Garcia, "Faut-il vraiment un interprète?" *Le Nouvel Observateur*, 15-21 October 1998; Pierre Merle, *Argot, verlan et tchatches*. (Toulouse: Editions Milan, 1997).

[42] See also Daniel Delas, "Le bilinguisme aujourd'hui. Quand les langues se mélangent", www.u-cergy.fr/article3774.html, article dated 27 April 2005 (accessed 10 April 2010). Delas notes that processes used in manufacturing slang are similar in all major cities, and in that respect are not particularly original.

[43] Béatrice Girard, "Savez-vous parler « djeun's »?", *Phosphore,* 249, March 2002.

some of these new words are echoed by other young people and even manage to find their way into standard-language dictionaries.[44]

A final point remains to be made before concluding. In recent years, along with a weakening of communitarian ideology and the attendant efforts to put a positive spin on suburban cultural production, sociologists have noted a decrease in enthusiasm in the press for the younger generation and its modes of expression. This change in attitude can be attributed to the riots that rocked the suburbs in 2005 and the questions that French society was forced to confront concerning the social divide and the resulting linguistic divide. Previously isolated voices were heard, such as those of Azouz Begag, Alain Bentolila and some socio-educators. They cautioned against the ideological craze for the so-called richness and creativity of youth language. In 2005 Frederic Potet's article, "Vivre avec 400 mots" generated a large number of letters from readers and comments in other newspapers and on blogs.[45] People became alarmed by the lexical and morphological poverty of suburban youth speech—a sign of non-integration—and its potential negative consequences in the classroom: "12 à 15% des jeunes en France vivent au-dessous du SMIC linguistique", the article said. Revaz adds:

> Dans certaines banlieues des ados se barricadent linguistiquement et, une fois enfermés dans leur prison de mots, ils ont peur du langage de l'école. D'identitaire, le code devient alors un facteur d'exclusion. A chacun son langage bien sûr, mais il est essentiel de savoir que d'autres manières de communiquer existent.[46]

In other words, originality in the spoken forms of the language where every youth can be creative with impunity, should not overshadow the learning of the normative language which will enable him or her to function adequately in society at large.

---

[44] For example, the words *beur, keuf, meuf, kiffer, ouf* and the expression *ça craint* have now entered the pages of the *Petit Robert*.

[45] Frédéric Potet, "Vivre avec 400 mots", *Le Monde*, 19 March 2005.

[46] Nadia Revaz, "Des mots des jeunes au langage scolaire", *Résonances*, June 2003, p.1.

Conclusion

The terminology in use (*le français jeune*, *la langue des jeunes*, *le jeune*) suggests that there is *one* unified variety of French, defined by age. However, other variables (diastratic, diatopic, situational, diachronic, gendered) cut across the speech of teenagers. Although plurality in youth speech is occasionally recognized by the press, this theme remains under-developed, and ultimately, it is a simplified and stereotyped picture of youth language that is imposed on the reader. Some specific linguistic aspects are developed at the expense of all others. We have discussed in particular the popularity of lexical items deviating from the norm, especially borrowings and verlan. These characteristics are associated with certain social groups (initially with 'trendy' youths, and later more with youths of the suburbs). Ultimately, the media represent and officialize a form of French which is largely fabricated and caricatured. Of course, we can be grateful to the media for attracting public attention to modern linguistic forms, but we cannot ignore the dangers of the approach they choose to take. The first is conceptual in nature: the fuzziness and confusion of the denomination 'youth French' are never adequately resolved. The second is social: by focusing too much on the creativity, the picturesque, the attractiveness of the language of certain disadvantaged groups, journalists conceal possible deficiencies in this language and the culture of confinement it can underpin. One might also regret that, ultimately, it is the perspective of adults which dominates—which is a constant problem when it comes to representations of youth, linguistic or other.

Integration or Interaction?
Disability in France Today

Sam Haigh

During the televised debate that took place between Ségolène Royal and Nicolas Sarkozy prior to the presidential elections of May 2007, one heated exchange, in particular, became the subject of subsequent media coverage and on-line discussion. It came about two hours into their two hours and forty minutes of debate, when Sarkozy introduced the subject of the schooling of children with disabilities. Stating that only 40 per cent of such children, in France, were currently educated in what he called "des écoles 'normales'", as against 100 per cent in some other Northern European countries, he pledged his commitment to rectifying the situation, declaring that it was important not only for those children themselves that they received mainstream education, but that it was even more important for nondisabled children since it would allow them to see, first hand, "que la différence est une richesse".[1] Royal, for her part, found such a proposition "scandaleuse", "le summum de l'immoralité politique", not because it prioritized the needs of able-bodied children, but because it was an empty pre-election promise that failed to take account of the fact that the

---

[1] The debate took place on 3 May 2007 on TF1. Accessed June 2008 at http://www.dailymotion.com/video/x1vpl6_debat-royalsarkozy-laccrochage.

government of which he was a part had so far acted counter to the interests of the very children whose cause he now seemed to be championing. She cited the case of Handiscol, an initiative that she set up in 1999, while *Ministre déléguée à l'enseignement scolaire*, in order precisely to ensure that children with disabilities should be able to attend mainstream schools by, amongst other things, providing 7000 new learning support assistants ("auxiliaires d'intégration scolaire"). According to Royal, it was the government to which Sarkozy belonged that was responsible for getting rid of these posts and dismantling Handiscol itself, ensuring that only half of the children with disabilities who were attending mainstream schools five years ago continue to do so.

This part of the debate elicited articles and blogs in which it was revealed that Handiscol still, in fact, exists, and where it was claimed that the numbers of disabled children at mainstream schools had actually risen since 1999. Here, a debate raged over whether Royal had deliberately lied about the facts, as well as over how many children with disabilities received more than a few hours' education per week, and over the number of *aide-éducateurs* and their relative lack of qualifications. It also led to the creation of "2700 postes supplémentaires d'auxiliaires de vie scolaire [et] [...] le lancement d'une plate-forme téléphonique d'information" and, consequently, to unprecedented amounts of enquiries from the parents of children with disabilities, ahead of the 2007 *rentrée scolaire*, all believing that it would now be possible to find a mainstream school place for their child.[2] What is perhaps most significant of all, however, is the simple fact that, in France, a debate about disability could elicit so much media and general public interest. As we shall see, in comparison with the US, Canada and the UK, most Scandinavian countries, and other European countries such as Belgium and Holland, France has historically lagged behind in terms of disability law and provision. That the issue was raised, and so contentiously, in the very public arena of the televised presidential debate is surely evidence of a sea-change that at last seems to be taking place, however slowly, in French attitudes towards disability.

---

[2] See Laurent Lejard, "Une Rentrée très politique", *Yanous!* (September 2007). Accessed June 2008 at http://www.yanous.com/espaces/parents/parents070914.html.

This change can in fact be seen to have begun in 2002, when President Chirac, just ahead of the EU's planned Year of Disabled People in 2003, announced that disability was to be one of the three *chantiers* of his second term of office, and appointed Julia Kristeva as head of a new *Conseil national handicap*. The Council's slogan is "sensibiliser, former, informer", and one of its key aims is to "changer le regard et le comportement de chacun vis-à-vis des personnes en situation de handicap".[3] Its remit, therefore, is to bring issues of disability into wider public, as well as political, view. To this end, Kristeva commissioned a series of six public-information broadcasts for television, presented various conference papers, wrote both academic and more widely accessible newspaper articles, as well as giving many media interviews, including one with Ségolène Royal herself.[4] At Chirac's request she also produced a report on the current situation regarding disability in France, which was published in 2003 as *Lettre au Président de la République sur les citoyens en situation de handicap*.[5] There was then a *tour de France des états généraux*, culminating in a conference in May 2005 addressed by the President and another book by Kristeva, *Handicap: le temps des engagements* (2006).

Most significantly in terms of actual, political change, though, was the introduction of a new law, "La Loi de l'égalité des chances, la participation et la citoyenneté des personnes handicapées", a law directly influenced by Kristeva's work and even modified, after its first reading in parliament in June 2004, following an open letter to Chirac in *Le Monde* on 16 October 2004 in which Kristeva protested that it did not go far enough. Finally passed on 3 February 2005, this law represented the first major piece of disability legislation in France since 1975 and, as Kristeva herself points out, it was designed specifically to introduce "des innovations radicales susceptibles de

---

[3] See the Conseil national's website: http://cnhandicap.org/index.asp.

[4] Julia Kristeva and Ségolène Royal, "Que faire pour les handicapés?" in *L'Express*, 11 April 2005. Accessed June 2008 at http://www.lexpress.fr/info/societe/dossier/-handicap/dossier.asp?ida=432551.

[5] Julia Kristeva, *Lettre au Président de la République sur les citoyens en situation de handicap, à l'usage de ceux qui le sont et de ceux qui ne le sont pas* (Paris: Fayard, 2003).

nous faire rattraper notre retard".[6] Like its earlier US and UK counterparts, the Americans with Disabilities Act (1990) and the Disability
Discrimination Act (1995), both of which have subsequently been
extended and modified, this law covers major, basic issues such as the
right to non-discrimination, the right to work and/or to reasonable
levels of benefits, the right to have access to public places and public
transport and the right to be educated alongside people without
disabilities. In other words, and in a discourse that is also familiar
from its Anglo-American counterparts, such a law is based on the
premise that the integration of people with disabilities into
'mainstream' society is the way to fight exclusion, and to achieve,
instead, equality, participation and citizenship in a modern world that
increasingly imagines itself as inclusive and tolerant of difference.

Exclusion, as Henri-Jacques Stiker showed in his
groundbreaking 1982 study *Corps infirmes et sociétés*,[7] has been one
of the primary characteristics of the history of disability. From the old
and new Testaments and antiquity to the Middle Ages, the
Renaissance and Enlightenment, to the nineteenth and twentieth
centuries, disability—in various ways and for apparently different
reasons—has been made to 'disappear'. This may have been through
sequestration (in 'leper colonies', religious communities or charitable
institutions); through an exclusion from the social into a life of
mendicancy; or through ideas of cure and eradication—from a biblical
belief in the miracle to an increased faith in medical technologies from
the nineteenth century onwards. As Kristeva adds, in her own
examination of the history of disability—one that is clearly influenced
by Stiker, whom she cites, but which is much more closely focused on
France—the current approach to disability is one that emerged in the
late-nineteenth century, and it is "[un] modèle médical [...] binaire".[8]
That is, one which sets up an opposition between "un individu frappé

---

[6] Julia Kristeva, "Handicap, différence et société", pp. 1-12 (p. 7). This article was
published online as part of the proceedings of a conference at which Kristeva spoke in
November 2006 at the University of Lyon. Accessed May 2007 at www.universite-
lyon.fr/servlet/com.univ.utils.LectureFichierJoint?CODE=1170088738809&LANGU
E=0&ext=.pdf.
[7] Henri-Jacques Stiker, *Corps infirmes et sociétés: Essais d'anthropologie historique*,
third edition (Paris: Dunod, 2005). First published in 1982 by Editions Aubier
Montaigne.
[8] Kristeva (2003), p. 17.

de déficiences et porteur de besoins" on the one hand and "une société dotée de pouvoirs médicaux, économiques et juridiques" on the other.[9] Such a model has meant that people with disabilities have effectively been excluded from the social and isolated as "objets de soins" in receipt of charitable aid rather than being viewed as fully-fledged citizens.[10] The alternative to such a model is usually seen, as it is by both Kristeva and Stiker, as the 'social model' of disability that has predominated in an Anglo-American context since the 1980s, and which informed 1990s disability legislation in both the US and the UK. Here, disability is seen to be produced not simply by physical or mental 'deficiencies' in isolation, but by the ways in which a given society interprets such deficiencies and by its refusal to adapt itself to them.[11] Despite the adoption of such a definition of disability into French law at various points in the 1980s, Kristeva feels that, until the 2005 law, the medical model has prevailed and the insights of a more 'social' approach have been largely ignored.

It is this, then, that provides the context of the debate between Royal and Sarkozy, for if people with disabilities receive an education at all in France it is still most likely to occur in a medico-educational institution designed for that purpose, mainstream schools never before having been obliged to find ways of educating people with specific needs. Obviously aware of this movement from exclusion to integration, both presidential candidates seem keen to position themselves at the forefront of France's race to 'catch up' with the progress made by other countries in the area of disability provision and the move towards a social model of disability. However, Stiker, for his part, takes issue with the notion that the discourse of integration is a new approach to disability at all. What he finds in his history of disability is that the impulse to exclude and eradicate has occurred *alongside* a professed will, in most periods and societies, precisely to integrate people with disabilities in some way. That it should be seen as a modern form of 'progress' from previous eras of

---

[9] Kristeva (2003), p. 17.
[10] Kristeva (2006), p. 7.
[11] See Kristeva (2003), pp. 27-8, p. 37. For a more detailed account of the social model of disability, see Michael Oliver, *The Politics of Disablement* (London: Macmillan, 1990). More recently, there have been calls by disability theorists to update the social model: see, for example, Mairian Corker and Tom Shakespeare (eds), *Disability/Postmodernity: Embodying Disability Theory* (London: Continuum, 2002).

'barbarity' is therefore not credible; rather, integration is but another
form of erasure, one that is more pernicious because more subtle, for it
can more easily pass unnoticed and the reasons behind it can be
masked.[12] Kristeva, too, is suspicious of the term integration: "il sent
la charité envers ceux qui n'auraient pas les mêmes droits que les
autres".[13] In other words, it remains part of a medical model which
pits 'society' *against* 'people with disabilities' and seeks eradication
of the latter by their absorption into the former. What I want to begin
by examining here is therefore not simply whether a move towards a
social model of integration 'really is' occurring, either in France or
elsewhere but, rather, whether the discourse of integration that
currently prevails in debates on disability really promotes equality of
participation. What form might a more adequate or appropriate alternative take—particularly within a French context, where the term
integration has such specific historical, political and cultural
resonances?

It may at first appear striking, as Kristeva herself points out,
that equality for people with disabilities has so far been the least
forthcoming in "le pays des droits de l'homme"—a Republic based on
the ideals of "liberté, égalité, fraternité".[14] However, as Kristeva
acknowledges, this is of course also a Republic built on notions of
abstract individualism, reason and universalism inherited from the
Enlightenment; a tradition of unity and indivisibility that has tended to
see difference as a threat to national coherence and as something,
precisely, which must be erased through integration. As many others
have pointed out, Enlightenment and Republicanist values were
actually based on a false universalism, one that proclaimed the
equality of universal rights while simultaneously enshrining "the
inequality of particular bodies" and excluding those bodies—female,
black, disabled—from citizenship.[15] Despite this, Kristeva is unwilling

---

[12] See Stiker, p. 14-15.
[13] Kristeva (2006), p. 4.
[14] Kristeva (2006), p.1.
[15] Lennard J. Davis, *Bending over Backwards: Disability, Dismodernism and Other
Difficult Positions* (New York: New York University Press, 2002), p. 26. See also pp.
107-12. Others make the same point in relation both to colonized subjects (see
Margaret Majumdar, *Postcoloniality: The French Dimension* [Oxford: Berghan,
2007], pp. 8-32) and, especially, women. Indeed, that this "crisis of French universalism" is at the heart of gender inequality is the basis of Joan Wallach Scott's

simply to reject either Enlightenment or Republican values. On the contrary, and in a move familiar from her previous work (notably *Etrangers à nous-mêmes*),[16] it is to the Enlightenment that she returns in order to find a means of recalibrating current French attitudes towards difference. In particular, she examines Diderot's 1749 text, *Lettre sur les aveugles à l'usage de ceux qui voient*, reading it as at the origin of the social model that has subsequently become associated with the Anglo-American approach, and therefore positioning France at the forefront of a "first wave" of disability rights.[17] She locates his efforts within a solidly Republicanist[18] framework, pointing out how he worked specifically "sur fond d'égalité des droits de l'homme", and that his aim was to have blind people recognized as both political subjects and equal citizens.[19] Of course, this is why the title and subtitle of her *Lettre au Président* echoes so obviously that of Diderot: she sees the ultimate aim of Chirac's *chantier*, too, as that of including people with disabilities within society as fully-fledged "sujets-citoyens",[20] and she feels that the inspiration behind it, similarly, is "en droit-fil de l'esprit des Lumières".[21] For Kristeva, one of the opportunities offered by Chirac's *chantier* is that of reaffirming and also renewing what she calls "le pacte républicain"; a means of enabling the Republic to fulfil its potential for real equality and universal rights.[22] As means of achieving all of this, she envisages not *integration* but, once again in resolutely Republicanist language, "une citoyenneté partagée" based on an *interaction* between people with and without disabilities.[23]

It should come as no surprise to those familiar with Kristeva's previous work that the new approach to disability that she envisages is

---

argument in *Parité! Sexual Equality and the Crisis of French Universalism* (Chicago: University of Chicago Press, 2005), as well as of Gisèle Halimi's "Un universalisme trompeur", in *La Nouvelle Cause des femmes* (Paris: Seuil, 1997), pp. 87-106.

[16] Julia Kristeva, *Etrangers à nous-mêmes* (Paris: Fayard, 1988).

[17] Kristeva (2003), p. 15-16; and Kristeva (2006), p. 6.

[18] I am using this term instead of 'Republican', as does Wallach Scott in *Parité* (cited above), to designate someone who upholds the principles of the republic since, as she points out, "almost everyone in France is a republican" (p. 165).

[19] Kristeva (2006), p. 6.

[20] Kristeva (2003), p. 30.

[21] Kristeva (2003), p. 14

[22] Kristeva (2006), p. 4.

[23] Kristeva (2003), p. 14, 28.

based not only on a reexamination of Enlightenment philosophy, but also on a call to psychoanalysis. For Kristeva, the desire to exclude disability, literally or via integration, has been born out of fear. Stiker, too, points to the fundamental unease felt by most people when faced with "les corps difformes et les esprits englués",[24] an unease that springs from the fact that "chacun a son 'autre' infirme qu'il ne peut pas admettre" and whom we are frightened to confront in the body of the person with disabilities.[25] This is not only because the deficient body serves to remind us that anyone, through accident or ageing, can become disabled at any time. More than this, it is because those who live with disability are "des personnes dont le corps et l'esprit interrogent l'identité même de notre espèce".[26] That is, they call into question what it is to be human, and are testament, in particular, to our fundamental vulnerability. And this, for Kristeva, is where psychoanalysis can serve as a model: Freud's discovery of the unconscious, she feels, was a discovery precisely of our constitutive vulnerability, a vulnerability that is revealed daily on the analyst's couch and that analysts have necessarily already recognized within themselves in order to enable them to be open to the vulnerability of others, to empathize with it and to share it.[27] This openness to the other and, in particular, this "écoute psychanalytique de la vulnérabilité",[28] is therefore the model that she proposes for the interaction that needs to take place between people with and without disabilities if any kind of "citoyenneté partagée" is to be realizable. Indeed, maintaining her rigorously Republicanist focus, she even goes so far as to call for the word "vulnérabilité" to be added as a fourth term to the Republic's *devise* of "liberté, égalité, fraternité".[29]

For Kristeva, then, it is about recognizing that "la vulnérabilité [...] [fait] partie intégrante de l'espèce humaine".[30] For Stiker, too,

---

[24] Stiker, p. x.
[25] Stiker, p. 7.
[26] Kristeva (2006), p. 1.
[27] Kristeva (2006), p. 9-10. She makes a similar point in an interview with Denis Poizat, published in the journal *Reliance*, 20.2 (2006), 8-10 (8).
[28] Kristeva, interview with Poizat, p. 11.
[29] Kristeva, interview with Poizat, p. 10. "Liberté, égalité, fraternité... et vulnérabilité" is also the title of the later version of "Handicap, différence et société" published in *Recherches en psychanalyse*, 6.2 (2006), 11-27.
[30] Kristeva (2006), p. 10.

disability (and, indeed, difference in general) needs to be reconceived as 'integral' rather than 'integrable' to the human condition: "[il faut] apprendre que la différence n'est point une exception, une monstruosité, mais quelque chose qui arrive dans le cours du monde".[31] For him, it is important to accept that 'reality' generates difference, including disability, and that "il est inscrit dans l'univers humain d'estimer la différence qu'il engendre".[32] As David Mitchell points out in his Foreword to the English translation of Stiker's book, if most eras have professed a will to integrate people with disabilities, none of them have committed themselves to a belief in the naturalness of physical and cognitive differences to the normative human condition.[33] Such an attitude would enable a move away from both exclusion and integration, towards a recognition of difference as 'normal' (in the sense of 'ordinary') and, to echo the title of one of Kristeva's articles, people with disabilities would have "[un] droit à l'irrémédiable".[34] One of the key aims of the *Conseil national handicap* is to effect a profound change in the way in which disability is *seen*, and the seven 90-second public-information films that Kristeva commissioned, and which were aired in May 2004 on France 2, 3 and 5 are, therefore, a central part of this work. As Ludovic Tomas points out in his review of them, "chaque spot est une fiction qui présente les difficultés rencontrées selon le type de handicap".[35] However, as he also points out, "*La caméra épouse le regard du valide*, souvent ignorant, parfois indélicat voire méprisant".[36] Each of them, in other words, privileges the nondisabled perspective of disability, and this is what is striking about Kristeva's work as a whole: that she takes so little account of the perspective of people with

---

[31] Stiker, p. 10.

[32] Stiker, p. 10.

[33] David T. Mitchell, "Foreword", in Stiker, *A History of Disability*, trans. William Sayers, (Michigan: University of Michigan Press, 2000), p. xi.

[34] Julia Kristeva's "Handicap ou le droit à l'irrémédiable" is an earlier version of "Handicap, différence et société", published in *Etudes*, 4025 (2005), 619-29.

[35] Ludovic Tomas, "Handicap. Pour changer son regard", *Journal de l'Humanité*, 4 May 2004. Accessed May 2007 at http://www.humanite.presse.fr/popup_print.php3?-id_article=393031.

[36] Tomas, my italics. Tomas does not appear to imply any criticism here.

disabilities themselves.[37] Echoing Sarkozy's comments on the importance for nondisabled children of being educated alongside children with disabilities, for Kristeva it is primarily nondisabled people who will gain from recognizing their own vulnerability in that of the disabled person, just as the inclusion of disabled people within the 'Republican pact' represents, above all, an opportunity for a renewal of Republicanism, indeed democracy, as a whole.

Such bias has not gone unnoticed within the French disabled community itself. For example, in his report on the 2005 *Etats généraux* conference organized and presided over by Kristeva, Laurent Lejard, editor of *Yanous!*—"le premier hebdomadaire francophone du handicap"—criticizes both the new *Conseil national* and Kristeva herself for not including any people with disabilities amongst "les 'spécialistes' du handicap" called to give papers on the subject, or amongst the sports people, media personalities and minor celebrities invited to sponsor this event and the *Conseil*'s other projects. Rather mockingly, Lejard asks: "croit-elle que le handicap est contagieux? Peur, angoisse, refoulement?"[38] Unfortunately, then, Kristeva would seem to be perpetuating the binary, medical model of disability—the sense of professionals and experts on one side and disabled 'patients' on the other—of which she is elsewhere so critical, thereby widening the divide between people with and without disabilities rather than working to promote real interaction and exchange. What I want to turn to here is the question of whether efforts are being made by people with disabilities themselves to offer new perspectives on disability—more practical perspectives, perhaps, that might enable precisely the kind of interaction and exchange envisaged theoretically by Kristeva.

Until recently, most writing about disability in France has taken the form of either short, educational, fiction aimed at children and adolescents or, for an adult readership, of testimony—either of able-bodied parents who have experienced the birth of a child with a

---

[37] This tendency is familiar, once again, from Kristeva's previous work on the foreigner, particularly in *Etrangers à nous mêmes*. Here, she similarly emphasizes the necessity of recognizing our own otherness as a prerequisite for building links with the others that are foreigners, but neglects the perspective of the foreigner him or herself.

[38] Laurent Lejard, "Faux Etats-Généraux, vraie dépossession", *Yanous!*, 27 (2005). Accessed May 2007 at http://www.yanous.com/news/editorial/edito050527.html.

disability, or of newly-disabled people, in the vein of Jean-Dominique Bauby's *Le Scaphandre et le papillon*, published in 1997 and made into a film in 2007. This tendency towards first-person, experience-based writing is, of course, to be expected, since the consideration of disability as a category of social exclusion is a more recent phenomenon than that of race, class, gender or even sexuality—and particularly in France. As Lennard J. Davis points out in his seminal work of disability theory, *Bending over Backwards*, even in a US context, "the political and academic movement around disability is at best a first- or second-wave enterprise", and thus remains heavily invested in identity politics.[39] Unfortunately, the discourses of sympathy, admiration and bravery that surround the marketing and reception of these kinds of texts frequently play on the fear of the able-bodied population that disability may strike their lives at any time too, and relief that it so far has not. As one reviewer of *Le Scaphandre et le papillon* notes, "the reason a person is going to read the book or see the film is to satisfy the fear of disability. Like it or not, there's the whole 'I hope that never happens to me' element in approaching this movie".[40] This kind of response does not necessarily lend itself either to interaction between disabled and nondisabled communities, nor to serious intellectual debate about the gulf between these two worlds.

Such interaction and serious debate is something that Stiker was keen to provoke when he published *Corps infirmes et sociétés* in 1982. He does consider the fear and unease of the nondisabled person but, unlike Kristeva, takes a resolutely disabled perspective on the history of disability. At the same time, he includes only occasional and oblique reference to his own personal experience of disability and this, especially in a French context, marks it out as very much ahead of its time. Stiker often writes in the first person, but he does so in a philo-sophical rather than autobiographical mode, as in this description of the newly disabled person's experience of disability:

> La représentation de moi-même, construite avec peine pour vivre, survivre, affronter des autres—avec la part de masques et de faux-semblants inévitables, avec les refoulements non moins inévitables... et nécessaire—, se brouille, vacille, se brise même. Je me croyais comme ceci... et voilà ce que

---

[39] Davis, p. 10.
[40] See http://www.goodnewsfilmreviews.com/2008/05/le-scaphandre-et-le-papillon-d-iving.html. Accessed April 2009.

je deviens! Je me croyais vu comme cela… et voilà comment j'apparais désormais![41]

Similarly, he discusses the way in which, for the disabled person, disability carries with it "ce besoin, très élémentaire et fruste peut-être, de ne pas être banni, incompris, étrange et étranger, à mes yeux d'abord, aux yeux des autres ensuite"[42] and, more, goes on to describe "l'énorme besoin d'imiter, de jouer sans cesse des mimes" that minimize one's difference, even enable one to 'pass' as non-disabled.[43] In other words, to integrate—an attitude towards disability which Stiker feels is experienced as much by people with disabilities as it is by those without, and which is inevitable when one lives in a culture that it is based both on a fear of difference, and on "la passion de la similitude".[44]

Stiker's early attempts to write a wide-ranging, philosophical yet personally informed, historical text that would generate serious academic debate is finally beginning to do just that, although it was not until the second edition was translated and published in the US that it finally received the academic attention, in France, for which Stiker had originally hoped.[45] It certainly finds echoes in the recent work of Alexandre Jollien, a philosopher who has cerebral palsy and whose first book, *Eloge de la faiblesse*, is autobiographical, but also resolutely not written as a testimony. Instead, it takes the form of a philosophical dialogue with Socrates on his own disability in partic-ular and on *la dissemblance* in general. Jollien's work bears striking similarities with that of both Stiker and Kristeva: he discusses the fear of nondisabled people when confronted with difference and the necessity both of recognizing one's own "faiblesse" and of enabling others to recognize theirs.[46] For him, too, "l'écoute amicale" is the primary way of undertaking what he terms "une recherche commune des solutions" between people with and without disabilities, and it is

---

[41] Stiker, p. 3.

[42] Stiker, p. 7.

[43] Stiker, p. 8.

[44] Stiker, p. 10.

[45] Indeed, it was this that led to the publication, in French, of the updated third edition to which I am referring here: as Stiker points out in his preface to the second edition, "Ma tentative demeure isolée. Je n'ai pas provoqué le débat que j'attendais" (p. ix).

[46] Alexandre Jollien, *Eloge de la faiblesse* (Paris: Cerf, 1999), pp. 51-54.

this that he aims to reflect with the "dialogue quasi socratique" in which his text is written.[47] Like Kristeva, he prefers the idea of redefining the terms 'normal' and 'anormal' to a discourse of integrating difference into 'the mainstream',[48] and where she describes the need to "changer le regard", he describes that of learning to "regarder autrement".[49] Like Stiker, he describes the enormous temptation, when faced with "le regard d'autrui", of trying to hide, to fit in, to integrate and, having spent most of his childhood and adolescence in a medico-educational institution, he also describes how difficult it was to leave and embark on a life in an outside world dominated by the experience of being looked at.[50] For Jollien, the experience of disability is one of being simultaneously visible (as disabled) and invisible (as a fully-fledged citizen): looked at but not recognized. As leading US disability theorist Rosemarie Garland Thomson puts it, the entire history of disability is one of "being on display", and of "being visually conspicuous while being politically and socially erased".[51]

It is this desire to move from 'visible invisibility' towards the real recognition of difference, as the prerequisite both of full participation and shared citizenship, that may also be seen to characterize the work of Delphine Censier. And her work, appropriately enough, takes the form not just of written autobiography but also, primarily, of photography. Censier was born with a disability, has been a wheelchair user from the age of six, and in her 2005 autobiography *Elle, Moi, une Autre*[52] she writes powerfully, like Stiker and Jollien, of the effects of "le regard des autres". Echoing Garland Thomson's work on freak-show exhibits,[53] she describes how

---

[47] Jollien, p. 63, 72.
[48] Jollien, p. 17, 98-99.
[49] Jollien, p. 72.
[50] Jollien, pp. 47-50.
[51] Rosemarie Garland Thomson, "Seeing the Disabled: Visual Rhetorics of Disability in Popular Photography", in Paul K. Longmore and Lauri Umansky, *The New Disability History: American Perspectives* (New York: New York University Press, 2001), pp. 335-374, p. 348.
[52] Delphine Censier, Elle, Moi, une Autre:'Gagner la vie' ou la reconquête d'une histoire perdue d'avance (Lausanne/Paris: Editions Favre, 2005).
[53] See, for example, Rosemarie Garland Thomson, *Freakery: Cultural Spectacles of the Extraordinary Body* (New York: New York University Press, 1996).

people with disabilities are made to feel constantly on display, "observés comme des bêtes de foire".[54] Like Jollien, she lived primarily in medico-educational institutions as a child and adolescent, and she details the experience—both there and in the countless hospitals in which she has continued to find herself since—of having her body regularly 'exhibited', literally 'laid bare' as a matter of routine, both for medical procedures and while being washed and dressed.[55] What is clear in all of these incidents is that it never occurs to any of the staff attending her that she (or they) may experience her body as anything other than simply an object of medical attention. Having managed, like Jollien, and with similar difficulty, to swap institutionalized living for a more 'normal' life in the mainstream community, she describes the moment when, during an evening with close friends, she revealed that she, like her doctors, had only ever been able to see and experience her body "à travers [s]on dossier médical, celui d'une patiente atteinte d'une maladie génétique au nom barbare: amytrophie spinale de Werdnig-Hoffmann de type 2".[56] Seeing herself primarily as "une jeune fille déformée, toute couturée de cicatrices", she felt unable to look at her own body properly, "[par] peur de découvrir un monstre".[57] Taking as a dare one friend's joke that she should force herself to move beyond her fear by having photographs taken in her underwear, without her body brace and other medical paraphernalia, she asked her carer Béatrice to be the photographer. The resulting photographs revealed to her not the 'monster' she had expected, but instead allowed her to see herself, for the first time, as "une femme à part entière",[58] and this led to her now vast collection of similar photographs which, since 2004, she has been exhibiting all over France and, more recently, on her website.[59]

All of Censier's photographs evoke the genre of 'soft' pornography, and picture her in sexually suggestive poses and in various types of satin and lace underwear in red, black or white.

---

[54] Censier, p. 94.
[55] Censier, p. 17-18.
[56] Censier, p. 7.
[57] Censier, p. 8, 9.
[58] Censier, p. 10.
[59] http://delphinecensier.com/.

Figure 1: "Rouge"

In her choice of what she calls "photos de charme", she is very obviously swapping one form of objectification (medical, as a disabled body) for another (sexual, as a female body). Indeed, it is as if she cannot imagine her body other than as objectified. For her, escaping the medicalization of her body clearly means performing a highly sexualized version of femininity—that is, in her words, becoming not only "une femme", but "une femme comme on peut en découvrir dans les magazines".[60] If these choices make Censier's photographs uncomfortable viewing from some feminist perspectives, from that provided by feminist disability theory, they are, at least, explicable. As many theorists of disability have pointed out, disability and sexuality are generally seen as mutually exclusive,[61] and disabled

---

[60] Censier, p. 9.

[61] See, for example, Tom Shakespeare, Kath Gillespie-Sells and Dominic Davies, *The Sexual Politics of Disability: Untold Desires* (London: Cassell, 1996) and Robert McRuer, *Crip Theory: Cultural Signs of Queerness and Disability* (New York: New York University Press, 2006).

women, in particular, are frequently subjected to what Garland Thomson, citing Harlan Hahn, calls "asexual objectification".[62]

This was precisely Censier's experience when, having removed her body brace for her photographs, she decided that she would like to replace her usual, heavy brace with a lighter, less noticeable one that covered less of her body and would therefore enable her to wear fashionable clothes and to feel her lover's touch on her skin. Her doctor, however, finds this request both baffling and unreasonable and his reply—"mais tu es handicapée, il faut assumer"[63]—reveals precisely an inability to see her, simultaneously, as both disabled and a sexual being. However, in the sexually suggestive poses and underwear that she chooses, and always pictured without her wheelchair or body brace, Censier's body conforms precisely to what Garland Thomson elsewhere calls "fashion's impossible standards".[64] As reported in most of the newspaper articles that cover her exhibition, and which are also included on her website, Censier is petite and extremely slim—"une petite poupée Barbie sexy", according to one interview.[65] Censier's photographs rarely picture her as simultaneously disabled and sexual, and thus she appears to have fallen into "passing as nondisabled" or "identifying against oneself",[66] and to have given into the great temptation, identified by both Jollien and Stiker, to imitate and therefore integrate. Indeed, she does admit that, initially, she wanted to use the photographs precisely to enable her to "[se] fondre au plus proche de la norme" and, at her very first exhibition (which she chose to hold at one of the insitutions in which she had previously lived), she was accused precisely of dishonesty by the former friends, co-patients and health workers there, who took issue with the artificiality of the photographs and felt betrayed by her

---

[62] Rosemarie Garland Thomson, *Extraordinary Bodies: Figuring Physical Disability in American Culture and Literature* (New York: Colombia University Press, 1997), p. 25-6.

[63] Censier, p. 140.

[64] Garland Thomson (2001), p. 363.

[65] Frédéric Vignale, "Interview de Delphine Censier, le Téléthon en 4 questions", http://www.lemague.net/dyn/spip.pip?article1671. As she reveals in her book, she has in fact suffered from anorexia (Censier, p. 43-44).

[66] Rosemarie Garland Thomson, "Integrating Disability, Transforming Feminist Theory", *NWSA Journal*, 14.3 (2002), 1-32 (15-17).

apparent attempts to hide her disability by failing to depict herself in her wheelchair.[67]

What such a view of Censier's work misses, however, is the element of performance that is central to her photographs (see figures 1-2). Her deliberate choices about costuming, props and photographic media, and her constant attention to the *mise-en-scène* and its artificiality are crucial. She is aware of arguments about the object-ification of women and, as she points out, "si une nana plantée sur ses deux jambes exhibait des photos semblables, on pourrait légitimement lui demander pourquoi"; and for this reason, she feels that "il ne faut pas perdre l'illusion créée. L'illusion de la femme sensuelle qui entre en contraste avec la femme en situation d'incapacité physique".[68] In fact, this is a contrast to which she actively draws attention, for she always travels with her exhibition and is present at it, in her wheelchair, revelling in the shock created by her presence and enjoying the moment when people realize that the woman in the photographs is the same person as the woman in the wheelchair.[69] In contrast to Kristeva's public-information films, Censier's presence at her exhibition actively encourages the possibility of social interaction between people with and without disabilities, especially since she actively engages with the people who have come to view the photo-graphs, approaching them or waiting to be approached and discussing her project, her life and her disability with them, or organising small conferences around the exhibition itself.[70] In many cases, according to Censier, the able-bodied people with whom she speaks share their own problems with her, and she frequently finds herself just as moved by the difficulties—physical or psychological—with which they have struggled, as they apparently do by hers.[71] For Censier, what these encounters reveal is neither a simple desire to shock, on her part, nor an impulse, on the part of the able-bodied, to construct themselves as 'normal' in relation to the 'deviant' body on display. Rather, they reveal a mutual recognition of difference—and one that, closely echoing Kristeva, Censier feels is possible only through "le partage".

---

[67] Censier, p. 178, 145-46.
[68] Censier, p. 175.
[69] Censier, p. 176-77.
[70] Censier, p. 172.
[71] Censier, p. 134-35, 178.

As she puts it: "la frontière de la différence s'estompait dans le part-age".[72]

Figure 2: "Noir et Blanc"

The work of Censier and Kristeva, therefore, takes different forms but envisages similar outcomes. Both, in different ways and from different perspectives, aim to change the way in which disability is perceived, and see integration as yet another form of invisibility rather than a positive move towards the recognition of disability as difference. Both, too, emphasize the practical aspects of such a vision. For Kristeva, the whole point of the 'philosophy of disability' that she sets out in her articles and reports is to inform and subtend the practical, political and legislative action which will enable the "citoyenneté partagée" in which all members of the Republic are recognized as fully-fledged citizens.[73] In the case of Censier, her much more direct, and personal, appeal for recognition and interaction has led her to an awareness of the same practical issues that Kristeva singles out as vitally in need of being addressed. For Censier, in particular, the kinds of issues that have traditionally been prioritized, such as physical access to buildings and public transport, have merely been the most

---

[72] Censier, p. 159.
[73] Kristeva (2005), p. 623.

visible means for "mainstream" society to appear to be taking action—by accommodating the apparent needs of people with disabilities, rather than recognizing their real needs.[74] Access to education and to work and/or benefits sufficient to enable people with disabilities to live independent lives outside of institutions are, for both women, the real priorities. Thus, in practical terms, Kristeva's theoretical idea of "une citoyenneté partagée" would entail a move-ment away from institutionalization, in which the specific needs of people with different disabilities cannot be catered for, towards a model of "accompagnement personnalisé", in which each person with a disability is enabled, financially and practically, to participate on an equal footing in mainstream society, and she emphasizes the necessity of proper training and qualifications for the "accompagnateurs" nec-essary for this.[75] Censier's emphasis, too, is on replacing institutional-ization with "accompagnement".[76] She writes about the enormous difficulty that she had in securing the necessary help to enable her to live independently, and of the real difference that good, professional, carers have made to her life. Once again, it is "le partage amical" that is necessary for these relationships to work but, on a more practical level, it is also funding, so that people with disabilities are no longer forced to live dependent lives, "prise en charge" by family members, partners or institutions.[77]

Despite the obvious similarities between her work and that of Kristeva, however, Censier declares herself unconvinced by the very political intitiatives in which Kristeva is involved. Three years after it was announced, she claims that Chirac's "grande cause nationale" is laughable, such are the practical and material difficulties that she continues to face on a day-to-day basis,[78] and the new law of 2005, which can be seen as the outcome of Kristeva's work and Chirac's *chantier*, was widely recognized by disability associations as not having gone nearly far enough.[79] Stiker, too, in the Epilogue to the

---

[74] Censier, p. 103.
[75] See Kristeva (2006), p. 3; Kristeva (2005), p. 623; and Kristeva (2003), p. 67.
[76] Censier, p. 60-61.
[77] Censier, p. 9, 102-03.
[78] Censier, p. 109.
[79] This is Royal's opening point in her interview with Kristeva, "Que faire pour les handicapés?" (p. 2), and it is also Lejard's general criticism in "Une Rentrée très politique", cited in note 2 above.

2005 edition of *Corps infirmes et sociétés*, feels that this law is just the same as the previous ones, introduces nothing new and uses the same language of deficiency. For him, "le législateur n'a pas changé de vision".[80] Censier is equally unimpressed by Sarkozy's discourse of "solidarité", which was to become a key term during his presidential campaign.[81] In a campaign video aired on 13 April 2007, for example, Sarkozy declared his solidarity with disabled people in ways, precisely, that called for a non-recognition of difference and a confidence, instead, in the benefits of integration: "Les handicapés ne doivent pas etre regardés comme des gens différents. Les handicapés, c'est nous […] Beaucoup de Français réclament la solidarité. Moi, je pense que s'il en est une catégorie qui en a besoin, c'est bien celle des handicapés et de leurs familles".[82]

This is, in fact, a line that Sarkozy then repeated, almost verbatim, over a year later when he addressed France's first National Conference on Disability in June 2008. In this 40-minute speech he promised to speed up the implementation of the 2005 law and to prioritize, in particular, precisely those areas that Kristeva had recommended to Chirac and that Censier also identified as urgent: access to work and school, and to the means of living independently.[83] In many ways, this was an expanded version of a speech that he gave in June 2007 at the 47th conference of UNAPEI (Union Nationale des Associations de Parents et Amis de Personnes Handicapées Mentales). He was the first president to attend this conference since 1975 (the same year as the introduction of the previous most substantial piece of disability legislation in France) and his decision to speak there was seen, in some quarters, as a direct result of his promise, in the pre-election debate with Royal, to make the education of children with disabilities central to his term of office should he be elected.[84] Here, as in his speech a year later, he frequently adopts a very Kristevan discourse, stating that:

---

[80] Stiker, p. 243.

[81] Censier, p. 96.

[82] Accessed September 2008 at http://www.dailymotion.com/video/x1pfqx_nicolas-sarkozy-je-veux-la-solidari_events.

[83] See http://www.dailymotion.com/mychannel/luciano75/video/x5qc1o_discours-de-nicolas-sarkozy-confere_news.

[84] http://www.lejdd.fr/cmc/politique/200723/handicap-sarkozy-s-engage_27394.html.

> Pour moi, le handicap ne doit plus être considéré comme une situation d'exception, à laquelle il est répondu par des solutions d'exception. Le handicap doit être considéré comme une réalité ordinaire de la vie. Je [...] suis convaincu que la scolarisation, c'est permettre que le regard porté sur le handicap change, que toute personne handicapée soit regardée et considérée comme un citoyen à part entière.[85]

Thus, Sarkozy does appear eager to be seen to be taking over where Chirac left off and to be fulfilling his pre-election promises to implement the 2005 law. At last, there appears to be a political will in France to make up some of the vast amount of lost ground since the 'first wave' of disability rights that Kristeva locates in the Enlightenment. Whether any of this will come to fruition remains, of course, to be seen and, just as Sarkozy's rhetoric of solidarity belies "un manque de conviction et de volonté de tous" for Censier,[86] so disability associations have been cautious in their responses to Sarkozy's elegant and apparently heartfelt speeches. L'APF (L'Assoc-iation des Paralysés de France), for example, generally praised his engagement in the project, but said that it hoped also "que Nicolas Sarkozy saura entendre la demande des personnes en situation de handicap qui ne peuvent plus, aujourd'hui, se contenter d'engage-ments politiques mais veulent des actes concrets".[87] For Royal, speaking in her interview with Kristeva in 2005, the real problem is still one of visibility:

> En France, nous sommes dans la même situation qu'il y a une ou deux décennies à l'égard des femmes. Aujourd'hui quand il n'y a pas de femme dans une réunion, on se dit qu'il doit y avoir un problème, alors qu'il y a dix ans cela ne choquait pas [...] Dans la société française, on ne voit pas les

---

[85] "Allocution de M. Nicolas Sarkozy, Président de la République, à l'occasion du 47ème Congrès de l'UNAPEI (Union Nationale des Associations de Parents et Amis de Personnes Handicapées Mentales)". Accessed April 2009 at: http://www.elysee.fr/-elysee/elysee.fr/francais/interventions/2007/juin/allocution_du_president_de_la_repub lique_au_47eme_congres_de_l_unapei.78442.html.
[86] Censier, p. 96.
[87] "Réaction de l'APF au discours de Nicolas Sarkozy tenu aujourd'hui au congrès de l'UNAPEI", 9 June 2007. Accessed April 2009 at: http://www.reflexe-handicap.org/-archive/2007/06/09/r%C3%A9action-de-l-apf-au-discours-de-nicolas-sarkozy-tenu-aujour.html.

handicapés. On ne les voit ni dans les administrations, ni dans les entreprises, ni dans les élus. C'est ce verrou-là qu'il faut faire sauter.[88]

In other words, if people with disabilities remain excluded from the decision-making processes that affect their daily lives—and this is just as much the case now as it was then—disability will remain invisible. It is only once this invisibility begins to be noticed, and steps are taken to effect change, that disability will be recognized as an 'ordinary' human difference, and people with disabilities will be enabled to live 'ordinary' lives. For the moment, as Royal tells Kristeva, it is simply to be hoped that "les nouvelles générations auront un regard différent sur le handicap. L'acceptation des diversités est en progrès".[89]

---

[88] Kristeva and Royal, p. 5.
[89] Kristeva and Royal, p. 6.

Identity and Ethnicity

Racaille versus *Flics*? Who's to Blame for Criminality and Delinquency in Franco-Maghrébine (*Beur*) Fiction?

Hélène Jaccomard

In the so-called *beur* corpus, a minority literature and, accordingly, aimed at contesting dominant views on Franco-Maghrebis,[1] *beur* subjects are frequently portrayed as juvenile offenders, and even hardcore criminals. Such a prevalence of delinquency and crime in this type of texts could lend itself to the charge of reinforcing prejudices. Harzoune blames *beur* writers for staying "à l'ombre d['eux]-même[s]"[2] in that they tend to reproduce preconceived ideas about *beurs* and Maghrebis currently spread by the media:[3]

> Tel qu'il se développe depuis maintenant plus de vingt ans, le débat public sur "l'insécurité" tourne autour de quelques thèmes centraux dont l'un des principaux est la relation supposée entre délinquance et immigration. Cette

---

[1] Franco-Maghrebis (or *beurs*) refer to offspring of Arab migrants born or living in France from an early age.

[2] Mustapha Harzoune, "Littérature : les chausse-trapes de l'intégration", *Mélanges culturels* (2002): 15-27.

[3] See, for example, Laurent Mucchielli and Véronique Le Goaziau (eds), *Quand les banlieues brûlent... Retour sur les émeutes de novembre 2005* (Paris: La Découverte, 2006) and Martine Valo, "Quand les Suisses parlent de nos banlieues", *Le Monde 2*, 102, 28 January-3 February 2006, 20-29.

> relation est elle-même double. Elle vise d'une part les étrangers proprement dit et [...], d'autre part, les "jeunes issus de l'immigration", pour la plupart de nationalité française, et en leur sein, plus particulièrement, les jeunes d'origine maghrébine et noire africaine.[4]

Nacira Guénif also deplores the portrayal of the delinquent *beur* as the "garçon arabe", who owing to his supposed machismo and his violence is considered guilty of a myriad of social evils, a *bona fide* scapegoat of a declining France.[5] To this sexualized representation one might add a broader geopolitical context whereby Arabs and *beurs* are the target of Islamophobic feelings, supposedly deemed to generate violence on a grand scale.[6] In the same vein as nineteenth-century bourgeois feared the new class of industrial workers, *beurs* are collectively viewed as the "new 'dangerous classes' of the 21st century".[7]

Some Franco-Maghrébine writers such as Mehdi Charef, Abdel Hafed Benotman or Mounsi have actually done time in jail, and infuse their writings with their first-hand experience. For instance, Benotman's *Les Forcenés* (2006) is a collection of short stories about prisoners he personally met in jail, paradoxically a universe not as unforgiving and violent as the 'outside' world.[8] Another reason for the prevalence of delinquency and criminality in *beur* texts might be found in the paradox encountered by *misérabiliste*[9] literature: how to show that injustice done to their Franco-Maghrébine characters turn them into anti-social protagonists, whilst at the same time proving that

---

[4] Laurent Mucchielli, "Délinquance et immigration : des préjugés à l'analyse", *Claris*, 2 (2002): 10-15 (10).

[5] Nacira Guénif Soulimas, *Des Féministes aux Garçons arabes* (Paris: Editions de l'Aube, 2004).

[6] Such is the plot of *Djihad,* a film by Félix Olivier (2006), which is remarkably non-judgmental about *beur* involvement in terrorism. Earlier fiction, too, is antipathetic to the media representations of *beur* youth as terrorists. See, for example, Nacer Kettane, *Le Sourire de Brahim* (Paris: Denoël, 1985).

[7] Alec Hargreaves, "Quel bilan ? La révolte des banlieues à travers les livres", *Le Monde Diplomatique*, November 2006, on-line archives: http://www.monde-diplomatique.fr/ (accessed 3 January 2008).

[8] Abdel Hafed Benotman, *Les Forcenés* (Paris: Rivages, 2006).

[9] The Dictionary of the *Académie française* gives the following definition of *misérabilisme*: "n.m. XXe siècle. Dérivé de *misérable*. Parti pris de faire apparaître, à travers une œuvre littéraire ou artistique, les aspects les plus sombres et pitoyables de la société, de l'humanité ; caractère d'une œuvre qui manifeste cette volonté."

beurs could be different—better citizens—given different attitudes towards them and different social conditions.

My hunch is that this apparent paradox is largely due to the adoption of unquestioned 'left realist' views on crime (and, in this instance, 'ethnic' crime), which, at the best of times, inform the most open-minded media and general public. In fact, left-leaning commentators share a consensus on the proximate causes of delinquency and crime propounded by social control theory, which is not without ambiguities. They tend to disagree, however, on the ultimate causes of delinquency and crime, as will be shown later by drawing on some prominent criminology theories. It is also my contention that a closer reading of the corpus shows that the representations of *beurs* as *racaille*—the insult brandished in November 2005 by Nicolas Sarkozy, then first *flic* of France—is not as monolithic as would seem at a cursory glance. First, before being represented as delinquents or criminals, *beurs* themselves are victims of crimes. Second, more recent writings in the corpus seem to contest the real-life schism between *flic* and *racaille* by placing at the centre of the stage *beur* policemen whose bi-cultural affiliations lead to the triumphant vanquishing of injustices, whilst others broaden the fight against prejudices by taking up other causes than the anti-racist, anti-Arabophobic one.

Racaille?

As sites of contestation, a large number of narratives denounce ethnic violence against *beur* subjects. Ahmed Kalouaz, in *Point Kilométrique 190* (1986) tells the true story of a man who, mistaken for an Arab migrant (he is in fact a tourist), is thrown out of a train window. This event took place in the wake of the 1983 *Marche des Beurs*, an historic moment supposed to herald a new era for *beur* political identity. Kalouaz wants to alert readers to the risks associated with becoming a visible minority in an intolerant society.[10] The plot of Azouz Begag's *Quand on est mort, c'est pour toute la vie* (1994) also originates from a news item—Morad, a young Arab, is killed by a taxi driver who overreacts when Morad jumps out of his vehicle to avoid

---

[10] Ahmed Kalouaz, *Point kilométrique 190* (Paris: L'Harmattan, 1986).

paying the fare. The judge concludes a *non-lieu* and the taxi driver is set free. Morad's brother, the narrator, expresses his anger at a whole system of oppression: "Je hais la justice, la police, les juges, leur intégration et leurs Droits de l'Homme".[11]

Ten years earlier, one of the first *beur* narratives, Nacer Kettane's *Le Sourire de Brahim* (1985), had already placed the blame squarely on the collusion between police and the justice system:

> Ce n'était pas le premier meurtre raciste dans la région. La musique était toujours la même. Celui qui tirait était souvent un ancien policier ou militaire à la retraite. [...] Là aussi la musique était toujours la même. Les magistrats trouvaient toujours un alibi à la 'défaillance' humaine. Le meurtrier, après avoir été gardé au secret quelque part, se retrouvait muté dans un autre département. [...] l'affaire était étouffée.[12]

One last example: Mehdi Charef opens up *Le Harki de Meriem* (1989) with the killing of Sélim, son of a *harki*[13] about to become a lawyer ("On comptait sur la réussite du fils pour effacer tout regret d'exil"[14]). The three racists who murder Sélim are further enraged when they find out that Sélim is in fact as much a Frenchman as they are. A more subtle analysis here links the murder to France's intolerance of diversity based on a fear of the Other in oneself.[15] Here again the perpetrators will escape punishment for their crime. And furthermore, the police are nowhere to be seen to protect *beurs* or Maghrebis against these aggressions.

In fact, the police are often the very perpetrators of notorious *bavures* against Arab-looking youths. As one instance among many others, Tahar Ben Jelloun's *Les Raisins de la galère* fictionalizes the infamous case of Hamed Khelkad (called Kamel Mellou in the novel) who is shot by police when he is wrongly suspected of being an Algerian terrorist. The perpetrators are given a rap on the knuckles: "REUB ABATTU—6 MOIS AVEC SURSIS".[16] Another case of

---

[11] Azouz Begag, *Quand on est mort, c'est pour toute la vie* (Paris: Gallimard Jeunesse, 1994), p. 9.

[12] Kettane, p. 132-133.

[13] *Harki* is the name given to Algerians who, during the Algerian War of Independence, joined the army or the police, sometimes by force, sometimes willingly.

[14] Mehdi Charef, *Le Harki de Meriem* (Paris: Mercure de France, 1989 [Folio, 1991, 1997]), p. 28.

[15] Julia Kristeva, *Etrangers à nous-mêmes* (Paris: Gallimard, 1988), p. 13.

[16] Tahar ben Jelloun, *Les Raisins de la galère* (Paris: Fayard, 1996), p. 54.

police wrong-doing is described in Kettane's *Le Sourire de Brahim*. Neo-nazis attack the narrator's *lycée* in a deprived suburb with large migrant populations; this is only made possible by police complicity with right-wing extremist groups.[17] Moreover, Kettane repeatedly mentions instances of violence committed in housing estates by police officers, some of whom were Arabophobic veterans of the Algerian War.[18]

Other types of violence, which could be called symbolic violence, also inhabit the corpus: *beurs* are excluded from work (for example, Mehdi Charef's *Le Thé au Harem d'Archi Ahmed* and Hamid Senni's autobiography, *De la cité à la city*); they are excluded from higher schooling (Soraya Nini's *Ils disent que je suis une beurette*); they are subjected to "*délits de faciès*"[19] in the metro or night clubs, and confronted to a host of lesser or greater obstacles to a proper integration into an intolerant society.[20] Nacer Kettane summarizes these in a conversation between Franco-Maghrébine youths:

> — T'as raison, lui dit Tahar, y'en a que pour les Dupont-Durand, dans ce pays ; à l'ANPE, on se fait jeter, aux H.L.M. on se fait jeter, dans les boîtes on se fait jeter, c'est vraiment la merde.[21]

These leitmotivs of actual and symbolic violence done to Franco-Maghrebis are offered as unequivocal explanations for literary characters being pushed to anti-social behaviours and acts against institutions. Strain theory of crime[22] gives credence to the fact that "anomie reduces the control of most social institutions (family, school, law) over individuals and exacerbates cultural economic sources of strain". Under some circumstances, referred to as 'ecological intensifiers', which include paucity of resources, male-

---

[17] Kettane, p. 67.

[18] Kettane, p. 162.

[19] This term denotes the singling out of individuals by police for identity control on the basis of their Arab looks, which might denote an illegal migrant.

[20] Mehdi Charef, *Le Thé au Harem d'Archi Ahmed* (Paris: Folio, 1983); Hamid Senni (with Brigitte Dusseau), *De la cité à la city* (Paris: L'Archipel, 2007); Soraya Nini, *Ils disent que je suis une beurette* (Paris: Fixot, 1993).

[21] Kettane, p. 155.

[22] Melissa Bull, "Social Explanations", in Hennessey Hayes and Tim Prenzler (eds), *An Introduction to Crime* (Sydney: Pearson Education Australia, 2007), pp. 197-214 (p. 203). See also Robert Agnew, "Foundation for the General Strain Theory of Crime and Delinquency", *Criminology*, 30 (1992): 47-87.

male rivalry or competition between classes, crime is a normal behaviour, even a better strategy than non-crime.[23] In essence "deprivation of wealth and power" causes criminal behaviours.[24] If some preconditions for social justice are missing, then "there is even an argument for disobedience or revolution".[25]

The other line of thought that arises from violence done to ethnic members of French society asks what type of justice system would achieve parity and proportionality of punishment in a society characterized by social injustices: "*retributivist* justice demands different treatment of difference" by handing out differential treatments to the criminal haves and have-nots.[26] In the French context, authors denounce time after time what can be termed the non-application of *retributivist* justice for their marginalized characters in search of the integration and social mobility promised by the Republican school. It is only logical that they should turn against the system if such promises are not kept. This interpretation appears in Djouder's *Désintégration*, a book-length plea for social justice for Beurs and Maghrebis:

> Nous les petits casseurs et les petits tagueurs de banlieue, qui commettons de petits délits, sommes des feux follets. Nous exprimons un millionième de la violence reçue. [...] Pas de république? pas de fraternité. Pas de fraternité? pas d'accueil. Pas d'accueil? pas d'appartenance. Pas d'appartenance? pas d'identité. Pas d'identité ? Pas de transmission? Pas de langage. Pas de langage? pas d'école. Pas d'école? pas de formation. Pas de formation? pas de métier. Pas de métier? pas d'argent. Pas d'argent? pas d'appartement. Pas d'appartement? pas de point de départ. Pas de point de départ? pas de sens. Pas de sens? pas de valeurs. Pas de valeurs? pas de république...[27]

This litany of negatives is meant to justify how hardship and survival in a society where a mere Arabic name spells discrimination lead to offenses committed by the victims, who deep down are not malicious,

[23] See, for example, Robert J. Bursik and Harold G. Grasmick, "The Use of Contextual Analysis in Models of Criminal Behavior", in J. David Hawkins (ed), *Delinquency and Crime: Current Theories* (Cambridge: Cambridge University Press, 1996), pp. 236-267.
[24] Bull, p. 206.
[25] Okeoghene Odudu, "Retributivist Justice in an Unjust Society", *Ratio Juris*, 16.3 (2003), 416–431 (425).
[26] Odudu, p. 426.
[27] Ahmed Djouder, *Désintégration* (Paris: Stock, 2006), p. 101.

just angered and sincerely desirous to escape their destiny. As Oxford jurist Okeoghene Odudu argues, "we should only punish those who have demonstrated that they are bad people".[28] 'Bad', not a moralistic term here, applies to criminals who harbour a desire to harm, show indifference to their victims, and who have no aversion to breaking the law, individuals who neutralize their acts by declining responsibilities or denying they have hurt their victims.[29] In other words the dominant discourse in *beur* fiction is that evil is not ethnically determined. This is supported by research of the 'left-realist' criminology school, which claims that anomie, marginalization in a materialistic society, impoverishment and racism are sufficient reasons for crime to be class-related, rather than culture-, let alone race-related.[30] And for *beurs* it is important to set the record straight on the causes of delinquency and crime.

In a humorous and even ironic way this is precisely what one of the very first *beur* texts, *Le Thé au Harem d'Archi Ahmed* (1983) did. With its crude realism, Charef denounced injustices, racism, poverty and the generational gap in the deprived suburbs. In the process the novel became a model for the *beur* novel and *beur* film. It portrayed a large number of *racaille*, no great criminals, rather unemployed, unschooled, bored young men with little to look forward to apart from money-making schemes, exploiting people weaker than themselves, prostitutes, gypsies, or country people. Their profile—young males from lower socio-economic classes, and limited education—corresponds closely to statistics about offenders in Europe, the USA and even Australia.[31] At the same time Charef's characters help their mates, save junkies from overdoses and keep a mad woman from jumping to her death on Christmas night... In short, they have good hearts.

One scene is central to an understanding of Charef's hermeneutics and how he skilfully negotiates the danger of having his

---

[28] Odudu, p. 426.

[29] Hennessey Hayes, "Interactionist Explanations", in Hayes and Prenzler, pp. 215-230 (p. 223).

[30] See Barbara A. Hudson (ed), *Race, Crime and Justice* (Aldershot: Dartmouth, 1996) and John Lea and Jock Young, *What is to be done about Law and Order?* (Harmondsworth: Penguin, 1984).

[31] See Hennessey Hayes and Tim Prenzler, "Victim and Offender Characteristics", in Hayes and Prenzler, pp. 78-95.

characters misconstrued as villains. In the Parisian subway the two main characters, Madjid and Pat, a non-ethnic young man, steal a man's wallet. A reddish country bumpkin ridiculed for his awkwardness in the capital city, the man notices the theft and immediately turns to Madjid who had strategically positioned himself next to his victim. Pat is already out of reach with the wallet. Madjid lets the man search him whilst at the same time berating him for his obvious racism, and indeed onlookers take Madjid's side. Nonetheless the thief is the young ethnic who will enjoy the spoils with his mate. To trap the racist at his own game, to "decline his stereotypes"[32] in both senses of the term, is a legitimate act of revenge for the *beurs*. The moral of the story is that racism is a crime of a higher order than theft and, therefore, a legitimate target for hard-done-by youngsters.

A less endearing exploitation of French people's supposed prejudices appears in Paul Smaïl's *Ali le magnifique* when the protagonist ("le bien intégré, bien dans sa peau, propre sur soi— l'exception aux statistiques. Inoffensif—voilà. Innocent. En blanc, d'ailleurs"[33]) is play-acting in the *RER* train as he is telling a plausible but wholly fabricated horror story on the Algerian War to an anonymous public, captive in their RER carriage and racked with guilt for this young man's sorry tale.

The conclusion of *The Thé au Harem d'Archi Ahmed* also dispels simplistic links between criminality and ethnicity, and clearly states the all-important unity within a social class. Madjid is caught by the police in a stolen van, and Pat escapes but decides to wait by the side of the road to get arrested too, out of solidarity with Madjid. Placed under the sign of friendship and carried out by a benevolent cop, the arrest does not resemble closure. Rather, prison might be the solution to their aimless drifting, a break in the possible escalation from petty theft to serious crime. Taking into account the author's own brush with the law, this ending suggests a belief in the rehabilitating power of prison for good-hearted delinquents.

The fundamental goodness of *beur* protagonists is a leitmotiv of the corpus. It finds its expression in characters whose civic spirit urges them to inflame their *cités*. Following in the steps of Tahar ben

---

[32] See Mireille Rosello, *Declining the Stereotype* (Dartmouth: University of New England Press, 1997).

[33] Paul Smaïl (alias Jack-Alain Léger), *Ali le Magnifique* (Paris: Denoël, 2001), p. 33.

Jelloun's *Les Raisins de la galère* (1996) with its university educated, righter-of-wrongs female protagonist, Faïza Guène writes about her narrator's "forts élans républicains",[34] a *pasionaria* fighting against injustices in a social context sympathetic to characters stereotyped along ethnic lines. In these two novels published ten years apart, would-be rioters have their energy turned into constructive social action and *participation citoyenne*.

Occasionally, writers refer to a mindset other than social constructivism. Mounsi, a singer and author of a fairly didactic autobiographical narrative, favours a psychoanalytical interpretation of the delinquent *beur*:

> [L]a délinquance, pour moi, ne fut jamais dans son essence qu'un geste pour redonner une puissance à mon père. C'est à la famille dans son tout que s'adressaient mes délits. Le premier hasard d'une casse m'a permis de rédimer en un instant l'infini de la soumission quotidienne de mon père.[35]

Interestingly, such an explanation is disqualified as a prejudice to be disregarded if serious research on *beur* delinquency is to make progress: "[L]aisser de côté des préjugés sur 'l'apathie' et la 'démission' des pères maghrébins face à leurs enfants nécessairement en difficulté".[36] That is to say that beneath the psychologization emerge societal views—at once reinforced and contested—on the link between criminality and ethnicity. Authors portray characters who might be excused for committing offences, suggesting that "the deprived have a weaker obligation to obey the law, or are only obliged to obey those from which they benefit".[37]

It is no wonder then that truly 'bad' *beur* characters remain an exception in the corpus. Also inspired by a news item, Paul Smaïl's *Ali le magnifique* (2001), mentioned above in passing, focuses on a serial killer whose schizophrenia is provided in a foreword as an (unconvincing) explanation for his personality and criminal acts. Like a madman, Ali, a highly unreliable narrator, remains impervious to other people's motives, thereby excluding himself from the social

---

[34] Faïza Guène, *Kiffe kiffe demain* (Paris: Hachette Littératures, 2004), p. 193.

[35] Mounsi, *Territoire d'outre-ville* (Paris: Stock, 1995), p. 67.

[36] Christine Delcroix, "Une expérience de mobilisation des pères de famille. Récit d'une recherche-action", *Claris*, 2 (2002), 19-21 (19). http://labreche.free.fr/textes/-Claris.bulletin_n=2.pdf (accessed 21 February 2008).

[37] Hudson quoted in Odudu, p. 423-424.

contract. Interestingly, in a text redolent with ruses (under the double-allegiance pseudonym of Paul Smaïl—the true author is Jack-Alain Léger, not himself a *beur*) meant to confuse the reader as to the identity and motives of the serial killer, the ending is strangely conventional. With no hint of irony, Ali, the hardened criminal, falls in love with a prison inmate and repents of his crimes. Even an evil being may turn good, given the right circumstances.

There also exist characters in the corpus whose anti-social madness finds its ultimate explanation in the deleterious *banlieue* from which they come. In Rézane's *Dit violent* (2006), Mehdi's violence is both verbal and imaginary. The open ending—does he carry out his plans for the suicide attack at a football match he has been daydreaming about?—does not allow the reader to know for certain whether his violence is ever actualized. The skill of the writer is never to alienate the reader from a protagonist who killed his father (a wife-basher) and barely restrains himself from murdering women who pay him for sex. Mehdi in Rézane's novel sees a society inimical to migrants and their children as being wholly responsible for his internal violence. And indeed, other writers, such as Abdel Hafed Benotman, explain such internal violence by the external violence *beurs* are constantly subjected to:

> Pris entre deux violences, celle du dedans et celle du dehors il forma en lui lentement, haineusement, huître inviolable, une perle noire. Perle prête à éclater le moment venu dans une violence que lui-même ne pourrait pas maîtriser. Faraht Bounoura avait la haine.[38]

This dialectic between inner and outer factors has been the source of a longstanding debate in criminology:

> C. Shaw (1929) argued that a comprehensive theory of delinquent and criminal behavior could be developed only through a simultaneous examination of the "inner personal world of the subject (i.e. psychological and motivation processes) and the group context that defined the situations for that subject. [...] Unfortunately subsequent development of criminology generally did not maintain a balanced perspective on the dual roles of group and individual dynamics in the aetiology of illegal behaviour. As a result, the discipline traditionally has been characterized by alternating periods in which

---

[38] Abdel Hafed Benotman, *Eboueur sur échafaud* (Paris: Rivages, 2003), p. 121.

one of these dynamics is given theoretical primacy while the other is relatively neglected.[39]

In the literary corpus examined here it would seem that the theoretical primacy of causes of crimes is given to the social situation of the subjects, with their psychological make-up being granted a much more secondary role. However, if one distinguishes, as the letter of the law requires, between delinquency and crime, then, it would appear that writers tend to attribute *crimes* to personality traits first, and a dysfunctional society second, whereas *delinquency* is entirely caused by an unjust society. In fact, if one takes into account the classic plot of *beur* fiction—victimization followed by delinquency—and the fact that authors show a marked preference for *beur* delinquents over *beur* criminals, their beliefs would seem nearer to the philosophy of the *interactional* theory of delinquency:

> [R]ather than seeing delinquency as a simple consequence of a set of social processes, an interactional perspective sees delinquency as both cause and consequence involved in a variety of reciprocal relationships over time.[40]

The reciprocal cause-and-effect mechanism of delinquent acts creates a prevalent youth sub-culture of violence against institutions as described by *banlieue* sociologist Mucchielli:

> Ensuite, une composante essentielle de cette sur-délinquance locale est sa dimension anti-institutionnelle. On peut parler ici d'une "violence contre les institutions" qui regroupe toutes les formes de dégradations et toutes les formes de violences exercées à l'encontre des biens et des personnes qui symbolisent les institutions.[41]

And who better than the police to symbolize these institutions?

Flics

Beur films and novels seem automatically to position the police on the other side of an unrecoverable divide. And yet, the fight for anti-racism and anti-discrimination might advance better if the French

---

[39] Bursik and Grasmick, p. 226

[40] Terence P Thornberry, "Empirical Support for Interactional Theory: A review of the Literature", in Hawkins, pp. 198-235 (p. 198).

[41] Mucchielli (2002), p. 15.

police were recruited among visible minorities. In the *banlieue* film par excellence, *La Haine*, a *beur* policeman has a minor role. Naturally, on his own he cannot stop "la spirale infernale des confrontations entre policiers et jeunes des cités".[42] In 2003 Renée Zauberman and René Lévy, both social scientists, concluded their study of the police, minorities and Republican ideals in France by saying that, although a prerequisite, "ethnic diversification is not in itself enough to suppress discrimination by the police and improve their relationship with minorities."[43] This is due in particular to "a specific set of political values that we called the 'Republican Ideal' based on an abstract conception of citizenship, denying any political significance to the personal identities of citizens."[44]

One novel in the *beur* corpus, Lakhdar Belaïd's *Sérail killer* (2000), explores how an ethnic police force could diminish racial tensions and help manage memories and revenge in a post-colonial era. This novel also suggests that causes for criminality and delinquency among *beur* and Maghrébine populations in France are to be found in history, an approach not prevalent in contemporary criminology but which would avoid the pitfalls of reductive left-realist analysis.

Sérail killers—the double entendre reflects the self-derision of the narrative[45]—adopts the conventions of a thriller: action-packed and suspenseful plot, misleading clues, corpses found with placards bearing the word 'traitor', an enquiry run by two complex and tormented police inspectors, and strong language. As is common in *polars* the novel is located in an urban setting, in this instance, Roubaix, known as "*bougnoule city*" owing to the fact that 50% of its population is Muslim and that it is home to the highest concentration of ex-*harkis* in the country.[46] This quirk of geography is the result of

---

[42] Hargreaves, n.p.
[43] Renée Zauberman and René Lévy, "Police, minorities and the French Republican Ideal", *Criminology*, 41.4 (2003): 1065-1100 (online, n.p., accessed 3 March 2008).
[44] Zauberman and Lévy.
[45] *Sérail* instead of *serial* plays also on the double meaning of *sérail*: not a harem, but insider knowledge as in the idiomatic expression '*être du sérail*'.
[46] Lakhdar Belaïd, *Sérail killers* (Paris: Gallimard, 2000), p. 16. For a fuller picture of the *harkis*, see Jean-Jacques Jordi and Mohand Hamoumou, *Les Harkis, une mémoire enfouie* (Paris: Autrement, 1999) and Géraldine Enjelvin "Les Harkis en France : carte

history, in this case the establishment of *harki* repatriation camps in northern France. Belaïd believes that the detective story is the perfect vehicle for speaking about History and politics.[47] In a sense, in some parts, the book sounds like a history lesson about the Algerian War of Independence and its effects on contemporary France, aimed both at the offspring of Algerians and the general French public.[48]

Characters in *Sérail killer* are shaped and determined by their origins, and above all, by their fathers' deeds during the Algerian War. As Belaïd explains in an interview,

> [c]e qui est important dans *Sérail Killers* c'est l'influence de la guerre d'Algérie sur les personnages, l'influence de ce que les parents ont vécu et ont transmis, même sans le vouloir, à leurs enfants, mais c'est aussi ce qui ne s'est pas dit. Ces silences, ces souffrances que les parents ont vécues, qui ont été transmises à leurs enfants sans qu'aient été expliquées les raisons de cette souffrance.[49]

Unlike the usual *beur* narrative's distribution of *beurs* and police on either side of the social order divide, this heavy determinism implies that *beurs* are no more, no less likely than any French person, to become criminals, delinquent or law-abiding citizens, even policemen. All, however, suffer from the burden of unspoken family and national history. Take for instance the narrator, Karim Khodja, a Muslim journalist who assists a Franco-Maghrébine inspector, Bensalem, also called '*rebeucop*', to solve the murder of two *beurs* (two more bodies, that of a prostitute and the Lady Mayor of Roubaix will appear later). In truth the word *beur* here more than anywhere is inadequate to describe these characters. As the author explains,

---

d'identité française, identité harkie à la carte?", *Modern & Contemporary France*, 11.2 (2003): 161–173.

[47] Hubert Artus, "Interview de Lakhdar Belaïd", *L'Ours polar* ([2000] 2007), online http://patangel.free.fr/ours-polar/auteurs/belaid1.php (accessed 29 January 2009).

[48] Although the most recent, this book is not the only one to use the genre for this subject. For instance, Didier Daeninckx's *Meurtres pour mémoire* (Paris: Gallimard, 1984), is a thriller on the surface, but a *roman à thèse* about the memory of WWII and the *Bataille de Paris* (the bloody repression of a peaceful march by pro-independence Algerian workers on 17 October 1961 in Paris). As to the silence on the Algerian War, it is the central motif of Mehdi Charef's *La Maison d'Alexina* (Paris: Mercure de France, 1999) and *A bras-le-cœur* (Paris: Mercure de France, 2006), Tassadit Imachit's *Une fille sans histoire* (Paris: Calmann-Lévy, 1989) and Nina Bouraoui's *Garçon manqué* (Paris: Stock, 2000).

[49] Artus, n.p.

> il n'y a pratiquement que des Français dans mon livre, mais des gens marqués
> par une histoire très traumatisante qui a été celle de la colonisation française
> en Algérie, de la guerre d'Algérie, de la gestion de la colonisation algérienne
> par la France, de la gestion de la guerre d'Algérie par la France, et de
> l'héritage que tout ça représente pour les jeunes Français issus d'une
> population algérienne qui vivent en France.[50]

For a better understanding of the work done by Belaïd on identity and
stereotypes, since it has a bearing on the interpretation of crime and
delinquency, it is important to outline the history of the two main
characters who represent the heterogeneity of Franco-Maghrébine
communities. Karim Kodja was born in France and is married to a
strong-headed Muslim, the daughter of a *harki*. As if simply to add to
the *effet de réel*, this fact is told matter-of-factly and has no direct
bearing on the plot. Kodja speaks like a modern San Antonio with a
smattering of Arabic (in its Algiers variant, to be more precise) and is
just about to start Ramadan when the story begins. Like the author's
own father, Kodja's father was sent to jail in Algeria for five years for
supporting Messali Hadj against the FLN. Kodja went to school with
Bensalem, son of a Kabyle freedom fighter who was thrown into
armed conflict alongside the French after his own father (Bensalem's
grand-father) was assassinated by the FLN. Not a *harki*, he was
nonetheless treated like a traitor to the war of Independence. In 1962
the Bensalems manage to flee Algeria to escape reprisals. Whereas
Kodja is a leftist intellectual, Bensalem is a member of the National
Front because he identifies with its staunch stance on law and order,
and also because the National Front presents itself as the party of
harkis.[51] Although he resigns from the party fairly promptly, his
image as a National Front supporter sticks. After years of antagonism
Bensalem calls on his old school-friend to help him with the enquiry.
Together they are indeed able to solve the crimes, and they are able to
do so as a direct result of their connection with the past history of
France and Algeria.

The motives for the first crime seem self-evident. Farid Hand-
Lounis, son of a *harki,* must have been killed by the Djafris, FLN
fighters, since both families were manipulated by the OAS into
destroying each other during and after the Algerian War. But the

---

[50] Artus, n.p.
[51] Belaïd, p. 87.

second body, also found with a placard bearing the words '*Traître et fils de traître*', is that of Ben Achour, son of an FLN militant, who has always despised *harkis*.[52] Kodja translates the first two murders into political terms but has to abandon his original line of enquiry, whereby the National Front would have blown on old coals to light the fire between the various Algerian factions in Roubaix so that the ensuing local civil unrest would have incensed the general population against migrants and their children. In fact, the book is an indictment of politicians, from extreme-right to socialists, for the way they instrumentalize migrants and *beurs*.

As Belaïd clearly stated in an interview, "au PS, il y a des gens qui ont clairement dit: '*si vous prenez des beurs [comme candidats], on part au FN*'."[53]

The denouement of the detective story demonstrates how ethnicity is utilized for political ends, by disguising political crimes as racist ones. Instead of the National Front being behind a conspiracy against law and order and using the dissensions between the various Algerian factions in France, ex-OAS men were planning to destabilize France, starting with Roubaix, a powder keg with its large immigrant population. Riots between various Algerian factions would have ensued, the army would have been sent in and the population would have demanded that all Algerian and *beurs* be extradited, like a *pieds-noirs* exodus in reverse.

Although the plot is a little far-fetched, *Sérail killer* nonetheless successfully breaks down the association between criminality and Arab ethnicity. It also broaches the issue of the trustworthiness of the population emerging from immigration. As written on the placards hanging around the neck of the corpses, the question is that of treachery. All characters must prove their loyalty to France in spite of their divisive family histories. Can Kodja trust Bensalem, son of a Kabyle and supporter of the French in Algeria? Can Bensalem trust Kodja, son of a Messalist? Can the reader trust the narrator and his *fausses pistes*? Belaïd brings to light the fact that a dual identity can be interpreted in incompatible ways. Intellectuals, like Homi Bhabha believe in the power of hybridity.[54] Subjects themselves seem to

---

[52] Belaïd, p. 78.
[53] Artus, n.p.
[54] Homi Bhabha, *The Location of Culture* (London: Routledge, 1994).

devalue it as a *bâtardise* based on shifting loyalties. The two main characters enact a third way: Kodja and Bensalem are not subjugated by their identity, yet it is their very personal history that allows them to find the real culprits. These two *beurs* shape their own identity, modify it, personalize it and in the end, elude an ethnicist, and potentially racist, discourse.[55]

This lesson is supported by a constant undercutting of ethnic stereotypes. In *beur* fiction Bensalem is the only main *beur* character who is also a policeman. In 'French' fiction it is also very unusual to have a practicing Muslim like Karim Kodja as a main protagonist. Far from being the typical *garçon arabe* he is a husband in love with his wife, who is actually a high achiever, a Muslim and an assertive character. Kodja, does not engage in religious propaganda. On the contrary, in one scene he berates an ex-drug addict, Helmut Stockaert, converted to Islam:

> — Dis donc Helmut-Abderrahmane, t'as pas honte de piquer la religion des Arabes? Tu crois qu'ils veulent de toi, les *kholoto*? [Arabic in Algerian slang] [...]
> — J'avoue. J'ai péché et mes frères là-bas m'ont sauvé.
> Là, j'éclate carrément:
> — *Wach*? Mais retiens-moi, Bensalem! je vais l'étrangler, cet envahisseur! Cet immigré de la religion! Tu nous prends pour une poubelle? L'islam ne peut pas accueillir toute la misère du monde! [...] Sous-développé! Métèque! mais comment voulez-vous que ces gens-là s'intègrent?
> Bensalem:
> — Arrête ta comédie! Ça y est, ils sont tous au bout de la rue.
> Moi, en nage:
> — Ce n'était pas de la comédie...[56]

As in the official Republican doctrine the place of Islam in France is resolutely in the private sphere. In this political thriller, *beurs* and Maghrebis are both victims, and upholders of the law. Crimes are committed as a result of unresolved historical memories and Arabo-phobia.[57] As in previous texts, albeit from another perspective, the main protagonists are innately good.

---

[55] This is also how Nacira Guénif-Soulimas sees the plight of Franco-Maghrebis (p. 183).
[56] Belaïd, p. 85-86.
[57] *Sérail Killers* is not the first detective story based on the Algerian War of Independence. In the 1970s and 1980s, such novels met with some qualified success,

The fight against the alleged correlation between delinquency and ethnicity is also found in yet another thriller, Akli Tadjer's *Bel-avenir* (2006). Tadjer unites *beurs* and police in an unusual fashion. First he establishes how *beurs* have developed a social conscience that now embraces all victims of an unjust society, not only the ones from their own communities. His protagonist becomes a journalist for a newspaper whose boss is trying to buy a good conscience by employing an "*Arabe de France*". Omar, however, refuses to be the token Arab. Instead of serving the cause of *beurs* ("ses congénères"[58]) as is expected of him, and, at the risk of losing a hard-earned job, Omar helps illegal migrants (*sans-papiers)* reduced to living clandestinely and delinquently, and dependent upon doubtful charity organizations. His support culminates in the final scene, set in a grand church. In the middle of a Christmas midnight mass attended by VIPs, wealthy citizens and representatives of the Republic such as the *préfet*, Omar organizes a demonstration by illegal migrants demanding that their visas be granted collectively. Ironically, the confrontation ends in the unexpected alliance between the demonstrators and the *flics* called to expel them. The police are headed by a high-ranking *brigadière*, who was brought up in the same *cité* as Omar. Apart from taking sides with Omar owing to their shared past, she decides to rebel against her orders to make amends for a *bavure* she committed years before. If such a demonstration can be called delinquency, its cause is again an unjust society, and therefore disturbing order is a legitimate act. The spectre of *communautarisme*, that anti-republican foe, is demystified with *beurs* and *flics* uniting in their fight for civil justice for all. The bigger crimes are the ones committed against powerless people. Moreover in order to work towards a moralized nation everyone has to get their hands dirty, make compromises, even breach the law. This

---

such as Gérard Delteil's *N'oubliez pas l'artiste* (Paris: Gallimard,1987), Jacques Syreigeol's *Une mort dans le djebel* (Paris: Gallimard, 1990), which was the winner of the Mystère de la critique prize in 1991, and Didier Daeninckx's *Meurtres pour mémoire* (1984). It is not, however, the usual form of the vast corpus on the Algerian War, as clearly emerges from Benjamin Stora's extensive works, *Le Livre, mémoire de l'histoire: réflexions sur le livre et la guerre d'Algérie* (Paris: Préau des collines, 2005); and *Le Dictionnaire des livres de la guerre d'Algérie: romans, nouvelles, poésie, photos, histoire, essais, récits historiques, témoignages, biographies, mé-moires, autobiographies 1955-1995* (Paris: L'Harmattan, 1996).

[58] Akli Tadjer, *Bel-Avenir* (Paris: Flammarion, 2006), p. 50.

agrees with Zauberman and Lévy's conclusion: in order to bring about the Republican ideal of a united nation "one must violate its principles, by highlighting precisely those traits the ideal wants to render inconsequential".[59]

The *beur* corpus is made up of many *romans à thèse*. Whether *polars* or not, they have a broader agenda than just showing *beurs* as victims who take their revenge, consciously or not, by offending or committing crimes. These texts are intent on breaking the chain of misery between ethnicity and violence; they find explanations sometimes in traumatized personalities but mostly in an unjust society. Only more recent writings, however, manage to go beyond social control theory and its aetiology of crime oscillating in varying degrees between personal and social causes, which seem now too hackneyed to be enlightening. Lakhdar Belaïd and Ali Tadjer show how militant action directed against the real culprits of an unjust society, the politicians and the powerful, instead of isolated and random acts aimed at ordinary citizens or institutions, would better serve Republican ideals which are unquestionably shared by their *beur* characters, whatever their past histories. In all the novels, however, violence, symbolic or actual, does seem more prevalent in other members of society than its Franco-Maghrébine members: *beur* texts are here to denounce the real criminals among us.

---

[59] Zauberman and Lévy, n.p.

'Je ne suis pas noir':
Global Football and (Post)Colonial France

Francesco Ricatti

Introduction

Intellectuals have argued in the past as to the soporific nature of football, as the new opium for the people or the new form of bread and circuses. Against this elitist interpretation, many scholars in recent times have argued that football is an important stage on which social tensions and alternative visions of society can be represented, acted out and lived through. Anthony King, for instance, states that "European football provides a prominent arena in which important social relations in European society are periodically made", and where key values and relations of contemporary society become intensely visible.[1] From a similar perspective, Alexander Nelson suggests that football is a "hotly contested forum for the expression of conflicting conceptions of nationhood and belonging".[2] According to others,

---

[1] Anthony King, *The European Ritual: Football in The New Europe* (Burlington, VT: Ashgate, 2003), p. 15, 32.

[2] Alexander Nelson, "World Cup Fever, Nationalism, and The Ambiguous Alliance of Nation-States and Transnational Corporations", *Critique: A Worldwide Journal of Politics* (Fall 2007): 1-11 (11), lilt.ilstu.edu/critique/FALL2007DOCS/Alexander-_Nelson_pdf.pdf (accessed 11 July 2008).

political and cultural élites use football to foster national unity in spite of social inequalities,[3] and transnational corporations use such imagined communities to acquire a local soul for their national brands and create consumer loyalty.[4] At the same time football also encourages "popular expressions of conflict and differences".[5]

Despite the importance of these innovative contributions, scholars who write about the social relevance of football too often forget to look at and analyse football matches and the (re)actions of football players on and off the field. Their focus is instead on how media, politicians and transnational corporations interpret and appropriate such events. In this way the emphasis is not on the power of football and its players in representing and influencing important aspects of our societies, but on how football and its players are manipulated by other actors within the broader social context.

In the past ten years, since France's victory in the FIFA (*Fédération Internationale de Football Association*) World Cup in Paris, the symbolic role played by the national football team in French society has been largely celebrated, debated and critically investigated by journalists and academics. This essay will recall key elements of this debate as well as contrasting the 1998 rhetorical celebration of *La France plurielle qui gagne* with two events in the 2006 World Cup. At this time the threat posed by French football players to the hegemonic construction of the French nation in Republican and (post)colonial terms emerged vividly. When using the term hegemonic we are refer-ring broadly to Gramscian theories.[6] For Gramsci, cultural hegemony is an essential and highly contested tool through which subaltern groups lacking in class-consciousness are controlled by the dominant class.

The French visit to Germany for the 2006 World Cup was characterised by two events that received a great deal of attention

---

[3] Richard Giulianotti and Gerry P.T. Finn, "Old Visions, Old Issues: New Horizons, New Openings? Change, Continuity and Other Contradictions in World Football", in G.P.T. Finn and R. Giulianotti (eds), *Football Culture: Local Contests, Global Visions* (London: Frank Cass, 2000), pp. 256-281 (p. 260).
[4] Paul A. Silverstein, "Sporting Faith: Islam, Soccer, and the French Nation-State", *Social Text*, 18.4 (2000): 24-53 (37-38).
[5] Giulianotti and Finn, p. 260.
[6] Antonio Gramsci, *Lettere dal carcere* (Turin: Einaudi, 1950) and *Quaderni dal carcere* (Turin: Einaudi, 1975).

from both the French and global media. The first of these was an argument between National Front leader, Jean-Marie Le Pen, and French defender, Lilian Thuram. Le Pen declared that he felt only the remotest attachment to the French team because its excessive number of black players made it difficult for him to feel that the team was truly representative of France. This identification of France as a white nation in relation to football essentially mirrored a similar discussion, also fostered by Le Pen, when the 1998 World Cup was played in France. He then argued that the French team was not authentic, because of the inclusion of an excessive number of players either born outside France or the sons of migrants, particularly migrants from former colonies. In 2006 Lilian Thuram, one of France's best and most respected players, replied to Le Pen's provocative assumptions of what it means to be French by declaring that Le Pen was ignorant of French history.

The second event considered in this essay took the global media by storm during the final of the 2006 World Cup between France and Italy, when the French captain Zinedine Zidane (the player who perhaps more than any other 'represents' the national side), head-butted the Italian defender, Marco Materazzi, who had possibly offended Zidane by referring to one of his relatives, most probably his sister. The head-butt cost Zidane a red card and contributed to the Italian triumph in that match. French, Italian and global media speculated for several days about the mysterious words uttered by Materazzi.

Our intention here is to challenge the Manichaean lens through which these kinds of events are often interpreted, by locating their importance in the agency demonstrated by the players and in the complex interplay of different temporal dimensions that the two events display. Drawing on the work of Homi Bhabha, the question that we wish to raise is whether these two football events contributed to "introducing a new time into meaning".[7] In other words, do such brief moments in French football challenge hegemonic assumptions about the French nation and society by posing a threat to their historical foundations?

---

[7] Homi K. Bhabha, "Postcolonial Authority and Postmodern Guilt", in L. Grossberg, C. Nelson, and P. Treichler (eds), *Cultural Studies* (New York; London: Routledge, 1992), pp. 56-68 (p. 68).

La France qui gagne?

Before illustrating these two episodes in greater detail, let us go back in time to 1998, a key year in the evolution of French football and in the creation of a controversial but undeniably powerful relation between football and the reconstruction or reinvention of a French national identity. As Hugh Dauncey and Geoff Hare argue, the 1998 World Cup became increasingly perceived as an opportunity to celebrate French *grandeur*.[8] Before the Cup, when few French people anticipated a French victory, the World Cup was seen more as an opportunity to display French economic, political and cultural power, along with the organisational skills of the public and private sectors, than an occasion to demonstrate to the world the ability of the French team to play football. However, by the end of the World Cup the triumph of the French team allowed not only journalists but also politicians and intellectuals to celebrate the apparent birth of a multiethnic and successful national identity.[9] The symbol of what we could call a multicultural nationalism was Zinedine Zidane, arguably the best football player of his generation. He became the symbol of successful integration while also maintaining a strong link with his Algerian Kabilie family. His insistence on his need as a migrant to work harder than others in order to achieve success recalls a trad-itional rhetorical discourse commonly used to cover or justify the class exploitation of migrants. It also recalls very similar words by Kopa(szewski),[10] a great French football player of Polish origins who, having changed his name and hidden his Polish background, took France to third place in the World Cup in the late 1950s.[11]

The multicultural and multiethnic French team that Zidane led to success was renamed *black, blanc et beur* (black, white and Arab), with a clear reference to the French flag and the multiethnic

---

[8] Hugh Dauncey and Geoff Hare, "Introduction: France and France 98", in H. Dauncey and G. Hare (eds), *France and The 1998 World Cup: The National Impact of a World Sporting Event* (London: Frank Cass, 1999), pp. 1-14 (p. 1).

[9] Kevin Connolly and Rab MacWilliam, *Fields of Glory, Paths of Gold: The History of European Football* (Edinburgh and London: Mainstream Publishing, 2006), p. 216.

[10] Geoff Hare, *Football in France: A Cultural History* (Oxford; New York: Berg, 2003), p. 123.

[11] John Marks, "The French National Team and National Identity: Cette France d'un 'bleu métis'", in Dauncey and Hare, pp. 41-57 (p. 48).

composition of the team. *La France qui gagne* became the symbol of a *la France au pluriel* and the successful integration of migrants from former colonies into French society. President Chirac and Prime Minister Jospin, who were from opposite sides of the political arena, both made use of the equation between the football team and the nation.[12] As Hobsbawn argues, an "imagined community of millions seems more real as a team of eleven named people".[13] Intellectuals such as historian Benjamin Stora and demographer Michèle Tribalat also appropriated this metaphor in a positive sense.[14]

This celebration has since been recalled and critically analysed by many scholars, most of whom have focused on the social relevance and the postcolonial nature of the celebration and its interpretations while overlooking the football event itself and the active role of the players.[15] Among the most perceptive analyses of the 1998 celebrations are those by Elizabeth Ezra and Paul Silverstein.[16] Both scholars remark how, far from representing a break from colonial and postcolonial hegemony, the appropriation of the event by journalists, politicians, intellectuals and the general public as a celebration of difference within a unified national identity based on the values of the French Republic was in fact largely consistent with it.

In the epilogue of her book on the French colonial unconscious, Ezra insists on the celebratory description of the French team as *black, blanc et beur*. While the use of this expression should be first of all related to the common use of the adjective *tricolore* to describe the team since the 1970s,[17] she emphasises how this expression does not

---

[12] Hare, p. 135.

[13] Quoted in Nelson, p. 6.

[14] See Hugh Dauncey and Geoff Hare, "Conclusion: The Impact of France 98", in Dauncey and Hare, pp. 205-221 (p. 218) and Hare, p. 135.

[15] See, for example, the following studies: Connolly and MacWilliam; Liz Crolley and David Hand, *Football and European Identity: Historical Narratives Through the Press* (London; New York: Routledge, 2006); Dauncey and Hare (especially their introduction, conclusion and the chapter by Marks); David Goldblatt, *The Ball is Round: A Global History of Football* (London: Viking [Penguin Books], 2006); and Hare.

[16] Elizabeth Ezra, *The Colonial Unconscious: Race and Culture in Interwar France* (Ithaca; London: Cornell University Press, 2000); Paul A. Silverstein, *Algeria in France: Transpolitics, Race, and The Nation* (Bloomington; Indianapolis: Indiana University Press, 2004); and Silverstein (2000).

[17] Crolley and Hand, p. 47

simply recall the French flag; in fact, it bears a remarkable resemblance to the caption of a famous 1941 poster showing an Arab, an African and a South Asian man under the French flag: "trois couleurs, un drapeau, un empire".[18] Thus, for Ezra the metaphor of the *black, blanc et beur* football team should be read not as a model of national unity but as "a new model of Empire", in which victory in a football tournament is used to reassure the French about the "loyalty of France's (post)colonial subjects".[19]

Silverstein's analysis is similar insofar as he focuses on Zinedine Zidane as the 1998 hero who became an emblem of successful integration *à la française*, where incompatible differences are apparently suppressed under Republican universalism.[20] In fact, Zidane was transformed into a symbol of the nation as a racial exception, a successful result of the *mission civilisatrice*, thereby justifying the hegemonic colonial perspective.[21] This interpretation is also consistent with the colonial construction of *la plus grande France* through the promotion of successful sportsmen from the colonies into honorary Frenchmen.[22] Yet, the difference that is continuously repressed in the case of Zidane and many other sporting champions re-surfaces, since it is at the core of French assimilationism and of Republican ideology itself.

The ephemeral nature of the 1998 celebration has also been emphasised by various scholars,[23] with particular reference to the failure of the first football match between France and Algeria, in October 2001, and Le Pen's surprising admission to the second round of the presidential elections in 2002 to the detriment of the socialist candidate. The match between France and Algeria in particular was transformed by young second-generation French people of Algerian background into a non-violent battlefield on which to reaffirm the

---

[18] Ezra, p. 146.
[19] Ezra, p. 151, 146.
[20] Silverstein (2000), p. 40-42 and (2004), p. 128.
[21] Silverstein (2004), p. 129.
[22] See David Murphy, "Life after the French Empire: Some Case Studies from Senegalese Culture" (2003) http://www.nuigalway.ie/french/documents/life-AfterFrenchEmpireCaseStudiesSenegalese.pdf, (accessed 4 July 2008).
[23] Crolley and Hand, pp. 161-163; Goldblatt, p. 769; Hare, p. 137; and Herman Lebovics, *Bringing the Empire back home: France in the Global Age* (Durham; London: Duke University Press, 2004), pp. 140-142.

complexity and contradictory nature of their own struggle for identity. Furthermore, Richard Giulianotti and Gerry Finn have argued that even before the World Cup started there were clear signs of deep contrasts within France's multiethnic society. In fact, they recalled the street riots that marked the start of the tournament and which involved "young, disenfranchised Parisians of North African extraction who had been effectively excluded from the commodified jamboree".[24]

Several commentators have remarked that the French team has always been characterised by ethnic diversity.[25] In fact, debates about the positive or negative contribution of migrants and the children of migrants to French football have been ongoing since the 1960s.[26] Thus the question is what it was in particular about the 1998 team that made it a national symbol of successful integration. The first and more obvious answer is that it was in fact the first French football team to win the World Cup. However, it has also been argued that the agenda for the discussion about the ethnic and racial nature of the French team was set first of all by Le Pen.[27] In 1996 and again in 1998, he criticised the large presence of players from former colonies, once even defining the team as an *épicerie* in reference to the many grocery shops managed by migrants.[28] Furthermore, the same ethnic diversity was somehow celebrated by Adidas, the major sponsor of the French team, opposing both Le Pen's racist statements and advertisements for Nike, Adidas' major rival in the transnational corporations' exploitation of the football market.

In summary, the sort of celebratory discourse that dominated the aftermath of the French victory in 1998 showed how its metaphorical power could sustain the rhetorical discourse of an imagined French multiethnic identity without actually being able to oppose the emergence of a much more complex and dramatic social reality. Once the carnival of celebration had ended, all the contradictions and problems of multiethnic French society re-emerged.

---

[24] Giulianotti and Finn, p. 261.
[25] Connolly and MacWilliam, pp. 205-207; Crolley and Hand, pp. 46-56; and Marks, pp. 47-55.
[26] Hare, p. 131
[27] Marks, p. 50.
[28] Lebovics, p. 137.

France's defeat in the 2002 World Cup and Le Pen's success in
the first round of the presidential elections soon made clear how the
euphoria of the 1998 World Cup had been nothing but a metaphor for
a national community that was imagined and had never existed. Using
the terminology applied by Neil Blain to the study of the relations
between sport, media and culture, one can posit that Zinedine Zidane
and the 1998 French team were perceived as a metonym of French
society whereas they were in fact used in rhetorical discourse as a
metaphor.[29] The metonym works on the power of a real-life
connection between an object and its referent. Zidane and his team
mates were a powerful metonym because they were actually part of
French society. The nationalistic character implicit in the identification of the team as a symbol of a multicultural France, however,
insofar as it hid the deep and controversial reality of this connection
under the rug of Republican values of integration and national unity,
transformed a powerful metonym into a weak metaphor, destined to
die at the first light of day, together with the carnival of extravagant
celebrations over the football triumph.

Je ne suis pas noir

Having recalled the French victory in 1998 and its appropriation by
various social actors, it is my intention to argue for two fundamental
antidotes that scholars should consider when writing about events of
such symbolic relevance in order not to remain caught in the same
dangerous attitude that they criticise in journalists and politicians. The
first is to analyse sporting victories simply for what they are, without
overcharging them with symbolic and metaphorical significance. This
may in fact have been the case of the majority of people celebrating
France's victory, in spite of the appropriation by political and cultural
élites (from Chirac to *Libération*). The second antidote is to refuse to
transform football players into puppets to be (dis)played for various
political and cultural aims. It is my intention to argue that this can be
done by considering football players as powerful, active, and
sometimes ambiguous, protagonists of the contemporary sporting and

---

[29] Neil Blain, "Beyond 'Media Culture': Sport as Dispersed Symbolic Activity", in A.
Bernstein and N. Blain (eds), *Sport, Media, Culture: Global and Local Dimensions*
(London: Frank Cass, 2003), pp. 227-254.

social arena. It is from this perspective that we shall consider the two episodes that respectively opened and concluded the French expedition to Germany for the 2006 World Cup.

The first episode saw Thuram taking a strong position against Le Pen's invention of France as a white country that should not be represented by a football team for the most part made up of players with African origins. Thuram was born in 1972 in Pointe-à-Pitre, Guadeloupe, and moved with his mother to France at the age of nine. Until his recent retirement from the football field due to heart-related problems, he had been the most important defender in the French team and the scorer of two crucial goals during the 1998 World Cup. He was also one of the few football players who wore glasses when appearing publicly. This may seem an insignificant aspect of his public life. It serves to characterise him, however, as a player and as an intellectual. He is probably one of the few players who can profess to loving Miles Davis and to avidly reading Frantz Fanon.[30] Furthermore, he is omnipresent in contemporary French media and always ready to promote the rights of marginalised people and the victims of colonial France as well as advancing a fairer and more sensitive reconstruction of colonial French history. He also took a very clear position against Sarkozy during the 2007 presidential election campaign, saying for instance that "on parle de 'lepénisation' des esprits, mais il y a aussi une 'sarkoïsation' des esprits".

Central to our concerns here, however, is a single sentence. It is a sentence that Thuram pronounced in response to Le Pen just before the beginning of the 2006 World Cup. In answering a question posed by a journalist regarding Le Pen's impression that there were too many *joueurs de couleur* in the French team, Thuram ironically replied: "moi, personnellement, je ne suis pas noir".[31] He then added that Le Pen was ignorant of French history. While the second part of his answer received strong attention from the media, it is the first part—*moi, personnellement, je ne suis pas noir*—that resonates so powerfully. Implicit in this ironic reply was the sharp refusal to be

---

[30] Andrew Hussey, "If You Can Keep a Cool Head", guardian.co.uk (2007), http://www.guardian.co.uk/sport/2007/mar/04/football.newsstory (accessed 16 July 2008).
[31] See http://www.lequipe.fr/Football/20060629_152835Dev.html.

reduced to a metaphor of negritude or to become the black puppet of Le Pen or any other politician or journalist.

If we relate this sentence to Thuram's constant recollections of the tragedy of slavery, the injustice of contemporary France, in particular in relation to the treatment of migrants, and the accusation that Le Pen was ignorant of French history, it becomes easy to see how the struggle for cultural hegemony can be articulated by a respected football player in all its complexity. The ironic sentence *je ne suis pas noir* reinforces Thuram's right to define himself as *noir* and *pas noir*, to emphasise a central historical aspect of his own life in the ways and in the terms that he considers most appropriate to a certain social, cultural, political and/or sporting context. It is also essential to emphasise that the term *noir* in French culture is inextricably related to colonial stereotypes, and since the 1980s the English term *black* has often been used instead,[32] as we have seen in the slogan 'black, blanc et beur'.

Thuram here clearly breaks the binary relations (black vs. white, majority vs. minority) around which the exclusion of the other is usually articulated by introducing a new time into the meaning of *noir*. Here the challenge to the literal meaning of *je ne suis pas noir* suggests that *noir* is no longer a natural attribute but a cultural one, which is hegemonically imposed within the (post)colonial logic that still informs debates on difference and multiculturalism in Republican France. For instance, speaking about football, African players are often described by the media as undisciplined and naïve but extremely powerful.[33] Here it is not difficult to see how the colonial stereotype operates in the cultural and sporting arena.

Thuram's words are particularly important because, as Laurent Dubois argues,[34] the genealogy of French political culture is to be found in a form of perennially deferred universalism where the 'other' is momentarily excluded. This allows France to celebrate its universalism, while in fact reinforcing structures of racial, ethnic and

---

[32] Dominic Thomas, *Black France: Colonialism, Immigration and Transnationalism* (Bloomington; Indianapolis: Indiana University Press, 2007), p. 11-12.
[33] David Hand, "Football, Cultural Identities and the Media" (2000), http://www.leisuretourism.com (accessed 4 August 2008).
[34] Laurent Dubois, "La République métissée: Citizenship, Colonialism, and The Borders of French History", *Cultural Studies*, 14.1 (2000): 15-34 (18-27).

economic exclusion.[35] The most striking example of the perversity at the core of Republican ideology is Opération Vigipirate, which was instituted by the French government in 1997 as a response to terrorism just a few months before the World Cup. As Laurent Dubois reports, "the soldiers conduct extensive identity checks against those who 'look' foreign, concentrated in sites of transit which those who live in the *banlieue* must pass through each day to go to work".[36] Here of course, foreign does not mean Italian or Portuguese or American; it means Arab, African, Muslim and black. That is, during the days in which *la France au pluriel* was being celebrated in the stadium and on the streets, the physical appearance of (post)colonial French citizens was still questioned as a sign of doubtful loyalty to the nation-state.[37] This paradox recalls Slavoj Žižek's interpretation of racism, according to which the physical features that mark foreigners as different become an "indicator of a more radical strangeness", something un-fathomable "that makes them 'not quite human'".[38] The 'other' is essentially perceived through a series of fantasies.

In the case of France's postcolonial society these fantasies are often structured around what Pascal Blanchard and Nicolas Bancel call "Les origines républicaines de la fracture coloniale",[39] and what Herman Lebovics calls the "imperial-republic syndrome".[40] This syndrome is still partially based on racial identification, but is also sustained by the idea that there are cultural differences which cannot be mediated, and certain lifestyles and traditions that are in-compatible.[41] As we shall see when speaking about Zidane, this pertains in particular to Muslims, who are identified, particularly by the media, as not being assimilable.[42] Essentially, the right to dif-

---

[35] Dubois, p. 20.

[36] Dubois, p. 16-17.

[37] Silverstein (2000), p. 31.

[38] Slavoj Žižek, "'I hear with my eyes': Or The Invisible Master", in R. Salecl and S. Žižek (eds), *Gaze and Voice as Love Objects* (Durham; London: Duke University Press, 1996), pp. 90-125 (p. 105).

[39] Pascal Blanchard and Nicolas Bancel, "Les origines républicaines de la fracture coloniale", in Pascal Blanchard, Nicolas Bancel and Sandrine Lemaire (eds), *La Fracture coloniale: La société française au prisme de l'héritage colonial* (Paris: La Découverte, 2005), pp.6-17 (p. 6).

[40] Lebovics, p. 5.

[41] Thomas, p. 27.

[42] Silverstein (2000), p. 31.

ference becomes the right of French society to remain 'untouched'. From this perspective Le Pen's extreme ideas are in fact a vivid and expressive manifestation of what is a much more diffuse national sentiment.

The perverse core of French republicanism is consistent with Žižek's critique of ideology, according to which ideology constructs the myth of an ultimate goal (for instance Democracy, or Republican universalism), and simultaneously constructs a historical Other (for instance the Jew, the immigrant, or the Arab terrorist) in order to justify the impossibility of this dream ultimately being fulfilled.[43] On the other hand, ideology also preserves us from the traumatic encounter with the Real, precisely affirming such impossibility (the terrorists are combated via laws and practices that violate all basic democratic principles). It is in this context that the challenge posed by Thuram comes to represent a counter-hegemonic threat to the French colonial syndrome. By refusing to be the 'Negro', he is reaffirming his right to live and define his identity within multiple, different, partial and interconnecting spaces where he can challenge any attempt to sustain racism through both the celebration and the refusal of (incompatible) physical and cultural differences.

Zidane's Head-Butt

During the final act of the 2006 World Cup, in the last minutes of the match between Italy and France, with the score tied at 1-1, a now (in)famous incident occurred: Zidane received a red card and was forced to leave the field after head-butting the Italian defender Materazzi, who was later accused of having made offensive and possibly sexist remarks against Zidane's sister. In the following days many newspapers, in France and around the world, speculated as to the racist nature of Materazzi's remarks;[44] at the same time they also insisted on the deceitful nature of the Italian player(s). In anticipated

---

[43] See in particular Slavoj Žižek and Glyn Daly, *Conversation with Žižek* (Cambridge: Polity Press, 2004).
44 Yasmin Jiwani, "Sports as a Civilizing Mission: Zinedine Zidane and The Infamous Head-Butt", *Topia: Canadian Journal of Cultural Studies*, 19 (2008): 11-33; David Rowe, "Media, sport e razzializzazione: la finale di Zinedine Zidane", *Studi culturali*, 4.2 (2007): 343-361.

contrast, the representation of the event in the Italian media insisted on the stupidity and gratuitous violence of Zidane's act. Moreover, the nationalistic defence of Materazzi by the Italian media emphasised his shrewdness as a positive and typical Italian attitude. In Italy Materazzi was received as a hero, and a particularly smart one. In October 2006 the biggest Italian publishing house, Mondadori, even published a book authored by Materazzi entitled *Che cosa ho veramente detto a Zidane* [What I actually said to Zidane], a humoristic collection of 249 possible offensive sentences, including "After Foucault's death French philosophy is crap". As David Rowe emphasises, this book emptied the event of its political dimension by showing (or, perhaps, pretending) Materazzi to have been Zidane's clever and ironic victim.[45]

If the Italian defence of its defender is not surprising, given his contribution to Italy's final victory, perhaps it is not surprising either that the football organisation, FIFA, and French president Jacques Chirac himself should show themselves so willing to preserve Zidane's symbolic and economic value. At the same time, FIFA also proved ready to exclude any suggestion of racism from the event. Zidane was received by Chirac with full honours, together with the rest of the team, to whom the president extended "l'admiration et l'affection de la nation toute entière", adding that "[la] France vous aime et vous admire"; and for Zidane he reserved particular praise, calling him "un virtuose, un génie du foot mondial et un homme de cœur".[46] This attitude was mirrored by FIFA, which, in an unprecedented decision, gave a three-match suspension to Zidane and a two-match suspension to Materazzi, who had not in fact received a red card during the match.

There are no doubts that during the incident both Materazzi and Zidane displayed a highly stereotypical masculinity. While Materazzi is a strong and energetic defender, who has built his career on athletic power and *gioco maschio*, Zidane is a football artist who has made an apparently simple and marvellous art out of impossible pirouettes around the ball. Moreover, Zidane was the most representative and celebrated player in the French team. Furthermore he was one of the *Galacticos*, the stars of Real Madrid, around whom the Spanish team

---

[45] Rowe, p. 356.
[46] Comments accessed on Youtube (4 August 2008) http://www.youtube.com/-watch?v=rPPnWtcsFYY (author's translation).

has reinforced its international fame in recent years, transforming a fascinating football team into a global multimillion-dollar brand. Yet it is also important to remember that Zidane had already been the protagonist of violent reactions against other players before the 2006 final. As Hugh Dauncey and Douglas Morrey suggest, Zidane's integrity as a footballer who plays by the rules is questionable.[47] Regarding the 2006 head-butt, the main focus of scholars has not been the event itself but the global resonance that it received in the news and the attitude that FIFA took towards it.[48]

Yasmin Jiwani, who has undertaken a thorough critical analysis of the English and French newspaper coverage of the event, emphasises the civilising mission that the state attributes to sport. This is a convincing argument that had already been put forward by Silverstein before the episode in question.[49] Furthermore, Jiwani frames media comments on the event within an orientalist discourse that uses images of savagery, violence and animalism to describe the actions of African and Arab athletes. This perspective also supports the gendered identification of the Muslim man as conservative, masculinist, fundamentalist and terrorist. In summary, Jiwani uses the celebration, fall and redemption of Zidane to show how the state and the media can appropriate sporting heroes' actions to hegemonically reinforce a (post)colonial construction of the nation. While Jiwani's article represents an important contribution to the debate on sport and national identity in France, it largely fails to address two central and strongly related aspects of the event: firstly, it understates the powerful and ambiguous relation between postcolonialism and transnationalism, failing in particular to acknowledge the role played by multinational corporations; secondly, it completely overlooks Zidane's active role in the event and its aftermath, unconvincingly representing a global football star as a sort of puppet in the hands of the French government, the football governing body FIFA and the national and international media.

---

[47] Hugh Dauncey and Douglas Morrey, "Quiet Contradictions of Celebrity: Zinedine Zidane, Image, Sound, Silence and Fury", *International Journal of Cultural Studies*, 11.3 (2008): 301-320 (307).

[48] I am referring in particular to the two most relevant academic articles written until now on the episode by Jiwani and Rowe.

[49] In both Silverstein (2000) and Silverstein (2004).

This first aspect is particularly important because, as Silverstein argues, concerns over Islam operate within a transnational space,[50] and the French state has often attempted to transform migrants into consumers,[51] particularly by attempting to create a capitalist Islam. Moreover, a large part of the French national side is made up of players from prestigious teams such as the Spanish clubs Real Madrid and Barcelona, the Italian clubs Milan and Juventus or the English ones Chelsea and Manchester United. As members of these teams, they participate in European and intercontinental competitions, and they are part of a global phenomenon that makes them popular all over the world, from Portugal to China, from Norway to South Africa. Furthermore, these markets assist the increasingly globalised nature of the football business.

Transnational corporations compete with the nation-state in the creation of new national and local identities and usually exercise a stronger influence on the representation of football events by the media.[52] It is important to be aware that national and local identities come to represent meta-commodities through which transnational corporations try to obtain customer loyalty.[53] It has already been emphasised how the media celebration of the multiethnic French team in 1998 was first of all an Adidas creation, fostered by advertisements that occupied media spaces, as well as real locations such as le Trocadéro in Paris.[54] From this perspective, globalisation does not simply homogenise;[55] on the contrary, it also fosters national, local and group identities, which are exploited by global capital and, in the case of football, primarily through the association between a brand and a player or a team.

If in Zidane's case the condemnation of his action as uncivilised can be framed within orientalist discourse, the public celebration of his long career and his redemption after the head-butt episode are also clearly related to the protection of the large economic interests of UEFA (the Union of European Football Associations), FIFA and of

---

[50] Silverstein (2000), p. 27; Silverstein (2004), p. 127.
[51] Silverstein (2004), p. 123.
[52] Nelson, p. 7.
[53] King, p. 200; Silverstein (2000), p. 37.
[54] Silverstein (2000), p. 40.
[55] Thomas, p. 14.

those transnational companies that sponsor the French team, Real
Madrid and Zidane himself. These economic and political interests
give enormous power to football stars like Zidane. In the case of a
player such as David Beckham, however, this power is mainly due to
the marketability of his body, his looks and his 'posh' wife. In
Zidane's case it is first of all related to his indisputable talent and his
history of successes. It is also a consequence of his ability to navigate
in the murky waters of contemporary football, always remaining at the
heart of the game but at the margins of the most dangerous whirlpools.
Dauncey and Morrey have emphasised the "inherent opacity of
Zidane's celebrity persona" and his unwillingness to be framed as a
symbol of ethnic minorities or political parties.[56] In the conclusion of
their article, they further argue that "Zidane's careful refusal to take
up ideological positions or explain his actions may represent a canny
negotiation of a global media arena in which the slightest utterance is
subject to fine scrutiny".[57] Importantly, they seem to be suggesting
that opacity, ambiguity and silence are not a sign of passivity on
Zidane's part, but rather the core of his agency. We should for
instance keep in mind his questioning during the trial concerning the
pharmacological products administered to Juventus players. During
his time at Juventus his body-weight increased significantly. Throughout the trial he maintained a substantially uncooperative attitude and
attributed the change in his body to weight-training.[58]

The construction of Zidane as a French national hero was not
simply carried out by the State, the media, the football teams where he
played and transnational corporations. It was also the flowering of the
role that Zidane played in the French team as a charismatic figure, a
great player and a fundamental point of reference for his team-mates.
When considering the head-butt it is important to recall two essential
elements that pertain more to football than to politics, economics or
colonial history. Firstly, Materazzi was the man who scored the goal
that gave Italy the 1-1 draw after France had scored with a penalty by
Zidane. Secondly, a few minutes before the head-butt Zidane had was-
ted a wonderful opportunity to score the victory goal. In other words,

---

[56] Dauncey and Morrey, p. 302.
[57] Dauncey and Morrey, p. 318.
[58] See "Un giorno in pretura: terzo grado, triplice fischio", broadcasted on the Italian
TV channel Rai 3, 23 February 2008.

just before the infamous accident, Zidane had twice come very close to becoming, once again, the French hero who brought the World Cup to the French nation. While it is not possible to argue with certainty that this purely sporting aspect had an influence on Zidane's loss of self-control, the head-butt cannot simply be read as a reaction to a racist or offensive comment on the part of Materazzi. And it is this aspect that is lacking from Rowe's interpretation of the event when he argues that, although Materazzi's comments were not strictly speaking racist, they need to be read within the framework of the sexual racism around which forms of oppression are often articulated.[59]

The "emasculation" that Materazzi perpetrated against Zidane,[60] by making offensive remarks about his sister, is symptomatic of an attitude—an undeniably despicable one—that is common among many football players, and it is not necessarily related to a postcolonial discourse. At the same time, we should avoid reading Zidane's reaction simply as that of the (post)colonial victim or, even worse, the reaction of a Muslim defending the honour of his family. Zidane was a football star who played an ambiguous and substantially hegemonic role within the context of transnational capitalism and identity-driven consumerism. While the episode was certainly appropriated by other social actors, who often demonstrated a (post)colonial attitude and what Silverstein calls "gendered imperial fantasies",[61] this should not cause us to overlook the role played by footballers in the social, political, economic and cultural arena. Zidane has often demonstrated his relative independence from those social forces that would like to push him to one side or the other of the political arena. For instance, he has variously defined himself as a Kabyle from La Castellane, a Beur from Marseille and a Frenchman.[62] Here it is not difficult to see how he makes use of references to his residential district and his city to create "third spaces" where his fragmented identity can be expressed in positive terms.[63] As Silverstein remarks, Zidane has always been a reluctant minority model and has often been accused of being a "virtual

---

[59] Rowe, p. 353.
[60] Rowe, p. 353.
[61] Silverstein (2000), p. 31.
[62] Andrew Hussey, "ZZ top", guardian.co.uk (2004), http://www.guardian.co.uk/-football/2004/apr/04/sport.features (accessed 4 August 2008).
[63] Homi K. Bhabha, *The Location of Culture* (London: Routledge, 1994), p. 38.

Arab".[64] The fact that his wife is Spanish and his children have Italian names also suggests that Zidane, while proudly aware of his background, lives the comfortable, transnational life of all football stars.

In conclusion, the cases of Thuram and Zidane demonstrate how nation-states and transnational corporations do not always have complete control of sporting events. As Nelson argues, "the agency (or just unpredictability) of individuals and groups is liable to inflect and complicate the resulting spectacles".[65] At the same time, the amplification of these episodes in the media, and the clear nationalistic and (post)colonial connotations that they assume, demonstrate how football does not simply mirror central aspects of contemporary society but largely contributes to the creation of discursive and material practices related to complex questions of local, national and transnational identity. Zidane's head-butt in particular represents one of those events where, as Rowe suggests, a short moment in time can be frozen and repeated an infinite number of times around the world, so that a myriad of historical and geographical connections become possible and visible.[66] These connections relate different worlds, meanings and emotions into an inextricable network that can be appropriated but never completely controlled by any of the actors involved. Sometimes, as in the case of Thuram's *je ne suis pas noir*, a new time can be introduced into meaning, so that players' agency challenges prevalent visions of histories, societies and communities. And at other times, as in the case of Zidane's head-butt, one of these frozen moments can threaten and reveal the hegemonic nature of the construction of national identities by the nation-state, transnational corporations and the media. Zidane's violent reaction can be taken as evidence that, as Žižek argues, what makes a person human is that s/he is much more than his/her symbolic identity and is in fact "a wealth of idiosyncratic features".[67] Most importantly these idiosyncrasies underline the failure of the symbolic order. Both cases demonstrate football's extraordinary potential to influence our world(s), behind and beyond its appropriation by nation-states, transnational corporations and the media.

---

[64] Silverstein (2000), p. 41; Silverstein (2004), p. 139.
[65] Nelson, p. 2.
[66] Rowe, p. 355.
[67] Slavoj Žižek, *Organs Without Bodies : Deleuze and Consequences* (New York; London: Routledge, 2004).

Tos Ethnic Identity in France through the Blogs of Young People of Portuguese Descent

Martine Fernandes

Translated from the French by Murray Pratt

> Il n'est pas illogique d'avancer que les enfants de migrants portugais, si leur 'part portugaise' résiste à la tendance d'étouffement des identités culturelles, pourront faire valoir la leur dans les espaces publics, et pas seulement comme référence d'origine ou sur un mode folklorique ou bien dans les espaces familiaux et associatifs.[1]

Portuguese migrants arrived in France in large numbers during the 1960s, fleeing the dictatorship of António de Oliveira Salazar (1928-1968) and colonial wars in Africa (Angola, Mozambique, Guinea).[2]

---

[1] Albano Cordeiro, "Les apports de la communauté portugaise à la diversité ethno-culturelle", *Hommes et Migrations*, 1210 (1997), 5-17 (http://www.adri.fr/HM/-articles/1210/1210a.html).

[2] This article first appeared in French as "'Miki-le-toss ou comment repérer un guech en quelques leçons': L'identité ethnique 'tos' en France à travers les blogs de jeunes lusodescendants" in *PORTAL Journal of Multidisciplinary International Studies*, 4:2 (2007), special edition "Contesting Eurovisions", edited by Dimitris Eleftheriotis, Murray Pratt and Ilaria Vanni. This version is available online at the following web-site: http://epress.lib.uts.edu.au/ojs/index.php/portal/article/view/521/444, and is re-produced in translation into English in the current volume with the kind permission of Paul Allatson (Editor). The quotation in the title is from the welcome page of a blog (http://miki-le-toss.skyrock.com). The terms 'tos' and 'guèch', analysed below, designate second-generation Portuguese immigrants. The term 'people of Portuguese

They experienced clandestine border-crossings, shanty towns, undocumented employment, racism and economic exploitation.[3] Even though the Portuguese today constitute one of the largest immigrant communities in France, they remain 'invisible', overlooked by researchers and public alike, because they are considered to be well-integrated, notably after Portugal's entry into the European Union in 1986.[4] However, as Albano Cordeiro has shown, the Portuguese have conserved their national identity and ethno-cultural practices thanks to their extensive network of clubs and associations: they have succeeded in integrating without integrating.[5] Due in part to their heritage, a generation of Portuguese descendants have, since the 1990s, entered into a phase of visibility.[6] Cordeiro's hypothesis, quoted in the epithet above, would seem to be proved by their public emergence in literature (Alice Machado, Carlos Batista, Brigitte Paulino-Neto), cinema (José Vieira), theatre (the company Cá e Lá), politics and public organisations Cap Magellan, Mémoire Vive), music (Da Silva, La Harissa, Less du Neuf) and the blogosphere. This progression towards increased visibility began in the 1980s with the 'tos' movement and the establishment of organisations for Portuguese youths, the March for Equality in 1983, and the co-foundation of Convergence 84. In the 1990s, identity demands grew, partly in response to Portugal's entry into the European Union, which reinforced a sense of Portuguese national pride among descendants (often with double nationalities), but also due to the increasing institutionalisation of ties

---

descent' is used here to render the author's original use of 'lusodescendants', which is used, notably by the Portuguese government, to designate the descendants of Portuguese expatriates globally.

[3] As recently as 29 January 2004, L'Humanité denounced the human trafficking of 350 Portuguese and 50 Malians in the west of France: "En deux ans, plusieurs centaines d'immigrés auraient travaillé dans trois abattoirs de l'Ouest dans des conditions proches de l'esclavage." http://www.humanite.fr/2004-01-29_Politique_-Un-trafic-de-main-d-ouvre-decouvert (accessed 16 October 2009).

[4] In France, the concept of integration is rarely brought up when it applies to European residents. Yet, more than thirty years later, most Portuguese resident in France retain Portuguese nationality and do not participate in French political life. See Cordeiro.

[5] Cordeiro, p. 111.

[6] See Jean-Baptiste. Pingault, "Jeunes issus de l'immigration portugaise : affirmations identitaires dans les espaces politiques nationaux", Le Mouvement Social, 4:209 (2004), 71-89.

between Portuguese descendants and their home land as well as a measure of French openness towards its immigrant communities.[7]

For Jean-Baptiste Pingault, the *tos* movement, like the *beur* movement, petered out at the end of the 1980s. He makes a distinction between the first generation of *Tos*, whom he characterises as left-wing militants, and more contemporary formations of Portuguese descendants, as symbolised by the association Cap Magellan which was founded by students in 1991. In this chapter, however, I aim to show that a *tos* movement persists today, as demonstrated in the thousands of online blogs maintained by teenage *Tos*, the term they continue to use to refer to themselves. This virtual ethnic affirmation is expressed through photomontages and ethnic symbols (the flag, the Portuguese national anthem) and by patriotic discourse. 'Miki-le-toss' is one of these blogs, offering a caricature of the teenager of Port-uguese descent in France through its use of French language mixed up with Portuguese, visits to Portuguese night clubs, the annual summer holiday in Portugal, pride in being Portuguese and the patriotism of the blog. Its interest lies at the same time in its demonstration of the existence of a *tos* community in France with its own ethnic practices and in denouncing a drift towards nationalism. I will therefore show that this identitarian affirmation, facilitated by the blogosphere, has something in common with the cultural nationalism of the Chicanos in the United States (a reference point for the Portuguese heritage rap group La Harissa). If these blogs allow for the expression and re-inforcement of a communitarian ethnic identity (which those com-mercial brands interested in targeting Portuguese descendants know how to exploit[8]), it is nonetheless an identity which poses no threat to European integration or to France.

---

[7] Jorge de la Barre, *Identités multiples en Europe: Le cas des lusodescendants en France* (Paris: L'Harmattan, 2006).

[8] Brands of clothing targeting Portuguese descendants have multiplied, within France and across Europe: they include V.I.P. (Very Important Portuguese), Emigrante, PLG Spirit, Mafiatos, Luso, Conquistadores Portugueses, Lusitanowear, Saudades-Wear, Lajet7toss, Costawear, Style, Bull-Rythmic and Mystika-prod.

100% Portuguese and Proud of it

Paris-based radio station Skyrock is the premier European blog editor, hosting more than 9 million blogs, mostly maintained by teenagers. Cyril Fiévet, co-author of *Blog Story* (2004), interviewed in *Le Monde*, explains that the success of the blog is due to the way it democratises public discourse. He continues, "il y a des millions de gens qui ne s'exprimaient pas auparavant, qui n'en avaient pas forcément les moyens, et qui décident de prendre la parole".[9] The multiplication of blogs maintained by people of Portuguese descent no doubt constitutes an unprecedented entry into discourse by this community. An internet search for the keywords 'Portugais' ('Portuguese') or 'Portugal' brings up millions of Portuguese heritage blogs. Although these share the characteristics of other teenage blogs (personal photographs, bands, etc.), they also constitute a discrete subgenre to the extent that they base themselves on the affirmation of a specific national pride ('100% Portuguese and proud of it'). Privileging communication within the group, blogs are a form of intimate diary, broadcasting "short notes, usually dated (by day and hour) [...] published in chronologically inverse order", and which are often linked to identitarian quests, notably among teenagers.[10] Sandra Calvert has noted the potential blogs hold for the analysis of the construction of identity among teenagers: "weblogs [...] may offer insight into the ways in which adolescents present themselves online, especially in terms of self-expression and peer-group relations, both of which impact the construction of identity."[11] Insofar as the technical characteristics of blogs (comments, links, multimedia[12]) favour the creation of virtual communities, they can also serve the construction of ethnic identities. Affirmations of identity can be found on the wel-

---

[9] O. Zilbertin, "Un Français sur dix a créé son blog sur Internet", *Le Monde*, 3 January 2006.

[10] Olivier Trédan, "Les weblogs dans la Cité: entre quête de l'entre soi et affirmation identitaire", *Marsouin: Cahier de recherche*, 6 (2005). Available online at: www.marsouin.org.

[11] Sandra L. Calvert and David A. Huffaker, "Gender, Identity and Language Use in Teenage Blogs", *Journal of Computer-Mediated Communication*, 10:2. Available online at: cmc.indiana.edu/vol10/issue2/huffaker.html.

[12] Many blogs contain links to videos (documentaries, songs, television extracts) hosted on *Youtube*.

come pages of blogs, in the specific iconographic content they deploy, and in the links they host, all of which concur in reinforcing an effect of community.

Ethnic identity, within the context of acculturation into a host nation, is linked to individuals' sense of belonging to a particular ethnic group, their sharing in one or more of the following elements: common origins, culture, religion, language and place of origin.[13] According to Jean Phinney, ethnic identity is a dynamic construction which is part of teenage development within complex modern societies, stretching from a lack of interest in childhood years through to the active take-up of an identity at the end of adolescence. This process (not completed in all cases) is dependent on social experiences lived within the family, the ethnic community and society at large:

> During adolescence, many youth, especially those from ethnic groups with lower status or power, may become deeply involved in learning about their ethnicity. This process can lead to constructive actions aimed at affirming the value and legitimacy of their group [...] or to feelings of insecurity, confusion, or resentment over treatment of their group.[14]

Starting with the welcome page, containing among other elements the name of the blog, the blogger's pseudonym and a description of the blog's content, Portuguese descendants affirm their ethnic identity and their patriotic pride in Portugal.

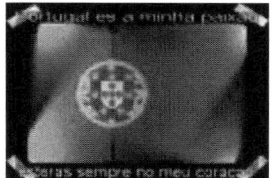

Figure 3[15]

---

[13] See Jean Phinney et al., "Ethnic Identity, Immigration and Well-Being: An Interactional Perspective", *Journal of Social Issues*, 57:3 (2001), 493-510.

[14] Phinney, p. 496.

[15] The description of the blog reads, 'fidel o portugal, PORTUGAL NO MEU COR-ACAO!!!!oué je sui fan de mon pays, portuguésa de alma é coracao!!!anti portugais arrete toi la, ta rien a voir ici!!!un gros bisou a tous, et surrt a tt les portugais demeran en france e que sentem falta da nossa terra!!bonne visite a tous!!'.

The names of the blogs and even the pseudonyms (in many cases the two elements are similar) often express teenagers' multiple identifications, whether local or national. The pseudonyms, identity markers which become the foundation of the bloggers' new online identity often contain 'Portugal' or 'Portugais' ('Portuguese').[16] In one instance (see fig. 3),[17] the pseudonym 'portugal-amo' ('I love portugal') is reinforced by the blog's title, 'portugal in the heart', as well as by the photomontage of the national flag and the legend: 'Portugal, you are my passion/ You will always be in my heart'. The names of other blogs contain references to Portuguese regions or villages (referred to using the term *le bled*[18]) as well as the numbers of French departments or the names of French cities, many of them referring to Parisian suburbs: 'portugal-77', 'portugal94-vitry', 'portugaise-du-93' and 'Minhota75'. Other names express national pride more directly, often in a humorous register referring to the sense of shame, whether in the past or present, in being Portuguese in France: 'super-portugais'; 'the Guesh: une portugaise parmi d'autres'; 'mister-portos'; 'Força Portugal'; 'portugais-loveur'; 'authentic-carai: portugues para sempre'; 'un Portos et Tos pour un'. This shame can be explained by the anti-immigrant racism experienced by parents in France and Portugal.[19] Like the descendants of Algerian residents who have reclaimed the term *beur*, Portuguese descendants revalorise the xenophobic terminology applied to the Portuguese in France (*Portos, Guech, Tos*) and invent new collocations (*Caraï*[20]). This contemporary practice by identitarian movements of ethnic minorities can be seen as a revalorisation of their experience in France.

---

[16] Trédan, p. 6.

[17] An example of the blogs that can be accessed from http://portugal-amo.skyrock.com.

[18] The term, of Moroccan origin, designates the parents' village of origin. It is also used in this sense by descendants of Algerian residents.

[19] In Portugal, during annual holidays, descendants of Portuguese living in France are called, among other names, *os Immigrantes* (Immigrants), *os Franceses* (French) and *os Abeques* ('Withs', a Portuguese pronunciation of the French word *avec* and referring to the phrase 'Viens avec moi' ['Come with me']).

[20] This comes from a vulgar word *caralho*. The orthography of all these terms fluctuates: *karaï* or *caraï*; *tos, thos* or *toss*; *guech* or *guesh*.

The description of the blogs often reinforces the function of the blogs' and the bloggers' names, by reaffirming ethnic identity and national pride:

> un blog 400% portugais pour représenter la plus belle communauté du monde: voili (sic) mon blog je sui un toss je m'apèle david j'ai 15 ans j'habite Sarcelles:tKt lE BlOg ki rEpReSenTe nOtRe notre beau pays LE PORTUGAL!!! Ici tu trouveras plein de montages concernant le PORTUGAL. Dédicaces a tous les PORTUGAIS qui abitent en france!!!![21]

In its escalation, this comes close to blind patriotism, using eulogy, superlatives and graphic inventiveness. Presentational content often includes dedications to the Portuguese in France, inserting the blogger within the community at the same time as offering homage to it. Equally, Portuguese heritage rap groups legitimate their existence through similar dedications and by proclaiming themselves to be 'representatives' of the community. For example, the song 'Y a des Karaïs' by the rap group Spe-6-Fik from the Parisian suburbs (Trappes 78) is one long dedication to young Portuguese in France: 'C'est pour ceux qui sont fiers du pays et des couleurs, fiers des anciens, fiers de leurs frères et de leurs sœurs, de nos valeurs, de l'histoire et qui ont leur main sur leur cœur quand ils entendent "Heróis do Mar" (the Portuguese national anthem)'. Spe-6-Fik claim to be 'Fier du pays que je représente', as do La Harissa, proclaiming themselves to be 'Les Portos du rap français' and affirming in 'Fils d'une nation' that '[o]n vient représenter du mieux que l'on peut notre peuple fier et org-ueilleux'. Each blog is also invested in a representational mission and addresses itself primarily to other Portuguese descendants.[22] The sense of ethnic self-glorification is reinforced by repetition, not only of the text but of the images too.

The iconographic content of the notes, which consist of an accumulation of personal photos (family, friends) or of ethnocultural photomontages, plays a part in the process of affirming ethnic identity. The same photomontages are repeated from blog to blog (extra-textuality) and reinforce community cohesion. The photomontages

---

[21] See portugais-du-69.skyrock.com, le-portuguais-95.skyrock.com, i-love-portugal.-skyrock.com.

[22] In some cases, didactic notes seem to be addressed, as will be discussed later in the chapter, to people other than Portuguese descendants, and there are indications that some comments are made by readers who are not of Portuguese descent.

bring together ethnic symbols (the national flag and anthem, the carnation) with other objects. For example, in one note the photo-montage consists of the national flag represented within an eye, sig-nifying Portugal's *saudade* or melancholy.[23] The adjacent text contains the lyrics of the national anthem. The most frequently used image, the flag, appears in photos (notably related to the soccer World Cup) and photomontages (on cars, motorbikes and clothing). Two re-current photomontages are of particular interest: the Portuguese flag superimposed on the map of France, and on the map of the world. The Portuguese flag on the map of France with the title 'invasion des Portugais en France' (see fig. 4) makes a claim for the recognition of the Portuguese presence in France, for the most part ignored by institutions and the media.[24]

http://laportugaise905.skyblog.com

Figure 4[25]

---

[23] See E. Lourenço, *Mythologie de la saudade: Essai sur la mélancholie portugaise* (Paris: Editions Chandeigne, 2007).
[24] See portugal.skyrock.com, ptiteportos33.skyrock.com/7.html and portugal-amo.-skyrock.com/24.html.
[25] The text reads "essayer dimaginer le nombre de portugais ki ya en france!!!!vous allez allussiner!!!ce n'est ke la pure vérité!!!(msg pour tt ceu a ki mon "culte portugais" ne plai pa!!!!!!) regardez tous autour de vous ya des portugais en france et c comme ca!".

The term *invasion*, often used in xenophobic discourse, is here taken up in a positive sense as a reminder that the Portuguese form the most numerous international community in France. The group Spe-6-Fik also point to this presence in 'Y a des Karaïs', the accompanying video for which figures in the blogs. The group enumerates French cities and departments: "Y a des Karaïs à Lille, à Brest, Bordeaux, Toulouse, Marseille, à Lyon, Strasbourg, Paris; 75-77-78-91-92-93-94-95." The Portuguese flag on the map of the world indicates the sense of belonging to a global community among Portuguese descendants and recalls that the Portuguese diaspora includes transnational practices.[26] In 'Fils d'une nation', La Harissa also position themselves within this global perspective: "j'vis en banlieue parisienne depuis mon enfance […] j'ai mélangé du hip-hop et de la musique de chez moi, du Luxembourg au New Jersey en passant par le Canada, en France, en Suisse, en Belgique, attachés à nos racines on met un point d'honneur à représenter les nôtres […] Epa, comme toi j'suis un enfant du pays sur cette planète." This global vision is maintained by the Portuguese government. Portugal effectively rediscovered its Lusophone status after its entry into the EU and reaffirmed its link with Portuguese-speaking communities through

> [l']institutionnalisation de la Communauté des Pays de Langue Portugaise (CPLP), [la] création du Conseil des Communautés Portugaises, [la] création des Rencontres Mondiales de Jeunes Lusodescendants organisées par le Secrétariat d'État aux Communautés Portugaises (SECP) (anciennement Secrétariat d'État à l'Émigration Portugaise), et enfin [la] décision d'accorder le droit de vote aux élections présidentielles à tous les Portugais quel que soit leur pays de résidence.[27]

Anchored within the community of a social network, Portuguese descendants display their attachment to Portugal through ties of affection, friendship or love. As Jorge de La Barre notes following an inquiry conducted among youths of Portuguese descent:

> Le fait de déclarer avoir des amis français et portugais est particulièrement associé à l'identification en tant que Français et Portugais, alors que le fait d'avoir des amis majoritairement portugais est particulièrement associé à l'identification en tant que Portugais. De même, le fait de se sentir plutôt

---

[26] See Caroline Brettell, *Anthropology and Migration: Essays on Transnationalism, Ethnicity and Identity* (Walnut Creek: Altamira Press, 2003).
[27] de La Barre, p. 85.

(voire très) proche des Français est particulièrement associé à l'identification en tant que Français.[28]

The technical functions of the blog (links, commentaries) also enable expressions of belonging to an ethnic community. The community of the social network is inscribed within hypertextual links to other blogs or ethnically defined sites (like the Portuguese dating site 'Lusomeet' spanning France, Luxembourg, Belgium, Switzerland and Portugal).[29] For Olivier Trédan, the blog "constitue en quelque sorte le lieu d'affichage des relations construites via le réseau Internet ou constitué dans le cadre d'une sociabilité physique".[30] By dint of being linked as a social network (blogrolling), a sense of belonging and the construction of a community is reinforced: "You are defining your community and telling others that you see yourself as the company you keep".[31] Networking of this kind is fundamental in that it also constitutes a sign of popularity. According to Biz Stone, "links are the currency of the blogosphere" and the expression 'links whore' is used to designate bloggers keen to be quoted.[32] Within the context of ethnic affirmation, this practice reinforces the sense of belonging and mutual recognition.

The blogs of Portuguese descendants show, if ever it was needed, that multicultural communities are a social reality in France. The French governmental organisation, the 'le Haut Conseil à l'Intégration' recognizes this, to a certain extent, on its official website:

[L]'histoire de l'immigration en France montre à l'évidence qu'aujourd'hui comme hier la grande majorité des migrants ont d'abord été 'accueillis' dans des communautés culturelles d'origine qui leur ont permis de sauvegarder au moins pour un temps leur identité avant de leur permettre de négocier avec la société d'accueil une nouvelle appartenance.[33]

However, the 'Conseil' immediately denies the juridical value of any political claim linked to ethic identity: "En France, toute référence à l'ethnicité d'une personne ou d'un groupe peut être légitimement

[28] de La Barre, p. 214.
[29] See www.lusomeet.com.
[30] Trédan, p. 3.
[31] Biz Stone, *Who Let the Blogs Out?: A Hyperconnected Peek at the World of Weblogs* (New York: St. Martin's, 2004), p. 101.
[32] Stone, p. 91.
[33] See http://www.hci.gouv.fr.

considérée comme contraire à l'ordre républicain, dans la mesure où elle met en question l'unité juridiquement intangible de la nation française". 'Cultural diversity' is contrasted with multiculturalism of the 'Anglo-Saxon' model, which would threaten national unity and social cohesion. Yet, by drawing to some extent on a US model of ethnic struggle, Portuguese descendants can situate themselves within a campaign for the recognition of ethnic identity.

Nossa raça é portuguesa

American rap music, which, at times, echoes ethnic claims, has some degree of influence on Portuguese descendants. One of the recurring photomontages on the blogs is entitled 'Mafia Toss'. This shows armed men, dressed in black, in the style of 'gansta rap'. One of the texts adds this commentary: "T'as un blem avec les Portugais ? T'en touche un, Tu nous touche [*sic*] tous." As we will see in more detail, it is effectively within a context of xenophobia, past and/or present, that these blogs emerge. The rap group La Harissa draws its inspiration from Latin music and civil rights struggles in the United States. Their first album, released in 1998, was called *Portos Ricos*. In the album *Conquistador* (2000), one song is called 'J'ai le touché latino' and in the album *Portugal Rap Star* (2001) another is called 'Nossa Raça' [Our Race], a Portuguese concept that recalls the Chicano concept of 'La Raza'. Far from being trivial, this possible reference to the Chicanos establishes a parallel between the situation of the Portuguese in France and the Chicanos in the United States. In fact, there are commonalities between these two communities. The Portuguese who reside in France originate in a poor, Latin, Catholic country. Often from rural backgrounds, they fled misery, crossed borders illegally (by foot, in cattle trucks) and occupied low-status jobs (construction, housework, agriculture). Like the Mexicans, their country is close to the host country (although it doesn't border it, as Mexico does the United States) and they have maintained a strong link with their country and language, notably as a result of return journeys. Finally, they represent a sizeable group and have come together in cultural organisations associated with football, folklore and religion. The two communities are, of course, different, in that one of them is situated within a European paradigm of North-South power relations reflecting former colonial strengths, and the other, existing within an American model of the same North-South power relations, has inherited the effects of both Spanish and US colonialism, notably in the way this plays out in terms of race. How then can the affirmation of identity by Portuguese descendants be compared to the cultural nationalism of the Chicanos?

Michael Hames-Garcia shows that there were three major components to Chicano cultural nationalism in the 60s and 70s: native claims, the defence of unity rather than emphasising internal differences, and a conservative ideology of the family.[34] This cultural nationalism, emerging within a context of discrimination and economic exploitation, enabled the creation of an oppositional political identity, founded on a national myth (the Aztec myth of Aztlán), which in turn permitted a territorial claim (for example, New Mexico and California). Aspects of these three components can be found in the blogs of Portuguese descendants, where cultural nationalism has a strong link with Portuguese nationalism, both contemporary and Salazarist: the foundational myth is that of the Portuguese 'conquerors' in the time of the 'Discoveries'; the defence of unity rests on the concept of the *raça portuguesa*; and the conservative familial identity, linked to Catholicism, echoes Salazarist values (God, the family, the homeland).[35] The heritage of Salazarism, which might seem paradoxical, is nonetheless not negligible since the generation of Portuguese ex-patriots was brought up during the dictatorship, which lasted more than half a century.

---

[34] Michael Hames-Garcia, "How to tell a Mestizo from an Enrichirito: Colonialism and National Culture in the Borderlands", *Diacritics*, 30:4 (2000), 102-122.

[35] Maria Filomena Mónica has shown that the elitist regime of Salazar reduced primary education from seven to four years and favoured religious teaching and nationalist propaganda. Portuguese exile is considered as a form of 'voting with one's feet' against Salazar. António de Oliveira Salazar was named as the Finance Minister in 1928 and was Prime Minister between 1932 and 1968. His dictatorial regime, with fascistic elements such as an emphasis on Portuguese youth and a state police (PIDE), was founded on the rejection of modernity and industry in favour of traditional agriculture and what he characterised as 'routine' (or effectively 'archaic') life. Held back by poverty and illiteracy, and called up to go and fight against independence movements in Portugal's African colonies in the 1960s, many young Portuguese chose exile in France. Following an accident in 1968, Salazar was replaced by Marcel Caetano who remained in power until 1974, the year of the peaceful Carnation Revolution, which instated democracy. Salazar died in 1970. See Maria Filomena Mónica, *Educação e sociedade no Portugal de Salazar* (Lisbon: Presença, 1978).

Portuguese descendants' patriotism is linked to Portugal's accession to the European Union. According to de La Barre, while Portugal has been traditionally nationalist because of its relations with Spain, it witnessed a resurgence of national pride after 1986. This nationalism, which at the same time was felt across Portuguese communities around the world, was encouraged by the Portuguese government:

> La politique du gouvernement pour les Communautés Portugaises privilégiera l'intégration sociale, civique et politique des citoyens nationaux résidant à l'étranger, au sein des différentes sociétés d'accueil; en prenant en compte l'importance croissante des lusodescendants dans l'affirmation et la visibilité du Portugal dans ces pays; en sauvegardant le patrimoine des racines culturelles et en préservant une identité enrichie par la culture d'induction; en alimentant la nécessité de sa valorisation culturelle, académique et professionnelle; en stimulant une intervention accrue dans le domaine public et politique aux divers échelons de la vie démocratique de ces sociétés; en promouvant un attrait pour une intervention plus intense dans le cadre de la démocratie participative.[36]

On the first anniversary of his coming to power (9 March 2006), President Cavaco Silva visited Luxembourg and encouraged the Portuguese of the diaspora not to forget their land, and to promote and defend the Portuguese language: "There is a Portuguese spirit that remains alive, and the Portuguese language and culture are the strongest expression of our Portugueseness."[37] Institutionally recognised, Portuguese descendants are encouraged to integrate at the same time as serving as ambassadors for Portugal.[38] They express their national pride by making reference at times to the founding heroes of the Portuguese nation (including Viriathe, Afonso Henriques and Vasco de Gama) who were notably restored to honour by Salazar in order to reaffirm Portugal's imperialist vocation. As the album *Conquistador* by the group La Harissa shows, Portuguese descendants prioritise within national history the period of the 'Discoveries' with

---

[36] de La Barre, p. 99.

[37] Our translation. See www.lusojornal.com/archives/unefr11.pdf (page 3).

[38] Notably, the Portuguese government created a 'charter for Portuguese descendants' destined for the under-thirties giving them privileges in Portugal and grants to undertake higher education in France.

its great navigators.[39] When reinstated within the context of conquest, the migratory experience of previous generations is reinterpreted in a positive light. La 'DeDiCaSSe a NoS PaReNtS' of the blog 'foda-se' deploys this strategy:

> À vous héros d'une autre époque, qui avez osé faire le grand saut, dans des conditions parfois inhumaines, et qui êtes allés jusqu'au bout de vos rêves .../ À vous qui avez été des précurseurs, des aventuriers courageux, qui avez osé défier l'inconnu en vous montrant entreprenants bien avant que vos enfants ne le deviennent .../ À vous, derniers grands 'navigateurs' portugais, bien portugais jusqu'au bout des ongles, et qui êtes pourtant perçus comme étrangers lorsque parfois vous revenez au Portugal... [40]

The organisation 'Cap Magellan: le Portugal sans clichés' has also adopted the French name of the Portuguese navigator Fernão de Magalhães, the first circumnavigator of the globe.[41] This organisation, whose president has at times been accused of nationalism, has largely contributed to the recognition of Portuguese descendants by the Portuguese and French authorities.[42] Pingault rightly notes the radicalisation of the identitarian discourse with Cap Magellan (whose members proclaim themselves to be Portuguese-speaking agitators) and the use of an 'ethnic logic' linked to cultural lobbying.[43] During the 2007 presidential elections, their website encouraged its readers to address the candidates: "Vous êtes français d'origine portugaise ou portugais vivant en France, vous avez un lien avec la communauté portugaise de France ou avec l'Espace Lusophone? Envoyez-nous vos opinions, revendications ou suggestions sur l'ensemble des thèmes liés à cette origine, culture, langue ou espace social."

The myth of the 'Conquest' has at the same time been upheld by the Portuguese government, which makes Portugal and its

---

[39] The fashion brand 'c-portugueses' ('Conquistadores portugueses') also exploits the national myth of conquest: "voila la nouvelle marque portugaise qui symbolise l'immigração mais aussi os navigadores portuguses [les navigateurs portugais] qui on découverent o caminho par as indias [le chemin des Indes] comme un certain Vasco da Gama car nous portugais nous somment des explorateur [*sic*]". See http://-conquistadores.skyrock.com.
[40] See http://foda-se.skyrock.com.
[41] See their website: http://www.capmagellan.org and the magazine *Cap Mag*.
[42] See Pingault.
[43] Pingault, p. 86.

communities into a deterritorialised nation linked by language.[44] This myth masks the true conditions of Portuguese emigration under Salazar and the long mistrust of the government and its official representatives in France by those who had left the country and who had long endured the Salazarist oligarchical system.[45]

The second component of cultural nationalism, the predilection for unity within the community, is evident in the blogs. The patriotic imagery and discourse used in the blogs is identical, regardless of whether it is deployed by girls or boys. Heterosexuality and mono-culture are the norm. Social class distinctions and internal tensions are not evoked, such as the differences between those living on the continent and on islands, from different regions, or identifying them-selves as French. The fashion brand 'VIP: Very Important Portuguese'[46] also uses national identification as a symbol of unity: 'Uma nação, Um Povo, uma Selecção'.[47] It is worth noting though, as de La Barre demonstrates, that Portuguese descendants who identify themselves as European (although this is unusual), French or Franco-Portuguese are generally better educated than those who affirm only their Portuguese identity. This drift towards nationalism, and its disregard of social and sexual differences within the Portuguese community, relies on the unifying concept of the *raça*.

Constituted as an independent monarchy in the twelfth century, Portugal is one of the oldest states in Europe. In the nineteenth century, the concept of the 'Portuguese race' was placed at the centre of Portuguese nationalism (with the language, territory, religion and certain historical events), notably by the republican Téofilo Braga. The myth of a Lusitanian race—linked to the Lusitanians whose chief

---

[44] Carlos da Fonseca, "Emigration et rhétorique impériale", *Migrances*, 15 (1999), 22-31.

[45] The current interest shown by Portuguese descendants in the promotion of the Portuguese language, which coincides with the decline in funds sent by Portuguese residents, remains suspect. Moreover, Ex-President Mário Soares, is considered to have encouraged Portuguese residents not to return to Portugal, with the exception of the most qualified. See Pingault.

[46] The brand defines itself as follows on its official blog: "[L]e premier concept mondial qui met en valeur sa communauté à travers une marque 100% Portugaise. Fournisseur PORTUGAIS, Banque PORTUGAISE, Designer PORTUGAIS." See http://www.viportuguese.com.

[47] 'One nation, one people, one selection' ('selection' referring to the national football team).

Viriathe resisted the Roman occupation from 147 to 60 BCE—goes back to the fifteenth century. The idea of a glorious Portuguese destiny linked to the 'Discoveries' dates to the sixteenth and seventeenth centuries, with the publication in 1572 of a collection of poems, *Les Luisades* by Luis de Camoens.[48] Drawing on superior Portuguese values linked to a mythical reinterpretation of the history of Portugal, the concept of the 'Portuguese race' is later taken up by the Salazarist dictatorship in an assertion against other European nations and as a justification of its colonial empire (the oldest and longest). Salazar declared 10 June, the date of the national holiday, the Festival both of the Portuguese race and of de Camoens, who died on 10 June 1580. The day was renamed, after the revolution of 25 April 1974, the 'Day of de Camoens, Portugal and the Communities'.

The concept of 'race' appears in the work of La Harissa, who define themselves as the 'voice of the sons of the nation'. In the song 'Nossa Raça' the chorus is unequivocal: "Portugal é nossa terra/ A mais bela com certeza/ Vamos là cantar com força/ Nossa raça é portuguesa [Portugal is our land/ Without a doubt the most beautiful/ Sing with force/ Our race is Portuguese]". The group situates itself in opposition to the French: "je n'oublie pas mes origines, ma culture, mon pays [...] 100% portugais je le suis et resterai/ Et j'en suis fier pour rien au monde je le changerai [...] / Il faut qu'on se serre les coudes/ Leur montrer qu'on est fier d'être portugais/ Toi-même tu sais qu'on est tous frères." The use of this concept, with its links to Salazarism and colonialism, is perverse in light of the group's criticism of the dictatorship that forced the Portuguese into exile and their celebration of the Carnation Revolution in the song '25 April'. It is even more so when one considers their call for a new revolution: "J'entends encore la foule qui dans la rue criait: *Revolução*/ Le prix que le peuple paye encore: *Liberdade* / Rien n'est terminé t'entends: *Revolução*." Some of the blogs, in line with this, call themselves 'povo lusitano' [Lusitanian people] or quote La Harissa and its concept of race directly in their introductory presentation or in a note.[49]

---

[48] José Manuel. Sobral, "De Casa a Nação: Passado, Memória, Identidade". Available online at: http://ceas.iscte.pt/etnografica/docs/vol_03/N1/Vol_iii_N1_71-86.pdf.
[49] See, for example, http://pikatchu602.skyrock.com/ and http://sportinguista92.-skyrock.com/2.html.

Finally, as with Chicano nationalism, Portuguese descendants' blogs praise the conservative values of the family, which are linked to Catholicism and to the Salazarist heritage. Maria Filomena Mónica has shown that Salazar, wanting to keep the Portuguese people in ignorance (those very people who would swell the number of the ex-patriots), reinforced the teaching of the Catholic religion in state schools. Key values, which for him were not up for discussion, were: God, the Homeland, the family and authority. The cult of the family and of patriarchy, linked to nationalist and fascist ideology, is visible in the organisation of Portuguese cultural organisations and the blogs. The photos and praise given to the family indicate the importance of group values. De La Barre shows that fraternity and the family are the values most often cited by the youths who identify as Portuguese. La Harissa also pays homage to Portuguese families, especially fathers, in 'A tous les papas portos'. This patriarchal ideology of the family is rarely called into question in the blogs, while it is at the root of family crises, as Serge Gordey shows in his documentary *Les Portugaises d'origine* (1984).[50]

La France aux Portugais

While the majority of the blogs are not anti-French,[51] some blogs are more nationalist than others, proclaiming the need for a choice between Portugal and France and Portuguese superiority. For example, a note entitled 'Portugal ou France' is accompanied by a photomontage of Portugal *versus* France and the text: "sa c un tages ke g fait/ alors dite moi vous preferer koi/ les portugais ou les francais/ perso moi c plutot le Portugal."[52] Another nationalist blog addresses itself exclusively to Portuguese readers. A photomontage with a no entry sign reads "interdit aux francais", while a note shows the map of France and Portugal with the text: "ou que l'on soit... quoi que l'on fasse... Le Portugal restera notre pays." Finally, a photomontage inviting readers to choose between France and Portugal receives pro-Portuguese

---

[50] Serge Gorday, *Les Portugaises d'origine*, Collectif Centopeia.

[51] The affirmation of Portuguese identity can be felt as nationalist: 'sur tou le blog je n'ai ke 1 truc a dire c O CHIOTE LE PORTUGALEEEEEE' (Florian). See the comments at http://vive-o-portugal.skyrock.com/5.html.

[52] See http://mi-portugais.skyrock.com/4.html.

comments, including a minority that are anti-French: "portugal la france ses 2 la merde."[53] The numerous photomontages inviting readers to leave comments in support of Portugal ("ceux qui aiment le Portugal dîtes le ici!!! Viva Portugal!! [Si Tu kiFfF le PoRtUg; dit le dans les com'S]")[54] only contain a few anti-French comments linked to the 2006 World Cup. In fact, nationalist blogs are most often rejected by readers, particularly those that make territorial claims.

A digital photo of graffiti reading 'La France aux Portugais' (see fig. 5), which rewrites the slogan of the extreme right 'La France aux Français', illustrates the number of Portuguese in France:

Figure 5

This nationalist note, with its territorial claim, troubles the apparent harmony of the group. Following on from messages of support ("Ué la France aux portugais, apres tout on la bien merité!!' [Ze-pekenia]") are messages varying in their hostility:

---

[53] See http://amour-portugais.skyrock.com/2.html and http://amour-portugais.-skyrock.com/5.html.
[54] See http://portugal-1719.skyrock.com/2.html.

'la france a l'algerie car nous on les a niqué en 1962 et oui' (hamza), 'je suis moitié française moitié portuguaise et je suis pas d'accord...le portugal reste le portugal et la france reste la france point final ... vive le portugal et vive la france.' (soso3786), 'mais putin on croirai lire un article d'un arabe raciste envers les français ! jsuis portugaise et jte di un truc FERME TA GUEULE! on a envahit la France ... pfff retourne chez toi si c'est pour dire sa! Quand on vit en France on doit se considéré comme français (jte demande pas de regnié t origines)! Et c'est à cause de gens comme toi ke le patriotisme en France meurt à petits feux.' (suck), 'Moi je suis Italien et je suis français avant tout. Vive la france, la France n'appartiendra jamais au portugais rêves pas lol mdr,' 'moi je suis francaise et bien francaise!!!! tauras jamais la france reve pas!!!!!!!!!!!!!!!!!!' (elodie)

Some oppositional voices appear, then, in the comments but are also in the minority in blogs such as 'Miki-le-toss'.

The blog 'Miki-le-toss', created by a teenager of Portuguese descent, is in the minority in its self-mockery and ironic vision of the *tos* community. It illuminates the sexist and reactionary tendencies of this community and draws a caricatural physical description of a *tos*. This playful depiction refers to the stereotype of Portuguese hirsuteness, the fashion sense of young Portuguese and the American influence. Every note starts with the phrase 'Parce que c'est un toss...' and, through photomontages and amusing texts in a mix of French and Portuguese, evokes the stereotypical life of Miki-le-toss, a working-class macho of Portuguese descent. The episodes of his life include: exclusion from French clubs and frequenting Portuguese ones; a taste for mechanics inherited from his father; sexism; a passion for football ('préfère Cristiano Ronaldo... à sa meuf'); affirmation of identity on the blogs (**"Parce que c'est un PortoSs, MIKI** représente le **bled** dans son Skyblog..."); a taste for French popular television; annual holidays in Portugal ("Parce que c'est un immigré, MIKI **aime** retrouver ses potes **du bled** *chaque année...* **Comme lui, ils habitent en France et attendent** avec impatience le mois d'août..."); folklore; ethnic fashion; family in Portugal ("aime retrouver **seus Abòs** [les grands-parents]... il les kiff"); family in general (**"aime plus que tout** sa familiazinha. **Même sa reum** qui le *saoul* souvent"); a taste for Portuguese food; social origin (son of Portuguese caretakers in Paris); the reprimands of the father who works on a building site; religion (mass on a Sunday). At the same time as it enumerates certain characteristics of the Portuguese community in France in this comic register (a comedy predicated on the recognition of the socio-cultural context and language which reinforce the sense of community), the blog criticises its conformism.

Figure 6

Another oppositional blog, 'foda-se',[55] is one of the few to explicitly disavow the notion of Portuguese 'community' and its commercial re-cuperation, notably by the manufacturers of ethnic fashion items:

> Le comble de tout ça c'est que les createurs de ses marques qui se revendiquent pleinement portugais ne sont même pas capable d'enchainer correctement un paragraphe en portugais ^^. Dans ce monde on est capable de tout pour se faire du blé.../ Vous qui portez ces marques 'tos,' vous expliquer que vous 'représenter' le Portugal mais ya d'autres moyens bien plus intelligents de 'représenter' sans forcement avoir besoin de porter ces t-shirts.

Conformism, essential in the construction of community, explains the lack of dissident voices in the blogs. Community cohesion is situated within the context of a xenophobia that reinforces ethnic solidarity. Anthony Smith has shown how the modern theorists of the nation, by concentrating on the elite, have not explained how nationalism can

---

[55] A Portuguese insult. See http://www.foda-se.skyrock.com.

exercise such a fascination among popular classes.[56] In the case of Portuguese descendants, the claim to an identity and to a 'special' dignity is fundamental.[57] In fact, if they are not nationalist per se, these blogs certainly belong to a movement reclaiming the memory and history of the Portuguese community in France. The blogs sometimes take a pedagogical approach and evoke, often clumsily, the history of Portugal, parents and Portuguese descendants.

Allusions to anti-Portuguese racism are ubiquitous in the blogs. Bloggers often warn their readers that any racist comment will be deleted: "Ce blog est consacré au PORTUGAL, les PORTUGAIS et tout ce ki concerne le PORTUGAL! Mes tes com et pour les rageux c'est en haut à droite Ok ! Merci..." "Enfin un blog spécial portugal!!!!!!!... pas de commentaire raciste etc!!!". A sense of marginalisation—segregation at work and in the school—is also mentioned in the blogs. As La Harissa put it in 'A tous les papas portos': "Quand tu t'appelles Da Silva ton ascension au niveau le plus haut est semé d'embûche... 10/20 de moyenne générale insuffisant Mr Sanchez ça vous dit l'approche du bâtiment... ici on tape dans le bâtiment on fait la relève de nos papas personne se plaint c'est comme ça la vie".

For Linda Alcoff, far from being strategies designed to threaten social harmony, ethnic identities have a history in realism: "A group's general position in the labor market, along with its specific historical experience [...] reinforces the salience of group identity in everyday life."[58] In this way, some notes reject Portuguese stereotypes and indifference or ignorance by adopting a didactic tone in order to present the history of Portugal and its culture. The bloggers use traditional maps, tourist or personal photos of the *bled*. They adopt conventional historical discourse or stereotypes of the 'ser Tuga é... ['to be Portuguese is...]' kind.[59] Some blogs evoke the difficult history of parents' migrations. They critically tackle the colonial wars in Africa and Salazarism and demand social recognition for their parents in

---

[56] Anthony Smith, "National Identity and the Idea of European Unity", *International Affairs*, 68:1 (1992), 55-76.
[57] Smith, pp. 63-70.
[58] Linda Alcoff, "Against Post-Ethnic Futures", *The Journal of Speculative Philosophy*, 18:2 (2004), 99-117.
[59] See http://meu-portugal.skyrock.com and http://portugais-loveur.skyrock.com.

France and in Portugal. A good example is this photomontage of the 'diplôme du portugais immigré':

Figure 7

Many blogs evoke with humour the particular language of the French Portuguese (spoken by parents and certain Portuguese descendants) with its mix of French and Portuguese (similar to the mix of English and Spanish spoken by some Chicanos):

> Tous les portugais, ont dans leurs famille, que ce soit leur mères, leur grand-mères, grand-pères, oncles..... quelqu'un qui fait un remix Français-portugais ! Qui s'embrouillent avec les 2 langues, et c'est trop marrant, ca donne des phrases qui veulent rien dire, ca me fait déliré! Lol /-Arrete de me chatiar = Arrete de m'embeter .../ -Ma qu'est que cé ce bourdel = Qu'est ce que c'est que ce bordel/ -Abre o frigo = Ouvre le frigo/ -Va comprar uma baguette = Va acheter une baguette/ -Quem é o counard que toque a la sounette à esta hora. Quel est le connard qui sonne à la sonnette à cette heure .../ -Tou minerve = Tu ménèrve.[60]

---

[60] See http://lindo-portugal.skyrock.com/17.html. The blog 'foda-se' calls this language *françiou* or *portuguesh*.

Equally, the blogs call for an ethnocultural contribution by Portuguese in France.[61] The blog 'foda-se', written by a teenager from Clermont-Ferrand, lists Portuguese shops, businesses and bands (notably a Portugo-Auvergnat rock group).[62] The history of France is also revisited in order to valorise Portuguese participation. For example, the photo of the name of an avenue in the sixteenth arrondissement of Paris, 'Avenue des Portugais', recalls the role played by the Portuguese in the First World War: "ah ca c une vré rue, elle represente celle la c BIEN!!!! C le moyen pour les portugai de se sentir + a laise en france lol, on se sen mieu qd mm, un peu com a la maison avc cette avenue! ms c qd mm mieu la baixo!!"[63] These blogs also contribute, in their own way, to a call for the memorialisation of Portuguese people in France, inspired by Portuguese organisations such as 'Memória Viva/Mémoire Vive' founded in 2003.[64]

Through their blogs, young people of Portuguese descent announce and construct a *tos* ethnic identity. First appearing at the beginning of the 1980s, this identitarian discourse is now more radical, thanks to the construction of Europe, a certain opening up of France and the rise of xenophobia. For historian Emmanuel Todd, interviewed in *L'Humanité*, "[o]ur society is becoming radicalized".[65] This *tos* identity is in a process of constant construction, both in the real and virtual worlds, and, despite the risk of political or economic recuperation, seems to reflect a necessary step in the construction of identity for young Portuguese descendants. In most cases, far from being 'models of integration' (failure at school, low-status work, the 'return' to Portugal), Portuguese descendants are preoccupied by their place in France and never refer to European identity in their blogs,

---

[61] See Cordeiro.

[62] See also the 'Lusopages', a Lusophone directory in France: http://www.-lusopages.com.

[63] *La baixo*, or 'down there', means the South in Portuguese. See http://www.-portugal-amo.skyrock.com/29.html. The blogger is not always aware of the reason for this street name. See the edition of 4 April 2007 of *Lusojournal*, one of the free newspapers for Portuguese in France (http://www.lusojournal.com) for an evocation of the commemoration ceremonies at Richebourg (where 1800 Portuguese soldiers are buried) and at La Couture.

[64] See http://www.sudexpress.org/.

[65] J-E. Ducoin, "Emmanuel Todd: notre société se radicalise", *L'Humanité*, 5 April 2007.

even if it is their double European belonging which facilitates their assertion of themselves as *Tos*. Critics like Anthony Smith have been led to question what it means to be European, and whether Europe might not be conceived of as the sum of its constituent nationalities and communities. Such is the case for Portuguese descendants. If the construction of a common European identity is to be welcomed, which remains to be seen, it will not be based on an assimilatory model of replacing national culture with a European one.[66] Indeed, what many European countries have in common is a dictatorial past, whether of the extreme left or right. As noted in *The Economist*, "[w]hen countries of 'Old Europe' were gung-ho to say governments should make a lot of noise about a common European culture, it was the young Hungarian culture minister who said, no, we shouldn't do that: propagating official culture was something the communists did."[67] This dictatorial and nationalist past is at the origin of the identity claims of numerous European ethnic minorities, and notably by the *Tos* in France.

And so we may well ask what genuine integration might really look like. First and foremost, integration requires a full education in both host and home culture. Indeed, for Phinney, an *integrated* identity is a strong ethnic identity (*tos*, in this case) allied with a strong national (French) identity.[68] It is the possibility of having a head of state from a working-class background called Maria da Silva or Mohammed Benguigui. Yet, for many of the upholders of 'integration', such a scenario remains unacceptable.

---

[66] Smith, p. 72.
[67] 'Charlemagne: Do as I Say or as I Do?', *The Economist*, 17 February 2007. p. 55.
[68] Phinney, p. 502.

Measuring Cultural Change in Contemporary France

The Natives Strike Back: *'L'Appel des Indigènes de la République'* and the Death of Republican Values in Postcolonial France

Kiran Grewal

Introduction

As the first modern nation state,[1] France has long prided itself on being a fully formed nation built on the principles of the 1789 revolution. French Republican values have allowed France to simultaneously assert a commitment to universalism—as *le pays des lumières* and the 'home of human rights'—and claim an exceptionality (*l'exception française*) which make foreign approaches (particularly Anglo-Saxon ones) to issues such as ethnic relations unacceptable. Moreover, traditionally this was also the approach taken by those seeking social change in France. Social justice movements in the past have generally attempted to use the language of 'Republican values' as the framework within which to situate their claims. Whether this took the form of Republican feminism or the *Beur* movement of the 1980s, the emphasis was on forcing the Republic to acknowledge and

---

[1] Rogers Brubaker *Citizenship and Nationhood in France and Germany* (Cambridge, Massachusetts: Harvard University Press, 1992), p. 35.

live up to the promises contained within its founding principles rather than a questioning of the principles themselves.

This has changed in recent years with the virtue of French Republicanism itself being challenged for the first time. Various events in the 1990s and early 2000s invoked suggestions that, rather than an aberration, certain forms of discrimination could in fact be linked to the founding myths on which French national identity had been constructed. With these suggestions, came calls for a radical overhaul of the very discourse of Republicanism. Furthermore, with the simultaneous problematization and ethnicization of the *banlieues* (poor housing estates on the outskirts of major cities) since the 1980s and the increased—and ever increasing—visibility of France's ethnically diverse citizenry, France's unresolved colonial legacy has emerged as an important site of contest.

In this context a new activist movement has made an important contribution to reopening and linking debates around race, gender and France's colonial history within the French public sphere. In January 2005 a group calling itself *le mouvement des indigènes de la République* (MIR) issued an online manifesto (appel) in which they declared "La France a été un État colonial… La France reste un État colonial!"[2] Since then, MIR and its sister organization, *les féministes indigènes* have created what up until the early 2000s had largely been missing from French public discourse: a postcolonial critique of French national identity, Republicanism and ethnic relations policies.

Sex and the Citizen

While this chapter will focus on ethnic relations in contemporary France, it is noteworthy that it is not only in terms of ethnicity that the concept of the abstract, universal citizen has come under attack. In the introduction to their collection of essays exploring new developments in French feminism, Roger Célestin, *et al.* identify an increased recognition within French feminist literature of the need to challenge the uncritical acceptance of the Republican myths of universalism and

---

[2] Mouvement des Indigènes de la République, "L'appel des indigènes de la République", 20 January 2005. Available at http://www.indigenes-republique.org/ (accessed 18 April 2009).

equality.[3] Both women's rights (centred around the *parité* movement) and gay rights activists (centred around the *Pacte civil de solidarité* or PaCS debate) in the 1990s sought to highlight that, far from being neutral, the abstract citizen was in fact a heterosexist and masculinist construction and in doing so opened up the possibility for questioning the very foundation of Republican values.

Documenting the seven-year *Parité* campaign Joan Scott explains:

> Unlike those earlier [feminist] movements, which took French republicanism to be immutable, the parité movement sought to change the terms of republicanism by addressing the very problem I thought was intractable: the problem of sexual difference [...] [S]ex had to be included in any conception of abstract individualism for genuine equality to prevail. The abstract individual, that neutral figure upon which universalism depended—without religion, occupation, social position, race, or ethnicity—had to be reconceived of as sexed. Here was the innovation: unlike previous feminisms, women were no longer being made to fit a neutral figure (historically imagined as male), nor were they reaching for separate incarnation of femininity; instead, the abstract individual itself was being refigured to accommodate women.[4]

While its ultimate effectiveness in redressing the sexually discriminatory culture of the French political sphere has been questioned,[5] the *parité* campaign in the 1990s can be seen to have made two important contributions to public discourse. Firstly, the *parité* movement reinvigorated debate about gender inequality in a period that had largely seen a decline in interest in the claims of feminism (in France and elsewhere). At the same time it highlighted a fundamental contradiction within the French Republican discourse of equality: as one of the founders of the *parité* movement, Claude Servan-Schreiber noted in an interview with the *New York Times*: "[e]xclusion of women has

---

[3] Roger Célestin et al. (eds), *Beyond French Feminisms: Debates on Women, Politics, and Culture in France, 1981 – 2001* (New York; Basingstoke: Palgrave MacMillan, 2003).

[4] Joan Scott, Parité! *Sexual equality and the crisis of French universalism* (Chicago; London: University of Chicago Press, 2005), p. 4.

[5] For a detailed review of the *parité* movement, the legislative changes and their subsequent impact on electoral trends see: Eléonore Lépinard, "Identity without Politics: Framing the Parity Laws and their Implementation in French Local Politics", *Social Politics: International Studies in Gender, State & Society*, 13.1 (2006), 30-58; and Danielle Haase-Dubosc, "Sexual Difference and Politics in France Today", *Feminist Studies*, 25.1 (1999), 183-210.

been part of France's political philosophy since the Revolution".[6]
While official French nationalist discourses took pride in the Revolutionary spirit of egalitarianism, the denial of full rights to women
including the right to vote until 1944 and the continued abysmal
record of women in public office served as a strong reminder of a less
exemplary history.

Unfortunately, while the *parité* movement started out with an
extremely radical agenda, as Joan Scott documents, it did to some
extent lose its revolutionary potential.[7] In this context she asserts that
it is unsurprising that the pro-*parité* philosopher (and wife of then
Prime Minister Lionel Jospin) Sylvaine Agacinski emerged as the
primary voice for the movement. While the early proponents of *parité*
sought a re-envisioning of French universalism, Agacinski relied on a
much more essentialist and less radical process of reasoning in her
support for the concept of *parité*: "Men and women, here much more
than elsewhere, have always sought to understand and to please each
other, and they have not been above borrowing from each other
qualities that might have been lacking in their own sex: a man with no
grace or a woman with no character would bore us".[8] In framing
parité in this way Agacinski actually used the movement to re-assert
l'exception française, distancing French gender relations from the
perceived 'battle of the sexes' model associated with the Anglo-Saxon
world and re-asserting hegemonic French discourses of gender and
nation. The outcome was a highly diluted re-imagining of both the
concept of Republican universalism and the abstract citizen:

> While *parité* wanted to *sex* the abstract individual as a means of *unsexing* the
> political body, Agacinski wanted to *sex* the political body, installing the
> heterosexual couple as the model of perfect complementarity. In this

---

[6] Cited in Scott (2005), p. 3-4.
[7] Scott (2005) argues that the PaCS debate of the late 1990s and particularly the
alleged threat to the institution of marriage and the family (and by implication the
nation) posed by full recognition of homosexual relationships played an important
role in reframing the debate. So too did the tactical need to distance the *parité* campaign from the stigma of Anglo-Saxon style "quota" or "affirmative action" policies
to avoid losing powerful supporters. Joan Scott, "Vive la difference!" in Célestin *et
al.*; and Éric Fassin, "The Purloined Gender: American Feminism in a French Mirror",
French Historical Studies, 22. 1 (1999), 113-138.
[8] Sylviane Agacinski, *Parity of the Sexes*, trans. Lisa Walsh, (New York: Columbia
University Press, 2001), p. 131-132.

essentialist view of things, *mixité* was not divisive or fracturing, she insisted, but unity, the unity exemplified by the reproductive couple merging to conceive a child.[9]

This approach served to de-legitimize or at least downplay other challenges and/or attempts to embody and demystify French universalism. As Éric Fassin writes in relation to the debate over same-sex marriage and PaCS:[10]

> In order to avoid the stigma of Americanization, the inventors of parité in politics were willing to say that it had nothing to do with (American-style) "quotas": women were no minority, since sexual difference was no ordinary difference, like class or ethnic differences; it was an essential, universal difference. This potentially essentialist argument served a strategic purpose: at first, it worked powerfully in the direction of equality—between men and women. But in the context of the debate surrounding gay and lesbian couples and families, it could also work, quite powerfully too, against equality—between heterosexuals and homosexuals.[11]

Not only did this less radical version of *parité* work to the disadvantage of gay and lesbian activists,[12] Agacinski's interpretation of Republican universalism also served to distance the *parité* movement from the claims that were emerging contemporaneously among France's growing ethnic minority population. In describing the only one essential, 'truly universal' difference to be that of sex, Agacinski instead sought to expressly dismiss other concerns, including those relating to ethnicity and religion as "muddying the waters".[13]

---

[9] Scott (2005), p. 119.

[10] *Pacte Civil de Solidarité* – the legal recognition of civil unions between heterosexual or homosexual couples, granting them similar rights as those previously only available to married couples.

[11] Éric Fassin, "The Politics of PaCS in the Transatlantic Mirror" in Célestin *et al.*, pp. 27-38 (p. 32).

[12] As Catherine Raissiguier documents it resulted in a number of significant amendments to the final version of the *PaCS* law, which reduced the rights same sex couples received: see Catherine Raissiguier, "The Sexual and Racial Politics of Civil Unions in France", *Radical History Review*, 83 (2002), 74-94.

[13] Sylviane Agacinski, "The Turning Point of Feminism" in Célestin *et al.*, pp. 17-22 (p. 18).

Race and the Republican Citizen

Even as dominant representatives of *parité* such as Agacinski sought
to distance their cause from issues relating to ethnicity in France, the
reality of French ethnic diversity was becoming increasingly difficult
to ignore. Describing an incident at *La Nuit des Césars*[14] in 2000 when
Cameroonian author Calixtha Beyala and Caribbean playwright Luc
Saint-Eloy interrupted the live broadcast to read a statement critiquing
the limited representation of ethnic minorities in French media,
Mireille Rosello writes: "the whole episode generated a French
discussion about a type of identity politics that theorizes ethnicity and
race as components of the Republican subject".[15] For a nation that had
constituted its identity on an abstract universalism this naming of
ethnic identity represented a major challenge. And yet the viability—
or even desirability—of a colour-blind Republic was being increasingly called into question.

The 1980s in France had seen the emergence of a strong anti-
racism movement, most particularly concentrated around the situation
of *Beurs*: second- and third-generation French residents of North
African heritage. In 1983 this movement had staged a nation-wide
march—dubbed *la marche des Beurs*—which had gained extensive
media and political attention, with the marchers received by then
President François Mitterrand at the Elysée Palace. For various
reasons (including close alliances between many of the leaders of the
movement and the *Parti Socialiste*) an essential characteristic of the
Beur movement had been its reliance on Republican principles as the
framework within which to situate its claims. And their efforts seemed
to meet with political will: there had been an initial flurry of political
activity in the Mitterrand years with special educational and social
programmes set up to address social exclusion.[16]

However, it had become increasingly evident over the course of
the next 20 years that the rhetoric of integration and equality was not

---

[14] The French equivalent of the American Oscars.
[15] Mireille Rosello, "New Gendered Mosaics: Their Mothers, the Gauls" in Céléstin *et
al.*, pp. 97-112 (p. 99).
[16] For a more detailed review of *Beur* activism in this period see Rachel Bloul, "From
Moral Protest to Religious Politics: Ethical Demands and Beur Political Action in
France" *Australian Journal of Anthropology*, 9.1 (1998), 11-30.

in fact delivering practical outcomes. While there had been a steady increase in the visibility of 'non-White' French public figures[17] and, as David McMurray noted in 1996, "a very high level of Arab content in all aspects of French popular culture",[18] *Beur* political activism had largely been replaced by disillusionment. Its leadership had been fragmented by political infighting. Many of its most educated and articulate members were now installed in bureaucratic or political positions, which challenged their allegiances,[19] while those the movement had sought to represent remained socially and economically disadvantaged in the increasingly stigmatized area of the *banlieue*. Sociologists Angelina Peralva and Eric Macé also note that ironically, while the *banlieue* was becoming increasingly problematized within French public discourse as the primary site of *'les violences urbaines'*,[20] the *Beur* movement had also served to reinforce the media linking of the *banlieue* with those French residents of (predominantly) North African background within the public imagination.[21]

In fact, there seemed to be an inherent paradox emerging: on the one hand, France's notion of civic citizenship sought to efface all forms of ethnic difference with the claim that "[i]n France, once

---

[17] From popular music (with the popularity of artists such as Khaled, Cheb Mami and MC Solaar) to sport (embodied in footballer and national hero Zinedine Zidane), literature (including popular and celebrated authors such as Calixtha Beyala, Azouz Begag, Tahar Ben Jelloun, and Assia Djebar, the first North African woman appointed to the *Académie Française*) to cinema (an example being the success of *banlieue* cinema, which provides a very multi-ethnic image of France), France's multi-ethnic reality has become increasingly difficult to ignore.

[18] David McMurray, "La France Arabe" in Alec Hargreaves and Mark Mckinney (eds), *Post-colonial Cultures in France* (London; New York: Routledge, 1997), p. 27.

[19] A recent example being anti-racism and feminist activist Fadela Amara who was selected by incoming president Nicolas Sarkozy for the position of junior minister on urban policy, a position which has resulted in her frequently being accused by the Left of having 'sold out' to personal ambition.

[20] 'Urban violence': the popular term used to describe urban unrest, criminality, delinquency and anti-sociality. As with many Western nations, there has been a focus in recent French media and public discourses on the perceived increase in *'les violences urbaines'* as the cause of general feelings of insecurity within French society.

[21] Angelina Peralva and Éric Macé, *Médias et violences urbaines: Débats politiques et constructions journalistiques* (Paris: La Documentation française, 2002), p. 19.

you're French, you're French and that's it",[22] and *communautarisme* presented as the antipathy of Republican national unity (*la République une et indivisible*). Yet on the other hand, it seemed the Republic itself was proving incapable of ignoring ethnic difference. While scholars within and outside of France documented high levels of cultural integration among second- and third-generation immigrants in France, particularly those of Maghrebin origin,[23] they continued to be disproportionately affected by unemployment and maintain a lower socio-economic status than their French counterparts.[24] Moreover, it was government institutions and policies that were failing them. As Friedrich Heckmann notes: "If [open policies towards naturalisation] and other aspects of general integration can be seen as a tendency toward the goal of 'integration' or acculturation, housing policy seems to totally run counter to this goal. It clearly leads to a marked pattern of segregation".[25] Similarly, Alec Hargreaves writes:

> [A] massive amount of research data has been produced during the last fifteen years by sociologists, political scientists and others showing that the second and third generation of minority ethnic groups [...] have overwhelmingly assimilated to the cultural norms dominant in France [...] In this respect, the

---

[22] Valérie Orlando, "From Rap to Raï in the Mixing Bowl: Beur Hip-Hop Culture and Banlieue Cinema in Urban France", *Journal of Popular Culture*, 36.3 (2003), 395-415 (398).

[23] Researchers have found that Muslim immigrant communities in France predominantly speak French, are open to inter-marriage, adhere to French cultural values and norms and have birth rates that increasingly mirror white French birth rates. Michèle Tribalat, Patrick Simon and Benoît Riandey, *De l'immigration à l'assimilation: enquête sur les populations d'origine étrangère en France* (Paris: La Découverte/INED, 1996); Michèle Tribalat, *Faire France. Une grande enquête sur les immigrés et leurs enfants* (Paris: La Découverte, 1995); Jonathan Laurence and Justin Vaisse, *Integrating Islam: Political and Religious Challenges in Contemporary France* (Washington D.C.: Brookings Institution Press, 2006).

[24] Cathy Lisa Schneider, "Police Power and Race Riots in Paris", *Politics & Society*, 36.1 (2008), 133-59 (137).

[25] Friedrich Heckmann, "Integration Policies in Europe: National Differences and/or Convergences?" *European Forum for Migration Studies*, Paper 33 (1999), p. 11. Available at http://web.uni-bamberg.de/ba6ef3/pdf/efms_p33.pdf (accessed 15 November 2006).

French model of integration has been highly successful. Its failures have been in social and economic policy.[26]

Even dedicated Republican feminist (and member of the Sarkozy government) Fadela Amara notes in her book, *Ni Putes Ni Soumises* the contradiction between her clear cultural affiliation with France and her identification in the key institution of the Republic, her primary school, as an *étrangère*:

> [C]'est dans le creuset de la République—l'école de mon enfance—, que j'ai véritablement senti pour la première fois que j'étais une étrangère, le jour où une institutrice voulant recenser les élèves étrangers, et pensant certainement bien faire, m'a demandé de lever la main. Et pourtant, selon la loi issue des accords d'Évian, j'avais la nationalité française.[27]

While Amara's own organization, *Ni Putes Ni Soumises* has remained (problematically) faithful to the language of French Republicanism even in light of this observation (discussed further below), the disconnect between the language of integration and the reality of racial/ethnic division in France was becoming increasingly difficult to ignore, a matter attested to by the mass riots which engulfed France for three weeks in late 2005.[28]

The 2005 Riots and *Les Territoires perdus de la République*

In November 2005, following the death of two young boys—one of Tunisian and one of Malian origin—who had been electrocuted while attempting to flee from police, riots erupted in *banlieues* across France. What followed was a period of intense political, media and public debate about the problematic situation of the French *banlieues*. The debate was not new but in fact reflected a culmination of many years of problematization.

---

[26] Alec G. Hargreaves, "An Emperor with No Clothes?", *Social Sciences Research Council Web Forum*, 28 November 2005. Available at http://riotsfrance.ssrc.org (accessed 16 April 2009).

[27] Fadela Amara, *Ni Putes Ni Soumises* (Paris: Éditions La Découverte, 2003), p. 19.

[28] For more on these riots and their aftermath see the contributions made by prominent researchers on contemporary French society to the Social Sciences Research Centre (SSRC) web forum available at http://riotsfrance.ssrc.org (accessed 16 April 2009).

The *banlieue* had historically been a zone on the periphery; firstly separating the working classes and poor from bourgeois intra-muros society and later a zone of immigration.[29] While the association of the *banlieue* with juvenile delinquency in media and academic discourse had been present since the 1960s,[30] there has been something of a consensus among academics that it was the 'hot summer of the Minguettes' *('Été Chaud des Minguettes')* that crystallized the stigmatization of the *banlieue* within media discourse.[31] 'The hot summer of the Minguettes' was in fact a series of uprisings which took place on the Minguettes housing estate on the outskirts of Lyon in the summer of 1981. This uprising was most notably marked by the images of cars set on fire by protesters.

Also at this time, the image became ethnicized. As Christian Rinaudo writes: "Lors de 'l'été chaud des Minguettes', les médias décrivent un univers ethnicisé dans lequel l'image de l'immigré se superpose à celle du jeune voyou".[32] Rinaudo goes on to quote from an article in the *Nouvel Observateur*,[33] which describes the *banlieue* of Lyon as "un repaire de jeunes Arabes en colère, chômeurs et plus ou moins délinquants".[34] The ethnicized and problematized world of the 'hot summer of the Minguettes' has remained in the French popular imaginary and has frequently been invoked subsequently in response to instances of urban unrest. As French sociologist Véronique de Rudder pointed out in an interview in 2002, "les jeunes impliqués dans les révoltes urbaines ne sont pas tous d'origine étrangère, mais fantasmatiquement, on ne voit que des jeunes basanés".[35] In this context, the 2005 riots presented what seemed to be yet another parallel to

---

[29] Henri Rey, *La Peur des Banlieues* (Paris: La bibliothèque du citoyen, Presses de la fondation nationale des sciences politiques, 1996).

[30] Guy Lochard, "La 'question de la banlieue' à la télévision française" in Marilia Amorim (ed), *Images et discours sur la banlieue* (Ramonville: Éditions érès, 2002), pp. 31-42 (p. 34).

[31] Lochard, p. 37; Christian Rinaudo, *L'Ethnicite dans la Cité : Jeux et enjeux de la catégorisation ethnique* (Paris; Montreal: L'Harmattan, 1999), p. 30; Macé and Peralva, p. 18.

[32] Rinaudo, p. 30.

[33] A respected, national mainstream magazine of the Left.

[34] Rinaudo, p. 31.

[35] Gérard Baudin and Philippe Genestier (eds), *Banlieues à Problèmes : La Construction d'un problème social et d'un thème d'action publique* (Paris: La documentation Française, 2002), p. 114.

the 'hot summer of the Minguettes': the same ethnically different young men[36] portrayed once again angry, unemployed and burning cars. Except this time it had resulted in the most intense period of civil unrest in France in nearly forty years.[37] And it had happened more than twenty years after these initial uprisings.

So where was the Republic going wrong? Cathy Lisa Schneider notes in her analysis of the riots that even as those within the community of Clichy (the Parisian suburb where the boys died) pointed to the ongoing problem of police brutality and racism as the initial cause of the riots, this issue was quickly subsumed by other discourses. Some right-wing political and public figures did draw links between the riots and the supposed 'cultural incompatibility' of certain immigrant communities. For example, a number of right-wing politicians, including the Acting Minister of Employment, Gérard Larcher, openly asserted that the practice of polygamy had contributed to the riots.[38] Other public commentators asserted a connection between the riots and Islam or the "dysfunctional sexuality of Muslim youths".[39]

However, while outrageous, these crude conflations of socio-economic factors with cultural and religious practices were generally rejected by the authorities. Hargreaves, writing immediately after the riots, remarked that, while in the past politicians had tended to blame the failure of integration policies on the unwillingness of ethnic minorities to adapt their Islamic beliefs, "senior officials have on this occasion paid closer attention to what is actually happening on the streets of the *banlieues*"; he went on to note: "[t]he public prosecutor in Paris, Yves Bot, Prime Minister Dominique de Villepin and most sections of the French media including right-of-center newspapers such as *Le Figaro*, have all stated firmly that Islamic organizations played no role in provoking the riots".[40] Instead, many journalists and public officials alike, including then Minister for the Interior (now President) Nicolas Sarkozy, drew on the image of the "lost *banlieues*

---

[36] Although this time not only North African but also Black. See Schneider.
[37] Alec G. Hargreaves, "*Indigènes*: A Sign of the Times", *Research in African Literatures*, 38.4 (2007), 204-216 (209).
[38] He even proposed new legislation banning what was already a prohibited practice, which then Prime Minister Dominique de Villepin signed (Schneider, p. 136).
[39] Schneider, p. 136; see also Hargreaves (2005).
[40] Hargreaves (2005).

of the Republic",[41] sites where Republican values needed to be reinstated, by force if necessary.[42] Thus, while unemployment, socio-economic marginalization of *banlieue* residents and ethnic discrimination were all recognized as key issues which needed to be addressed, Republican values were once again presented as the solution. Yet, while the *Beur* movement had largely adhered to this framework without challenge in the past, the climate in 2005 suggested that resorting to the mythical virtue of Republicanism would not be sufficient this time.

Confronting the Past: The Ghosts of Colonialism

Although much of the enthusiastic *Beur* activism of the 1980s had withered, the early 2000s had marked a renewed period of pressure on France to confront its colonial past. In particular, with the Algerians identified as the most 'problematic' immigrant community in France,[43] there had been pressure for France to deal with the most sensitive of its colonial legacies: the Algerian War. In his 2002 book, leading Algerian war historian Benjamin Stora commented that "[t]he more the Algerian War fades away, the more this repressed history haunts French society".[44] On the one hand, public debate on the French use of torture in the Algerian War, most notably instigated by the confessions of former military chief of Algiers, General Jacques Massu and General Paul Aussaresses in 2001 led to some of the first official recognitions of the human rights violations committed by the

---

[41] Frédéric Viguier, "The Lost *Banlieues* of the Republic?", *French Politics, Culture and Society*, 24.3 (2006), 1-4.

[42] The most infamous example of this discourse being Sarkozy's controversial statement that he intended to "nettoyer au Kärcher" the "racaille" of the *banlieue*. See Philippe Ridet's article, "Nicholas Sarkozy droitise son discours pour attirer l'électorat du FN", *Le Monde*, 23 June 2005, p.8.

[43] See Alec Hargreaves, Immigration, 'Race' and Ethnicity in *Contemporary France* (London: Routledge, 1995), pp. 152-59; Benjamin Stora, *Le transfert d'une mémoire: De l'"Algérie française" au racisme anti-arabe* (Paris: La Découverte, 1999) and *Histoire de la Guerre d'Algérie* (Paris: La Découverte, 2002); Richard L. Derderian, "Algeria as a lieu de mémoire: Ethnic Minority Memory and National Identity in Contemporary France", *Radical History Review*, 83 (2002), 28-43; and Jennifer Howell, "Reconstituting Cultural Memory through Image and Text in Leïla Sebbar's Le Chinois vert d'Afrique", *French Cultural Studies*, 19.1 (2008), 57-70.

[44] Stora (2002), p. 20.

French army during the war.[45] On the other hand, there had been political attempts to re-assert a 'positive' side to the French colonial enterprise, most particularly in the form of the controversial *Loi française n° 2005-158 du 23 février 2005 portant reconnaissance de la Nation et contribution nationale en faveur des Français rapatriés.*[46]

In his response to the riots, French sociologist Stéphane Dufoix pointed to a number of events in 2005—including MIR's *appel* and the controversy surrounding the 23 February law—in which the inter-related issues of French colonial history and contemporary race relations were reintroduced into French public discourse. This led him to remark that "[t]he issue of the state recognizing historical traumas and discriminations is not new. Yet it has shown some very interesting developments in the last year and a half".[47] These public responses were to be contrasted with those of the state. As Hargreaves comments, while there had been renewed efforts by French authorities to address the issues being raised again during the riots, notably the social, economic and racial discrimination many residents of immigrant origin continued to experience, "there was a growing danger that, in its dance of the seven veils, the Republic would be perceived to be an Emperor with no clothes, unable or unwilling to redress discriminatory practices which sometimes emanated from agents of the Republic itself".[48] It seemed the official, uncritical and timeless resort to Republican rhetoric was no longer going to be accepted as a sufficient response.

In the year following the riots, another major event sparked further debate about France's colonial past. A film titled, *Indigènes*

---

[45] Following a campaign by human rights organizations *la ligue des Droits de l'Homme* and Human Rights Watch, Aussaresses was indicted on charges of 'apologizing for war crimes' and 'torture'. He was convicted of the former but found to be covered by an amnesty for the latter by the *Cour de Cassation*.

[46] Article 4 of which stated: "Les programmes scolaires reconnaissent en particulier le rôle positif de la présence française outre-mer, notamment en Afrique du Nord, et accordent à l'histoire et aux sacrifices des combattants de l'armée française issus de ces territoires la place éminente à laquelle ils ont droit." This law was subsequently repealed in January 2006 due to intense public pressure (see Howell, p. 59).

[47] Stéphane Dufoix, "More than Riots: A Question of Spheres", *Social Sciences Research Council Web Forum*, 28 November 2005. Available at http://riotsfrance-.ssrc.org (accessed 16 April 2009).

[48] Hargreaves (2005).

emerged as a surprise hit both within France and internationally.[49] Not only was it made by French-Algerian director Rachid Bouchareb with a substantial budget[50] and featured *Beur* actors in the four main roles, it also painted a less than glorious picture of France's treatment of the colonial soldiers during World War Two. By depicting the role played by colonial soldiers in the liberation of France from Nazi occupation, and the racism they encountered along the way, the film presented a provocative postcolonial commentary on the idealized French Republic of traditional nationalist discourses. It simultaneously demonstrated the injustice experienced by colonial soldiers who faced discrimination both during and after the war (when they were denied equal pensions with their French counterparts) and highlighted the important national contribution that had been made by the forefathers of the very population most resented in contemporary France, the North Africans.

As an indicator of the reaction the film provoked, the government announcement of a long-lobbied for change in policy on colonial war veterans' pensions coincided with the release of *Indigènes,* leading to a suggestion that it was in fact the film that had prompted this official change of heart.[51] *Indigènes* also undoubtedly contributed to the ongoing discussion about the relationship between the French colonial enterprise and the fraught nature of contemporary French ethnic relations. This was a discussion another recent initiative was eagerly promoting and, thanks to the overlap in the name (*indigènes),* the film provided publicity for the movement which had emerged in early 2005 seeking a radical revision of the Republic's simultaneous colonial and postcolonial status.

---

[49] It was a box office success, won Jamel Debbouze the award of Best Male Actor at the Cannes Film Festival in 2006 and was nominated for an American Academy Award in 2007 in the category of best foreign film.

[50] Hargreaves writes that Bouchareb was able to raise a production budget of almost EUR 15 million, a substantial amount by French standards and reflective of what Hargreaves describes as, "a sea change in the status of minority ethnic artists" (2007, p. 205-06).

[51] Hargreaves (2007), p. 204.

Developing a 'Postcolonial Anticolonialism': *Le Mouvement des indigènes de la République*

As noted above, MIR emerged as a movement in early 2005 with the publishing of an online *appel*. While academics, politicians and journalists continued to debate the extent to which the *malaise* in the *banlieues* could be remedied by the restoration of Republican order, MIR's agenda left little doubt where it stood on the rhetoric of Republicanism:

> La décolonisation de la République reste à l'ordre du jour ! La République de l'Égalité est un mythe. L'État et la société doivent opérer un retour critique radical sur leur passé-présent colonial. Il est temps que la France interroge ses Lumières, que l'universalisme égalitaire, affirmé pendant la Révolution Française, refoule ce nationalisme arc-bouté au "chauvinisme de l'universel", censé "civiliser" sauvages et sauvageons. Il est urgent de promouvoir des mesures radicales de justice et d'égalité qui mettent un terme aux discriminations racistes dans l'accès au travail, au logement, à la culture et à la citoyenneté. Il faut en finir avec les institutions qui ramènent les populations issues de la colonisation à un statut de sous-humanité.[52]

This express rejection of *les Lumières* and the reference to the ongoing significance of France's colonial past was in sharp contrast to the *Beur* movement's appeal to Republican values to counter the racism and social exclusion they experienced. Moreover, rather than seeking to assert their rights as French citizens like any other, MIR seemed to be going out of its way to stress difference. They had adopted a label—*indigènes*—which had in fact been a pejorative term used during colonial times to refer to colonized populations. So too in their slogan, *va t'faire intégrer !* they had made a play on the common insult *va t'faire foutre* and turned it into an outright rejection of the policy of integration.

While MIR were not the first to point to the inherently problematic language of integration,[53] by adopting this provocative slogan and choosing to identify themselves as *indigènes* they openly

---

[52] Mouvement des Indigènes de la République (2005).

[53] The North African sociologist and writer Azouz Begag had already pointed to the underlying implication contained within integration that it was the insufficient efforts of ethnic minorities that explained its failure. This had led to him being appointed as 'Minister for Equal Opportunities' in June 2005, a position from which he subsequently resigned in April 2007.

confronted a fundamental paradox that had long been present within the French public discourse. As *porte-parole* for the movement, Houria Bouteldja exclaimed in an interview:

> [I]ssu de l'immigration', ça suffit, ça fait quatre générations et on est toujours 'issus' de l'immigration […] [L]a réalité, c'est qu'on ne sera jamais français, puisque être français, c'est appartenir à une espèce de caste. C'est une espèce d'honneur et n'est pas français qui veut. Et comme l'a très bien dit Le Pen, être français, ça se mérite! C'est Le Pen qui le dit mais c'est toute la société qui le pense. Nous, on ne peut pas y prétendre parce qu'on est trop basanés et on ne sera jamais assez blancs pour être français, quoi qu'on dise et quoi qu'on fasse. Donc on est systématiquement obligés de faire nos preuves qu'on est bien civilisés, qu'on mérite d'être français, etc. etc.[54]

While in theory they were all French citizens, the reality was that a distinction was all too often drawn between *les Français de souche* and *les étrangers*, based purely on ethnic difference. This had sometimes taken the form of the qualifier 'of immigrant origin' described by Bouteldja, which is applied regardless of how many generations of integration into French society the individual may have had. Other times French citizens had simply been identified as *étranger*, regardless of their citizenship status, as Fadela Amara's school experience discussed above demonstrates.[55] While up until this point this reality had simply led to further resort to the language of Republican universalism and egalitarianism (including by Amara herself), MIR represented a radical shift by simply refusing to engage with this traditional rhetoric:

> Rien n'y fera et on peut avoir toutes les cartes nationales qu'on pourra, on aura toujours un corps, un visage qui nous stigmatisera, et cela parce que la Nation française est ethnique. Elle est ethnique. Donc, tant qu'on ne reviendra pas de manière radicale sur ce qu'est la Nation et tant que la Nation et la République ne seront pas redéfinies, ça ne sert à rien pour nous de nous prétendre français.[56]

By asserting that the Republic was in fact an ethnic nation Bouteldja was challenging the very foundation of French national discourses on

---

[54] Chiara Bonfiglioli, "Entretien avec Houria Bouteldja, porte-parole du Mouvement des indigènes de la république", 10 December 2006. Available at http://www-.indigenes-republique.org/spip.php?article599 (accessed 27 June 2007).

[55] See also Hargreaves (1995), p. 32.

[56] Bonfiglioli.

citizenship. Since the time of the First Republic, France had distinguished itself from other nations (such as Germany) by adopting a *jus soli* approach to citizenship. With the heavy investment in the Republican education system, it had always been official rhetoric that French citizens could be created through the fostering of shared cultural values. And yet, as discussed above, the reality for many non-white French citizens had proved otherwise. So why keep turning to Republican values, MIR asked, when regardless of the extent of cultural adherence, they would still always be treated as outsiders?

Instead MIR has sought to confront its 'otherness' head on. Bouteldja has emerged as something of a public figure in recent times in France, doing many radio and television interviews. In each she has openly asserted her identity as Algerian *and* French but Algerian first and foremost. Further, while many *Beur* activists have been at pains to stress their commitment to secularism, Bouteldja has openly called herself a Muslim. This is significant not because of Bouteldja's personal religious conviction but the fact that the descriptor 'Muslim' has a specific ideological meaning in France. As MIR point out, the term 'Muslim' has been used as a conflated ethnic, religious and political label that has all too often been invoked—both during colonial times and in contemporary France—as a justification for exclusion or marginalization.

During the colonial period, the Muslim beliefs of colonized peoples justified their denial of French citizenship rights,[57] while in contemporary French discourses the construction of 'hereditary Muslims' has justified the claim that certain immigrant (generally North African) populations are simply un-integratable into French society.[58] Some prominent *Beur* figures have found themselves caught between their own personal lack of religious affiliation and their presentation in dominant public discourse as 'Muslim representatives'.

---

[57] While Jewish Algerians were granted full citizenship in 1870 under the Crémieux Decree, *Décret n° 136, 24 October 1870*, Muslim Algerians retained the status of "subjects" and were required to apply to be 'naturalised' upon demonstrating a "French way of life": Patrick Weil, "Le statut des musulmans en Algérie coloniale: une nationalité française dénaturée" *EUI Working Paper* HEC No. 2003/3, European University Institute Florence, Department of History and Civilisation, pp. 6-7.

[58] Jim House, "Muslim Communities in France" in Gerd Nonneman, Tim Niblock and Bogdan Szajkowski (eds), *Muslim Communities in the New Europe* (Reading, Berkshire: Ithaca Press, 1996), pp. 219-235 (p. 224).

This has particularly been the case with young *Beur* women whose statements against the patriarchal and sometimes abusive environments within which they have been raised has all too easily conformed to the dominant French understanding of Islam as an inherently misogynistic and barbaric religion.[59]

In this context Bouteldja's open declaration of herself as a Muslim (irrespective of the extent of her faith) provides a powerful counter-discourse. For one, her status as an independent, articulate and assertive woman rebuts the traditional presumption within mainstream French discourses that Muslim women are downtrodden, passive victims of their culture. Additionally, she reclaims an aspect of her identity that has frequently been deployed in dominant French discourses as part of the process of 'Othering' those of North African origin. If she is to be constructed as 'always already Muslim' by virtue of her ethnic origin, why should she not choose how this label is applied? For similar reasons, while she does not wear the *hijab*, she is frequently photographed wearing a headscarf traditional to Algerian Berber women, which she teams up with fashionable modern 'French' clothing.

This bold assertion of an Algerian identity, in light of the problematized nature of Algerians in France (mentioned above) is intentionally provocative. So too, in selecting 8 May 2005 as the date of the movement's first march, MIR directly sought to reopen the unhealed wound of the Algerian War in French public discourse. In fact 8 May 2005 marked the sixtieth anniversary of a date MIR argued was illuminative of France's Republican paradoxes: while 8 May 1945 has traditionally been celebrated in France as the day of

---

[59] For example while most of the spokespeople of the *banlieue* feminist organization *Ni Putes Ni Soumises* have been openly critical of Islam and declared their own lack of religious belief, a discussion on Muslim women's sexuality on the French television channel *Arte* on 8 February 2005 featured representatives from *Ni Putes Ni Soumises* as representatives of "young Muslim women in France". For more on this see Kiran Grewal, "The Threat from Within: Representations of the *Banlieue* in French Popular Discourse" in Matt Killingsworth (ed), *Europe: New Voices, New Perspectives* (University of Melbourne: Contemporary Europe Research Centre E-Book, 2007), available currently at http://www.cerc.unimelb.edu.au/publications/-Europe%20new%20voices%20ch3.pdf. See also Ruth Mas, "Compelling the Muslim Subject: Memory as Post-Colonial Violence and the Public Performativity of 'Secular and Cultural Islam'", *The Muslim World*, 96 (2006), 585-616.

liberation from German occupation, it also marked the massacres at Sétif and Guelma in Algeria, events which historian Mohammed Harbi describes as "the real beginning of Algeria's war of independence".[60] In marking the anniversary of these two events, MIR has sought once again to highlight the inter-relationship between French discourses of freedom, equality and humanist universalism and the reality of its colonial violence.

Finally, the establishment in 2007 of a specific feminist arm of the movement, *les féministes indigènes*, added an important layer to the debate. The other major *banlieue* organization to emerge in recent times—the feminist group *Ni Putes Ni Soumises*—had by this stage increasingly lost credibility among *banlieue* residents and postcolonial scholars alike due to its unquestioning adherence to Republican rhetoric, its co-option by mainstream politics and its perceived contribution to the further demonization of men of the *banlieue*.[61] The image of the 'good Republican *beurette*' and her evil counterpart the un-integrated (un-integratable?), '*garçon arabe*', had fitted all too neatly into the discourse of "the lost *banlieues* of the Republic".[62] With gender relations in the *banlieue* portrayed as a battle of the sexes compared with the relationship of complementarity experienced by French men and women (as the above example of Agacinski demonstrates), *Ni Putes Ni Soumises* seemed to further justify the social exclusion of at least male *banlieue* residents. As a result, while politicians and the media alike called for a reinvigoration of Republicanism in the *banlieues*, others began to question the extent to

---

[60] Mohammed Harbi, "Massacre in Algeria" (trans. Barbara Wilson), *Le Monde Diplomatique*, May 2005. Available at http://mondediplo.com/2005/05/14algeria (accessed 16 April 2009).

[61] In an illuminating example of the tense nature of *Ni Putes Ni Soumises'* relationship with *banlieue* residents, *Libération* journalist Marie-Joëlle Gros provides an account of a meeting at a local high school between members of *Ni Putes Ni Soumises* (NPNS), students and *banlieue* residents: Marie-Joëlle Gros, "Ni putes, ni soumises, ni comprises" *Libération*, 6 March 2003, p.16. See also, Nacira Guénif-Souilamas, "Ni Pute, ni soumise ou très pute, très voilée?" *Cosmopolitiques*, Vol. 4 (Juillet 2003), 53-65; Nacira Guénif-Souilamas and Éric Macé, *Les Féministes et le garçon arabe* (Paris: Éditions de l'aube, 2004); Grewal 2007(a) and 2009, "'Va t'faire intégrer!': The *appel des féministes indigènes* and the challenge to 'Republican values' in Postcolonial France" *Contemporary French Civilization*, 33.2 (2009), 105-133.

[62] Guénif-Souilamas and Macé (2004).

which this approach really offered any solution to problems of racism *or* sexism (in the *banlieue* and outside).

Les féministes indigènes, drawing on and contributing to the new (and exciting) body of postcolonial feminist scholarship which was also emerging in France, sought to further complicate the links between racism, class discrimination and sexism. Declaring themselves daughters of Solitude (one of the leaders of the French Caribbean slave insurgents) and Algerian war hero Jamila Bouharid, *les féministes indigènes* affirmed:

> Nous, en tant que femmes vivant en France, héritons des acquis des luttes des féministes françaises. Mais en tant que femmes racialisées, nous remettons en question les diktats de l'universalisme blanc et masculin et du féminisme blanc qui dénient toutes autres visions du monde ou vécus. Le féminisme occidental n'a pas le monopole de la résistance à la domination masculine.[63]

In making this statement, *les féministes indigènes* noted the paradoxical status of French Republican feminism within the colonial period: while French women struggled to assert their rights (as the *parité* campaign demonstrated), the language of feminism *had* been deployed all too frequently to justify the denial of full citizenship rights to colonized peoples. As Julia Clancy-Smith writes, the situation of colonized women was central to the *mission civilisatrice*:

> By 1900 issues of sex and gender, particularly the status of Arab women, came to be privileged in debates over Algerian male suffrage. Manipulated as a political and rhetorical strategy, female status was marshalled to refute the notion that the Arabs' assimilation to France was desirable or even possible.[64]

Moreover, metropolitan French feminists were frequently critical of the colonial administrators during this period, not for their racist attitudes but rather for their failure fully to enact the civilizing mission. These feminists themselves frequently employed highly racist and imperialist discourses in their description of the plight of their

---

[63] Les féministes indigènes, "L'appel des féministes indigènes", 26 January 2007. Available at http://www.indigenes-republique.org/spip.php?article667 (accessed 24 April 2009).

[64] Julia Clancy-Smith and Frances Gouda (eds), *Domesticating the Empire: Race, Gender and Family Life in French and Dutch Colonialism* (Charlottesville; London: Virginia University Press, 1999), p. 155-56.

colonized counterparts.[65] As a result, *les féministes indigènes* called for a new form of feminism: one which recognized the intersecting and mutually reinforcing nature of race and gender discrimination.

This public call for political activism was paralleled by an increased academic interest in the area. In a special edition of the journal *Nouvelles Questions Féministes* (linked to *les féministes indigènes* webpage), the editors note that

> [s]'il existe une question féministe qui mérite approfondissement parce qu'elle est compliquée et recouvre des enjeux fondamentaux pour nos existences, c'est bien celle des imbrications structurelles entre l'oppression fondée sur le sexe et les oppressions fondées sur l'appartenance à une race, ethnie ou culture, regroupée ici sous l'appellation 'racisme'.[66]

In another edition of *Nouvelles Questions Féministes,* explicitly citing the influence of Latina, Black and postcolonial feminism, Patricia Roux, Lavinia Gianettoni and Céline Perrin explain, "nous concevons le genre, l'hétérosexualité, la classe sociale, la race et la nationalité comme des systèmes sociaux et politiques structurés par des rapports de pouvoir", before going on to stress the interconnected nature of these systems and structures of power: "les mécanismes par lesquels les rapports de sexe, de race et de classe se renforcent mutuelle-ment".[67] In the same edition, veteran French feminist Christine Delphy rejected what she saw to be the "false dilemma" that had been created in French public discourse through the posing of feminism and anti-racism in opposition to each other.[68]

The simultaneous highlighting through both scholarship and activism of the interconnected nature of racism and sexism is perhaps

---

[65] For further discussion of this paradoxical relationship between French metropolitan feminist activism and the colonized female population see Clancy-Smith and Gouda; Sara Kimble, "Emancipation through Secularization: French Feminist Views of Muslim Women's Condition in Interwar Algeria", *French Colonial History*, 7 (2006), 109-28; and Grewal (2009).

[66] Natalie Benelli, Christine Delphy, Jules Falquet, Christelle Hamel, Ellen Hertz and Patricia Roux, "Les approches postcoloniales : Apport pour un féminisme antiraciste" *Nouvelles Questions Féministes*, 25.3 (2006), 4-12 (4).

[67] Patricia Roux, Lavinia Gianettoni and Céline Perrin, "L'instrumentalisation du genre: une nouvelle forme de racisme et sexisme", *Nouvelles Questions Féministes*, 26.2 (2006), 92-108 (92, 93).

[68] Christine Delphy "Antisexisme ou antiracisme: un faux dilemme", *Nouvelles Questions Féministes*, 26.2 (2006), 59-83.

the most important new development in French political, academic and public life. By stating in their *appel* that "[d]ans notre société, racisme et sexisme sont intimement imbriqués", *les féministes indigènes* sought to avoid the trap, which *Ni Putes Ni Soumises* had fallen into, of being forced to choose between their ethnic identity and their gender identity. Moreover, they showed their cynicism for employing the language of Republican universalism and egalitarianism in the context of a nation which had far from satisfactorily achieved these lofty goals:

> Dans une société 'francepaysdesdroitsdel'homme', structurellement inégalitaire et patriarcale, NOUS, descendantes de colonisé-e-s et d'immigré-e-s lançons un appel aux femmes et aux féministes qui s'estiment victimes de violences sexistes et racistes à nous rejoindre en vue de contribuer à l'émergence et à la construction d'une parole FEMINISTE POLITIQUE, égalitaire et autonome qui interpelle l'ensemble de la société française dans sa gestion des questions concernant les femmes venues ou vivant dans les pays du sud.

Instead, *les féministes indigènes* have sought to engage with issues such as violence against women in a manner that is sensitive to the various, often conflicting, demands placed on ethnic minority and immigrant women by both the dominant society and their particular ethnic minority communities. In doing so they have proposed what could be the most sophisticated attempt at an anti-racist, feminist politics France has seen and, arguably, a potential role model for organizations in other pluri-ethnic Western liberal democracies.[69]

---

[69] The problematic pitting of feminist and anti-racist discourses against each other has been noted by scholars working in a variety of contemporary western national contexts: see for example Kiran Grewal, "'The Young Muslim Man' in Australian Public Discourse", *Transforming Cultures eJournal*, 2.1 (2007), 116-134. For the Australian context, see Christina Ho, "Muslim Women's New Defenders: Women's Rights, Nationalism and Islamophobia in Contemporary Australia", *Women's Studies International Forum*, 30 (2007), 290-98. For her part, Sherene Razack has written on this issue in the UK and Scandinavian context—see Sherene Razack "Imperilled Muslim Women, Dangerous Muslim Men and Civilised Europeans: Legal and Social Responses to Forced Marriages", *Feminist Legal Studies*, 12 (2004), 129-74. For the Canadian context, see *Looking White People in the Eye: Gender, Race, and Culture in Courtrooms and Classrooms* (Toronto; Buffalo; London: University of Toronto Press, 1998).

Conclusion

The last twenty years have seen some significant shifts in French discourses of nation and citizenship. Frustrated by the ongoing failure of the idealized Republican values to deliver on their promises of *liberté, égalité, fraternité*, various social movements have contributed to a problematization of these values. While dominant political and media discourses have continued to invoke the rhetoric of 'salvation through Republicanism', new voices have also increasingly been heard in the public sphere: voices that are less willing to accept the virtue of France's dominant national myths uncritically. By placing Republican values in a historical and social context, both activists and scholars have convincingly argued that these values themselves are heavily implicated in the continued inequality and discrimination present within French society. Moreover, they have argued that it is only through a radical overhaul of the French nation state and its discourses of nation and citizenship that France will be able to emerge as a truly equitable and egalitarian society.

In particular, France has experienced increasing pressure in the last decade to confront its colonial past as a means of establishing a less tense relationship with its postcolonial population. A significant contributor to the development of this discourse has been the collaborative movement of postcolonial scholars and activists, *le mouvement des indigènes de la République* (MIR). In the short time it has existed MIR has simultaneously provoked debates about ethnic difference, the ongoing significance of French imperialism and the relationship between sexism, racism and colonialism. In attempting to construct an *anticolonialisme postcolonial*, MIR reflects a new era in France: one where open debate about ethnicity is no longer dismissed as an 'Anglo-Saxon' contamination with no relevance in the 'exceptional universalism' of the Republic. With the movement continuing to grow, representatives such as Houria Bouteldja emerging as prominent figures in the French public sphere and MIR now attempting to form its own political party, it seems the time has come for France to make its own rich contribution to the developing area of postcolonial studies.

Soukaz in a Staccato Mode

Lawrence R. Schehr

Lionel Soukaz is a radical queer film- and video-maker, though, I would add as an immediate caveat, that such appositional phrases must be engaged and deconstructed, not only for inherent reasons, but also for the destabilizing instrumentality of Soukaz's project that itself puts such easy labeling always already in doubt. He was a *compagnon de route* of many in the original French gay liberation group, *Front Homosexuel d'Action Révolutionnaire*, which began in 1971; amongst the co-founders of this group were Françoise d'Eaubonne (1920-2005) and the extremely influential Guy Hocquenghem (1946-1988), who died of AIDS-related complications. Soukaz and Hocquenghem work-ed together on *Race d'ép* (1979), a long documentary chronicling a history of homosexuals and homosexuality.[1] Their collaboration was a formative one, and indeed, Soukaz has used one of Hocquenghem's most notorious slogans as a title for a recent film, *Notre trou de cul est révolutionnaire* (2006). From his very first films, including *The Boy-friend*, which came out, as it were, in 1975, Soukaz regularly uses available techniques, first with film, then with video and its current computer-based avatars, to interrogate the position of the subject, ultimately queer and invariably male, the collective, again queer and

---

[1] See Guy Hocquenghem, *Race d'ép : Au siècle d'images de l'homosexualité* (Paris: Hallier, 1979).

male, and the political. Far from being mainstream, Soukaz has perhaps been sidelined from a general public consciousness by his own radicality of subject and technique, yet there is a certain viral video currency, as he continues to post numerous videos on Daily-motion.[2]

What does it mean in this case to interrogate the position of the subject, and specifically, in a day and age in which there is a relative freedom of mores for the middle-class subject in the urban Western world, and this in spite of the constraints of globalization and the imposed consumerism of a free-market economy? In Soukaz's case, we can focus on one strand in particular, though it is not the only one: the position of the gay male subject. Though it is always somewhat arbitrary to give an initial moment, I would nevertheless define the founding and first activities of the FHAR as the starting point, a moment at which the clinical word 'homosexual' is still used, as if it were the only available non-pejorative word. By 1979, with the publication of the volume *Race d'ép*, and eight years into the movement for gay liberation, the social situation had radically changed, as is evidenced by the classic linguistic move of empowerment through the appropriation of the vocabulary of the other: so the pejorative term *pédé*, turned into *verlan*, becomes *d'ép* and the appropriation of language is a significant sign of social change, relative 'acceptability', and even the legal change a few years later (in 1982), when the age of consent for same-sex sexual activity finally becomes the same as that for heterosexual activity.[3]

So on the one hand, Soukaz's work is a regular and timely documentation of the changes in the positions of the gay subject, one that literally moves from the shadows and margins to the center; it is a record of what discourses are possible (in the Foucauldian sense) for

---

[2] I should like to thank Lionel Soukaz for having provided me fascinating personal insights into his work and for his generosity in giving me copies of many of them. I should also like to thank Yekhan Pinarligil for having made the meeting between Lionel Soukaz and me possible. Soukaz's filmography for this chapter is made up of the following films: *The Boyfriend* (1975); *The Boyfriend II* (1976); *Ixe* (1980); *La Loi X* [also known as *La Nuit en permanence*] (2001); *Notre trou de cul est révolutionnaire* (2006); *Race d'ép* (1979); *Le Sexe des anges* (1977); *La Télévision nous encule* (2002).
[3] Julian Jackson, "Sex, Politics and Morality in France, 1954-1982", *History Workshop Journal* 61:1 (2006), 77-102.

that subject and in what space (intellectual, visual, geographic, discursive, and so forth). As we shall see below, there will always have been a gay Paris, but Soukaz's camera, even early on, reinforces the visibility of the once marginalized subject through its witnessing of that subject. But on the other hand, there is at work a second dynamic, which is, of course, the specter of AIDS, the first cases of which appeared in 1981, and which did not begin to decline in the West until the advent of combination therapy about a decade and a half later. Thus accompanying the discourse of liberation, as it makes its first quantum leap by the end of the seventies and the beginning of the eighties is what starts as an impossible discourse and finishes as a discourse of death and mourning. As the character, Muzil, based on Michel Foucault, puts it in Hervé Guibert's *A l'ami qui ne m'a pas sauvé la vie*, in a moment set in 1981: "Un cancer qui toucherait exclusivement les homosexuels, non, ce serait trop beau pour être vrai, c'est à mourir de rire".[4]

The advent of combination therapy has vastly reduced the mortality rate of HIV infection in the West and, in his recent work, Soukaz turns away from recording a specific gay subjectivity and focuses on a more general politics that is both oppositional and leftist in nature. I would hypothesize that the relatively diminished necessity, urgency, and even moral obligation of representing and documenting the destruction wreaked by AIDS is at least one of the factors that has allowed Soukaz to turn toward a more general sense of liberatory politics, one that seemed promised in the manifestos of FHAR, but one that necessarily became detoured by the omnipresence of the epidemic.[5] Regardless of the seeming turn in his work, part of which obviously also has to do with generally changing mores and legislation, including the PACS (1999), Soukaz's work continues to document the changing post-modern subject, and this with a fairly simple, albeit never simplistic, style.

---

[4] Hervé Guibert, *A l'ami qui ne m'a pas sauvé la vie* (Paris: Gallimard [Folio], 1990), p. 21.
[5] The reader should understand that when I am writing of the diminished current need for documenting gay individuality as it has become normalized in the wake of combination therapy for HIV+ infections, I am speaking only of HIV+ infections in the West. Moreover, as the recent recrudescence of infection rates itself demonstrates, there is continued need for documentation and knowledge in all forms.

In and of themselves, Soukaz's techniques do not constitute a wide range of possibilities, but consist of a set of formal camera positions, uses, and tricks instrumental as a means of varying what might otherwise be perceived by the director and his audience as a heteronormative approach to story-telling. In short, their primary function is to destabilize the positions of viewer and viewed and to recast both into a questioning mode, in an invention of or an appeal to alterity. The techniques function to destabilize subjectivity by putting into question the relation of self, or indeed, the *effet de soi*, to others and to the Other (in a Lacanian sense), as well as to the (Lacanian) notion of the Real into which language cannot go. In so doing, these "technologies of the visual", to use the felicitous expression that Lester Faigley has used as an article title, serve to question both the sense of community and the seemingly inviolate inevitability of the progress narrative of the political.[6] Indeed, the very ideals of the liberation movements ironically coincided with the end of the *trente glorieuses* and the initial conceptions of the post-modern by Jean-François Lyotard, among others.[7] Lyotard, in particular, in questioning the possibilities of a master narrative, implicitly is also questioning the continued viability of a progress narrative.[8]

---

[6] Lester Faigley, "Technologies of the Visual". http://www.cwrl.utexas.edu/-~faigley/work/material_literacy/technologies.html (accessed 26 January 2009).

[7] The expression *les trente glorieuses*, coined by Jean Fourastié, refers to the period from 1945 to 1974. I would argue that the first texts of what would come to be known as post-structuralism or deconstruction were Roland Barthes's *S/Z* (Paris: Seuil, 1970) for the former, and Jacques Derrida's *De la grammatologie* (Paris: Minuit, 1967) and "Structure, Sign, and Play in the Discourse of the Human Sciences" (in Richard Macksey and Eugenio Donato (eds), *The Structuralist Controversy: The Languages of Criticism & the Sciences of Man. 40th Anniversary Edition* [Baltimore: Johns Hopkins University Press, 1970]), the latter based on a talk Derrida had given at Johns Hopkins University in 1966. In both instances, in their strategies of eviscerating the certainty of the structure and the event, these works are the roughly simultaneous *mises-en-pratique* of what Jean-François Lyotard, for one, is theorizing in his work on the post-modern, as he declares that there are no more "grands récits".

[8] Here, it would be tempting to create a parallel between the techniques favored by Soukaz on the one hand and the fragmentary approach (as opposed to a left-leaning progress narrative) to the individual favored by Gilles Deleuze and Félix Guattari in such works as *Capitalisme et schizophrénie. L'Anti-Œdipe* (Paris: Minuit, 1972). But it may also simply be a symptom or a sign of the times: the deconstruction of the *bel canto* line of popular song, not by the simplicity of 1950s popular music, but by the

Three simple examples will suffice here to demonstrate this change in form. In *Ixe*, one of the director's most stirring, daring, and ambitious films, Soukaz uses a flashing, repetitive, and insistently haunting reproduction of images and actions, often disquieting ones that mark the subject as compelled and as incapable of escaping the containment or situations of heteronormativity, regardless of what he does. Yet it is the camera technique that counts—the queering, iterative approach that forces the viewer to take into account normalized queer subjectivity. It is thus the actions of the character plus the perceptions thereof that allow for the freedom that direct revolt cannot produce. In a more recent film, *La Télé nous encule*, Soukaz projects images, sounds, and disembodied voices, that is to say, to use the technical term, prosopopeiae, from television onto early twentieth-century pornographic images on glass, scenes that depict scenes of anal intercourse. Thus does Soukaz willfully conflate the literal and figural meanings of *enculer* in order to bring an entire set of discourses into question. Finally, in a short recent 'documentary', Soukaz repeatedly screens a clip of Nicolas Sarkozy misspeaking, in order to reinforce the spectators' sense of the absurd posturing associated with the political. While none of these techniques is itself extremely innovative, it is the underlined, emphatic, and unconditional use of simple, low-cost, filmic language, in a staccato and often looped style with jump cuts and syncopated rhythms, compounded with a modicum of clever editing, that marks Soukaz's originality as a film-maker and that drives his queer, or even post-queer, points home.

In Soukaz's work, the categories of the subject, the collective, and the political evolve together, but not necessarily harmoniously or synchronously, and Soukaz uses his staccato camera-work to under-line his ideological position, which is a general technique of de-familiarization of the human, in order to produce a queer *cinéma d'auteur*. Starting at the beginning of the age of gay liberation and its battles, continuing through the age of AIDS in which film becomes a protest, a record, a *memento mori*, and an act of mourning, and to that end, we should consider Cyril Collard's *Les Nuits fauves* (1992) as the prime example, and still pursuing a wider political agenda as we speak, Lionel Soukaz blazes a singular path as an independent film-

---

percussive insistence of the bass line and the qualities associated with the 'air guitar' of late-1960s and early-1970s progressive rock.

maker and witness. He rearticulates the position of the subject as one in which it is perversely situated at the loci of representing not only sexual desire but also the interpellation, in the Althusserian sense, of the subject through ideological state apparatuses, a Foucauldian notion of discourses and power as expressed in notions of social construction.

Yet throughout, there is a resolutely deconstructive position, sometimes marked by the mourning associated with AIDS, the mourning associated with the death of a generation, sometimes merely marked by a puckishness or a *jeu d'esprit*. Soukaz uses the camera to mark this permanent difference of the self from any fixed position. Images disconcert, disidentify, and inscribe Derridean *différance*. Indeed, in works like the recent *La Télé nous encule*, Soukaz accommodates a discourse and an imagery that move the film away from the identitary, and that combination simultaneously distances the spectator from a solidary position of subjectivity or even complacency and moves the viewer toward a vision that Soukaz disharmoniously forges with his spectator, one that I should not hesitate to call 'post-queer' in its destabilization of identity and representation.

Perhaps Soukaz's most famous work is the documentary written and produced by Guy Hocquenghem, *Race d'ép*, a full-length history of representations of male homosexuality in the late-nineteenth and entire twentieth centuries that starts with the homoerotic photographs taken by Wilhelm von Gloeden, the German photographer who had a fondness for mock-classic poses from Sicilian boys and adolescents through the movements of liberation in the late-twentieth century, or as it is put in the first part of the film, "de Gloeden jusqu'à la porno-graphie actuelle". Yet Soukaz's techniques in this film, consonant with those in *Ixe* as well as in a variety of his films before and after, bring us not to a documentary position of filming what is there to be filmed or of minimally investing, through filming, in the represent-ation of what is there, but rather to a construction of the queer object as the object desired by the camera. In *Race d'ép*, Soukaz offers re-creations of the photographs, as he uses adolescents to mime the pre-history of the stills that wound up in von Gloeden's collections.

Thus, for Soukaz, the history of the present moment, the moment filmed in a documentary, is one to be created through a con-structed history that is not necessarily inherent in the moment of production. Soukaz therefore creates a kind of protocol or fiction of social constructivism for his topic, and the topic is, in the early years, invariably a politicized version of male homosexuality, to be transformed, as time goes by, into a more generalized politics. It is a social constructivism that places both the Foucauldian notion of social construction and any lingering concepts of an ahistorical homo-sexuality into question. Through what amounts to a spasmodic tech-nique, the use of voice-overs, and a surrealistic sense of Eisensteinian montage, Soukaz structures his films so as to create a history of male homosexuality that is always already queered by its effects and affects.

This is already obvious from early films like *The Boyfriend* and *The Boyfriend II*, which date from 1975 and 1976 respectively, and which are among his earliest works, that show the primary technique of the Kuleshov effect, a kind of montage that depends heavily on an intercutting to create filmic meaning, that, different from the more formal, dialectical approach taken by Sergei Eisenstein in the Odessa Steps sequence of *Battleship Potemkin*,[9] for example, allows the view-er seemingly to make sense of the splicing, the oppositions, and the odd pairings.[10] Thus the viewer is given a power, or seemingly given a power, to make meaning and to construct the object on screen. In these two early films of Soukaz, it is clear that the viewer, targeted as both male and homosexual, is asked to piece together fetishized body parts, particularly primary and secondary sexual organs including lots of images of genitalia and posteriors, but also including shot after shot of attractive young men, often in same-gender groupings. The viewer then constructs a homoerotic universe within the realm of the familiar, as if these men, taken as objects, were forming a *bande à part*, thereby marking the territory as an appropriated cityscape, much as Guy Hocquenghem would do in *Le Gay Voyage*, which would appear in 1980.[11]

In these early films then, the director appropriates a well-de-fined, easily readable space, that of Paris, marked by familiar sights

---

[9] Sergei Eisenstein, *Battleship Potemkin* [*Bronenosets Potyomkin*] (1925).

[10] The Kuleshov effect, named for the film theorist and director Lev Kuleshov, involves an intercutting of film segments so as to induce a perception in the mind of the viewer. A simple illustration of it can be seen in *Hitchcock Loves Bikinis* (anon., no date), http://www.youtube.com/watch?v=hCAE0t6KwJY (accessed 26 January 2009).

[11] Guy Hocquenghem, *Le Gay Voyage. Guide et regards homosexuels sur les grands métropoles* (Paris: Albin Michel, 1980).

such as the Eiffel Tower, Notre Dame, and the *bouquinistes* along the *quais de la Seine*, and queers it, as if to say to the viewer, now *not* exclusively coded as gay and male, we are here, we are everywhere, and we have appropriated this space as a counterspace. We, silent, invisible, or vocal and visible, appropriate this most iconic of spaces that is Paris as our own and we choose to fill it, not with the stuff of which heterosexual and heteronormative dreams are made, but rather with sexualized bodies and sex organs that will be devoted to acts of sodomy. And yet, through a second kind of cutting, beyond the Kuleshov effect, Soukaz goes even further in his revolutionary occupation of space by occupying the soundtrack in a perverse, deconstructive fashion.

Soukaz uses familiar music and lyrics and turns them on their head by reassociating them with images of same sex desire. So, in this first film he uses familiar music by Edith Piaf (1915-1963), which he will also do, for example, in *Le Sexe des anges*, songs that every listener or viewer would instantly recognize—'La Vie en rose' is part of our collective cultural consciousness. And while we recognize that Piaf, like Judy Garland (1922-1969), is (or was, for this is generational) a gay icon, Soukaz is not building on that iconicity in any direct fashion, but is taking the sound, the plaintive voice that always had a kind of 'tear' in the throat, what Barthes calls "le grain de la voix",[12] and sets that tear or lump against homoerotic images. Shorn of her iconic status, Piaf is seen to speak directly for/about/to gay men and their images instead of being in a situation analogous to theirs.

This divorce from iconicity that particularly occurs with Piaf is repeated with a divorce from the heteronormativizing 'boy loves girl' topos that is the mainstay of popular music. So, in *The Boyfriend*, for example, Soukaz co-opts the very heterosexual Yves Montand (1921-1991) singing 'Les Grands Boulevards' with its theme of the Baudelairean *flâneur*, as well as the song 'Everybody's Doing the Riviera', from the oh-so-straight musical *The Boyfriend*. The director juxtaposes, as we have already seen, sound and sight to render both queerly in an estrangement, a defamiliarization in the formalist sense, that puts into question any pre-established sexual hierarchy that would

---

[12] Roland Barthes, *Le Grain de la voix. Entretiens, 1962-1980* (Paris: Seuil, 1981).

give priority to heterosexuality and heteronormativity. In a later film, *Le Sexe des anges*, Soukaz will repeat his gesture by off-setting soundtracks of the straight Johnny Hallyday (1943-) singing 'A plein cœur' and (the incidentally gay) Charles Trénet (1913-2001) singing 'J'ai mordu dans le fruit de la vie'. If Trénet was himself gay, this personal position did not affect the unabashedly straight and hetero-normative lyrics of his songs. Yet Soukaz upsets the possibility of straight reading by setting these songs against scenes of bumper cars, Arab music played with or against Tati on the Boulevard Barbès, a shot of Jean-Louis Bory's book, *La Peau des zèbres*,[13] a scene of Narcissus falling in love with himself / his image, and the use of exclamatory slogans as political statements, calls to action, and de-constructive or rhizomatic ploys that, along with the fractured sound-tracks and the repetitive close-ups on male body parts (not to mention man-on-man action), turn this into a Deleuzian game of plug-ins and desiring machines.

Even in these early works, such as *The Boyfriend II*, the director uses the art of juxtaposition, as we have seen, to decenter the positions of safety on screen. Here then, he uses a heterogenous collection of texts by authors such as Gabriel Matzneff, Jean-Louis Bory, Tony Duvert, Pier Paolo Pasolini, and himself to destabilize the process by which something might congeal into orthodoxy or heteronormativity. As he moves from these early works to the epoch-making *Le Sexe des anges* (1977, though it seems to have been recut in 1981) and *Ixe* (1980) with its frenetic, repetitive close-ups, his initial acts of juxta-position and montage are replaced or replenished by more com-plicated combinations. If in *The Boyfriend II*, for example, Soukaz offers us a shot of a guy penetrating himself with a Coke bottle, that is an illustration, certainly, of Guy Hocquenghem's famous phrase "notre trou de cul est révolutionnaire", a title, as I have said, that Soukaz would use in a 2006 film, when, oddly, it is no longer the case.

But in *Le Sexe des anges*, the director offers a far more complex scenario in which the Che- or Castro-like politics of slogans replaces any simple act of revolt. Thus we learn that "sexuality should be as easy to understand as rock lyrics" and that "industrial society re-cognizes only one sexuality". Now it would, I think, be easy to argue

---

[13] Jean-Louis Bory, *La Peau des zèbres* (Paris: Gallimard, 1969).

that such facile statements, aside from the self-contradiction of the first, for the director makes it anything but easy, are no more powerful and perhaps even less so than an image of a Coke bottle being inserted into an anus. Yet Soukaz goes on in *Le Sexe des anges* to ramp up the power of his message by breaking it down, by offering it in contradictory fragments and by holding it up to the values of a society that he feels is a corrupt, evil one, yet one that he knows is the only one that provides a platform onto which this queerness can be constructed.

In part, the complexity arises because of the juxtaposition of whole scenes against one another and not merely shots, as is often the case in the earlier films. So, in one compelling sequence, there is a game of strip chess, with each captured piece being worth a particular sex act: thus the capture of the queen leads to an act of fellation and the capture of the king leads to an act of sodomy. Soukaz, however, refuses to simplify the position of the subjects, so this game is played between two adolescents, one of whom starts out in sequins; and it is, of course, never clear if the loss of a chess piece, given the consequences, is indeed a loss. This scene is soon followed by one in which a teacher or schoolmaster seduces, albeit forcibly, an adolescent in his charge. It should be said that, especially in the early films, Soukaz is pushing the limits and indeed thumbing his nose at French law, which, at the time, set the age of eighteen as the consensual age for same-sex sexual activity between men, so that his insistence here and elsewhere on ephebophilia (and even, arguably, pederasty) is a brave, if not necessarily laudable, act. In the scene just mentioned, however, following on as it does from the chess game, which would arguably be innocent (if not legal), since it involves two teenagers and not a difference in generations or power, Soukaz manages to question any position of accreted power, any position of regularized difference. He seems to be questioning how or why we make an artificial distinction between activities that are remarkably similar, and while some might question his amoral position, Soukaz is still asking a valid deontological question.

Again, it is not so much the individual scenes but the myriad juxtaposition between and among them. Here we hear André Bourvil (1917-1970) singing 'Bonjour Monsieur le maître d'école', only to have it followed by a scene of love-making between two 19- or 20-year olds, who have sex to Édith Piaf's 'L'Accordéoniste', followed by sailors, or men dressed as sailors (for this is, after all, the era of disco and the Village People) who romp around to 'By a Waterfall', an iconic thirties song from a Busby Berkeley film, *Footlight Parade* (1933), followed by 'There is nothing like a dame', from Rodgers and Hammerstein's musical comedy *South Pacific*. In the latter case, we are spurred on by the strange connection of the Genet-inspired sailors (think of *Querelle de Brest*, especially in the film version by Rainer Maria Fassbinder[14]) with the fact that the Rodgers and Hammerstein song is performed by sailors, at least one of whom is in drag. Thus through this *Entfremdungseffekt*, Soukaz makes every performance, every position a drag show: we are in drag regardless of what we are wearing or doing.

In these early works, Lionel Soukaz develops a filmic vocabulary that he will continue to use throughout the next quarter of a century of film-making. Here then, I should merely indicate three additional elements that will develop throughout the eighties, ones that seem to be natural outgrowths of the destabilized, rhizomatic positions he has shown in these early works. First, he will turn the camera on himself, in a film such as *Ixe*, in which he becomes his own protagonist. Yet in so doing, he does not abandon any position I have just described; rather, his own position becomes a queer performance of self, a mixture of the politically incorrect and the engaged. The camera work, the subjectivity, and the drug-related velocity of the film all are exponential increases over what we have seen heretofore: interiority replaces the occupation of Paris, self replaces other, adult replaces ephebe, and speed rules. Strangely, in retrospect, this shift to the personal as political occurs at exactly the same time as AIDS begins to appear, but, of course, it will not be known as what it would become for a few more years. So, the disco years, internalized and expressed in this film, still play out in seeming innocence.

Second, and in seeming contrast, or perhaps through this reperspectivization, Soukaz's films become increasingly political. This is no surprise given the time period we are talking about; as queer liberation develops and as AIDS turns into an epidemic, it is natural for there to be a turn taken away from the solipsistic world of *Ixe* and toward a politicized one in which society itself is repeatedly and soundly condemned. Soukaz's work develops a moral, or at least

---

[14] Jean Genet, *Querelle de Brest* (Paris: Gallimard [L'Imaginaire], 1981); Rainer Maria Fassbinder, *Querelle* (1982).

an ethical position as this politics develops. Simultaneously, there is a turn within what is framed by the camera: as his sense of the political develops in later films, he tends more and more to let the event he is filming dictate the form and shape of the documentary. Thus, films are event-driven and cohere because of content and not because of any formal imposition.

Finally, Soukaz does use a set of techniques that remark the space as a constructed one: he often has recourse to a double technique that he uses as a critical one of politicians he does not like, of laws of which he does not approve, or of social situations that he finds intolerable: he writes or scrawls over pictures, to make them ridiculous. So, in a short film, *La Loi X*, there are dancing, superimposed 'X's and 'O's on politicians' bodies and faces, figures that will morph into dancing, scrawled genitalia. He uses a similar technique in *La Télévision nous encule*, but in other works, instead of resorting to this childish scrawling, he returns to earlier techniques, as in *Ixe*, in which he uses repetition, rapidity, and ridicule to make fun of Nicolas Sarkozy and others of his ilk.

Where do we ultimately place Lionel Soukaz in the spectrum of gay French film-makers filming gay subject matter? It is hard to say, in that he doesn't ever buy into the collectivity we would associate with the team of Olivier Ducastel (1962-) and Jacques Martineau (1963-), for example, or the singularity, brooding or otherwise, we would associate with directors like Patrice Chéreau (1944-), François Ozon (1967-), André Téchiné (1943-), or Sébastien Lifshitz (1968-). Clearly, Soukaz's positions go hand in hand with those of Guy Hocquenghem: an engaged story-telling process, a political positioning that endlessly reinscribes the personal at the level of the political, but a use of technique that is far different from Hocquenghem's lyricism, however. Still, throughout, Soukaz continues the joint project that they worked on together. He seizes the hurled epithet of *Race d'ép*, and turns it on its head, taking what is known as empowerment from an insult, much as 'queer' has become the word of choice since the 1990s in the English-speaking world.

He also, throughout his work, maintains distance from both the organized, communautarian, citified collective of homosexuality as well as from the alienated, singular, outcast position. Soukaz's particular spin on the position of the politicized queer subject thus continually queers it (or him) to place that subject in a vacillating position that continues to mime the Kuleshov effect: a montage suitable to the apocalypse of the AIDS generation, an apocalypse that Soukaz seems successfully to have survived to continue to make extraordinary films in the twenty-first century.

Hidden Violences: Work and the Working Class in Recent French Film

Martin O'Shaughnessy

One of the not insignificant trends in recent French fiction and doc-umentary cinema is a renewed attention to class inequality and the world of work. For fiction cinema, the origins of the trend can be traced back to the middle of the 1990s, when films like *La Cérémonie* (Chabrol, 1995), *Etat des Lieux* (Richet, 1995), *Marion* (Poirier, 1996), *En avoir (ou pas)* (Masson, 1995), *La Vie rêvée des anges* (Zonca, 1997) or *Marius et Jeannette* (Guédiguian, 1997) were released. At this early stage, the main focus was on manual work and the working class or what remained of it. While the same group would still be at the centre of films like *Ce vieux rêve qui bouge* (Guiraudie, 2000), *Trois huit* (Le Guay, 2000), *Marie-Line* (Charef, 1999) and *Selon Matthieu* (Beauvois, 2001), another cluster of films turned their attention to the world of management. Beginning with Cantet's *L'Emploi du temps* (2001), it continued with *Elle est des nôtres* (Alnoy, 2002), *Violence des échanges en milieu tempéré* (Moutout, 2002), *Sauf le respect que je vous dois* (Godet, 2004), *Fairplay* (Bailliu, 2005) and *La Question humaine* (Klotz, 2006). Centring on the relationship between a management trainee and his factory-worker father, Cantet's *Ressources humaines* (1999) straddles the two groups and problematises any over-neat separation between them. Beginning perhaps a little later with Hervé Le Roux's *Reprise* (1997), documentary showed a sustained interest in the same subjects. Its main interest has been in the working class, in films like Trillat's *Les Prolos* (2002) and Lemaire-Darnaud's *Paroles de Bibs* (2001), and more specifically in that class's losing fights against factory closures, with *Rêve d'usine* (Decaster, 2002) and *Les Sucriers de Colleville* (Doublet, 2002) being notable examples. Fewer documentaries have focused explicitly on management, a film like *Ma mondialisation* (Perret, 2005), being an obvious exception. The recent and very successful (for a documentary) *Ils ne mouraient pas tous mais tous étaient frappés* (Roudil and Bruneau, 2005), which looks at bullying at work, draws together experiences of workers from a factory, a shop and a care-home and a middle manager.

While there are clear convergences between the fictions and the documentaries, it would be a mistake to look for over-precise parallels. Many of the documentaries that engage with work might also be seen as anti- or counter-globalisation films, a group into which the fictions fit far less obviously, even if globalisation is part of the context from which they emerge. The documentaries tend to limit themselves to the workplace or working life and are more focused on the collective than fictions, which are more interested in small groups and individuals and which tend to insert work into the broader pattern of lived experience. Despite the differences, the two groups of films do converge in two important and interconnected ways. Firstly, they draw attention to the working class at a time when it has become a quasi-invisible social group. Secondly, they point to relations of power and domination in the workplace, a relatively taboo subject in the present period, primarily due to the decrease in working-class cohesion, visibility and combativeness. The decline in ideological differences between major parties of left and right and their convergence on values and policies supportive of neo-liberal glob-alisation has meant that it is increasingly seen as outdated to promote the politics of class or class struggle. Opposing this contemporary 'consensus' politics, the films seek to drive class inequality and workplace-based oppression back to the surface. Denying the apparent pacification of the social, they collectively suggest that a violence is being done that is all the greater for its invisibility.

What is called the 'social question' has haunted the Republic since the nineteenth century. The legal and political equality to which it has laid claim has historically been undermined by a socio-economic inequality in the face of which official egalitarianism could easily be dismissed as an alibi for class domination. Fraternity, another key republican value, also rang hollow as long as the working class were condemned to social marginalisation. The integration of the worker into the nation was a long, slow process in which parties of the left (the Communists, the Socialists) and Trade Unions played a central part, despite an often ostensible commitment to internationalism. Hard-won reforms (paid holidays, the welfare state) and workplace and political representation gradually brought about the conflictual integration of the class and made the contradiction between republican values of equality and fraternity and real social conditions less flagrant. The full employment, economic growth and relative democratisation of consumerism in the post-war economic boom of the *Trente Glorieuses* seemed to have completed this long-term trend towards social inclusion. However, the last thirty or so years have seen a dramatic reversal in the state of affairs.[1] High unemployment has become a constant feature of French life. The old Fordist enterprises have been broken up. Where once there was the promise of stable, lifelong employment, we now see a diversification of statuses. If a core of full-time and relatively protected workers remains, subcontracting and a massive turn to temporary contracts have meant that the old stability has gone and that mass precariousness has returned.[2] Workers' capacity to mobilise has been severely curtailed in the process, with large-scale closures in industries like coal-mining, steel or ship-building where there were the strongest traditions of militancy. The Renault factory at Billancourt, the most emblematic bastion of worker power, is now an empty shell. At the same time, liberal globalisation's weakening of economic boundaries has meant that workers in different countries are effectively placed in competition with each other so that decent pay and social conditions can be recast as competitive disadvantages and one set of workers played off against another. Workers who demonstrate too much determination to defend

---

[1] On this issue, see Robert Castel's seminal *Les Métamorphoses de la question sociale: une chronique du salariat* (Paris: Fayard, 1995).
[2] The best account of the transformation of traditional Fordist industries is Stéphane Beaud and Maurice Pialoux, *Retour sur la condition ouvrière: enquête aux usines Peugeot de Sochaux-Montbéliard* (Paris: Fayard, 1999).

conditions or statuses find themselves facing the threat that their employer will shift production overseas.

This substantial weakening of the working class's position has been accompanied by a sharp decline in its public visibility. At the time of the 2002 presidential elections, *Le Monde,* France's leading newspaper, published a special section called "Enquête sur la France des oubliés" ("Inquiry into the France of the forgotten ones"), a large part of which was devoted to the workers. One journalist, Eric Dupin, noted that the 'mainstream' left (the Socialist and Communist parties) no longer mentioned the working class. He also evoked its 'de-proletarianisation', its loss of support amongst workers. While the once mighty Communist Party is now a shell of its former self, the Socialists have become a party of government which now refuses to make a specifically class-based appeal. Both parties rely less and less on worker membership.[3] Once a social group seen by many as the motor of history, the workers are now more likely to be seen as *ringards* or old-fashioned, their place as the visible outsiders of the Republic taken by the youth of the *banlieue* and the children of immigration.[4] The progressive worsening of their status and conditions is thus accompanied by a loss of public voice and visibility, a symbolic defeat laid over a social and political one.[5] It is in the space of this double defeat that a cinema figuring class and work must now carry out its own symbolic labours.

Full of symbolic resonance, Chabrol's *La Cérémonie* is a good place to begin an examination of how French fiction cinema has occupied this space. Released in 1995, the year of the mass public-sector strikes that showed that not all French workers were cowed, the film centred on the relationship between a self-satisfied bourgeois family and their new female servant. Although the family owe their wealth to industrial production, they live in a country château. The main social organisation in the local village is the Catholic relief

---

[3] "Enquête sur la France des oubliés", *Le Monde*, 2 June 2002.
[4] On the failure of the left and the unions to recruit the children of immigration, see Olivier Masclet, *La Gauche et les cités: histoire d'un rendez-vous manqué* (Paris: La Dispute, 2003). On the way immigrants have replaced workers as 'visible outsiders', see Michel Cadé, "A la poursuite du bonheur : les ouvriers dans le cinéma français des années 1990", *Les Cahiers de la Cinémathèque*, 71 (2000): 59-72.
[5] On this double defeat, see Jean-Louis Comolli, "Travail au noir", *Images Documentaires*, 37/8 (2000): 101-120.

agency which devotes itself to gathering clothes for the poor. As the film proceeds, we learn that the servant has a secret, her illiteracy, which she is desperate to hide. She pretends to be short-sighted, but the family take her into town and buy her glasses, thus seeming to confirm their benevolence. If her opinion is sought on any matter, she tends to reply "je ne sais pas". When her secret is finally forced into the open by the daughter of the family, she responds in kind by revealing that the daughter is pregnant. Things predictably turn nasty when she is fired and she and her postmistress ally turn the family's shotguns on them. The family might seem to be innocent victims had we not witnessed their smug superiority and the quiet struggle that develops to control the servant's time and whereabouts. This is announced by the very early sequence at the railway station when, having arrived on an earlier train than anticipated, the servant appears in a part of the station where she is not expected. It continues when, having been pressured to work on a Sunday to prepare food for a birthday party, she does not remain behind to serve the food, much to her mistress's surprise and indignation.

The film is interesting in the way it seems to suggest a new state of class relationships in France that seems remarkably like a lurch back into the past, as if suggesting that the long, slow conquest of a social place by the Republic's lower orders had never taken place. The tranquil rural setting, the château residence, the assured superiority of the family, the servant who has no opinions or access to the written word, the Catholic charity helping the poor: all seem from an earlier, even a pre-revolutionary period of unchallenged social domination. But rather than suggesting that class struggle has disappeared, the film would seem to show how, deprived of a voice, it has gone underground, manifesting itself in silent struggles, like that over the servant's time and location, or bursting out in acts of apparently motiveless destruction, as in the closing slaughter or, in a lighter mode, when the postmistress and the servant throw their charitable donations back in the astonished givers' faces. Part of the film's beauty lies in its capacity to leave the world it shows suspended between two interpretations of social interaction. As she moves from being an object of charity to apparently flagrant ingratitude, the servant seems to belong to an older social order where those at the bottom can only be the 'deserving' or 'undeserving' poor. Yet at the same time, through her different 'resistances', she would seem to embody a recalcitrant subjectivity and a refusal of unchallenged bourgeois rule. Disrupting the apparently consensual face of the social order, showing a resistance driven underground and deprived of words, the film seems remarkably apposite to its period.

Another film that refused the appearance of consensus was Laurent Cantet's widely praised *Ressources humaines*. In its early stages, the film seems to speak of a society in which class struggle is a thing of the past. The hero is studying management in Paris. He has come to the provincial factory where his father, a manual worker, has spent his career to undertake some work experience. His chosen speciality is human resources and the particular task he allots to himself is a study of the application of the then recent legislation limiting the normal working week to 35 hours. He devises a survey that will invite all the workers to give their opinions. The film would seem to speak of a situation in which all voices count equally, all are integrated (one stated aim of the 35-hours legislation was to create jobs for the unemployed) and class boundaries have weakened so that the sons of workers can become managers. But, like *La Cérémonie*, the film soon finds hidden barriers and violences beneath the consensual surface. Impressions start to change as soon as the hero, who has initially been blocked from access, tours the factory floor. As his father proudly shows him the machine where he has carried out the same repetitive task, day after day, year after year, a foreman approaches and tells the father he is slowing the work-rate. The worker on the next machine makes a barking noise while staring at the foreman. This is the first sign of a different reality where older workers are devalued and in which the workers generally seem to have no voice, the barking being emblematic both of voicelessness and a refusal of silencing. Other signs soon follow. The hero finds a new social distance between himself and friends he has left behind. A Parisian-based, management trainee, he now speaks a different language and cannot fit easily into the group. He is also excluded from certain management-level discussions, with doors shut in his face and blinds drawn, in a way which again points to something hidden. He only stumbles on what is going on when, working without permission on the computer of the Director of Human Resources, he finds a letter announcing a set of redundancies that includes his own father. Management has cynically been using the 35-hour issue (and the hero's 'consultation' exercise) as a distraction to cover its real intentions. The hero turns to the representative of the CGT (Confédération Générale du Travail), the trade union historically close to the Communist Party, but she tells him she cannot act unless there is some proof of his claims, as people see her as an old-fashioned class warrior out of touch with the present. The hero has to break into the factory offices at night and paste multiple copies of the tell-tale letter to the glass front door to force what is hidden to the surface. The workers now mobilise and a strike is called with the CGT representative, no longer the speaker of a 'dead' language, at its head.

While *Ressources humaines* seems in some ways like an old-fashioned piece of agit-prop, in other ways, like *La Cérémonie*, and for some similar reasons, it is very specific to its historical moment. At an earlier time, class difference and class struggle were something that could be found at the surface. Now, it is as if they have been driven underground, deprived of a voice and visibility. The hero's identity between classes might have been used to point to a new era of fluid boundaries. Instead, his uneasy in-between position—not yet of management, no longer of the workers—is used to highlight the barriers that still exist. The social inclusion signalled, at a general level, by the 35-hour legislation's avowed intention to distribute work more evenly and, at a more local level, by the hero's poll of the workers, is given the lie by the redundancies, the ruthless elimination of the older worker and the pretence of consultation. Only the closing strike gives the workers an authentic public voice, but this is a voice rooted in conflict.

Set in a provincial town, *Ressources humaines* is predominantly a local drama. It only opens onto something beyond itself when we briefly learn that the company figured is part of a group that uses the threat of exporting jobs to lower wage economies as a form of labour discipline. Moutout's *Violence des échanges en milieu tempéré* engages in a more rounded way with some of the dynamics of contemporary globalisation. The film tells the story of a young management consultant newly recruited to a leading Paris-based man-agement consultancy company called MacGregor. The young hero is given the task of carrying out an audit of a provincial French company that is being prepared for take-over by a leading foreign firm. The hero initially believes that his role is to help make an already profitable company more efficient. He slowly comes to realise that his real task is to identify the areas of the company's activities that can be lopped off to guarantee the high profits that will keep foreign shareholders happy. Worse still, the interviews he carries out with individuals reveal themselves to be a mechanism for selecting those who will be fired or kept. The implicit criteria are the willingness to take on new tasks, even if it means evicting those who have habitually done them, to work to higher cadences and to commit to 'flexible' hours. The implication is that a worker injured by a workplace accident and a mother with time commitments to her family will not be kept on due to their 'unfitness' for the new 'flexible' regime. Whereas the workplace was once one of the cornerstones of republican integration, guaranteeing people a productive social place, albeit a subordinate one, it has now become a place, the film suggests, of a ruthless selection that produces exclusion not integration, a process all the more violent for the way it targets people as isolated individuals in a way destructive of collective ties.[6]

The violence done at the human level is mirrored by what occurs spatially. Historically, French life has always been marked by the tension between an over-powerful Paris and the rest of France. This *tension* mutates to become something more akin to a *dislocation* in *Violence des échanges*. The consultancy company is signalled as something foreign by its name, 'MacGregor'. The buy-out is by a foreign multi-national. While the people who work in the French company are only associated with the provincial town, the hero moves between the provinces and Paris, even as his colleagues travel between the capital and foreign places of business. A spatial dislocation, already signalled in *Ressources humaines,* is confirmed here. While the transnational, Paris-based company is locked into global flows of power, the provincial has been cut adrift. As causality moves out of story space into the global ether, the Republic as agent of national integration seems to fade out of the picture.[7] Something similar can be seen in the recent documentary *Ma mondialisation*, within which a factory owner recounts how he has been forced willy-

---

[6] For a more developed account of the three films discussed so far, see Martin O'Shaughnessy, *The New Face of Political Cinema: Commitment in French Film since 1995* (Oxford: Berghahn, 2007), especially chapters four and five.
[7] For a more general account of the dislocation of national space in recent French social-realist film, see Martin O'Shaughnessy, "Eloquent Fragments: French Fiction Film and Globalization", in *French Politics, Culture and Society*, 23:3 (2005): 75-88.

nilly to adapt to global economic forces, shifting production overseas and breaking the traditional paternalist link between boss and worker, production and locality.

While *Ressources humaines* explored the tension between individual career and collective solidarity, *Violence des échanges* focuses more exclusively on the individual. By refusing to lend himself to the company's underhand behaviour, the hero of the former is able to re-establish solidarity with the group, even if he knows he has been detached from his class of origin. His personal, ethical decision can thus still open onto a politics. *Violence des échanges* is less positive in this respect. The decision its hero takes is framed as a purely ethical choice between wrecking his own career and destroying the working lives of others. He makes the wrong choice, but in any case there is no collective resistance with which he might have aligned himself. The need for such a thing is signalled near the end of the film when the production manager of the French company, someone loyal to all his workers, says that they must now resist but this is not followed up. The individualisation and isolation of the workers in the face of inhuman management is thus mirrored by the individualism implicit in the purely ethical choice that the film stages. Perhaps inadvertently, through its own structure, it thus suggests that the atomisation of the social has gone further than it seems to have in *Ressources humaines*.

Sophie Bruneau and Marc-Antoine Roudil's recent documentary *Ils ne mouraient pas tous* (2005) develops the same sense of atomisation. It figures, firstly, the encounter between therapists who specialise in work-related problems and four individual workers and, secondly, a discussion between the therapists about how the world of work has changed. Each worker represents a different type of activity. One works on a production line in a factory. The company she works for has been cutting the workforce by eliminating slower workers and by increasing the cadences for those that remain, who consequently find themselves under ever greater pressure. The woman finds that, even outside the factory, she is incapable of slowing down and that stress inevitably overflows inter her personal life. Any complaints from workers are taken as a sign of personal inadequacy. At the opposite end of the scale is a manager who has led a team of salespeople. His philosophy has been to try and get the best out of each person. New management has come in and adopted what is essentially a Taylorist system of organisation whereby interaction with the client is divided up into components with each allotted a calculated amount of time. Seeking to increase productivity, the company has pared down time allocations, putting more pressure on workers while raising sales targets to drive up profitability. Finding this system of management inhuman, the manager has sought to act as a buffer between his team and the externally imposed pressures and has cracked up. Reflecting on the interviews together, the therapists discuss the patterns they have noticed. A point that they make is that each of those who has been pushed to breaking point has initially been a passive collaborator with the system and has failed to react when others were the target of the inhuman pressures exerted. Another point that they agree upon is that while none of the managerial methods used are necessarily new in themselves (Taylorism dates from the 1910s), what is new is the isolation of workers in their encounter with the systemic as exemplified by the individualisation of measures of performance. Where collective resistances were once possible, individuals are now set in competition against each other. Pressures that previously triggered mechanisms of solidarity are now internalised as individual pathologies.

Amplifying and continuing the work of the therapists, the film resists the inhuman processes it describes. If, as an opening sub-title notes, "la souffrance subjective de ceux qui travaillent est invisible sur les lieux mêmes du travail", it works to bring what is hidden into public visibility while restoring a voice to those who have been effectively silenced.[8] While the focus on therapists runs the obvious danger of reducing systemic violences to the level of the personal psyche, the closing discussion forcefully reconnects the psychological to the social and the political. At the same time, the film uses the close collaboration of the therapists to point to an alternative mode of social organisation rooted in shared values, voluntary co-operation and pooled expertise that is in stark contrast to the enforced competition and atomisation experienced by the private-sector workers shown in the

---

[8] It might seem ironic that the film grants only the therapists access to the closing discussion of the systemic, seemingly mirroring the relegation of its worker-witnesses to the domain of personal experience. However, through its own publicness, the film effectively allows the workers to break out of the private domain to address an audience.

interviews, even if it too is under threat due to the increasing penetration of private-sector managerial practices into the public sector. In the golden age of the welfare state, the state system's ability to provide shared public services was indicative of social solidarity and a desire to integrate all into the national community. In the current period, the film would suggest, the state system serves to pick up the walking wounded generated by the contemporary organisation of labour, not so much an agent of integration as a bulwark against disintegration.[9]

A similar sense of atomisation of social relations, of hidden violences and of passive acquiescence is generated by Godet's recent fiction *Sauf le respect que je vous dois,* a film which begins with a car driven by the hero apparently trying to force another off the road and then challenges us to understand why this act of violence has taken place. A flashback, the main body of the film, takes us into an apparently cordial workplace where a team of salespeople seem to work in harmony. Slowly, in a way reminiscent of *Ressources humaines*, clues emerge that allow us to construct a rather different picture. The hero finds he has been moved from one office to another for no apparent reason. It emerges more broadly that the workers are expected to work overtime, as and when the company requires, irrespective of their personal lives. The hero's friend resists and is put under pressure to give in or leave. A solution seems to be reached when the friend is offered a computer to take home so that he can do extra work there if necessary. Puzzlingly, we find that the friend has been sacked. We then witness his suicide. This is the trigger that explains the act of violence that begins the film and which we now come to understand as the hero's attempt to remonstrate with his boss, who dies in the crash. The missing piece of the jigsaw is found when

---

[9] Something similar might be concluded from Bertrand Tavernier's *Ça commence aujourd'hui* (1998), a film set in the context of the social decay and fragmentation that scar a French town after the closure of its pits. Whereas once the school might have served as a symbol of republican integration of the children of the working class, its head-teacher hero is now called upon to deal with a series of problems that testify to social disintegration. The landscape of the town is still marked by the pitheads that serve to remind us how visible miners, as leading symbols of worker militancy, once were. Now, the head teacher has to bring a lorry driver to the school to remind the children what a worker is.

the hero discovers that the boss had accused his friend of stealing the borrowed computer.

More interesting than the ins and outs of the plot is the film's exploration of workplace dynamics in a context of intimidation and increasing pressure. The hero's friend is the only person who enters into outright public resistance. Others, including the hero, are initially passive, or, worse still, blame the friend for his refusal to conform. Paralleling what we saw in *Ils ne mouraient pas tous*, the film thus shows a pattern of atomisation, of individual failure to act and of collective failure to mobilise. As in that film and all the others discussed, workplace violence takes on the character of something hidden that has to be forced to the surface. In this specific case, the uncovering of what is hidden takes the generic form of a murder mystery: why did the hero force the other car of the road? The publicly visible death (of the boss) contrasts with the lack of public attention given to the friend's suicide and the failure to connect the two events. When people say there has been a death, only the hero and a journalist reply that there have been two. The high-profile death thus serves to bring the other death to visibility while paradoxically underlining the public invisibility or work-related oppressions.

Nicolas Klotz's *La Question humaine,* the final film we will consider here, likewise takes the form of a mystery, albeit a more intellectually ambitious one. Klotz and his writer Perceval have so far made three films that explore, in their different ways, the Republic's disavowed exclusions. Their first film, *Paria* (2000), looked at the treatment given to people living on the streets of Paris. Their second, *La Blessure* (2003), looked at the inhuman treatment of migrants being expelled from France. Rounding out the trilogy, *La Question humaine* looks at the inhumanity practiced in the world of work. Its hero is a psychologist, but unlike the therapists of *Ils ne mouraient pas tous,* his role is not to help the victims of workplace oppression but to help select those who will be weeded out. Like the heroes of *Violence des échanges* and *Ressources humaines,* he seems initially unaware of the monstrosity with which he is colluding. His psychological pro-filing suggests a new phase in workplace oppression that no longer stops at exterior, measurable evidence of suitability but seeks to probe the human interior to identify what can be mobilised for profit or provides an obstacle to it.[10] The hero's realisation that something is wrong begins to dawn when he is asked by one of his German-owned company's managers to investigate the chairman whose behaviour is said to be causing concern. While researching the chairman's past, he unearths a connection to the Second World War. The chairman is the child of someone who committed wartime atrocities while the man seeking to be rid of him is one of the children born of the Nazis' attempt to selectively breed a new race. At the same time, someone is sending the hero strange letters where apparently anodyne phrases from contemporary management reports are mixed with phrases taken from Nazi material relating to the Final Solution. Too subtle to simply suggest the dubious parallel between the Genocide and the contemporary world of work, the film is nonetheless pushing us to see that the same instrumental rationality might connect them both, subjugating the human to the inhuman while eliminating those seen as obstacles to the goals of racial purity or profitability. The reference to genocide takes to its extreme point something that seems to haunt these films explicitly or implicitly. The sense that one side (the working class) has been defeated, that inhuman logics are being applied in the world of work, that resistance now falls to individuals or small groups, and that many collaborate actively or passively with monstrous logics: all these traits mean that, rightly or wrongly, the shadow of the Second World War period in some ways hangs over the films.[11] This was a time, of course, when the Republic had abdicated its responsibilities, when previously integrated citizens were stripped of their nationality and when independent trade unions were outlawed.

---

[10] This kind of job interview or workplace appraisal is one of the most characteristic scenes of work-related fictions. Seen in films like *Etat des Lieux*, *En avoir (ou pas)*, *La Vie rêvée des anges* or *L'Emploi du temps*, it shows how workers must often reveal intensely personal details about themselves in a way that highlights contemporary asymmetries of power.

[11] The films of Guédiguian repeatedly invite parallels between anti-Fascist resistances and the struggle for survival by the remnants of the working class. *A la vie, à la mort* (1994) evokes, for example, anti-Francoist resistance, while *Marius et Jeannette* connects back to the experience of Communists imprisoned during the Occupation. For a discussion of the use of the word 'totalitarian' to describe the functioning of contemporary business, see Jean-Pierre Le Goff, *La Barbarie douce: la modernisation aveugle des enterprises et de l'école* (Paris: La Découverte, 2003).

Conclusion

The films considered converge in some important ways. All tend to suggest that the contemporary world of work is a place of hidden violences. It is because of this, no doubt, that there is an element of mystery in them: something ugly, perhaps murderous, which is not initially perceptible, needs to be driven to the surface to give the lie to the illusion of consensus or of social inclusiveness. Rather than being one of the key sites of republican integration, work now seems to be the place where social atomisation is generated. The films diverge in that some figure the violence witnessed as specifically class-related while others frame it more broadly as a struggle between the human and the inhuman. In the former group, what emerges is the undoing of the historical integration of the working class. In the latter, the social bond itself is at stake. Amongst the former, a film like *Ressources humaines* suggests all is not lost, that the working class can rediscover a voice and return to visibility but only through overt struggle, genuine integration of a subordinate group inevitably being con-flictual.[12] In contrast, a film like *La Cérémonie* suggests class struggle has been driven underground and can only re-emerge through explosions of violence. Where the struggle is between the human and the inhuman, the only type of choice available is an ethical one: characters can choose to collaborate or to enter into a purely in-dividual resistance. In contrast, where the struggle retains a class dimension, as in *Ressources humaines*, individual ethical decisions can still open onto a more properly political position. Whatever the case, the world of work, as seen by the films discussed, would now seem to be a site where core republican values no longer apply and a socially atomised and territorially dislocated Republic can no longer integrate.

---

[12] On the necessity of real struggle to a democratic politics, see, for example, Chantal Mouffe, *On the Political* (London: Routledge, 2005).

Reordering Regionality

May-June 1968.
Reflector and Vector of a Nation's Diversity:
The Case of Strasbourg, Alsace

Chris Reynolds

Introduction

An investigation of the 1968 events in Strasbourg in relation to the plurality and diversity of France is significant in two respects. Firstly, the specificities of the Alsace region in terms of its culture, history and geographical location led to a revolt that lies beyond the dominant narrative of 'May '68'.[1] This chapter will argue that such regional departures, largely airbrushed from conventional representations, are indicative of the plurality of France. Secondly, it will be argued, through an examination of the post-'68 years in Alsace, that the events were a vector in encouraging an affirmation of the nation's heterogeneity. 1968 will be described as paving the way for a shift in how the State perceived regional identities as well as ushering in a new indigenous generation that has been much more comfortable and forthcoming in coping with the inherent French/German duality of

---

[1] For a discussion on the issue of a dominant narrative see Michelle Zancarani-Fournel, *Le Moment 68. Une histoire contestée* (Paris: Seuil, 2008); Chris Reynolds, "May 68: A Contested History", *Sens Public,* 26 October 2007; Kristin Ross, *Mai 68 et ses vies ultérieures* (Paris: Complexe, 2005); or Isabelle Sommier, "Mai 68: Sous les pavés d'une page officielle", *Sociétés Contemporaines,* 20 (1994).

Alsatian identity. 1968 therefore provides a striking example of the consequences of the plurality France enjoys as well as being a catalyst in the acceptance of such diversity.

Historical Context

The history of the Alsace region is characterised by a high level of flux. Between 450 BC and the 1648 Treaty of Munster, control of the region passed from Celts to Romans, from Romans to Franks, from Franks to Germans before it became part of the Holy Roman Empire in the later tenth Century. The Peace of Westphalia of 1648 signalled the beginning of a direct two-way power struggle between France and Germany that has shaped the contemporary cultural identity of Alsace.[2] Over the next three centuries the region changed nationality five times. From 1648 until the Franco-Prussian War it was part of French territory.[3] Between 1871 and the conclusion of the First World War it was under German control before once again forming part of France until the Second World War.[4] The Nazi occupation brought with it significant difficulties for the region[5] before it was eventually freed and has since become an integral part of French territory.

One of the principal consequences of this highly unstable past was the emergence and consolidation of a hybrid cultural identity that drew on both German and French influences and traditions. When one considers that "Un Alsacien né en 1865 et mort en 1945 a reçu cinq nationalités différentes, alternativement allemande et française"[6] there can be little doubt as to the existence of a very specific mindset in the region, one grounded in a bi-polar identity. A recurring feature each time the region changed hands in the past was a determined effort on the part of the new 'masters' to impose a cultural hegemony mainly

---

[2] For a more detailed overview of this early history see Philippe Meyer, *Histoire de l'Alsace* (Paris: Perrin, 2008).

[3] For a closer examination of this period see Bernard Vogler, *Histoire culturelle de l'Alsace. Du Moyen Age à nos jours, les très riches heures d'une région frontière* (Strasbourg: La Nuée Bleue, 1993), pp. 183-204.

[4] See Bernard Vogler, *Histoire politique de l'Alsace. De la Révolution à nos jours, un panorama des passions alsaciennes* (Strasbourg: La Nuée Bleue, 1995), p. 222-23.

[5] For discussion of the issue of collaborators, for example, see Jean Ritter, *L'Alsace* (Paris: PUF, 1985), p. 62; and Vogler (1995), pp. 264-66.

[6] Meyer, p. 390.

through the eradication of all traces of the former's cultural imprint.[7] This trend had obvious connotations for the regional identity and was one that was given even greater strength and resonance in the aftermath of the Nazi occupation.

From 1945 to 1968, the process of imposing a French identity was afforded an added impetus as a result of the need to exorcise any German (thus Nazi) influences from French soil.[8] Importantly, the duality that underpinned Alsatian culture and society became more commonly viewed in a pejorative light by the native population. In this period described as "l'éffondrement de la vie culturelle régionale",[9] anyone proclaiming the need to foster and maintain this identity was associated with those pushing the autonomy agenda, thus collaborators. German was forbidden in schools and Volger's description of perceptions of the dialect gives some idea of the position the Alsatian identity found itself in during this period: "Le dialecte tend peu à peu à être considéré comme une tare, une maladie honteuse, un comportement préjudiciable à la francophonie, l'expression d'un sous-développement culturel, tout juste bon pour valet de ferme, rimeur du dimanche ou autre amateur de grosses farces".[10]

The difficulties faced by the region in the years leading to 1968 are clear. Such a difficult past, and the consequences it led to, created a specific way of life and attitudes in the region. This is exemplified in how 1968 was experienced there. An examination of how the crisis was played out in Strasbourg provides a valuable insight into how local specificities brought about an upheaval that does not fit the stereotypical view.

Pre-'68 Strasbourg

Like everywhere else in France in the build-up to 1968, in Strasbourg there were little or no obvious signs of the upheaval that was just

[7] These are described as cultural *épurations* in Pierre Klein, *L'Alsace inachevée* (Colmar: Jérôme, 2004), p. 19.
[8] Gireg Aubert and Aurélie Sonocinski, "1945-2004: le regain du régionalisme", *News d'ill*, 75, February 2004, pp. 14-15.
[9] Vogler (1993), p. 461.
[10] Vogler (1993), p. 462.

round the corner.[11] Such apparent calm was both reinforced by and
reflected in the great stability that characterised the economic and
political landscape. Economically, Strasbourg was in a relatively
strong position. Having benefited from the government sponsored
délocalisation programme, together with the advantages associated
with its proximity with Germany, unemployment was amongst the
lowest in the country. In comparison with the rest of France, both
Strasbourg and the region in general were in good economic health.[12]
Such stability was equally evident in terms of the political landscape.
Since coming back to power in 1958, Gaullists had completely
dominated the Region with the General held in very high esteem as
the saviour of French Alsace.[13] The economic and political stability
enjoyed since de Gaulle's return fed into, and was arguably shaped by,
an inherent conservatism often described as a prominent feature of the
Alsatian mentality.[14]

A quick glance at the University of Strasbourg of the 1960s
reveals similar experiences to elsewhere in the country.[15] The number
of students was growing exponentially, courses were seen to leave
graduates ill-prepared for the modern world of work, and the government reaction to the baby-boom (i.e., the hasty construction of new
buildings (namely *l'Esplanade*) was both protracted and perceived as
falling short of meeting growing needs.[16] However, the one episode

---

[11] For a discussion on the validity of the surprise element of the 1968 events see
Reynolds (2007), p. 12-13.

[12] For an overview of the economic situation in the region at the time see Léon Strauss
and Jean-Claude Richiez, "Le Mouvement social de mai 1968 en Alsace: décalages et
développements inégaux", *Revue des sciences sociales de la France de l'Est*, 17
(1989-90), 117-21; Yvonne Wendling, *Les Feuilles de mai 68 à Strasbourg* [Mémoire
de Maîtrise], University of Strasbourg, 1992, p. 14.

[13] See Vogler (1995), pp. 292-298; Wendling, pp. 14-17; Strauss and Richiez, p. 119.

[14] Ritter, p. 69.

[15] For analysis of the problems experienced within the university system nationally
see Christine Musselin, *La Longue Marche des universités françaises* (Paris: PUF,
2001); Didier Fischer, *L'Histoire des étudiants de 1945 à nos jours* (Saint-Amand-
Montrond: Flammarion, 2000); Antoine Prost, "1968: Mort et naissance de
l'université française", *Vingtième Siècle*, 23 (1989).

[16] See Agnès Ackner, "Révolte de mai 1968" in [No editor provided], *Encyclopédie
de l'Alsace* (Strasbourg: Publitotal, 1982), p. 6369; Pierre Feuerstein, *Printemps de
révolté à Strasbourg, mai-juin 1968* (Strasbourg: Saisons d'Alsace, 1968), pp. 16-17.

that does point to some degree of divergence relates to the famous *Situationniste* scandal of 1966.

Throughout the 1960s the University of Strasbourg had one branch of the *International Situationniste* (IS). Marginal and made up of a handful of highly militant students, the Strasbourg branch nevertheless created a huge controversy when it managed to take control of the *Association Fédérale Générale des Etudiants de Strasbourg* (AFGES) at the beginning of the 1966 academic year. In so doing they were handed a say in the management of the university restaurant, a Corsican holiday camp and given control of a two-million-franc budget.[17] Such responsibilities in the hands of a group who—via their outrageous pamphlet *De la misère au milieu étudiant*[18]—made clear their intentions to destroy every element of the university system, created panic amongst the authorities and were the focus of sustained national media attention.[19] Tension mounted as the *Situs* pursued their inflammatory tactics through increasingly provocative texts and actions. The scandal was eventually brought to a head when they decided to close down the *Bureau d'Aide Psychologique Universitaire* (BAPU).[20] This move provided ample ammunition for the university authorities to step in, strip them of their responsibilities and exclude some prominent members from the university for life.[21] There then followed a long period where the case was brought before the courts.[22] Despite this process continuing until the spring of 1968, in the meantime any *Situationniste* influence had dissipated with the Strasbourg branch riven with conflict and even excluded from the IS.[23] Locally, this episode had, by the eve of 1968, exacerbated the national

---

[17] See Feuerstein, p. 20; Georges Livet, *50 années à l'université de Strasbourg* (Strasbourg: Société Savante d'Alsace, 1998), p. 159.

[18] For details of the extraordinary coup by which the *Situationnistes* distributed their pamphlet see Livet, pp. 155-57; [No author's name provided], "De Strasbourg, Lettrisme et Situationnisme hier et aujourd'hui", *Cahiers/Chroniques,* 3, Université de Strasbourg, pp. 61-63.

[19] Feuerstein, p. 20.

[20] Livet, pp. 159-60.

[21] [No author's name provided], "10 jours qui ébranlèrent Strasbourg ou l'internationale situationniste se donne en spectacle", *Gros sel*, 8 (1968), p. 56.

[22] Remy Amann, *Le Scandale de Strasbourg ou l'épisode situationniste de la capitale alsacienne*, [Mémoire de Maîtrise], Université de Strasbourg, 1990, p. 131.

[23] Wendling, p. 23.

phenomenon of indifference amongst the student mass.[24] The silent majority of students increasingly perceived political issues as the domain of an excitable minority intent on wreaking havoc via extremist ideology. Largely apathetic, they preferred to concentrate on their studies despite grounds for discontent with the system.[25]

It would be wrong to state that the Strasbourg '68 is ignored in the dominant representations of 1968. In fact, due largely to the influence of *Situationniste* ideas and language on the spectacular elements that dominate the stereotypical image of the French 1968, one could be forgiven for interpreting the events in Strasbourg as very much fitting the mould of the conventional representation.[26] The following detailed reconstruction of these events problematises such an assumption.

6-18 May

The spark that triggered the Strasbourgeois events originated in Paris. However, despite clearly drawing on events in the capital, the trajectory was soon to differ between what took place in the Latin Quarter and on the Esplanade.[27]

On 6 May in reaction to the events of the previous three days in Paris, a minority of students in the Arts faculty responded to the *Union Nationale des Etudiants de France* (UNEF) call for a strike in

---

[24] Fischer, p. 382.

[25] Feuerstein, p. 17.

[26] In the vast majority of texts on 1968 that make any mention of Strasbourg it is generally only to highlight the role of the *Situationnistes*. For example, see Jacques Capdevielle and Henri Rey, *Dictionnaire de Mai 68* (Paris: Larousse, 2008), p. 392-93.

[27] A range of sources, including interviews with participants, consultation of Archives in *Les Archives de la Ville et de la Communaute Urbaine* (which houses an excellent collection on May '68) as well as the following texts, were used to put this chapter together: Françoise Olivier-Utard, "Les 'événements' de mai 68 en Alsace", *Almémos*, 12 June 2008, pp. 2-5; Hervé de Chalendar, "Mai 68, Un printemps en Alsace", *L'Alsace*, special edition, February 2008, pp. 4-11; Wendling; Strauss and Richiez, pp. 121-28; Jean-Paul Haas, *La Révolution inutile* (Strasbourg: Oberlin, 1987); Acker, pp. 6369-74; Feuerstein, pp. 24-57; [No author's name provided], "Le mai de Strasbourg. Chronologie des mouvements étudiants qui se manifestent à Strasbourg en particulier durant le mois de mai et juin 1968", *Bulletin d'information,* Université de Strasbourg, 15, 1968, pp. 118-24.

solidarity with their Nanterrois counterparts. The movement quickly brought together 500 students in the *Aula* (the grand reception hall) of the *Palais Universitaire* (PU) before 1000 demonstrators made their way to the city centre on a march that culminated in a sit-down protest in front of the offices of the local newspaper *Les Dernières Nouvelles d'Alsace* (DNA). The university strike movement quickly spread to the seven faculties where students, teachers and senior figures in the university milieu focussed on the need to discuss and organise a coherent movement.[28]

By 10 May, the idea of worker-student solidarity was floated during discussions, and the decision was taken to occupy the PU, an action facilitated by the *nuit des barricades* in the capital. Having spent the entire evening listening to radio reports from Paris, the Strasbourgeois students occupied the PU, declared the university autonomous and flew the red flag from what has been described as the "symbole de l'université".[29] There was a considerable turnout for the 13 May nationwide demonstration and one-day strike in protest against police repression of Parisian students. However, unlike elsewhere, in Strasbourg this would not be a significant turning point. Despite bringing some 10,000 people on to the streets from across society, the strike was far from widespread and the rebellious contagion sweeping the country would take somewhat longer to reach l'Alsace (and not simply because of the geographical distance at play).

In the meantime, the university movement continued to take centre stage. On 14 May, the Minister for Education, Alain Peyrefitte, granted official permission to the University of Strasbourg to undertake an experiment in autonomy.[30] Despite rejecting this move as an isolationist tactic, the university movement established many *commissions paritaires* which set about formulating proposals for the reform of the university system. As the strike movement in the world of work showed signs of falling into line with what was happening nationally,[31] students began to emphasise the need to bridge the gap between the university and the factory. 18 May signalled an important

---

[28] Feurestein, p. 23-24.
[29] Interview with Lucien Braun, who was a young lecturer at the University of Strasbourg in 1968, 27 June 2008. See also Haas, p. 2-3.
[30] Feurestein, pp. 30-33; Acker, p. 6371; Haas, p. 6-7.
[31] Strauss and Richiez, pp. 121-24.

shift in the events in Strasbourg with the beginning of a veritable strike movement marked with the occupation of the first-class waiting room in the city's train station.

18-28 May

Over the course of the next ten days, in both the public and private sectors, the strike movement spread.[32] By 28 May the stoppages had reached their high point, by which stage a feeling of worry was prevalent amongst local authorities and the conservative population. With one eye on the situation in Paris, officials in Strasbourg were faced with a situation that saw the strike spreading across a range of sectors, the increased involvement of the main trade unions, move-ment from the political opposition,[33] the occupation of the local theatre and the intensification of the university movement. By 21 May, the local population could be forgiven for believing that the region was being consumed by the revolutionary fervour they had been reading of in the newspapers and hearing on the radio. Faced with these conditions, local Gaullists began to react. On 22 May they issued a statement in which they declared that "La République est en danger".[34] However, despite unquestionably marking an escalation in the gravity of the local crisis, this period also saw what had been a relatively contained and measured university movement overstep the boundaries of the acceptable in a series of actions that ultimately would trigger the beginning of its demise.

On 21 May, the Strasbourgeois population woke to the news that in the early hours of the morning the word *révolution* had been daubed on the *Monument aux Morts* in the city centre.[35] The student

---

[32] Strauss and Richiez, pp. 124-28; Acker, p. 6372.

[33] Strauss and Richiez, p. 141-42.

[34] Wendling.

[35] This episode had always been one of the mysteries of the events in Strasbourg as no-one ever accepted responsibility and no-one was found guilty. A huge polemic broke out in the aftermath as students went as far as to produce a tract with drawings of the location so as to highlight how it was impossible for them to have carried out such an act. In so doing they always implied that it was clearly an act by the opposition to cast derision on the student movement. The mystery was eventually solved in 2008 when one student from the time eventually explained how she was present when two bourgeois students decided to carry out this provocative act with no

movement was immediately held responsible for this "erreur à ne pas commettre",[36] and the reaction from the general public was one of revulsion. The masses, who had until then quietly stood back and observed this movement develop, were given a reason to no longer be simply the 'silent majority'. Such irresponsible and disrespectful actions were the proof required that the movement in Strasbourg was none other than a provincial branch of the anarchic nonsense of the *gauchistes troublions* in Paris. 24 May would be the next notable date in the creation of local opposition to what was perceived as an increasingly uncontrollable student movement. The day began with students marching to the *Pont de l'Europe* on the border with Germany to welcome Daniel Cohn-Bendit back to France following his famous *interdiction de séjour*.[37] Despite his non-appearance, the act of welcoming the 'German anarchist' and the disturbances that accompanied the ensuing protest were evidence enough for the conservative population that the students were intent on replicating the *chienlit* of the Latin Quarter. This impression would be confirmed later that same evening. Following de Gaulle's failed address, students in Strasbourg gathered in their occupied faculties and listened as their Parisian comrades yet again fought pitched battles with the police on one of the most intense nights of trouble in the capital. A decision was taken that the best way for students in Strasbourg to show solidarity would be to equally take to the streets.[38] As the student demonstration reached the city centre it was faced with local police and CRS who were not keen on seeing the violence of Paris replicated in Strasbourg. The students nevertheless managed to build a barricade and prepared to defend it.[39] During the inevitable police charge, there was minimal violence, only a handful of arrests and little damage. However, the fact that the students had dared construct a barricade in an affront to local authority was clearly a step too far. As if to confirm the ab-

---

other motive than the thrill of such a serious transgression. See Elisabeth Schulthess, "Mai 68: Le Révelation de Bichette sur 'l'affaire du Monument aux Morts'", *L'Alsace,* 20 May 2008.

[36] Interview with Georges Foessel, who was a young archivist in 1968 and is responsible for the outstanding collection of material on the '68 events in Strasbourg available in the Archives de la Ville, 20 June 2008.

[37] Utard, p. 4.

[38] Feurestein, p. 43-44.

[39] For details see Feurestein, p. 43; Livet, p. 199-200.

surdity of what was happening and intensify accusations of *chienlit*, a local homeless person (named Celestin) who had become the mascot of the student movement was ceremonially nominated the Dean of the *faculté de lettres* following his heroics in clashes with the police.[40] From this point the student movement had lost all credibility in the eyes of the local population and the tide was beginning to turn against it. By 28 May, the strike had reached its high point. However, as discussed below, the convergence is not simply coincidental: with the conclusion of the Grenelle negotiations, this date also signalled the end of this crucial and eventful period as well as the tipping point of what was to be tolerated in Strasbourg.

28 May-1 June

The combination of the concessions offered at Grenelle and the *chienlit* of the previous week spurred a push for a return to reality. Gaullist supporters signalled their desire to finish with this movement during a gathering at the now symbolically charged location that was the *Monument aux Morts*.[41] This backlash was given even greater impetus when, on 30 May, de Gaulle's defiant speech struck a chord with the local population and inspired them to take matters into their own hands. The General's call for defence committees to be established around the country to protect the Republic was immediately met by André Bord who created *Comité d'Action Civique* (CAC) in each commune in what Strauss and Richiez describe as the "contre-offensive politique".[42] As some of the biggest and most important factories voted for a return to work, such as the Peugeot factory on 31 May, the students were becoming increasingly isolated.

On Saturday 1 June, another demonstration was planned in support of General de Gaulle with its finishing point the *Monument aux Morts*. What started out as a 1500 strong demonstration that marched peacefully around the city, ended with 5-6000 people at the *Place de*

---

[40] De Chalendar, p. 7.
[41] Feurestein, p. 47. It is also worth noting that a national meeting of *Anciens Combattants* had been held in Strasbourg between 23-27 May. This undoubtedly heightened tension and demonstrates the significance of the war in this region. See *Les Dernières Nouvelles d'Alsace,* 17 May 1968, p. 23.
[42] Strauss and Richiez, p. 143.

la République. Here, a number of speakers, including André Bord, addressed an already tense crowd. Word soon spread that a red flag was flying from the PU—which, under a kilometre away, directly facing the *Monument aux Morts,* was in full view of everyone at the meeting. A number of demonstrators decided to march on the PU to tear down this insult to the Republic.[43] Meanwhile, students who had been sunning themselves on the steps of the PU were shocked to see several hundred armed and angry protestors charging towards them.[44] Panicking, they barricaded themselves inside the building. However, such measures could not prevent the attackers from gaining access to the PU via its many different entrances. For a brief period there was a toe-to-toe battle between the students and the assailants. The latter caused significant material damage by breaking windows and ransacking offices as they fought their way into the building. They also left a number of students injured before the police managed to separate the two sides. There then followed a prolonged stand-off during which the CRS protected the students from any further attacks by constructing a human cordon between the PU and the Gaullist supporters massed at the foot of the steps. Negotiations on the possibility of removing the red flag were eventually brought to a close when it was agreed that the tricolore and the European flag would accompany the red flag of the students.[45] This extraordinary episode signified the divide between the student movement and the general population that had had enough of the defiant attitude towards authority experienced for almost four weeks. The rest of the month would see the gradual decline and demise of the university revolt.

June 1968

On 2 June, an agreement was reached to take down the red flag and negotiations began on the possibility of locking the PU overnight. By 7 June, the isolation of the students, exacerbated by the re-opening of secondary schools and the end of *lycéen* participation, was such that

---

[43] Strauss and Richiez, p. 50; Haas, p. 14.
[44] Jean Michel Mehl was a student at the university of Strasbourg in 1968 and his father was Dean of the Theology Faculty. Interview, 24 June 2008.
[45] For more detail on this critically important moment see *Les Dernières Nouvelles d'Alsace,* 2-3 June 1968, p. 21-22.

they felt the need to put a *service d'ordre* in place to protect their occupations. Between 8-10 June, the Strasbourgeois movement was reinvigorated as it hosted a national meeting of representatives from 13 different universities around the country that had been working on proposals for possible higher education reform. However, despite three days of discussion, no solid conclusions were reached and when the meeting was brought to a close on 10 June it was done so with a sense of failure.[46] Over the next four days, the movement was dealt a number of further blows. Firstly, a demonstration organised on 12 June in protest against the violence at Sochaux only managed to bring together 500 people and ended with the CRS entering the PU. Then on 14 June the *Conseil Universitaire* was dissolved and the occupation of the Arts faculty was abandoned. On 15 June, Strasbourg was once again the host of a mass meeting. This time, however, it brought together students not from around France but from around Europe in a bid to draw some common conclusions from what had just been experienced. However, these *Assises Internationales* went virtually unnoticed and failed to reach any solid conclusions. As the month carried on it was agreed to lock the PU overnight (17 June), the tricolore replaced the red flag (18 June), and the turnout for a joint meeting between students and teaching staff was virtually nil. On 23 June, the first round of legislative elections saw the Gaullists sweep to a huge victory without the need for a second round: all 13 sitting deputies were re-elected.[47] The students were on holiday and the Strasbourgeois '68 was over or as one anonymous tract ironically put it, "Si le mouvement baisse et l'occupation cesse, c'est parce que la vacance des grandes valeurs provient de la valeur des grandes vacances".[48]

---

[46] Feurestein, p. 57.

[47] Bernard Vogler, *Nouvelle Histoire d'Alsace. Une Région au cœur de* l'Europe (Toulouse: Privat, 2003), p. 273.

[48] Anonymous tract in "Les événements de mai 68 à la faculté des lettres de Strasbourg", Documents legués aux archives par Marc Schweyer, Archives de la Ville, Strasbourg, Box 114Z, No. 5, pièce 3.

A Divergent '68?

There can be no question that the Strasbourgeois revolt of 1968 was sparked by and drew inspiration from the capital. However, to assume that events in the Latin Quarter were somehow replicated in Strasbourg is to negate the specificities of this city's upheaval and contribute to the dilution of 1968's diversity.

In order to make sense of what took place it is necessary to consider the regional, historical, political and cultural aspects that set this city and region apart. For example, perhaps the most prevalent impression is that 1968 in Strasbourg was experienced with a certain degree of *sagesse* or, as one tract from 10 June put it, "Strasbourg, toujours à l'avant-garde du retour à l'ordre".[49] This is reflected in the virtual absence of violence. In fact there was very little tolerance of any excesses in terms of street protests and on the one occasion that students did overstep the mark, the revulsion of the general public was matched only by the hard line of the local police chief who declared the next day, "J'ai donné l'ordre de charger et de la faire vig-oureusement. J'en prends la responsabilité, il y a des limites à ne pas dépasser. Nous ne tolérons pas que Strasbourg devienne une ville de barricades".[50] Also worth pointing out is the fact that at no stage was there any real sense that the city was on the verge of paralysis.[51] There was a general strike but it was not widespread and never matched the exploits of other cities.[52]

Two reasons in particular help explain why this was the case. Firstly, as mentioned previously, the Strasbourgeois population was inherently conservative and one that found comfort in the stability and order that characterised Gaullist France. One only has to consider the great upheavals experienced across the region's tumultuous history to understand the population's desire to maintain some degree of stability. As Lucien Braun explained, "C'est germanique, il y a l'esprit

---

[49] Archives de la Ville, Box 114Z, No. 2, pièce 11.
[50] Livet, p. 200.
[51] De Chalendar, p. 9.
[52] As Strauss and Richiez argue, despite an intensification of the strike movement towards the end of May, the aim on behalf of the Trade Unions was to strengthen their hand in forthcoming negotiations, and the strength of the movement at this stage should be read as a result of this desire and not as fitting the nationwide trend of a complete standstill. Strauss and Richiez, p. 129.

germanique en Alsace […] On aime l'ordre ici […] c'est une tradition germanique".[53] Therefore, there was not the general propensity for radical change so prominent elsewhere, which explains why the movement very rarely stepped over the boundaries or showed very little tolerance for those elements that did. The impact of the proximity of the German border was also not without significance. Whilst other parts of the country soon found difficulties in providing the basics, and in particular petrol, such a degree of shortage was not to be experienced in Strasbourg. Anything running short, as Foessel explained, could simply be bought across the border: "Il ne leur manquait pas de nourriture, il ne leur manquait pas d'essence, d'argent […] et tout ça grâce à la proximité de l'Allemagne".[54] An anecdote concerning the impact of this geographical circumstance concerns the electricity supply for the region. Georges Foessel explained how his concern for the impact of a strike by *Electricité de Strasbourg* (EDS) was tempered when he visited their headquarters during the revolt. He was brought to an area and shown a lever that permitted the regional grid to be switched to the German system in the event of a strike.[55] This anecdote sums up just how the proximity of Germany and the cross-border ties that had been created over the years provided the grounds for specific characteristics that set Alsace apart, and, as Foessel argued, "ont fait que le mouvement finalement paraissait plus agaçant qu'autre-chose".[56]

The conservative nature described above is also a significant factor in making sense of the degree of isolation felt by the student movement in Strasbourg. Such was the detachment between the university and the general population that Georges Foessel described it as "un volcan sur une banquise".[57] Although the idea of a complete divorce between the student and worker movements is an increasingly common feature of dominant narratives of 1968, there is evidence that whilst contact was difficult, efforts were made on both sides to exploit the potential of the situation,[58] and, as Boris Gobille argues, "[à] des

---

[53] Braun, Interview.
[54] Foessel, Interview.
[55] Foessel, Interview.
[56] Foessel, Interview.
[57] Foessel, Interview.
[58] Reynolds (2007), p. 5.

échelles plus fines, locales, voire personnelles, la rencontre a bien eu lieu".[59] However, this was not the case concerning the movement in Strasbourg. Despite a certain degree of effort, there was a profound mistrust on behalf of the workers that stood in the way of any fruitful contacts.[60] In fact, and despite some sporadic strikes, the disunity and dispersion that characterised the strike movement in the region in general reflects the reluctance of the working class to become involved in what was in Strasbourg essentially perceived as a student movement.

However, care must be taken regarding the use of the term 'student movement'.[61] As a result of the ever-narrowing history of the events, any mention of students in 1968 tends to conjure up images of radicalised elements with utopian ideals whose only intent was to bring down the entire political system with no idea of how it would be replaced. All too often, the *Situationniste* past in Strasbourg leads to an easy assimilation of the '68 events there within this dominant narrative. However, as Amman argues, "[v]ouloir attribuer aux Situationnistes Strasbourgeois une participation majeure [est] un jugement abusif, d'ailleurs très favorable aux spéculations les plus fantaisistes".[62] Firstly, by 1968 the main protagonists of the *Situationniste* movement in Strasbourg were no longer around and those that were there were extremely critical of what was happening.[63] In one tract they even went as far as to claim that "l'étudiant n'a décidémment rien compris".[64] Such criticisms stemmed from the fact that the Strasbourgeois student population—contrary to popular myth—was, from the outset, dedicated to putting together a serious movement whose aim it was to work on proposing reform of the system. One only has to consider the quantity of declarations, proposals and general output of the university reformist movement in

---

[59] Boris Gobille, *Mai 68* (Paris: La Découverte, 2008), p. 55.
[60] See interview with Jean Kaspar in De Chalendar, p. 25.
[61] For discussion of limitations associated with such a term in this context, see Reynolds (2007), p. 8.
[62] Amann, p. 140.
[63] For more details see Amann, pp. 138-50.
[64] Anonymous tract in "Les événements de mai 68 à la faculté des lettres de Strasbourg", Documents legués aux archives par Marc Schweyer, Archives de la Ville, Strasbourg, Box 114Z, no. 5, pièce 1.

Strasbourg to understand where the priorities of this movement lay.[65] The numerous *Commissions Paritaires* from the seven different faculties benefited from the genuine interest in formulating proposals to improve the existing system as well as the active participation and close alliances with significant members of the teaching corps. As Jean Dewitz explained, "l'implication de pas mal d'enseignants […] a donné un aspect presque officiel au mouvement […] qui a fait que Strasbourg est devenu un pôle qu'on a pris au sérieux".[66] This aspect, in many respects, can help explain one of the most interesting developments of the Strasbourgeois '68.

The fact that the then Minister for Education Alain Peyrefitte gave permission for the University of Strasbourg to carry out an experiment in autonomy is, as François Igersheim argues, what sets the Strasbourgeois '68 apart.[67] Following a lengthy conversation between Peyrefitte and representatives of the University, the Minister seemingly conceded to one of the principal demands of the student movement.[68] There are several possible explanations for this extra-ordinary set of circumstances, unique in 1968. It could be argued that Peyrefitte was simply appeasing the students in such a huge city by giving the impression of offering them what they wanted in order to prevent them from joining the more radical elements of the '68 revolt, or, as Foessel described it, "un peu de farine à moudre".[69] This interpretation is given even greater weight when one considers the government's desire to see such a symbolic and dangerously located university (in terms of the risk of contagion from German elements) kept out of the seemingly uncontrollable movement developing in Paris. There is also the question of the significance of the term 'autonomy' for this region. Could the choice of this term—laden with pejorative historical significance—have been a strategic choice on behalf of the minister to conjure up the spectre of past errors and in so doing discredit the movement in the eyes of the general population?

---

[65] The collection of les Archives de la Ville are dominated by the work of the various *commissions paritaires* and underline the importance of the reformist sector in the Strasbourg university movement.
[66] Jean Dewitz was a student of German at the University of Strasbourg in 1968. Interview with author, July 2008.
[67] François Igersheim in Livet, p. 171.
[68] For details of how this conversation unfolded see Livet, pp. 188-91.
[69] Foessel, Interview.

For, as Dewitz explained, "effectivement dès qu'on parle de l'autonomie, Paris se fâche".[70] One could also argue that the movement in Strasbourg was at the very front line of the reformist elements of the national 1968 movement. The serious nature of the movement and the determination to focus efforts on future reform was so obvious that that Peyrefitte genuinely saw what was happening there as providing fertile ground for the discovery of possible solutions to the undeniably problematic system of higher education.[71] The prominence of Strasbourg in the reformist drive is underlined by the hosting of the *Assises Générales* in June 1968 which brought together fourteen universities from around the country. Finally, it is also true that Edgar Faure, Minister responsible for reforming the system of higher education in the aftermath of 1968, consulted a number of people prominent in the various *commission paritaires* around the country with Strasbourg once again playing a central role.[72] As Bernard Carrière, describing some of the key elements of the reformist drive in Strasbourg, argued, "[à] certains égards, la Loi Faure puis d'autres qui ont suivi ont repris ces concepts".[73]

Therefore, in terms of the actual events of 1968, it is clear that whilst Strasbourg cannot be considered in isolation to what was happening nationally and in particular in Paris, it is equally true that the capital cannot be considered as representing the Strasbourg revolt. However, when one juxtaposes the dominant narrative of the '68 events with a close regional analysis it becomes clear that important differences and elements are being squeezed from the history of 1968. One very symbolic example of this in terms of what happened in Strasbourg concerns the extraordinary events of 1 June. In the stereotypical image of 1968 the students are often framed in direct opposition with the police and in particular the CRS. On June 1 in Strasbourg the students were protected from attack by a crowd of marauding Gaullists by the CRS at the steps of the PU.[74] Describing

---

[70] Dewitz, Interview.

[71] Livet, p. 201.

[72] "Des représentants de l'université de Strasbourg ont été reçus par M. Edgar Faure", *Les Dernières Nouvelles d'Alsace,* 6 September 1968.

[73] *Les Dernières Nouvelles d'Alsace*, 18 May 2008, p. 10.

[74] There is a photo showing the CRS at the foot of the steps of the PU with their backs to the students and facing the Gaullist demonstrators in Les Archives de la Ville, Box 114Z, No. 6, Pièce 1.

what happened, one journalist pointed out that "il est paradoxal de voir les CRS et les gardiens de la paix empêcher les Strasbourgeois d'enlever le drapeau rouge qui flotte sur leur université".[75] This is indeed May '68 *à l'envers*, problematising the progressively diluted history of these events and flagging up the inadequacy of the dominant narrative in reflecting the heterogeneous nature of the national 1968 movement. Such incompleteness is given even more significance when one considers how 1968 would become a turning-point in the development of the region's cultural identity.

Consequences

Alsace was not immune to the generic changes engendered by the events of 1968. The stereotypical break with archaic structures that dominates conventional representations was obvious there also. Social mores were relaxed, teacher-taught relations became less formalised, and structures became less hierarchical in the workplace. There were, however, some areas that, although commonly linked to the 1968 events, took on a specific regional dimension that highlights how the diversity outlined above did not simply stop with how the events were played out. For example, in the aftermath of the revolt, the University of Strasbourg experienced significant structural change that to this day marks out 1968 as a definitive reference point in this institution's long history.[76] The University was split into three separate institutions in a bid to meet the challenges that the '68 revolt had exposed and, as Alacandre explained, "[s]i l'on fait un bilan de '68 en Alsace, il faut insérer cette question sur le plan universitaire".[77] Another regional specificity concerns one of the most commonly cited trends described as emanating from 1968: the ecology movement. The role of Alsace in

---

[75] *Les Dernières Nouvelles d'Alsace*, 2/3 juin 1968, p. 22.

[76] The History section of the website for what became Université Marc Bloch explains "Mai 68 ébranle les structures traditionnelles et remet en question une université qui se sclérose. En juillet 1968, une loi d'orientation de l'enseignement supérieur est votée. La Faculté ouvre à nouveau ses portes en octobre, partant sur de nouveaux principes tels que : pluridisciplinarité, autonomie, participation", http://www-umb.u-strasbg.fr/c1.php3?Id=001&cadre=c1 (accessed April 2009).

[77] Jean-Jacques Alcandre experienced the events of 1968 at Nanterre and later moved to Strasbourg where he is a lecturer at the Université Marc Bloch. Interview with author, 24 June 2008.

bringing this to the fore was paramount.[78] Many of those active in 1968 were integral to the struggles against the construction of the Marckolsheim and Fessenheim nuclear sites in the early 1970s. They brought with them a similar mentality as well as forms of action and methods of organisation that had proved so effective in 1968. The prominent *soixantehuitard* atmosphere has led analysts and particip-ants to draw a direct link between 1968 and such anti-nuclear activities. Equally evident in such struggles was an increasingly prominent sense of regional fraternity reflecting the change in attitudes that the 1968 events helped bring about.

Reticence in the affirmation of their complex dual identity was prominent amongst the Alsatian population during the 1945-68 period.[79] In many domains, commentators and analysts point to a before and after May '68. Such a model fits an examination of the development of Alsatian cultural identity. Bernard Vogler states that, "[l]'effervescence suscitée par l'agitation de mai conduit à une décrispation, un déblocage après le sentiment de culpabilité qui a étouffé l'Alsace depuis 1945".[80] Volger goes on to identify three distinct periods that help map out the impact of this change. The first period delineated (1968-74) is characterised by a surge in interest in all things concerning Alsatian culture and identity. As early as June 1968 a group known as *le Cercle René Schickele* was founded with the intention of bringing the issue of bilingual education back to the table.[81] A new generation of singers and musicians, epitomised by Roger Siffer, emerged, apparently unashamed to proclaim their dual identity through song, dance and theatre.[82] Such evident trans-formations were given further credence during the anti-nuclear demonstrations as the issues of ecology, bilingualism and the affirm-ation of cultural identity through music found common ground and popular support.[83] Despite this renaissance in regionalism—and arg-uably in a bid to avoid any problematic association between regional-ism, politics and the shame of the collaborationist past—there were no

---

[78] Vogler (2003), p. 321.
[79] Vogler (2003), pp. 284-86.
[80] Vogler (1993), p. 465.
[81] Aubert and Sobocinski, p. 14.
[82] Aubert and Sobocinski, p. 14; Vogler (1993), pp. 493-500.
[83] Jean-Claude Richez, "Mouvements culturels en Alsace" in [No editor provided], *Encyclopédie de l'Alsace*, 9, 1984, p. 5923.

significant political parties with traditional regionalist agendas that
came to the fore during this period.[84] The second phase that Volger
describes spans 1975-79 and is one that is characterised by a boom in
publications and other outlets for the affirmation of the Alsatian
culture. As Richez points out, "[a]près avoir 'découvert' leur langue et
leur passé, les militants culturels affirment vouloir prendre en charge
la parole des créateurs d'aujourd'hui en se donnant des moyens de
production".[85] In many respects, such developments confirmed the re-
emergence of the regional identity. It was equally during this period
that mainstream political parties began to sit up and take notice of this
increasingly prominent facet of regional society.[86] The integration of
regional issues coincided with the third of Volger's periods and is
marked by the adoption of a text entitled *la Plateforme de Selestat* by
all the major left-wing forces in April 1981.[87] In a bid to force the
future government's hand in the run-up to the elections, this text sets
out demands in relation to bilingual education, signage and media
presence for the dialect. 1981 marked a realisation of this growing
desire to see regional issues—based on the importance of culture and
language—become unavoidable aspects of French national politics
and society.[88] This third and final period saw the implementation of
the decentralisation policies under Mitterrand, which can be seen as
not only a confirmation of the need to recognise such issues but
arguably the culmination of a struggle resuscitated from the embers of
May-June 1968.

Today problems remain.[89] Many elements continue to cause
controversy and debate.[90] The regional dialect remains under threat as
does its place in the education system. The lack of generational
transfer and question marks over the utility of such a dialect in an
increasingly globalised society are just some of the challenges facing

---

[84] Aubert and Sobocinski, p. 14.
[85] Richez, p. 5293.
[86] Richez, p. 15.
[87] Richez, p. 15.
[88] Richez, p. 5293.
[89] For an overview of current issues see Meyer, pp. 388-98.
[90] None more so than the rise of the extreme right towards the end of the 1990s in the
region. For a discussion of this issue and how it reflects a very bleak outlook for the
region see Alain Bihr, "L'Exception alsacienne", *Le Monde Diplomatique*, May 1998,
pp. 16-17.

this significant facet of the region's identity. However, the existence of this identity is no longer in question, nor—and perhaps more importantly—is there any evident shame attached to its affirmation. In fact, the duality of Alsatian culture and identity, born out of the region's geographical and historical specificities, is increasingly perceived as a strength both within the region but also on a national level. Vogler goes on to identify specific elements and how they have evolved over the years, such as the University system, cultural politics, theatre, the arts and museums.[91] In each case 1968 can be highlighted as a significant turning point, a period that seems to have provided an opportunity for a reinvigoration of the region's cultural identity.

What explanations can be proposed to help us understand why 1968 was to prove so fundamental in this domain? The answer is twofold and can be found in a change in the rapport between state and region (and applicable on a national level) but perhaps more significantly in the impact of the new '68 generation. Around the country, the events of 1968 saw those without a voice suddenly demand a greater say in how their lives were governed. In universities, factories, schools, shops, almost everywhere grievances were brought to the fore. Significantly, one of the common trends running through these divergent groups was the prominence of youth. Young people, across the country, and across the board, took a stand demanding change, adaptation, modernisation and a break with the past. The great strength of this generation was not only its size but also it wider, less insular perspective (brought about by a whole raft of socio-economic changes that characterised the *trente glorieuses*). Drilling down to a more local scenario such factors are key considerations in Alsace.

A generation of young people who had been denied access to their own regional identity as a result of a set of circumstances that took place beyond their control and at a time that must have seemed light years away was provided with a clean slate. The possibilities of breaking down the structures that governed their society and drawing on the international element of 1968 (all the more evident in Alsace due to proximity with Germany) provided this generation with the chance to reclaim an identity that until then was not compatible with

---

[91] Vogler (1993), pp. 465-522.

the circumstances and mentalities that had governed Alsatian as well as national politics and society since 1945. 1968 provided the grounds for the re-emergence of the hybrid culture so often described as the Alsatian complex. From this point on it was possible to reclaim this bi-polar identity without any direct association with the mistakes of the past and therefore any confusion with the struggle for autonomy. The Alsatian identity (both elements) found its place in France and, as we have seen, would go on from strength to strength.

Such progress was facilitated by (and arguably precipitated) a shift in how the centralised state perceived and managed the regions in the long process that, started in the aftermath of 1968, culminated in the 1982 Deferre reform and the passing on of considerable regional independence. Given the post-'68 trajectory in this domain, the influence of the 1968 events in encouraging the diversity and plurality of Alsatian cultural identity is certainly difficult to ignore.

Conclusion

Even before the events of 1968 had ended, a trend emerged that saw this period become the focus of much analysis and discussion. As the years have gone by, the decennial anniversaries—and the hike in interest that has accompanied them—have been crucial in shaping the dominant image. By 1998, this image had become increasingly narrow to the point that *les événements* ran the risk of being reduced to nothing other than a jovial, Parisian, student-based revolt that led to many changes, some of which were hard to pin down while others were questionable. However, the fortieth anniversary marks a potentially significant turning point. There has been a noticeable trend amongst historians to go beyond the narrow, dominant perspective.[92] For example, the role of the working class and the nature of the huge 1968 strike movement have been given more emphasis.[93] Also, there

---

[92] See, for example, Fournel; Philippe Artières and Michelle Zancarini-Fournel, *68 Une histoire collective [1962-1981]* (Paris: La Découverte, 2008); Gobille; Dominique Damamme, *Mai-Juin 68* (Paris: Editions Ouvriers, 2008).
[93] Xavier Vigna, *L'Insubordination ouvrière dans les années 68* (Rennes: Presses Universitaires de Rennes, 2007).

has been an effort to de-centre '68 analysis in a bid to break down the over-emphasis on the Latin Quarter.[94]

However, this is just the beginning of a very difficult process of undoing forty years of analysis and coverage in a bid to repackage the history of 1968 in France in order to reveal its true complexity and magnitude. This chapter aims to encourage this process through one particular aspect: the need to map the events of 1968. If the divergences of Strasbourg are anything to go by, it is evident that a push to identify, highlight and showcase other regional departures is paramount in telling the full story of 1968 in France. Moreover, the need to reframe the 1968 events within a regional context is given even greater credence when we consider their impact on the Alsace region. For, as this chapter has demonstrated, not only did the '68 events in Strasbourg reflect and emphasise the nation's diversity, they also provided the grounds for the renaissance of Alsatian cultural identity and as a result encouraged an acceptance of the plurality of France.

---

[94] Chris Reynolds, "Understanding 1968–The Case of Brest", *Modern and Contemporary France,* 16.2 (2008), 209-22.

French Unity and the European Union: The Role of French Regions

Angela Giovanangeli

Translated from the French by Travis Watters

In France, the term 'national unity' is a slogan that remains the prerogative of politicians from both sides of politics concerned with expressions and phrases that speak of the importance of French cohesion.

The subject of French national unity is vast, touching the heart of France's political, economic and social structures, including education, work, linguistic policy, the legal system and social assistance. The notion of unity within the territorial context, especially that of the French regions, is of particular interest for certain reasons: French regions are closely connected to the administrative division of France, which is tied to the policy of national unity. An historical study of the territorial evolution of France highlights the fact that, since the *Ancien Régime*, the territorial division of France has been executed with the express purpose of unifying the French territory politically. European integration, however, has introduced a new way of viewing the role of the European regions. It involves considering regions no longer as divisions within a nation, but rather as areas capable of dialogue with other regions of European Union member nations.

In this study regarding the idea of French national unity, European integration will be examined, as well as how it coexists with policies in place in France, a country that favours the cohesion of State. It will seek to determine whether the European Union's regional policy, which encourages co-operation between regions of different European countries, calls into question the notion of unity in France, and will focus in particular on the regional groupings of the Upper Rhine and the Basque Country. These ideas will be considered in the context of ongoing debates amongst thinkers like Robert Lafont who argue that Europe is a way for French regions to regain their voices,[1] while others like Pierre Lellouche insist that European integration is a vehicle for reinforcing French national policy.[2]

More generally, and in order to justify our interest in the words 'national unity', a rapid examination of a few speeches given and words published by political figures over the course of the last few decades will attest to the difficulty of the term 'unity'. By way of an example, the second volume of Charles de Gaulle's *Mémoires de guerre* is entitled *l'unité* and retraces the period from 1942 to 1944. This book provides a taste of what was the objective of Gaullist politics in the context of the year 1942. It portrays the cohesion of French resistance as an "instrument valable dans la lutte contre l'ennemi et, vis-à-vis des alliés, un appui essentiel pour ma politique d'indépendance et d'unité".[3] In this context, the word 'unity' clearly refers to that of a France divided between the German occupation and the multi-factional resistance, where the word 'unity' becomes the leitmotiv of a nation torn apart by war and political ideologies. But this term also reveals a significant preoccupation of General de Gaulle: for him, unity is the general response to French national crises.

Some examples of the use of the term 'unity' also appear in connection with other politicians. On 29 August 2004, at the time of the kidnapping of two French journalists in Iraq and within the context of the new law prohibiting "conspicuous" religious symbols, the

---

[1] Robert Lafont, *La Révolution régionaliste* (Paris: Gallimard, 1967), p. 16.

[2] Pierre Lellouche, *Illusions gauloises. Plaidoyer pour une France debout* (Paris: Grasset, 2006), p. 87.

[3] Charles de Gaulle, *Mémoires de guerre. L'unité : 1942-1944* (Paris: Plon, 1956), p. 50.

France 2 news bulletin broadcast a speech given by the then-President Jacques Chirac. The *France 2* presenter described this speech as "un appel à l'unité nationale". Chirac described the tradition of equality, respect and protection of the free practice of all religions in France as the "ciment de notre cohésion nationale".[4] This theme is reminiscent of an article published in *Le Monde* on 27 December 2003, where Chirac declared himself in favour of a law prohibiting the wearing of religious symbols for national cohesion and in order to avoid division.[5] In a more recent article, *Le Nouvel Observateur* on 20 August 2006 published the main points of a keynote address given by Ségolène Royal at the *fête de la rose* in Frangy-en-Bresse (Saône-et-Loire), in preparation for her candidature in the presidential elections of 2007. During her speech, Royal affirmed her support for Mitterrand's ideology, and passed it on to a 2006 audience. For her, "les paroles de François Mitterrand allaient droit à l'essentiel. Nous pouvons retenir le devoir d'unité: sans elle, rien n'est possible".[6] Finally, on 6 May 2007, Nicolas Sarkozy called the French to unity on the occasion of his victory in the presidential elections. He asked the French to "donner l'image d'une France réunie, rassemblée." He also declared that "il n'y a qu'une seule France".[7] These examples illustrate how the political framework changes, but the theme of French unity remains at the centre of the French national interest of major political players.

Yet, parallel to this idea of French unity resides a unity that is contested. Historians such as Suzanne Citron demand a re-examination of the past in order to shatter the myth of a united France.

---

[4] 'Verbatim' *Le Monde.fr*, 29 August 2004 (accessed online 30 August 2004), and the 8 pm *France 2* evening news from 29 August 2004.
[5] "M. Chirac prône le 'sursaut républicain' et interdit le voile à l'école", *Le Monde/Sélection hebdomadaire*, Saturday 27 December 2003.
[6] "Les principaux points du discours-programme", *Le Nouvel Observateur*, 20 August 2006,
http://permanent.nouvelobs.com/cgi/edition/qobs_imprime?cle=20060820.OBS8817 (accessed online 21 August 2006).
[7] "Sarkozy remercie ses partisans à la Concorde", http://www.france2.fr (accessed online 7 May 2007).

Others, such as Colette Beaune, speak of France in the plural, or of 'two Frances', a two-faced France hidden behind the illusion of unity.[8]

French unity is also contested by the emergence of new territorial identities. These new expressions of identity are created by formations in contemporary society, especially due to European integration, which require a new way of understanding the territorial area.

In the context of the regionalisation of France, the evolution of the concept of French unity is all the more intriguing, given that the region is perceived as being capable of breaking or reinforcing the unity of France at two levels. The first is at the sub-national level, where the battle over the regionalisation of France has enlivened debate since the nineteenth century. The other is at the super-national level, within the framework of European integration. Today, the French regions are at the centre of controversies concerning the national cohesion of France. Some political thinkers note that a deepening of the role of regions at these two levels highlights the unity of France. Others see in this only the division of the nation, hence the paradox of the unifying aspect of French regions.

The 1960s was a period of reflection in terms of French regionalisation. The arrival of the notion of Europe—the European Community at the end of the 1950s—and of discussions about the regionalisation of France in the 1960s, evolved alongside each other. In his work *La Révolution régionaliste*, Robert Lafont explains that, in the context of the 1960s, the idea of Europe stirs up contradictory positions for regional nationalists. On the one hand, Europe adds another layer of administration and threatens regional identity. On the other, it is a way for regions to reclaim their voices, insofar as Europe is able to "desserrer l'étau du centralisme français".[9]

In a more contemporary context, the politician Pierre Lellouche refers to the notion of Europe in terms of nationalism. For Lellouche, Europe is an "illusion gaulloise", which the French dream of glorifying and converting "en une espèce de 'France en plus grand', où nos autres partenaires ne seraient en quelque sorte—et pour leur

---

[8] See Suzanne Citron, *Le Mythe national : l'histoire de France en question* (Paris: Les Editions ouvrières, 1987) and Colette Beaune, *Naissance de la Nation France* (Paris: Gallimard, 1985).
[9] Lafont, p. 16.

plus grand bonheur!—que les démultiplicateurs de la puissance nationale, du modèle hexagonal",[10] as it were. Lellouche highlights the paradox that has emerged from European discourse—a discourse which, since 1958, has called for the free circulation of goods, assets and people, while the debates favouring the construction of Europe have leaned little by little towards "une rhétorique antimondialiste de préférence nationale élargie",[11] i.e. a new nationalism that would foreground the nation. For thinkers such as Lellouche, the construction of Europe leads to nationalistic thought, which clearly underlines the existence of the nation.

Defining 'Region'

In France, the notion of regions is both ancient and modern—ancient in the sense that France is a patchwork of cultural and linguistic identities attached to the past and to regional identity. It is new in the sense that the administrative division of France into regions took place in the 1980s. Certain modern-day regions in France evoke historic regions—Brittany and Alsace, for example. Other regions are new creations with no ties to history or culture. The Centre, for example, is a purely administrative name explaining the geographical position of the region.

In the European context, the meaning of the word 'region' is problematic, since "du fait de l'attitude des différents Etats membres, les Régions ne sont pas égales devant l'Union européenne".[12] The word "region" carries different connotations depending on the country in question: *Länder* in Germany refers to a federal administration; for France, the word *région* signifies a decentralised administration with limited powers; in Greece, local administrative divisions refer to an extremely limited governmental authority.

---

[10] Lellouche, p. 87.
[11] Lellouche, p. 90.
[12] Michel Thys, "Régions" *Eurinfo*, 291 (December 2004/January 2005), monthly newsletter, pp. 3-6 (p. 4).

French Regions in the Debate on Unity

After long debates reaching back to the nineteenth century on the problems linked to centralisation (an historic trend in France), and after the increasing number of talks over the course of the twentieth century, the speech given by General de Gaulle in Lyon on 24 March 1968 proclaimed that "[l]'effort multiséculaire de centralisation… ne s'impose plus désormais".[13] This speech on the necessity of de-centralisation in France ended disappointingly, with a vote against the idea of regionalisation, the theme of the referendum that resulted in the resignation of President de Gaulle in 1969. Yet, the idea of reforming the territorial divisions of France was taken up again by Maurice Couve de Murville's government, which drew up a referendum law leading to the creation of regions in France. The report, prepared by the *Délégation à l'Aménagement du Territoire et à l'Action Régionale* (DATAR) in 1970, defined the regionalisation of France and highlighted the problems created by centralisation: economic instabilities, social inequalities and political tensions between the French departments. Reinforcing regional power was, to politicians, the answer to this instability. It was only in 1982, after the Socialists came to power, and with the Defferre laws, that regions became fully-fledged administrative units (law no. 82-213 of 2 March 1982). Since 2003, regions have become an essential characteristic of the Republic, appearing in the French Constitution.[14]

Throughout these debates, the same theme has dominated and reflected the institutional evolution of France, oscillating between centralisation and decentralisation.[15] The movement of this pendulum, swinging between a centralising State and decentralisation, shows the

---

[13] Bruno Rémond, *La Région : Une unité politique d'avenir* (Paris: Editions Montchrestien, 1999), p. 11.

[14] Constitutional revision—loi constitutionnelle n° 2003-276 du 28 mars 2003 relative à l'organisation décentralisée de la République. For further information see no. 75 of the J.O., 29 March 2003, p. 5568.

[15] This is a phenomenon that has existed since the feudal era, by nature decentralised, followed by the monarchy, which brought the kingdom together under a single unit of power, culminating with the absolutism of Louix XIV. Then came the Revolution and Bonaparte, establishing a strong centralised system, followed by the Third Republic, which instated parliamentary democracy, while still allowing the State to dominate. Finally, the decisive debates between 1968 and 1981 on the regionalisation of France.

concern modification of the territorial and administrative divisions of France caused in terms of national unity. For example, when France was divided into regions in 1982, political discourse clearly reassured the French public that national unity was not in danger. In the final paragraph of article 59 of the law of 2 March 1982, the legislator asserted that "la réunion et l'organisation des régions en métropole et Outre-Mer ne portent atteinte ni à l'unité de la République, ni à l'intégrité du territoire".[16] Since their creation, regions have kindled much controversy and continue to be contested even today. Articles addressing the failure of regions in France[17] clash with research indicating that "les enquêteurs sont de plus en plus souvent convaincus que la région est l'unité politico-administrative d'avenir (65% en 1990 contre seulement 59% en 1986)".[18] The failure, according to critics, is in fact due to a lack of efficiency and a lack of power in the political decision making process.[19] Despite the fact that, since the law of 13 August 2004, the regions have found themselves endowed with more and more responsibilities in terms of economic development, regional development, education, professional training and health, a paradox exists in that the State is still omnipresent. As Dumont highlights, "l'Etat garde un rôle prépondérant, comme l'illustre le maintien de certains services de l'Etat aux différents échelons territoriaux".[20] Indeed, this is a unique situation when compared with administrative structures elsewhere in Europe, in the sense that France has established a double administration "dépendant l'une de l'État et l'autre du conseil régional, chacune en charge d'opérations relevant de logiques comparables sur le même territoire".[21] This is unlike other European regions where "les

---

[16] Rémond, p. 32.
[17] See Patrick Le Galès and Peter John, "Is the Grass Greener on the Other Side? What went Wrong with French Regions, and the Implications for England", *Policy and Politics*, 25.1 (1997): 51-60.
[18] Rémond, p. 7.
[19] Le Galès and John, p. 51. This article notes that, despite an increase in the allocation of the regional budget since the 1980s, the regions have very little influence in the French political system.
[20] Gérard-François Dumont, *Les Régions et la régionalisation en France* (Paris: Ellipses, 2004), p. 142.
[21] Dumont, p. 142.

exécutifs régionaux sont chargés d'appliquer les lois nationales dans leur ressort géographique".[22]

Another paradox that emerges is linked to the way in which the French State uses its regions to finance sectors that should, by law, be financed by the State itself. According to the law of 29 July 1982, the State has put in place contracts defining the actions that the State and regions commit to undertake during a certain period.[23] These contracts are called State-Region plan contracts and, within the framework of regional development, give the State the right to obtain funding from the regions for sectors for which the State is responsible, such as higher education and research. The State must pay an amount, but, according to Dumont, it has only paid part of the promised amounts, or with unjustified delays.[24] As a result, regions are at the service and under the authority of the State for matters of development concerning only a section of the territory. This financial dependence highlights the fact that the country's unity is still seen by the State in terms of central domination.

Taking these various factors into account, it is difficult to measure the success of the introduction of regions. Moreover, the economic and demographic disparities between the regions indicate that unity in these territorial domains has not been achieved, despite all the regional reforms. French regions present great demographic disparities: the most populous region of France is Ile de France, with 11 million inhabitants, whereas Corsica has only 0.3 million inhabitants.[25] Inequality is also seen in other areas, such as the rate of employment, due to differing economic histories (Nord-Pas-de-Calais, Languedoc-Roussillon, Lorraine and Corsica are the regions most affected by a low employment rate, whereas Rhône-Alpes is experiencing strong economic development).

The success of regionalisation is sometimes explained by politicians by the fact that regions can today intervene more efficiently in areas such as secondary education. Yet, as Dumont explains, despite the decentralisation of power since the 1980s, regulatory legislative powers belong to the State alone: "Dès qu'une politique

---

[22] Dumont, p. 142.
[23] Contracts to present date: 1984-1988, 1989-1993; 1994-1999, 2000-2006.
[24] Dumont, p. 59.
[25] Estimates: INSEE 2001.

régionale suppose une réglementation, les institutions nationales sont seules habilitées à édicter des normes qui, au demeurant, ne peuvent être différentes d'une région à l'autre".[26]

In the European context, the issue of regions is not confined to the national level, but spills over to affect the construction of Europe. The European Union has added an additional dimension to France's territorial administration. That is, development in France is no longer carried out only at the national, regional, departmental, intercommunal or municipal levels; regional development also occurs at the European level. Furthermore, Europe is changing the relationship between Paris and her regions. Paris, who has for centuries dominated the French territory, must now, in a sense, share this privilege with Brussels, the capital of Europe.

The voice of the French Region in European dialogue

The goal of creating the Common Market in the 1950s was to develop a common economic zone, in order to improve the standard of living for the six original member countries. The first treaties (the Treaty of Paris in 1950 and the Treaty of Rome in 1956) focussed on economic exchanges between the member countries. The Treaty of Rome makes little reference to regions, but, in the context of the economic development of member countries, mentions the importance of harmony between regions of member countries and that "les écarts entre les différentes Régions et le retard des moins favorisées" must be reduced.[27] It was only on 18 March 1975 that the European Regional Development Fund, the ERDF, was created to help regions that, for various reasons, were in need of financial assistance (industrial redevelopment, compensation due to the negative effects of community policy, economic instability caused by the joining of new Member States). The European Community grew, and, as a result, was confronted with the problem of member countries with regions lagging in

---

[26] Dumont, p. 106. It is important to note that the regions in Belgium have legislative power, the *Länder* in Germany each have a constitution, while in Spain, Catalonia and the Basque Country have increased power in terms of legislative and regulatory decisions.

[27] Claude de Granrut, *Europe le temps des Régions* (Paris: Librairie Générale du Droit et de la Jurisprudence, 1994), p. 22.

economic development. It was for this reason that the European
Council of Paris, in 1972, entrusted to the European Commission the
drawing up of a proposition concerning the establishment of a Regional Fund in order to help the regions of the EC that were the most
disadvantaged in terms of funding for industrial investments, services
and infrastructure. This marked the beginning of Community regional
policy, but, it is important to note, it was a policy in keeping with the
national policy pursued by the States in question.

With European integration, the regions of France were vested
with a new role, as Claude de Granrut, a member of the Committee of
the Regions in 1994 explained: "Un processus de planification
régionale triangulaire, Région-Etat-Commission, se met en place. Il
confère aux Régions une sorte de statut d'interlocuteur de la
Commission. Il les renforce dans leurs compétences économiques et
d'aménagement du territoire".[28] Indeed, the regional economic disparities highlighted by the European Commission in the 1980s
propelled the regions to the fore of their countries' economic policy.

The evolution of the role of the region continued during the
1990s. The Treaty of the European Union, also known as the Treaty of
Maastricht, signed in December 1991, created additional space for the
regions, firstly with the establishment of the Committee of the
Regions,[29] then with the principle of subsidiarity desired by the
regions, and finally with the regions' right to "siéger au Conseil des
ministres dans les matières qui relèvent de leurs compétences, pour
autant qu'elles y soient habilitées par l'Etat central".[30] The scope of
regional activities was at first limited to five areas: economic and social cohesion, health, education, trans-European infrastructure and
culture. With the Treaty of Amsterdam, it was extended to the following areas: social policy, the environment, employment policy,
professional training and transport. Until the end of the 1990s, the
State was France's sole interlocutor with the Commission. Since the
reforms of 1999, the regions have had the ability to legally negotiate

---

[28] Granrut, p. 23.
[29] As indicated by Granrut, the Council and the Commission consult the Committee of
the Regions on all issues of specific regional interest. The Committee may put forth
opinions by its own initiative. For the regions, this means an institutional presence in
the European Union. Granrut, p. 29.
[30] Thys, p. 4.

the management of structural funds directly with the European Commission. It is true, as Granrut states, that there has been progress in the evolution of dialogue between the regions and the European Commission. We may even note that the regions have acquired more administrative power since their creation. It must be remembered, however, that in its mission to preserve the country's national cohesion, the French State has implemented a legality control allowing the State to maintain its right of surveillance over decisions made by local authorities. Although the regions have a certain level of independence concerning the direction to be taken in regards to their local area and the nature of the dialogue they would like to establish with the Commission, the State reserves the right to make all final decisions. The orientation of this policy is clearly determined by the policy of national unity set out in the French Constitution.

Since the Treaty of Maastricht, very few initiatives concerning the regions have been outlined. The Treaties of Nice and Amsterdam did not develop the issue of regions. It is true that the Committee of the Regions remains a consultative body, or even a limited power. Nevertheless, this study aims to see how the programs developed for the regions in Europe—especially the programs facilitating co-operation between regions of different countries—coexist, in the case of France, with the country's unity.

Certain regions in France are currently reinforcing their economic and cultural collaboration with other regions in Europe. In fact, the regions are even recognised for the central role they play in the economic construction of the European Union. A quick look at the European Commission's regional policy website provides evidence of the contribution made by regions within the framework of the global economy. According to the Commission, the regions of the European Union are the first to be affected when economic changes occur at the world level. It is for this reason that it is necessary to manage each nation's economy through the regions.[31]

Several initiatives have been implemented in order to facilitate and encourage links between the regions of the European Union. The fact that communication tools such as the trans-national blog *Tales from the Borderland* exist (launched in August 2007 with the goal of

---

[31] See the European Commission's website: http://ec.europa.eu/regional_policy/-policy/why/index_fr.htm (last accessed 26 August 2009).

informing cross-border communities) is proof of the links between European regions, and highlights the dialogue that goes beyond national borders. Moreover, projects encouraging co-operation be-tween regions with common goals, and competitions promoting the concept of regions also deepen the dialogue between the regions of Europe.

The competition for innovative action and programs such as INTERREG (inter-regional co-operation) are some examples of this co-operation. The first competition for innovative action was launched by the European Commission in 2004, with the goal of showcasing regional initiatives. The *Créanautes* project from the Limousin region in France won one of these prizes (amongst seven other European regions) for a project that exhibited the region's uniqueness.[32] Seven teams of young people were sent out for this project, with the mission of finding the "happening" places in the Limousin region. The result: a series of seven films was produced, showcasing the region's strong points.

This journey draws parallels with the school book *Le Tour de la France par deux enfants*, published in 1877 and written by Augustine Fouillée under the pseudonym of G. Bruno (and used in French primary schools until the 1950s). Bruno's book recounts a journey taken around France by young people. The story's objective is to acquaint children with the French territory and its activities, and subsequently link all of France through a feeling of shared nation-hood, common destiny and national identity within the framework of the national policies of the Third Republic. The Limousin project begins with a similar format, but in contrast to Bruno's schoolbook, the journey occurs to showcase the region's difference and specificity, and is a way of highlighting its strong points. The project's logo depicts seven young people with cameras in a yellow bus. Its poster, too, features this idea of recording and capturing images of regional activities.

In the same vein, the INTERREG program was created at the beginning of the 1990s, with the help of European funding, to promote projects and communication between the regions of several European

---

[32] http://ec.europa.eu/regional_policy/innovation/pdf/award/limousin.pdf (accessed 17 September 2007). For further reading: http://www.ianis.net/about/Lists/newsletter/-IANIS_NL_May_2004.pdf (accessed 17 September 2007).

countries, particularly member countries of the European Union. The program's objective is to group cross-border, trans-national and inter-regional regions in order to improve the economic and social cohesion of the European zone.

The goals of these projects vary according to the economic, industrial or technological interest of the region. By way of example, a project's theme could be the sharing of common borders, ecological research, coastal conservation, industrial interests, or the reduction of suburban violence. The INTERREG newsletter speaks of the import-ance for regions of working and learning together in order to reduce the social and economic disparities generated by the ever-increasing integration of European countries and the competition brought about by an increasingly global exchange system.[33] During a conference held in June 2007, the commission member responsible for regional policy, Danuta Hübner, noted that in order to confront global eco-nomic competition, regions should create ties between themselves, to align themselves with innovation coming out of countries such as Japan and the United States. She also stressed the necessity of creating a regional brand to better attract investment to European regions.[34]

The recognition of regional identity features in these interregional projects, as in the ALICERA project (Action Leaning for Identity and Competence in European Rural Areas), for example. This INTERREG project, begun in 2005, is an education program in rural areas involving seven regions in five European countries, including Brittany in France.[35] In the context of an exchange of ideas between young people working in rural areas, it is also a question of realising that regional identity can be a way to achieve better economic success. Within this project, for example, a visit to farms in order to learn more about regional produce is also a way to increase regional identity and knowledge levels.[36] Two key elements of this European regional policy must be noted: the promotion of a regional identity and the

---

[33] *INTERREG IIIC* Newsletter No. 1, November 2003, www.interreg3c.net (accessed 25 June 2007).

[34] Danuta Hübner, *Regions of the Future: Innovation, Regional Development and Cohesion Policy*, IANIS + Annual Conference, Bilbao, 15 June 2007, pp. 1-5.

[35] The other countries are Germany, Latvia, Hungary and Austria. See www.alicera.-org.

[36] *ALICERA News*, Issue no. 4, June 2006, p. 6. www.alicera.org (accessed 17 September 2007).

grouping of regions beyond national borders. In regards to French policy, these two concepts seem to be at odds with the idea of national unity, especially that of the Third Republic, which worked to erase all notions of regional diversity.

Certain factors of INTERREG projects must be considered in greater detail to determine whether a grouping of regions from different countries would result in the unifying aspect of a State being called into question. In the case of France, the fact that the State still reigns supreme in decisions regarding national issues has been emphasised, yet this grouping of European regions raises other cultural and legal issues.

The European regional policy initiatives of particular interest are those concerning the border zones of different countries. Cross-border co-operation distinguishes itself from other co-operation between European regions by the fact that regions share a common border, i.e. a common geographical space. A shared border also implies historical ties between these neighbouring regions. It is even possible that, at certain times, these regions were part of the same national area (like Alsace, which was part of Germany between 1870 and 1918, then between 1940 and 1944) or of the same linguistic or cultural area (like the French and Spanish Basque Country). This is why it seems logical to focus this study on the national policy of unity in France, compared to the nation's territorial administration, while concentrating on cross-border co-operation. This study begins with the idea that if a threat to the cohesion of France existed, due to the ties between European regions being deepened because of European Union regional policy, this would be evident in the regions with the most historical, linguistic or cultural ties, such as the Upper Rhine and the Basque Country.

The Upper Rhine is a co-operation between the borders of France, Switzerland and Germany. It is one of the oldest partnerships between border-sharing regions, dating from the 1960s, and began with the goal of creating economic stability between these regions. Today, the partnership has taken on various forms, including a cultural and educational dimension.

Owing to geographical similarities, common economic interests and similar historical ties, the Upper Rhine appears to be a zone that could easily free itself from the national yoke, to create a new entente founded on striking similarities. A school textbook was compiled by these regions to identify their social, historical and linguistic similarities.[37] Yet, a conference on the intercultural connections of the Rhine revealed that cultural issues were at the root of the failure of certain common projects, notably between the French and German regions.[38]

The cultural differences cover several domains: geographical, linguistic and historical. These differences are first visible in regards to the territories themselves, as the divisions are not uniform. As already mentioned, the meaning of the word "region" differs depending on the territory. Alsace is a region, Switzerland has five cantons (Bâle, Bâle Ville, Campagen, Aargau, Soleure and Jura), while in Germany there are two *Länder* (Bade-Wurtemberg and Rhineland-Palatinate). The way in which each division is administered in regards to the national power is different, the German *Länder* being federated and enjoying greater autonomy than the French regions, which are part of a highly centralised administrative structure. Concerning intercultural communication, in addition to French and German, the official languages, the presence of six local languages must be taken into account in this grouping (Frankish, Northern Alemanic, Badois, Alsacian, Southern Alemanic and Swabian).[39]

Added to this are factors tied to historical culture. The historian Birte Wassenberg cites the difficulties created in the cross-border project of the schoolbook for the Upper Rhine, whose goal is to "sensibiliser les jeunes à ce qui les unit, les différencie et ce qui peut rassembler".[40] Wassenberg explains that the chapter on history in this textbook is lacking, "en raison du désaccord des partenaires transfrontaliers sur la nécessité et la manière de décrire la deuxième guerre mondiale et ses conséquences pour le Rhin supérieur".[41] These difficulties are not limited to the past, but also affect the domain of work. Another example given by Wassenberg explains that in the

---

[37] "Vivre dans le Rhin supérieur. " *Manuel pour une Europe sans frontières.* http://www.crdp-strasbourg.fr/allemand/Manuel_RS/index.php (20 November 2007).
[38] Birte Wassenberg, "Le management interculturel des relations transfrontalières, l'exemple du Rhin supérieur" in Marie-Thérèse Bitsh (ed), *Le fait régional et la construction européenne* (Brussels: Emile Bruylant, 2003), pp. 405-430.
[39] Wassenberg, p. 408.
[40] "Vivre dans le Rhin supérieur." *Manuel pour une Europe sans frontières*, p. 1. Cited in Wassenberg, p. 416.
[41] Wassenberg, p. 416.

conventions regarding the signing of contracts, the French are vaguer concerning a project's settlement date, whereas a German expects a specific duration to be indicated for each activity covered by the contract.[42]

These intercultural problems have given rise to training programs seeking to inform participants in cross-border projects of the possible communication difficulties involved with these common projects. Despite the visible similarities between cross-border regions and the logic behind economic and cultural co-operation between them, the problem of culture exists and goes back to both political and historical structures, as well as to ways of thinking and acting. To aid in understanding the intercultural difficulty involved in a grouping of regions and, in this case, the French, Swiss and German cultures, a study carried out by Jacques Demorgon on the cultural complexity and interculturality,[43] highlights the genesis of the opposing political organisation in Germany and France, a key factor in the cultural antagonisms between the two countries. Demorgon contrasts the policy of unification pursued in France under the *Ancien Régime* and the Republics, with the policy of plurality and diversity in Germany.[44] This comparison underlines the fact that the policy of national unity in France is closely tied to the cultural elements that determine the thoughts and social and political behaviours of the individual, as is the case with the French in the common projects mentioned in the INTERREG program. In summary, the political structure of a country will have consequences for its culture. Demorgon proposes a geo-historical approach as a way of understanding cultural differences. In France, a long period of royal culture was followed by a market culture defined by successive complex crises (empires, restorations, republics and revolutions), while in Germany, "en raison d'une romanisation repoussée et d'une christianisation partielle ou tardive", community-based societies existed for longer.[45] This late evolution

---

[42] Wassenberg, p. 416.

[43] Jacques Demorgon, *Complexité des cultures et de l'interculturel contre les pensées uniques* (Paris: Anthropos, 2004). See, in particular, the chapter entitled "Contre les pensées uniques", pp. 285-304.

[44] Demorgon, p. 290.

[45] Demorgon, p. 291. Demorgon defines community-based societies as being "constituées par des groupes limités d'êtres humains tirant leur subsistance de la

from community to State stresses the notion of territory, or, as Demorgon explains, "un fort attachement à l'environnement naturel et humain",[46] which explains, in the context of Germany, "la solution politique du Fédéralisme pour ne pas détruire ces attachements locaux et régionaux".[47] This can be taken further with Alain Touraine's assertion that some countries without a long tradition of a Nation State, such as Germany and Italy, disassociate the notions of nation and State (*Deutschtum* compared to *Deutschland* or *italianità* compared to *lo Stato italiano*). This stands in contrast to France, which "reste attachée à l'identification de la nation et de l'Etat, proclamée et réalisée par la Révolution française",[48] even in the context of European economic and political integration. This different political genesis in Germany and France, and this different way of understanding the nation, identify the reason why intercultural problems could emerge, and may also explain the differences that exist in regards to communication.

The following anecdote illustrates the antagonisms that appear concerning communication:

> [Q]uand les conférenciers français s'expriment, les conférenciers et les auditeurs allemands sont peu satisfaits. Ils trouvent les exposés brillants en ce sens qu'ils jettent des lueurs dans toutes les directions mais ne constituent pas un sens clair et cohérent. Les exposés sont ressentis comme des morceaux de bravoure verbale, finalement superficiels, des jeux de langage. Du côté français, les exposés allemands sont souvent jugés longs, peu originaux, peu enrichissants, trop pédagogiques.[49]

In an attempt to explain communication difficulties, Demorgon's idea of "deux pôles, entre autres" in communication will be used, namely "l'explicite et [...] l'implicite".[50] The German and the Swiss tend to be rather more explicit (the meaning of words must be made clear) while the French are often implicit in their conversation (the meaning

---

chasse et de la cueillette. Elles étaient caractérisées par une globalisation du rapport à l'environnement naturel et surnaturel".
[46] Demorgon, p. 294.
[47] Demorgon, p. 294.
[48] Alain Touraine, "Existe-t-il encore une société française ?" in Dominique Schnapper and Henri Mendras (eds), *Six manières d'être européen* (Paris: Gallimard, 1990), pp. 143-171 (p. 152).
[49] Demorgon, p. 295.
[50] Demorgon, p. 295.

of words must be alluded to).[51] What is most interesting in this theory of the explicit and the implicit is its link with a country's nation policies. Demorgon points out that countries with strong religious, political and cultural unity, such as France and Japan, have no need to make the meaning of all their words clear, since words are understood through shared symbolic, cultural, political and social allusions. In countries composed of many States, such as Switzerland, Germany or even the United States, explicit language and very precise communication is needed, due to socio-historical and cultural roots not being shared. In the French context, national policy favours the unity of the country, where "[u]ne communication plus implicite ne pourra exister que dans un contexte social commun. À partir des mêmes expériences communes, les références seront comprises".[52] Common experiences are justified by the successive unifications of France: the Roman Empire, Christianity, the evolution of the national territory, linguistic unity and secularism. This point of view sheds light on the differences encountered in the world of Franco-German affairs in cross-border projects, for example.

The Basque Country has also been involved in the implement-ation of projects made possible through European co-operation. To begin with, the common European project entitled *Eurocité*, a network linking French and Spanish Basque cities, will be examined. The project involves the creation of communication (cross-border, trilingual Internet), transport (TGV planned) and education networks (Euro-Institut planned).

To determine whether this kind of project brings about modifications of France's national cohesion, the place occupied by the Basque Nationalist Party in these two countries will be highlighted. We begin with the assumption that if the bringing together of the Basque country, through European Union regional projects, were likely to bring about a deeper identification with the region, this would manifest itself in support for a political party that represents the regional or even historical identity of these regions in the two countries.

A study carried out by Jean-Marie Izquierdo found that the Basque Nationalist Party (BNV) in Spain occupies an important place

---

[51] Demorgon, p. 296.
[52] Demorgon, p. 296.

in this country. It is a party that "puise sa légitimité dans l'histoire du nationalisme basque tout entier, il occupe une position privilégiée au cœur des institutions basques et espagnoles".[53] Founded in 1895, the party has a determining role within the government of the Basque Country, governing alone or in coalition for nearly thirty years. The Spanish Basque Country has enjoyed autonomous administrative powers since 1979, and has institutional visibility in Spanish life. In France, the Basque Nationalist Party (PNB) is in a different position. The party remains almost unknown to the French residents of the French Basque Country, and obtains minimal results in elections.[54] This distinction in the institutional visibility of the political party is in fact linked to the French policy of national unity, which continues to be felt for the following reasons, despite the new area heralded by European integration. Firstly, the territorial division where the Basque Country is located is part of the Pyrénées Atlantiques department, which is also home to a Béarnaise minority. These identities are located in the Aquitaine region where all departments are part of a national whole, sharing institutions, a legal system and similar administration. The provinces that were historically part of Basque identity are today tightly integrated into the national identity, making it difficult for a political party such as the PNB to pursue a policy based on regional identity.

Next, and in the context of the Basque *Eurocité* project, the grouping of regions sharing a similar past demonstrates that the national policies of a State are a determining factor in co-operation between regions. The communication problems encountered in the Upper Rhine are also felt in the Basque Country of France and Spain. From a linguistic point of view, the Basque language is spoken very little in France, due to the linguistic uniformity imposed in the nineteenth century. It must also be noted that in the Basque Country in

---

[53] Jean-Marie Izquierdo, "Rôle(s) et statut(s) du parti nationaliste basque en Pays basque français et espagnol. L'incarnation du paradoxe régionaliste des trajectoires françaises et espagnoles" in Pascal Delwit (ed), *Les Partis régionalistes en Europe, Des acteurs en développement* (Brussels: Édition de l'Université de Bruxelles, 2005), pp. 197-215 (p. 197).

[54] At the 1998 regional elections, the PNB received 3.8% of votes (counting only Basque constituencies, if we take into account total figures for the department of Pyrénées Atlantiques, the PNB received 1.8%, while the PNV received 19.4% of votes). Izquierdo, p. 206.

France, a major portion of the population originates from other areas of France. On the other hand, Basque is very much alive in Spain and even dominates the Spanish language within the region. When it comes to learning a foreign language, the French and the Spanish in the Basque Country show a preference for learning English, rather than the language of their cross-border neighbour. As a result, publications and colloquiums arising from this cross-border co-operation necessitate the use of French, Spanish and sometimes even English.[55]

Conclusion

A country's national unity is measured in terms of political, legal and cultural factors. European integration, it is noted, coexists in parallel with a strong French national policy, which continues to influence the political and cultural aspect of the country. For France, the European Union has added a new dimension to the region, but rather than putting the idea of national unity in peril, the structures in place (such as education and political institutions) protect the unity of the State. The construction of Europe has invested the region with a role requiring the accentuation of its diversity and regional identity, in order to increase the economic sector for the benefit of the national interest. Yet, regional power remains in the sectors that least antagonise national cohesion, such as economic development, infrastructure and culture, steering clear of domains of national significance, such as justice, police, defence and international relations. It should be noted, however, that European integration has given a new voice to the French regions. The regions are endowed with the ability to communicate directly with Brussels. This co-operation also implies changes in regards to the law. In order to respond to the new legal structures presented by the grouping of common projects between European regions, France has had to put in place methods adapted to cross-border co-operation. It would be pertinent to see how these conventions will be adapted as European integration is deepened. For the

---

[55] Izquierdo presents a series of differences between the French and Spanish Basque Countries and highlights their linguistic, historical and economic imbalance.

moment, these conventions are signed within the limits of the powers of local authorities, while respecting international commitments.[56]

---

[56] According to the law of 6 February 1992 concerning the territorial administration of France, local authorities, and groupings with other foreign local authorities, may sign conventions within the limits of their authority and in accordance with article 131 of the French constitution, respecting international commitments. It should be noted that the methods for each grouping vary according to the grouping. For example, the most successfully completed is that between France, Germany, Switzerland and Luxemburg with the Karlsruhe agreement (1996). See also Pierre Gévart, *Comprendre les enjeux de la décentralisation* (Paris: l'Etudiant, 2006), p.152.

Haunted Europe: Virilio and Sangatte

Russell West-Pavlov

In December 2002, a group of Belgian journalists, investigating the living conditions of illegal asylum seekers hiding out in the disused World War Two bunkers along the Channel beaches near Calais were told a strange story. Some of the refugees claimed that they had been attacked by the police. Plain clothes police had arrived at the bunkers where they had sought refuge after the closure of the Sangatte refugee camp. Thinking they were volunteers from a charitable organization bringing food, the refugees went out to meet them, only to be brutally beaten up by truncheons. Then the attackers set fire to the bunkers, incinerating the few possessions the *sans papiers* had stored there:

> Le témoignage des migrants est explicite: trois hommes en civils se sont approchés d'eux en leur promettant de la nourriture, les ont molestés et ont volontairement mis le feu au blockhaus à deux endroits différents […] Les forces de l'ordre ont mis le bunker à sac puis ont allumé un feu, soutiennent des migrants, qui n'ont pas déposé plainte.

How did they know that the attackers were policemen, the journalists asked? Because of the flashing lights on their car, the refugees replied in halting English. The inspectorate of the *police nationale*, by contrast, reviewing the case, claimed the inflagration in the bunkers had been caused by a candle falling over, and that none of the refugees had been there when their men, passing by on a routine patrol, had discovered the fire.[1]

In this article, I suggest that this miniscule anecdote, taking place on the French coast on the site of the erstwhile line of fortifications known as the Atlantic Wall, and staging a brief skirmish between the French forces of law order and asylum seekers from beyond the borders of Europe, can be read as symptomatic of the current anxieties around the new frontiers of the European Union.

I begin by exploring the notion of postcolonial haunting which allows a site from the past to be re-encoded in the present as bearer of resurgent cultural anxieties. I then examine the anthropomorphic nature of the Atlantic Wall bunkers as the identificatory structure which permits the re-inscription of the bunkers within the con-temporary invasion rhetoric of illegal immigration. On the line marking the erstwhile outer limits of Hitler's Fortress Europe, a conflict between natives and interlopers reverses the terms of an earlier invasion narrative, only to demonstrate the recurrence of past border paradigms in the present day. I go on to show how the high-velocity warfare which supplants the bunker nonetheless preserves an archaic form of pedestrian warfare, a mythological category filled by the figure of the refugee as invader. Yet for all the evidence of a historical causality which enables the contemporary re-inscription of resurgent topoi of invasion, the bunkers also document the historical contingency of borders, a central determining factor in patterns of illegal migration. Finally, I examine the morphology of the Sangatte camp and its uncanny resemblance to the Channel Tunnel in its proximity. Such resemblance embodies the manner in which borders call forth the very transgressions they claim to prevent, thus highlighting the ultimate futility of the sealed borders which tarnish the grand project of European unity.

The article thus suggests that a reading which oscillates between past frontiers, frontiers whose traces, in this case, are still ev-ident in their monolithic brittleness, and present frontiers, as evinced in these media reports, or in fictional accounts of frontier trans-gressions, may teach us about the manner in which the contemporary

---

[1] RTB TV5, "Hôtel Plage" (also contains a digest of an article from *Le Monde*, 7 December 2002). http://archives.rezo.net/zpajol.mbox/200212.mbox/%3Ca05100317-ba17860e4629@%5B195.132.116.210%5D%3E (accessed 10 January 2007).

frontier is staged and defended. The article sets up a dialectical relationship between two conceptual complexes. On the one hand, I undertake a reading of the bunkers of the Atlantic Wall as analysed by the theorist of architecture, space and speed, Paul Virilio, who devoted an essay and an exhibition of photos to these relics of the Second World War in the mid 1970s.[2] His remarkable *Bunker archéologie* presciently predicts the paranoid structures of the twenty-first century EU border politics. On the other hand, I embark upon a reading of the topography of the Sangatte refugee camp near Calais, opened in 1999 to accommodate thousands of illegal refugees attracted to the area because of the proximity of the Calais-Dover ferry port and the Channel train tunnel, two means of gaining entry to the United Kingdom without passing through the airports and their attendant visa checks. I argue that the very topography of the Sangatte camp replicates that of the bunkers which, upon its closure, would take up its role as place of refuge and/or of incarceration. In the words of Paul Virilio, speaking twenty years before of the same bunkers: "l'habitant de ces lieux de péril […] possède déjà cette rigidité cadavérique que la protection de l'abri était censée lui éviter".[3] But I also suggest that this curious historical isomorphism indicates, conversely, that the borders may generate, by a paradoxical causality, the very transgressions they ostensibly control.

Haunted Europe

Sneja Gunew has coined the term of "haunted nations" to describe the manner in which contemporary multicultural nations, such as Canada and Australia, are persistently worried by the spectral traces their colonial pasts manifest in the present.[4] The bunker photographs collected by Virilio may appear so ghostly precisely because they embody the 'haunting' of European nations by their imperial and colonial pasts.

---

[2] Paul Virilio, *Bunker archéologie* (Paris: Centre Pompidou/Centre de création industrielle, 1975).
[3] Virilio (1975), p. 13.
[4] Sneja Gunew, *Haunted Nations: The Colonial Dimensions of Multiculturalisms* (London: Routledge, 2004).

The Atlantic Wall bunkers may be read as referring back to a moment in Europe's past where its colonial activities abroad abruptly erupted within the heart of the continent. Facism has been interpreted as "European colonialism brought home to Europe by a country that had been deprived of its overseas empire after World War I".[5] Anticolonial critics such as Césaire or Fanon did not see Nazism as an aberration of European Enlightenment. On the contrary, they read it as Europe's shocked encounter, on its own continent, of colonial practices hitherto only known elsewhere. Europe "ne pardonne pas à Hitler […] le crime contre l'homme blanc, […] d'avoir appliqué à l'Europe des procédés colonialistes dont ne relevaient jusqu'ici que les Arabes d'Algérie, les coolies de l'Inde et les nègres d'Afrique".[6]

The Atlantic Wall bunkers, though apparently unconnected with Europe's colonial past, may mark the site, strategically located at the interface of the European continent and the global oceans, where the concrete causal connections between a European colonial past and a European federal present are suddenly borne out. Raymond Williams has spoken of residual, dominant and emergent cultural elements.[7] The Atlantic Wall bunkers are an example of the "haunting" of European nations because residual moments of the present (the abandoned bunkers) become the bearers of a once-dominant, now-spectral past (the colonial period)—or residual moments of the past (the brief eruption of Fascist madness on European territory) are translated into the dominant modes of the present (the half-century of European federal stability and prosperity). The temporality of the residual trace preserved across time translates into the spatiality of the littoral. Residuality proceeds by metonymy; it is the marginal, not the central element, which resurges in the next epoch. One can concur with Foucault's assertion that "l'espace lui-même, dans l'expérience occidentale, a une histoire" by articulating this history along the margins of its spaces, something that Foucault himself does: "On pourrait faire une histoire des limites—de ces gestes obscurs,

---

[5] Robert Young, *White Mythologies: Writing History and the West* (London: Routledge, 1990), p. 8.
[6] Aimé Césaire, *Discours sur le colonialisme* (1956; Paris: Présence africaine, 1962), p. 12-13; see also Frantz Fanon, *Peau noire, masques blancs* (1952; Paris: Seuil/Points, 1971), pp. 72-3.
[7] Raymond Williams, *Marxism and Literature* (Oxford: Oxford University Press, 1977), pp. 120-27.

nécessairement oubliés dès qu'accomplis, par lesquels une culture rejette quelque chose qui sera pour elle l'Extérieur; et tout au long de son histoire, ce vide creusé, cet espace blanc par lequel il s'isole, la désigne autant que ses valeurs".[8] Significantly, in confirmation of this paradigm, it is along the *littoral*, "le seuil continental", "aux limites des terres", "aux limites des terres émergées", as Virilio does not tire of pointing out, not at its heartland, that Europe finds its determining cultural pattern.[9]

Anthropomorphism

Yet the Atlantic Wall bunkers function as a focus for contemporary anxieties of immigration in the first instance via a central topos of European Enlightenment, that of the anthropocentric universe. In Virilio's remarkable exhibition catalogue *Bunker archéologie*, which gathers the haunting black-and-white photographs he took in the late 1950s and early 1960s of the crumbling monoliths of the Atlantic Wall, this is not immediately evident. One aspect which contributes to the otherworldly, eerie quality of Virilio's bunker photos is the utter absence of human figures in their panoramas. The dunes and the ruined bunkers of the Second World War are deserted, and have been so for decades.

In the wake of the closure of Sangatte, however, the bunkers once again were peopled by threatening foreigners. This resurgence of the past is uncannily foreseen in Virilio's commentary in a quite tangential manner. He describes in a parenthetical observation the responses garnered by his maverick interest in these monoliths from the recent past. The bunkers are identified with the erstwhile occupiers, and are hatefully adorned with swastikas and anti-German slogans:

> L'identification de cette construction à l'occupant allemande, comme si celle-ci en se retirant avait oublié son casque, ses attributs, un peu partout le long de nos rivages [...] certains bunkers servaient encore à l'affichage de graffitis hostiles, les flancs de béton se couvraient d'insultes contre le boche, de croix

---

[8] Michel Foucault, *Dits et écrits 1954-1988*, ed. by Daniel Defert and François Ewald (Paris: Gallimard, 1994), IV, p. 752-53; I, p. 161.
[9] Virilio (1975), p. 9, 35.

gammées et l'intérêt que je semblais leur porter en les mesurant ou en les photographiant, renvoyait parfois sur moi cette hostilité.[10]

In a sense, this metonymic identification of bunker and local subject is encoded in the bunkers' morphology from the outset. Virilio notes that "[le]s blockhaus étaient anthropomorphes, leurs figures reprenaient celles des corps".[11] The bunker is itself an anthropomorphic construct, modelled on the human body, as becomes clear, for instance, in the profiles of fire-control towers looming among the pines of *les Landes* like Easter Island statues.[12] This anthropomorphism is not new. It is evinced in the sartorial vocabulary omnipresent in the eighteenth-century science of fortifications invented by Vauban (*cuirasse, chemise, revêtement, épaulement*,[13]), inherited by the bunkers of the Atlantic Wall.

In conducting this backward-looking genealogy of the an-thropomorphic nature of the bunker, it becomes possible, conversely, to explain the resonances extending in the other direction, which allow the military ruins, at early-twenty-first-century Sangatte, to be identified with a foreign threat from the middle of the previous century. The vocabulary of military threat was ubiquitous in the media reports on Sangatte.[14] It is perhaps hardly surprising, then, that in the wake of the closure of Sangatte, when asylum seekers took refuge in these readymades, they drew the wrath of the police, who appeared in plain clothes to set fire to the bunkers in an attempt to drive out these invaders. The asylum seekers, like the original builders of the Atlantic Wall, were foreign occupiers. But rather than coming from the sea like the invasion forces the bunkers were supposed to resist, the refugees were, in parallel to the erstwhile German occupiers, "an enemy within" (a phrase used by British politicians to describe asylum seekers).[15] This is the first of the reversals which we will encounter, again and again, in the complex network of relationships between the

---

[10] Virilio (1975), p. 10.
[11] Virilio (1975), p. 10.
[12] Virilio (1975), images pp. 90-93.
[13] Virilio (1975), p. 37.
[14] See for instance, Matthew Tempest, "Duncan Smith: Keep Sangatte Refugees Out". *Guardian Unlimited*, Friday 24 May 2002. http://politics.guardian.co.uk/homeaffairs/-story/0,,721376,00.html (accessed 10 January 2007).
[15] Matthew Tempest.

bunkers of the Atlantic Wall and the asylum seekers taking refuge there following the closure of the short-lived but notorious Sangatte camp.

Speed and its Others

The anthropomorphism described above became the identificatory vehicle allowing the abandoned bunkers to re-emerge as the site of a post-imperial haunting—a haunting otherwise highly unlikely given the massive shifts in military technology which have intervened since the Second World War. Virilio maintains, in a series of works around this theme, that speed increasingly determines warfare: "Après les distances d'espace et de temps, la *distance vitesse* abolit la notion de dimension physique"; "*la valeur stratégique du non-lieu de la vitesse a définitivement supplanté celle du lieu* et la question de la possession du Temps a renouvelé celle de l'appropriation territoriale".[16] The vehicle and the projectile increasingly coalesce, till they become one, stripped even of their human inhabitants (one thinks of pilotless cruise missiles and high-speed drones): "le projectile et le véhicule forment un mixte que le cybernétique va parachever en évacuant l'homme du système d'arme (par la robotisation)".[17] The bunkers mark the last spectacular appearance of the immobile fortress as a threshold phenomenon. Some, like the huge bomb shelters of the Third Reich, marked the advent of total warfare. Other bunkers served to launch the first stratospheric missiles (the V1 launching ramps in Normandy[18]) thus inaugurating their own final obsolescence. Virilio comments that

> [c]es blocs de béton étaient en fait les derniers rejetons de l'histoire des frontières, du *limes* romain à la muraille de Chine; les bunkers, ultime architecture militaire de surface, étaient venus s'échouer aux limites des terres, au moment précis de l'avènement du ciel dans la guerre [...] L'histoire

---

[16] Paul Virilio, *L'Espace critique* (Paris: Christian Bourgeois, 1984), p. 19; *Vitesse et politique: Essai de dromologie* (Paris: Galilée, 1977), p. 131. For a very recent reformulation of these theses, see "Ctheory Interview with Paul Virilio—The Kosovo War Took Place in Orbital Space: Paulo Virilio in Conversation with John Armitage", trans. by Patrice Riemens. http://www.ctheory.net/articles.aspx?id=132 (accessed 10 January 2007).

[17] Virilio (1975), p. 16.

[18] Virilio (1975), images pp. 110-111.

avaient changé de lit une dernière fois avant le saut dans l'immensité de l'espace aérien.[19]

Virilio's Atlantic wall bunkers are frozen objects. They are signs of a bygone age of war. Immobilized in their anachronistic emplacements, stranded in the air by the shifts of the dunes, they are left behind by the passage of time.

It is not inappropriate, then, that the bunkers on the Atlantic coasts, monuments to a form of static defence outstripped by the velocities of stratospheric war, come to house a new generation of pedestrians—the refugees on foot between the Sangatte camp and Sangatte town, or between the camp and the Channel Tunnel entrance. Significantly, Virilio notes the re-emergence of peasant conflict below the threshold of modern technologized warfare, his examples being Napoleon's disastrous Peninsula campaign and the Vietnam war:

> Les premières guerres 'modernes' sont celles de l'empire napoléonien. [...] Pourtant, cette grande armée triomphante qui va bouleverser la politique des états européens de façon irréversible subit un grave échec en Espagne. [...] la masse et la puissance totalitaires sont impuissantes devant l'ancienne méthode, celle du combat paysan. Tout au long de l'histoire qui va suivre, et malgré l'accroissement exponentiel des possibilités de destruction des armées modernes, on assistera, à des périodes constantes, à la répétition de ce premier échec dont le conflit vietnamien est l'exemple récent.[20]

What re-emerges under the threshold of Virilio's scenario of high-velocity-warfare is the humble foot-soldier ("l'histoire en commence au ras de sol, avec des pas"[21])—the tramping refugees making their paths across the fields, combated by the CRS as a new generation of third-world enemies.

It may appear excessive to interpret the contemporary refugee on the coasts of Europe as an avatar of earlier invaders. Yet the vocabulary of the media coverage certainly invites such an interpretation. And there may also be a historical causality which makes the modern flows of asylum seekers a direct concomitant of the end of older forms of warfare, with the resulting prosperity and peace of Europe powerfully attracting immigrants from elsewhere. Thinking within the

---

[19] Virilio (1975), p. 9.
[20] Virilio (1975), p. 20.
[21] Michel de Certeau, *L'Invention du quotidien. I : Arts de faire* (1980; Paris: Gallimard/Folio essais, 1990), p. 147.

military paradigm, Virilio observes that "[l]a conquête scientifique des énergies et de la vitesse n'est donc que celle de la réduction et de la contraction du monde. Face aux spectaculaires dégâts des *explosifs* de l'arsenal militaire, ceux de ses *implosifs* restent curieusement dissimulés".[22] Transferred back to the domain of global flows of immigration, the notion of 'implosion' might be coeval with the waves of asylum-seekers which European nations, recognizing in them the avatars of earlier threats, persist in combating with military technology—barbed-wire, helicopters, warships, infra-red night-vision equipment, internment camps—and which the media describe employing an array of equivalent metaphors. The contraction of the world is precisely the factor that makes the refugee the civil inheritor of the barbarian hordes or infidel armies at the gates of Europe. Globalization, in other words, produces new forms of invasion.

The bunkers commemorated in Virilio's work, relics from the first truly global war, simultaneously mark the first and last global conflict in human history till now. With their monolithic im-movability, "l'échec était inévitable et la configuration géographique du continent allait apporter une confirmation à l'analyse de Mao"[23]—namely, that "un état comme celui du IIIe Reich a, dès sa naissance, fondé toute sa vie politique et militaire sur l'offensive. Celle-ci enrayée, son existence prend fin".[24] The bunkers of Fortress Europe thus inaugurated a new form of aggressive global mobility. That mobility would be janus-faced, manifesting a neo-colonial mobility of global capital, and a neo-colonial flow of impoverished refugees, asylum seekers, *Gastarbeiter* and other migrant labourers. These semi-legal or illegal refugees constitute an 'implosive' phenomenon because they pose the greatest threat from within the nation, like the *Gastarbeiter* who refused to go home.

Contingency

Yet, for all the evidence of a historical causality which underpins the contemporary re-inscription of past artefacts such as the bunkers with resurgent topoi of invasion, Virilio's work also documents the

---

[22] Virilio (1975), p. 18.
[23] Virilio (1975), p. 26.
[24] Virilio (1975), p. 25.

historical contingency of borders. And it is this contingency, as much
as historical causality, which determines patterns of migratory
movement.

Virilio's photographs document a paradoxical tension between
the Neolithic monumentalism of the imposing structures constructed
along the French Atlantic *littoral* by the Todt Organisation's slave
labour—and the inevitable decay of these gigantic structures exposed
year in, year out to the sun, the wind and the waves. The sepia tint of
the photos and their desert-like dune background contribute to the
suggestion that the Atlantic Wall bunkers are the relics of an ancient
era. Whence Virilio's archaizing concept of an *archéologie* of the
bunker.

Virilio's photographic studies of the Atlantic Wall bunkers
powerfully reveal both their solidity and their instability. By dint of
furnishing a visual referent which indexes both the past-ness of the
bunkers and, paradoxically, their present-ness, he unintentionally
creates a material metonymy for the conceptual functioning of the EU
borders. By virtue of their location along the Atlantic sea coast, the
World War II bunkers come to signify a later political border oddly
identical with that of Axis-controlled Europe. It is of little importance
that in the 1950s, when Virilio took his photos, the EU was in its
infancy; nor is it of great import that in the mid-1970s, when the
photos were exhibited at the Centre Pompidou, the question of borders
and asylum politics had not reached its subsequent fraught status;
here, authorial intentions have little bearing upon the prescience of the
photographic texts themselves, upon their uncanny ability to embody
what Glissant had termed the "mémoire du futur".[25]

The bunker is a material signifier of what Virilio calls "nations
fortifiées" (47). As stranded, archaic reminders of a brutal line of
demarcation in a now unimaginable European military conflict,
Virilio's bunkers show the contingency of borders. By virtue of the
absolute anachronism of the bunkers, Virilio unwittingly demonstrates
how a border can appear immutable, but, because it is without foundations, is entirely contingent upon political factors, can disappear, can
shift, can be reconstituted. Borders are mere legal constructs, with
material results nonetheless of the most brutal kind. But because they

---

[25] Edouard Glissant, *Le Discours antillais* (Paris: Seuil, 1981), p. 138.

are contingent, as the border-crosser knows,[26] they evince loopholes and irregularities.

The bunkers display their inherent temporal contingency, a contingency expressed in their very principles of construction. As Virilio points out, the casemate is absolutely solid in itself, but lacking in foundations:

> Alors que la plupart des bâtiments sont enracinées dans le terrain par leur fondation, pour la casemate celle-ci n'existe pas, le centre de gravité en tient lieu ; d'où la possibilité d'un certain mouvement lorsque le sol avoisinant subit l'impact des projectiles. [...]
>
> Dans les constructions de brique et de pierres, c'est-à-dire dans les assemblages des éléments discontinus, l'équilibre des bâtiments est fonction du rapport sommet-base. Dans la construction en béton-masse, c'est la cohésion du matériau lui-même qui doit assumer ce rôle : le centre de gravité tient lieu de fondation.
>
> Dans le coulage du béton, il n'y a plus alors d'intervalles ; tout est compact, le coulage ininterrompu évite au maximum les reprises qui affaibliraient cette cohésion générale de l'ouvrage.
>
> Le bunker n'est pas réellement fondé ; il flotte sur un sol qui n'est plus un socle à son équilibre, mais une étendue mouvante et aléatoire qui s'apparente, en la prolongeant, à l'étendue marine. C'est cette autonomie relative qui équilibre la flottaison du bunker en assurant sa stabilité au milieu des modifications probables du terrain environnant.[27]

The bunker, as a physical marker of the border, is an analogy incarnate of all borders—rigid, naturalized, but entirely contingent. The slippage the bunker is prone to lays bare the contingency of the border it once marked out—and by the same token, the contingency of those which have since shifted elsewhere, borders no longer naturalized by their institutional embedding in the ground of the nation. In their positioning along the French *littoral*, Virilio's bunkers illustrate, *pars pro toto*, the dynamic existence of the EU. Its borders are in fact flexible—they are expanding on its outer eastern and south-eastern limits, being suspended within Europe itself. But at the same time, the EU borders are also being increasingly 'harmonized' (at summits in Tampere in 1999, Dublin in 2003, and The Hague in 2004)

---

[26] "Nous qui avons réussi à passer entre les mailles du filet", in the words of a character in Ben Jelloun's *Partir*. Tahar Ben Jelloun, *Partir* (2006; Paris: Seuil/Folio, 2007), p. 18.

[27] Virilio (1975), p. 32, 40.

so as to present no loopholes to the outside world. The EU is undergoing a creeping process of bunkerization.

The Atlantic Wall, "une hyper-structure appliquée à la défence d'un continent" as Virilio accurately says,[28] can be understood as a prophetic avatar of the present day EU with its increasingly well-policed borders; both undertakings display a hubristic "immensité du projet".[29] The loopholes—"l'embrasure [...] la fente de visée" in Virilio's bunker language[30]—become rarer and rarer, despite the pro-liferation of outer borders with the addition of new members. Yet the work which must be invested in the construction and maintenance of these borders betrays their utter contingency, and thus their ultimate fragility.

Fatal Attractions

Sangatte was a site symptomatically marking of one of these loop-holes, a fissure revealing, but only provisionally, the contingent nature of the EU and its constituent boundaries. The Atlantic Wall bunkers are material signifiers of the contingency of borders. So too was the Sangatte camp, a nearby neighbour of the Atlantic Wall, and for some of its inhabitants, their temporary abode before the bunkers them-selves.

The Sangatte campy was itself a contingent construction, which by its very spatial location and morphology, told of the gaps appearing between the contingent border regimes of Europe. The Sangatte camp was created as a result of the large numbers of so-called illegal refugees coming to Calais, on the English Channel coast. They were attracted by the still generous political asylum regulations in Britain, the presence of support networks as a result of Britain's colonial heritage, and the possibility of gaining entrance to the UK more easily via the Dover-Calais ferry traffic or the Channel Tunnel than via British airports. Moreover, France had no legal basis at that stage to expel these immigrants, though these would be subsequently tightened up. Thus Sangatte arose as a result of discrepancies between the

---

[28] Virilio (1975), p. 28.
[29] Virilio (1975), p. 9.
[30] Virilio (1975), p. 39.

various EU asylum regulations. It made concrete in spatial terms a set
of legal loopholes at the interstices of two juridical borders.

The camp was opened in 1999 by the French Red Cross at the
behest of the French government in order to provide a viable solution
to the provisional alternatives hitherto made available by the town of
Calais. It was originally intended to house 500 people, but eventually
accommodated over 1,500 at any one time. 50,000 refugees passed
through until its closure in late 2002. The closure was the result of an
agreement brokered between David Blunkett and Nicolas Sarkozy,
which traded the forcible closure of the camp on the French side for a
drastic tightening-up of British asylum laws. After its closure, groups
of refugees took refuge in the church of St. Pierre in Calais, until CRS
units cleared that sanctuary. Groups of refugees roamed the streets of
Calais in January and February, camping in the open or even taking up
residence in some of the abandoned bunkers along the coast.
Humanitarian organizations attempted to provide some sort of
emergency service, and to prevent harassment and violence to
refugees by the French police.

The Sangatte camp thus coalesced around a loophole in European immigration regulations, itself embodied in the nearby Channel
Tunnel. For quite some time it was possible for refugees to take a train
from Calais-Frethun to Paris, and then buy a Eurostar ticket for the
passage through the tunnel to London, without having to leave the
customs area. From 1999 onwards, however, this path was closed off
to all travellers without EU passports or a visa for Britain.[31]
Nonetheless, refugees continued to try to pass through the tunnel by
other means—on foot, hidden in containers or truck on the shuttle
trains.

The morphology of the Sangatte camp itself strongly resembled
that of the tunnel in whose proximity it was located. A long fenced-in
access road, forming something like a wire tunnel, led to the com-
pound where the hangar cum warehouse was located, with its
successive embedded cavernous spaces of tents and containers. The
Sangatte camp thus presented a reversed isomorphism, a spatio-
material chiasmus of the Channel Tunnel entrance. There, at the

---

[31] "Grenzgeographie Sangatte" [*Anarchitektur: Produktion und Gebrauch gebauter
Umwelt*, Pamphlet 03], p. 6. Available as pdf document at http://www.anarchitektur.-
com/aa03-sangatte/aa03-sangatte.html (accessed 10 January 2007).

Coquelles terminal, a bulbous wire-compound containing car- and truck-terminals, with ticket offices, duty-free shops and passport control, as well as a turn-around loop for the shuttle trains, funnels the Eurostar and freight trains into the tunnel itself, a long cavern which reverses the morphology of the Sangatte camp access-track.

The camp and the tunnel thus evince striking similarities, similarities which, however, suggest that around apparently stable borders, inside and outside can constantly be reversed in relations of chiastic symbiosis. This is also true of the bunker itself, as Virilio observes: "Désaffecté, l'ouvrage s'inverse sans canon, l'embrasure ressemble à une porte ornée de reliefs, avec ses redans verticaux".[32] Indeed, the fulcrum position of the Atlantic Wall bunkers, situated on a coastal border which is nonetheless within the EU borders (in relation to the UK) as well as marking its outermost limit (in relationship to the Atlantic) typifies the ambivalent reversibility of these frontier bulwarks.

At an extremely formalistic level, then, the respective sites, Sangatte and the Tunnel entrance in their specific morphologies already perform the relationships of perverse attraction which connect them. The Sangatte warehouse was, after all, conceived originally as storage space for the tunnel building materials—what was once stored there became constitutive of the tunnel as an open-closed space, as a highly-monitored route to freedom. Sangatte, from the outset, flowed into the tunnel, indeed, made the tunnel by flowing into it. The border functions as a generator of positive feedback, provoking an upward spiral of self-intensifying dynamics. The border, in other words, creates the refugee before the latter even tries to cross it. Virilio quotes Heidegger: "Le combat désigné ici est un combat originaire car il fait tout d'abord surgir les combattants en tant que tels".[33] Conversely, only a fluid, porous border, of the sort which can be found within the EU for the citizens of the 'older' EU countries, can maintain a negative feedback relationship which generates broad equalities rather than striking inequalities—of movement, of wealth, of knowledge.

Sangatte was situated on an ambivalent border—on one which had once been an outer border of Hilter's *Festung Europa*, sealed by

---

[32] Virilio (1975), p. 12.
[33] Virilio (1975), p. 5.

the concrete bunkers of the Atlantic Wall, but which is now an inner European border. It is this place on an inner European border, at a fault line between two sets of asylum regulations, which made the English Channel coast such a significant site for prospective asylum seekers. The camp, then, by virtue of its morphological properties, tells the story of its own emergence. And that story is focussed on the tunnel, itself a material embodiment of an embrasure within the European borders.

Giorgio Agamben has recently explored the camp as the epitome of the modern political phenomenon of *homo sacer*, the figure who marks, within the polis, its constitutive exterior: "The life [...] of the sacred man [...] [is] a threshold of indistinction and of passage between [...] exclusion and inclusion [...] [the sacred man] dwells paradoxically in both [the city and outside it] while belonging to neither".[34] Sangatte may have been an exemplification of Agamben's camp to the extent that for a short period it embodied spatially a site within Europe but also communicating with its outside. It was a location where, temporarily, the borders of Europe came undone; more fundamentally, however, by signalling the contingency of Europe's borders, it also pointed up Europe's dependence upon a gesture of exclusion to constitute itself. The bunkers briefly regained an erstwhile meaning in the wake of the camp's closure. At that moment they spectrally reactivated a half-forgotten episode of the history of the *littoral*, bringing earlier instances of Europe's exclusionary history back to mind. A. J. Greimas has commented that

> [le] langage spatial apparaît ainsi, dans un premier temps, comme un langage par lequel une société se signifie à elle-même. Pour ce faire, elle opère d'abord par exclusion, en s'opposant spatialement à ce qui n'est pas elle. Cette disjonction fondamentale qui ne la définit que négativement permet d'introduire alors des articulations internes qui l'enrichissent en signification.[35]

Such comments must be read today ironically, taking over-literally the notion of enrichment. Such a sceptical and abrasive reading would see the closure of borders, despite worries about resurgences of Europe's

---

[34] Giorgio Agamben, *Homo Sacer: Sovereign Power and Bare Life*, trans. by Daniel Heller-Roazen (1995; Stanford: Stanford University Press, 1998), p. 105.

[35] A. J. Greimas, "Pour une sémiotique topologique", in Manar Hammad, Eric Proovost and Michel Vernin (eds), *Sémiotique de l'espace: Architecture, urbanisme, sortir de l'impasse* (Paris: Denoël/Gonthier, 1979), (p. 14).

past along its frontiers, as a further avatar of a long history made up by aggressive acts of constitutive border-marking. Sangatte and the abandoned bunkers along the Atlantic *littoral* are reminders of that history, from which much is still to be learnt.

Paris *au pluriel*

.

A Many Splendoured Thing?
Plural Visions of the City in *Paris, je t'aime*

Ben McCann

> But then, nothing is as like a city as the cinema. Each is a mesh of signs and an open-ended proliferation of perspectives [...] Each of them, no less, is a potentially inexhaustible anthology of stories.[1]

Paris, je t'aime (2006) is a portmanteau film in which eighteen international directors each shot a five-minute segment addressing a particular aspect of life in Paris.[2] Using the romantic vicissitudes and dislocations of urban life as an ongoing structuring device, eighteen of the city's twenty *arrondissements* are visited in a random order, with

---

[1] Gilbert Adair, *Flickers: An Illustrated Celebration of 100 Years of Cinema* (London: Faber & Faber, 1995), p. 146-7.

[2] The films in order of appearance are: *Montmartre*, directed, written by Bruno Podalydes; *Quais de Seine*, d. Gurinder Chadha, w. Paul Mayeda Berges, Chadha; *Le Marais*, d/w Gus Van Sant; *Tuileries* d/w Joel and Ethan Coen; *Loin du 16ème*, d/w Walter Salles and Daniela Thomas; *Porte de Choisy*, d/w Christopher Doyle, in collaboration with Gabrielle Keng, Peralta & Rain Kathy Li; *Bastille*, d/w Isabelle Coixet; *Place des Victoires*, d/w Nobuhiro Suwa; *Tour Eiffel*, d/w Sylvain Chomet; *Parc Monceau*, d/w Alfonso Cuaron; *Pigalle*, d/w Richard LaGravanese; *Quartier des Enfants Rouges*, d/w Olivier Assayas; *Place des Fêtes*, d/w Olivier Schmitz; *Quartier de la Madeleine*, d/w Vincenzo Natali; *Père-Lachaise*, d/w Wes Craven; *Faubourg Saint-Denis*, d/w Tom Tykwer; *Quartier Latin*, d. Gérard Depardieu, Frederic Auburtin, w. Gena Rowlands; *14ème arrondissement*, d/w Alexander Payne.

events in each one gradually uncovering Paris's diversity and heterogeneity. The film's rationale can best be summed up by its producer, Emmanuel Benbihy, who states that the project "s'inspire de la pluralité du cinéma dans un endroit mythique: Paris, ville de l'amour".[3] This plurality is interrogated in a variety of ways, including the intermingling of genres, various visual styles, different filming techniques, the inclusion of French and non-French actors and directors, the use of transitional scenes, and the use of interconnected introduction and epilogue sequences.

This chapter intends to do three things: it will briefly explore the potential of the portmanteau film for developing alternative production models in French cinema; it will demonstrate how the *Paris, je t'aime*'s treatment of the city offers an intriguing re-conceptualisation of this most familiar of cinematic sites; and finally, it will show how the film's diverse themes—racial bigotry, grief, class conflict, lost love, found love, and cultural difference—explore

---

[3] The mission statement continued: "Each director has been given five minutes of freedom, and we, as producers, carry the responsibility of weaving a single narrative unit out of those twenty moments. The 20 films will not appear in the order of the *arrondissements*, from one to twenty, but rather, in a pertinent narrative order, initially unknown to the audience. They will be fused together by transitional interstitial sequences, and also via the introduction and epilogue sequences of the feature film. Each transition will begin with the last shot of the previous film and will end with the first shot of the following film, and will have a threefold function: 1) The first is to extend the enchantment and the emotion of the previous segment, 2) The second is to prepare the audience for the surprise of the next segment, and 3) The third is to provide a general, comfortable and cohesive atmosphere to the feature film. The delightful and brief interludes of these transitions will enable the viewer to slide from one world to the next, featuring a recurring and unexpected character. This mysterious character is a witness to the Parisian life and helps create a continuous narration. It appears both in and in-between the films. In addition to the information these transitions will provide about the city and its people, their tone will be intentionally light often referring to famous scenes easily attributed to the history of Paris cinema. Similar specifications will be followed by the composer who will supervise the musical fusion between the films and the transitions as he creates the musical score of *Paris, je t'aime*. Considering the common theme of Paris and Love, the fusion between the films and the transitions, the fast pace of a fluid and complete story-telling, *Paris, je t'aime* will not be just another 'anthology' picture. It will be a unique collective feature film that will constitute a two-hour cinematographic spectacle whose original structure will make for a dramatically different experience for its global audience." http://www.imdb.com/title/tt0401711/plotsummary (accessed 1 February 2008).

notions of diversity and difference and emblematise the current socio-political complexities of Paris. Due in large part to its plurality of form and content, I propose to contextualise *Paris, je t'aime* within a broader consideration of travelling cultures and global flows, of mobility between margin and centre, between French and non-French film productions, and the crossovers across national boundaries. The film exploits its plural format to move beyond a series of unconnected vignettes towards a more coherent interrogation of travel and movement within the modern city.

The Portmanteau Film

Broadly speaking, a portmanteau film (also referred to as an 'omnibus film' or 'anthology film') is a film consisting of several different short films tied together by a single theme, premise, interlocking event, or parallel narrative.[4] These short films are generally directed by a different director, and revolve around recurring places or objects that bind diverse individuals and groups together despite the discrete narrative segmentation. As David Scott Diffrient argues, part of the portmanteau film's appeal is its ability "to re-invigorate film narrativity through a decidedly de-centered, constantly shifting cine-matic speech-act".[5]

Portmanteau films, by dint of their compactness, require a different kind of story-telling. For Carina Chocano, the best short films "abandon narrative conventions and formula [...] to burrow in odd, tiny places and root out unexpected characters and swift, stealthy, merciless stories".[6] In *Paris, je t'aime*, each director's segment is

---

[4] Examples of portmanteau films include *Invitation to the Dance* (1956), *The Yellow Rolls-Royce* (1964), *New York Stories* (1989), *Four Rooms* (1995), *The Red Violin* (1998) and *Coffee and Cigarettes* (2003). In 2007, another portmanteau film— *Chacun son cinéma*—was commissioned for the sixtieth anniversary of the Cannes Film Festival. The project restricted the thirty or so filmmakers to three minutes per episode on any subject that reflected what festival head Gilles Jacob called "their state of mind of the moment as inspired by the motion picture theatre".

[5] David Scott Diffrient, "Stories that Objects Might Live to Tell: The 'Hand-Me-Down Narrative' in Film", http://www.othervoices.org/3.1/sdiffrient (accessed 1 February 2008).

[6] Chocano, http://www.calendarlive.com/printedition/calendar/cl-et-paris18may-18,0,1215577.story (accessed 1 February 2008).

limited to around five minutes, compelling them to employ a narrative economy that means not only that a story be told, but that it also fits into an overall thematic framework. Commenting on this constraint, Yann Tobin writes: "cinq minutes, assez pour apprécier les bijoux, et assez court pour supporter un mini-*pensum*".[7] Formally, the film's plurality is impressive. There is a diversity of genres (the vampire film, the kung-fu film, the silent comedy, the melodrama, the *comédie sentimentale*), a diversity of registers (social and political comment, intimate chamber piece, impressionism, expressionism, pantomime) and a diversity of cinematic styles (flashback, voice-over, tracking shot, speeded-up images, saturated colour). This plural approach to the look and feel of Paris permits each of the directors to "vagabonder à leur guise [et] radicaliser l'affirmation d'un style, repeindre la capitale aux couleurs d'un imaginaire personnel".[8] Thus, contributors to a portmanteau film are empowered to memorialize their own auteurist flourishes and challenge existing stereotypes of a particular cinematic city.

The perennial dilemma in a portmanteau film is whether the film has been successful not only in differentiating the styles and concerns of its directors within the context of the individual episode (after all, who wants to see eighteen films about Paris that are photographed, designed, edited, and performed in exactly the same way?), but also in convincingly hooking together the segments seamlessly enough that at first glance one could suppose that the film had been made by one filmmaker from one single script.[9] In the case of *Paris, je t'aime*, some directors manage to achieve this more convincingly than others, which inevitably leads to an overall narrative

---

[7] Yann Tobin, "*Paris je t'aime*: L'auberge parisienne", *Positif*, 545/6 (2006), 133. For instance, the episodes of *11'09"01* were all obliged to be the same length: eleven minutes, nine seconds, and one frame. *Lumière et cie* (1995) celebrated the centenary of film by obliging the directors to film their entries with a Lumière camera, to shoot without synchronised sound, to shoot no more than three takes, and to restrict the length to 52 seconds, the approximate running time of the earliest films.

[8] Frédéric Strauss, *Télérama*, n° 2929, 4 March 2006.

[9] Equally, distributors and exhibitors often allude to the difficulties inherent in persuading audiences to take a gamble on a portmanteau film. Hannah McGill argues that "[i]t's a tough sell […] Shall we go to the cinema tonight? Shall we see a movie or ten little bits of movies? I know which I'd chose." http://entertainment.timesonline.-co.uk/tol/arts_and_entertainment/film/article1893852.ece (1 February 2008).

unevenness and tonal inconsistency.[10] However, given the format of the portmanteau film, the audience is guaranteed not just perpetual shifts in register, pace, and genre, but also the implicit promise of something different occurring at regular intervals throughout. As Tobin concludes, "la 'séquence suivante' se fait attendre avec excitation: quel quartier? quel cinéaste? quels comédiens? quel genre du film?"[11]

Paris, je t'aime successfully brooks these challenges by setting the action within a defined space, thus providing a more profound investigation of the themes and issues raised in the various narratives. By highlighting the centrality of Paris to the audience, the film comes equipped with a built-in structure that is immediately recognizable to the vast majority of spectators. Such a strategy was adopted for the 1965 portmanteau film *Paris vu par...*, in which six members of the Nouvelle Vague movement (including Jean-Luc Godard, Eric Rohmer and Claude Chabrol), shot six short films in a different area of Paris. *Paris, je t'aime* is a virtual rebooting of *Paris vu par...* through its use of various Paris neighbourhoods as a framework for its narrative criss-crossing. However, in a break with the first film, the 2006 version—in recognition of the city's contemporary multicultural and international diversity—incorporates only a handful of native French directors.[12]

The sprawling complexities and diversities within the real city are treated by drawing together eighteen different views of Paris by a variety of international directors. The film seeks to map out a coherent vision of the contemporary metropolis by presenting its national and international audience with a compartmentalized Paris. This is clear from the opening title credits, before the beginning of the narrative proper, in which brief snapshots of Paris flash up on the screen. The idea of the city as 'coming attraction' is implicit from the outset, enticing the viewer with images of tourist iconography (the metro, Arc de Triomphe, bridges, dawn breaking over Notre-Dame) and then confirming them with a shot of an illuminated Eiffel Tower accompanied by exploding fireworks. This opening section underlines

---

[10] The Coen brothers' *Tuileries*, for example, or Alexander Payne's *14 ième arrondissement* are segments which humorously interrogate the nature of city living.
[11] Tobin, p. 133.
[12] The contributing French directors are Bruno Podalydès, Isabel Coixet, Sylvain Chomet, Olivier Assayas, Fréderic Aubertin and Gérard Depardieu.

the way in which *Paris, je t'aime* has been globally marketed as a branded love-letter to Paris. It is implicit in the film's publicity material, in which the shape of the Eiffel Tower constitutes the 'A' of 'Paris' and a large red heart figures prominently on the inter-nationally-released poster. Moreover, the two taglines for the film— 'One City. 10 Million Hearts. One Love Story. One Film.' and 'Fall in love with Paris 18 times'—appeal to the universal understanding of Paris as *the* typical site of love and romance. By marketing the film as a romantic love letter to that most familiar of film cities and by premiering the film at Cannes, producers Emmanuel Benbihy and Claudie Ossard use the format of the portmanteau film to gain maximum exposure and financial profit.[13]

Such decisions have far-reaching industry implications, not least in France. *Paris, je t'aime*, by virtue of its transnational cast and multi-lingual soundtrack, reflects the national and the global film industry's growing interest in serving as many different markets as possible simultaneously. By having Gérard Depardieu next to Nathalie Portman next to Ludivine Sagnier next to Bob Hoskins, the film allegorises cinema's ongoing attempts to create a transnational product which can be linguistically, structurally, and aesthetically appreciated within a global context. As Martine Danan reminds us, since the mid-1980s, French government officials have frequently stated the need to boost the international presence of French cinema in order to effectively combat the pressure of globalizing economic forces and stronger competition from Hollywood blockbusters. The financially ambitious projects that followed (for instance, *Valmont* [1989], *L'Amant* [1992], and *Le Cinquième Elément* [1997]) not only followed the Hollywood mode of production, but also adopted "a text-ual strategy similar to their Hollywood counterparts in an effort to target global markets".[14] These strategies include selecting general interest themes, an emphasis on action, the inclusion of international actors, the choice of a glossy aesthetic, and, perhaps most crucially,

---

[13] The history of the portmanteau format has developed concurrently with the rise of the international film festival scene, whereby producers, exhibitors and buyers regard the format as a commercially risk-free venture drawing together the cream of Europe's *auteur* fraternity. Accordingly, *Paris, je t'aime* was chosen to open the 'Un Certain Regard' section at Cannes.

[14] Martine Danan, "French Cinema in the Era of Media Capitalism", *Media, Culture & Society*, 22 (2000), 356.

"the downplaying or erasure of cultural references unknown to or confusing for foreign spectators".[15] Danant continues:

> Even though these films are regarded as 'French', their texts bear little mark of 'Frenchness' other than through superficial or stereotypical images as seamless and impersonal as advertising. Therefore, these depthless commodified images detached from the complexity of history and from concrete, situated life can function as 'postnational' spectacles able to appeal to both international and national audiences.[16]

The tourist appeal and aspirations of the postnational film are crucial, as these films play with many of the common mythical spaces associated with a particular city. Many reviews of *Paris, je t'aime* in both French- and English-language publications tended to highlight this 'postnational' aspect, in which the film's aesthetic mixes and muddles a number of traditional stereotypes associated with cinematic depictions of Paris. Richard Schickel's opening remarks in his *Time* review of the film is indicative of this: "How wonderful to be a filmmaker in Paris! Every morning you step out the door into the greatest standing set in the world. It's not just the places all of us tourists know—the Tuileries, the Eiffel Tower, the Latin Quarter—it's the anonymous streets where the food in the humblest bistro makes your mouth water, the women are always pert and smartly dressed, the men rueful and wise".[17] Likewise, *Variety* applauded "a two-hour experience that acknowledges the idealized Paris people carry in their heads",[18] while another review simply concluded "Travel agents, start your engines".[19] *Libération* scorned "Une ville décor, où personne ne travaille, ne vote, ne souffre d'autre chose que de maux de cœur", concluding that "[l]e problème ici, c'est que ce regard extérieur est immédiatement synonyme de tourisme". [20]

---

[15] Danan, p. 356.

[16] Danan, p. 356.

[17] Richard Schickel, "The Exquisite Films of Paris", *Time*, online: http://www.time.com/time/arts/article/0,8599,1619767,00.html (accessed 1 February 2008).

[18] Lisa Nesselson, "Paris je t'aime", *Variety*, online: http://www.variety.com/index.asp?layout=features2006&content=jump&jump=review&dept=cannes&nav=RCannes&articleid=VE1117930546&cs=1&p=0 (accessed 1 February 2008).

[19] 'Paris je t'aime', online: http://www.grouchoreviews.com/index.php?module=Movie_Reviews&func=display&id=2823 (accessed 1 February 2008).

[20] Philippe Azoury, "Paris en goguette américaine", *Libération*, 18 May 2006: http://www.liberation.fr/page.php?Article=382895 (accessed 1 February 2008).

I would argue that *Paris, je t'aime* belongs to that group of films such as Jean-Pierre Jeunet's *Amélie* or Luc Besson's *The Fifth Element* which are representative of these postnational trends. Although not as bombastic or aggressively marketed as these forebears, *Paris, je t'aime* does attempt to elide cultural specificity, linguistic difference, and topographical heterogeneity into a more cohesive cultural product. Similarly, whereas European cinema can be broadly characterised as possessing non-linear narratives, temporal and spatial ambiguity, and open-ended conclusions, *Paris, je t'aime*, like many other postnational films, opts for less complex narrative strategies and a more clear-cut resolution; in short, a Hollywoodised ending. *Paris, je t'aime* and the portmanteau film represent a new direction in cinema, offering new ways in which global film industry imperatives can be co-opted into the service of a film style that is based on a plurality and diversity that seeks to actively elide, rather than expand, the specificity of national cinema.[21]

Walking the City

Aside from its formal aspects, the potential of *Paris, je t'aime* to re-present a particular type of emergent French film in the new millennium can be seen in its relationship to urban space, and with more specifically with what Wendy Everett has called 'fractal films'. Everett defines a fractal film as a "filmic portrayal of urban space which is no longer shaped by the linear mappings of modernity, but is posited as both entirely random and at the same time structured by complexity, simultaneity, and violent encounters".[22] She suggests that in recent years a new genre of films has emerged that is predicated on the notions of mistaken identities, chance encounters, coincidence, and the interdependence of human and social networks within specific cities. Fractal films develop further the concept of the city as the prototypical site onto which interweaving stories and random

---

[21] It is telling that the subtitle for *Paris, je t'aime* is "Petites romances de quartiers", whereas that of Michael Haneke's *Code Inconnu* (2000), a very different interrogation of life in modern Paris in a globalized age, is "Récit incomplet de divers voyages". One alludes to resolution and narrative closure, the other to fragmentation and disjunction.

[22] Wendy Everett, "Fractal films and the architecture of complexity", *Studies in European Cinema*, 2:3 (2005), 159.

encounters are projected and also permit a deeper understanding of the topographical specificity of the city. Because fractal films often eschew reliance upon conventional and overly familiar spatial signifiers, a greater spatial sensitivity towards the city is produced by filming in the streets of Paris.[23]

If the multiple realities embodied in the parallel or intersecting stories of fractal films, offer, as Everett argues "neither stasis nor closure, but merely ongoing change and process"[24], then *Paris, je t'aime* fits neatly into this formulation. Portmanteau films often knit together several disparate unrelated stories via larger, often contextual themes, and as such it fits into the fractal film's preoccupations with randomness, intricacies and entanglements. True, the film does provide a sense of closure, not least through the way in which each of the eighteen stories resolve themselves. However, given that there are eighteen parallel stories—and the coda sees two characters from different films (Gena Rowlands and Bob Hoskins) enter the diegetic world of two others (Juliette Binoche and Ben Gazzara)—as well as numerous interstitial sequences, snap-shot images of the protagonists moving forward with their lives at the end of the film, and the use of subtitles to inform the viewer of the current location of the action suggests less a sense of closure, but instead reinforces a sense of open-endedness typical of life in the modern city. There is a sense of circuitousness and cyclicity that the film's neat ending does not entirely efface. The film's opening prefigures this haphazardness. Several small 'screens' emerge from the black title card containing snatches of dialogue that will be heard more fully later on in the film. The sounds emanating from each of these 'screens' gradually mingle into one cacophonous sonic tapestry that anticipates the randomness and disparate narrative fragmentation that follows. Ultimately, the modern European metropolis—of which Paris is the paradigmatic example—no longer functions according to what Georg Simmel called "punctuality, calculability [and] exactness"[25]; instead it is distinguished by

---

[23] Everett includes three recent French films in her study: Alain Resnais's *Smoking/No Smoking* (1993), Michael Haneke's *Code Inconnu* (2000), and Jean-Pierre Jeunet's *Amélie* (2001).

[24] Everett, p. 163.

[25] Georg Simmel, "The Metropolis and Mental Life", in P.K. Hatt & A.J. Reiss (eds), *Cities and Society: the Revised Reader in Urban Sociology* (New York: Free Press, 1951), p. 638.

haphazardness and diversity. The inherent plurality of the city is visible in the genetic makeup of its narrative structure, transforming Paris into a disjunctured space.

I would argue that several of the characters in *Paris, je t'aime* are denied a fully visible or mappable city. This topographical uncertainty is mirrored in the emotional and physical bonds between the city's inhabitants: people get lost, look at maps and guide-books, run after each other through streets and cemeteries. In this way, *Paris, je t'aime* fits into Michel de Certeau's configuration of what the modern city has come to embody. De Certeau begins his seminal essay "Marches dans la ville" with a description of the view of New York City from a skyscraper. From this perspective, thanks to distance, the city is reduced to a legible plan, a 'concept city'. In ascending the skyscraper, the subject shakes off the multiplicity of the streets, becoming a reader rather than a participant when his altitude "transfigure en voyeur". Positioned in this way, the viewer can delight in "le plaisir de 'voir l'ensemble', de surplomber, de totaliser le plus démesuré des textes humains".[26] De Certeau also describes the city's inhabitants as a "grouillement [...] de singularités", their trajectories are random and non-sequential, and their "jeux de pas sont façonnages d'espaces. Ils trament les lieux".[27] Thus a viewer standing atop the skyscraper remains alien to the inhabited world below, whilst those who walk the streets become active participants. Though individually illegible, the aggregate of many such movements constitutes the story of urban life. Accordingly, *Paris, je t'aime* is punctuated by the type of chance encounters between strangers, opportunities seized and missed, language difficulties and other barriers to communication described by de Certeau as typifying modern life in the city. The film eliminates topographical confusion by employing intertitles to inform the spectator as to the location of the current story. This is analogous to the viewer atop a skyscraper who attempts, from a distance, to map an ordered legibility onto the whole. Thus, the city can be 'read' from on high, conforming to a plan, comprehensible only because its constituent intricacies and entanglements have been compressed.

---

[26] Michel de Certeau, *L'Invention du quotidien, Vol. 1 : Arts de faire* (Paris: Gallimard, 1990), p. 140.
[27] De Certeau, p. 147.

The final segment, Alexander Payne's *14ème arrondissement*, proposes a reading of the city that combines the *flâneur*'s joy of the unsuspected discovery with the liberating power of travel to facilitate new interpretations of the city. Carol, an American postal worker, proceeds to recount, in heavily accented French, a recent journey to Paris. She begins at street level, engaging in the kind of pedestrian wanderings that de Certeau referred to as a "une géographie seconde, poétique".[28] However, when she stands on the observation deck atop the Tour Montparnasse, she is granted a changed perception of the urban landscape. When de Certeau stood on top of the World Trade Centre, he occupied the privileged position of 'seeing the whole'. Likewise, Carol's elevated view "mue en lisibilité la complexité de la ville" and "fige en un texte transparent son opaque mobilité".[29] Like de Certeau, Carol seeks to attain clarity and legibility through distance and simplification. When she descends to street level, her view of Paris demonstrably changes; she feels more at home, and undergoes an epiphany in a park. Though her accented French labels her an outsider, she concludes that "c'était le moment que j'ai commencé à aimer Paris, et le moment que j'ai senti que Paris m'a aimé aussi". It is this notion of Paris as a site of transit and hospitality that I will turn to in the final part of the paper. Where better to situate these narratives of chance, coincidence and contingency than the post-modern city?

Paris as 21st Century City

Unlike *Paris vu par...*, released around the heady era of the Situationists and the 1968 *événements*, *Paris, je t'aime* does not issue profound statements about the state of French society, nor is there a sense that its participants are engaged in an urgent collective project of the kind typical of *11'9"01*. However, this is not to play down the relevance *Paris, je t'aime*'s interrogation of contemporary urban politics. One of the more pragmatic qualities of the portmanteau film is that a collection of short films can be rushed into production far more quickly than a feature film, which in turn allows directors to comment on current affairs in a way that more conventional film-making rarely can. Thus, Europe's (and in particular France's) current

---

[28] De Certeau, p. 158.
[29] De Certeau, p. 141.

preoccupations with migration, immigration, and border porosity are arguably better served in a film like *Paris, je t'aime*, which smuggles a more radical political agenda into its conventional picture-postcard trajectory. By examining the extent to which numerous comings-and-goings take place in Paris, the film calls attention to the porosity of national borders and at the same time exposes the asymmetrical power relations between hosts and migrants, and Western Europe and America and its 'Others'.

The film explores a world increasingly determined by traffic across national boundaries, by migration, exile, displacement, by mobility and rootlessness, and by the clash or amalgamation of cultures and languages. By my reckoning, fifteen of the eighteen films are narratives predicated upon traffic and movement. Whether that may be an irate Parisian looking to park a car, an American postal worker on holiday, a couple reunited to finalise a divorce, a Nigerian cleaner seeking a better life in Paris, or a travelling salesman hawking products to Chinese hairdressers, the film skilfully intimates how cities such as Paris are the locus for a whole range of comings, goings, tensions, reunions, and voyages of (self)-discovery. As such, it functions as a version of a particular type of plurality, depicting the city as a sociologically diverse space in which different races, colours and nationalities attempt to cohabit. Such concepts are amusingly exemplified in a number of the segments,[30] but they are treated more profoundly in three of the films.

In Walter Salles's film, *Loin du 16ème*, a young Spanish-speaking nanny sings a lullaby to her child, leaves her cold wintry HLM in Bobigny, takes a crowded metro to a fashionable apartment in the 16th *arrondissement*, and sings the same lullaby to the child of her rich employers. The film is a lucid portrayal of an uprooted immigrant forced to leave her child, move across town, and care for somebody else's baby. That the director is Brazilian, and the actress (Catalina Sandino Moreno) is Colombian adds an extra layer of intertextuality by suggesting that the global business of film-making might facilitate career movement and enhanced opportunity for some, but at the same time creates disparities and discrepancies for other transnational

---

[30] Steve Buscemi plays a hapless American tourist verbally and physically attacked at a metro station for 'making eye contact'; Nick Nolte argues with his French-speaking daughter; Englishman Bob Hoskins is unable to communicate with his French wife.

migrants. Furthermore, this briefest of glimpses of the *banlieue* (it is the only time in the film that Paris *extra muros* is depicted) evokes one of French cinema's most recent pressing dichotomies, namely the city/*cité* binary, in which the disadvantaged *cité* exists as a site of containment of the marginal or threatening 'Other', distancing it from the city. The segment plays on the incommensurability between the various spaces and places in Paris—and primarily those of the bourgeoisie—and the confined apartments on the perimeter of the capital inhabited by immigrants and their families.

Elsewhere, in Oliver Schmitz's *Place des Fêtes*, a Nigerian cleaner is knifed by a gang of white Frenchmen in the eponymous square and slowly dies. While he is being comforted by a black paramedic, he utters the ironic line 'Lagos c'est plus sûr'. Here, Paris is represented as a dangerous site, where racially-motivated violence is directed towards the 'Other'. The segment demonstrates further France's problem with coming to terms with what Carrie Tarr has called "a fluid, multiethnic postcolonial society".[31] In Schmitz's vision of contemporary Paris, the city's inhabitants are treated with a sense of distance, and suffer from a lack of rootedness and an inability to integrate into the city. As such, both segments epitomize the ongoing attempt to smuggle into *Paris, je t'aime*'s metanarrative a more radical critique of the film's dominant discourse of inclusivity.

A different kind of fear is explored by Vincenzo Natali in *Quartier de la Madeleine*. Here, an American backpacker comes face to face with a vampire and eventually decides to become one himself. For Martine Beugnet, the reappearance of the vampire in contemporary French cinema "hints at a diffuse, collective unease about the nature and effects of globalisation".[32] Although the depiction of the vampire in *Paris, je t'aime* is eerily disquieting, it is nowhere near as unsettling or metaphorically charged as the figures in *Trouble Every Day* (2001), *Demonlover* (2002) and *L'Intrus* (2004). Nonetheless, the segment highlights the dangers residing within the romantic sites of Paris and suggests that vampirism thrives within the global city, functioning as a monstrous representation of insatiable

---

[31] Carrie Tarr, "Transnational Identities, Transnational Spaces: West Africans in Paris in Contemporary French Cinema", *Modern & Contemporary France*, 15:1 (2007), 65.
[32] Martine Beugnet, "Figures of Vampirism: French Cinema in the Era of Global Transylvania", *Modern & Contemporary France*, 15:1 (2007), 77.

greed and a compelling indication of the city's fluid and breachable borders. Traditional representations of the vampire tend to focus on the figure's invisibility and elusiveness, which in a modern context can again be related to current concerns over clandestine immigration.

It is revealing that these segments are directed by non-French directors and that each sets forth a Paris that emblematises certain aspects of the contemporary multicultural European city. It is depicted as the principal site of the conflicts and negotiations that take place against various heterogeneous languages, codes, and customs that define the contemporary cosmopolitan landscape. The film's protagonists face one another across a series of cultural divides that pull them apart and fragment the city. The depictions of eighteen different areas of the city allow a geographical fluidity that is easier to achieve than in a conventional two-hour film. Although the representations of Paris in *La Haine* (1995), *Chacun cherche son chat* (1995), *Amélie* (2001), and *Caché* (2005) are all highly effective in exploring particular Parisian zones and their marginalised opposites, these films are all bound by narratives that remain closely aligned to a specific space, such as a café or apartment block. On the other hand, the portmanteau format of *Paris, je t'aime* permits a rigorous interrogation of the plurality of contemporary Paris by short-circuiting narrative and spatial conventions. It configures Paris as a centripetal space; the end-point for travellers and migrants that also happens to be a locus of fragmentation and difference. Although the film tends to underplay the vexed relationship between travel, tourism and colonialism, it is aware that migration into and through the city has brought about a transformation of the cityscape itself.

Thus we can argue for the usefulness of the portmanteau film in supporting radically differing interpretations of modern city living. Not only does this reveal something of the genre's versatility, but also offers a documentary snapshot of a particular time and place. For all its ludic play with form and content, reliance upon star actors, and picture-postcard aesthetic, the film is a profound meditation on the current fluidity of borders and frontiers within the French capital, and, by extension, the rest of Europe.

Conclusion

The Paris in *Paris, je t'aime* is a convincingly mapped-out social space. It offers up familiar and unfamiliar environments where communication is hindered and human interaction often depreciated. Yet despite the problems associated with surviving in the city, the warp and weft of city life is also conceived as a conciliatory space where modes of affinity can be reforged and the vexed issue of migration can be renegotiated. As demonstrated, the portmanteau film is a useful tool in critiquing the many codes and customs of the contemporary urban cosmopolitan landscape. *Paris, je t'aime* is a paradigmatic example of an emergent form of cinema based upon chaotic spatial and narrative configurations. The film is less a travelogue than a kaleidoscopic view of the many moods the city inspires. It plays with the stability and instability of modern Paris—the familiar and unfamiliar architecture, spatial configurations, and traditional sites of French cinema—and situates them within a space of social and ethnic differentiation. A more unfamiliar Parisian terrain is on display here, praised by the *Los Angeles Times* as "the dynamic, varied metropolis that it is (and not the Eiffel Tower-themed repository for gamines and baguettes it's often shown to be)."[33]

Paris, je t'aime attempts to investigate the schisms and pressures found in any global city and co-opts them into a narrative pattern that maps out the individual and collective human destinies of the city's inhabitants. The increasing permeability of national borders as well as the recent changes in the geopolitical, socio-economic, demographic and cultural make-up of Europe (such as the processes of European integration and the dissolution of the Eastern Bloc) have had a profound impact not just on European filmmaking and film viewing practices, but also on the way in which we navigate around our cities. The film proposes a trajectory that links Parisians and non-Parisians together in a conceptual bond. By pulling together divergent and distinct plot strands, the portmanteau format attempts to apply order on a fragmented metropolis, and in turn becomes an apt metaphor for the plurality, heterogeneity and fragmentation evident not just in this globalized world, but also in the means by which these stories are

---

[33] Chocano.

recounted. As Diffrient reminds us, "the multi-story episodic film—
quite literally a *plural text* brimming with autonomous, discretely
demarcated tales strung together like beads—would seem to epitomize
the era".[34] Thus Paris itself can function as a representation of the
portmanteau and plural city insofar as it embodies the contradictions
and incongruities of our postmodern age.

Postscript

It is worth recalling that *Paris, je t'aime* was filmed in Paris in the
autumn of 2005, during the time of the riots that engulfed the city's
banlieues and then the rest of France. As Susan Hayward reminds us,
film narratives call upon "the available discourses and myths of its
own culture [which] work to construct a specific way of perceiving
the nation".[35] Thus, by the time the film premiered at Cannes, six
months later, *Paris, je t'aime* could be framed as an official version of
a socially cohesive Paris in which harmony and understanding had
replaced fracture and conflagration. Now the city was a place where
transnational forms of citizenship and multi-sited modes of belonging
could be forged and negotiated, and the hybridized culture thriving
within the city limits be embraced. This is exemplified in Gurinder
Chadha's segment, *Quais de Seine*, in which a young Frenchman falls
in love with a Paris Muslim girl. Their potential union suggests a way
forward for this newer, more inclusive and cohesive France, and as
such represents the ability of cinema, portmanteau or otherwise, to
embody the discourse of nation construction.

---

[34] Diffrient. After the success of *Paris, je t'aime*, three more versions, set in London,
New York and Tokyo, have since gone into pre-production.
[35] Susan Hayward, *French National Cinema* (London: Routledge, 1993), p.15.

Belleville *au pluriel*: Representations of a Parisian Suburb in the *Néo-Polar*

Carolyn Stott

At first glance, one of the advantages of Belleville is the unique view it offers of the city it overlooks. A closer look at the suburb uncovers an astonishing blend of architecture, of social strata, and of race; estimates of the number of different cultures represented within its boundaries vary between forty and eighty. Belleville today spans four *arrondissements*: the 20th, the 19th, the 11th and the 10th. The views held by other Parisians of this suburb are diverse; a nature-lover would no doubt mention the five kilometres of public parklands, lake, cliff and panoramic views comprising the magnificent *parc des Buttes Chaumont;* an Epicurean's first thought would be reserved for the twice-weekly *marché de Belleville*, reputedly the cheapest in Paris; an architect would evoke the curious mix of old and new buildings in various states of disrepair; a *cinéphile* would cite the suburb as the birthplace of cinema and home to Léon Gaumont's motion picture production business; and a historian would undoubtedly make reference to the tombs of the rich, famous, and occasionally infamous, buried within the limits of the extraordinary *Père Lachaise* cemetery.

Of course, the seedy side of Belleville, so well-suited to the *noir* genre, would also rate a mention, although the legitimacy of the widely held claims that the suburb rates among the least respectable in Paris, has long been debated; figures from 1995 published in *Le*

Nouvel Observateur[1] demonstrate, for example, that peripheral suburbs such as Belleville are much safer than the centre of Paris, with five times less crime per head of population committed in the 20th arrondissement than in the 1st.

This chapter focuses on the choice of Belleville as backdrop for numerous French films and novels in the detective genre, with a particular emphasis on the diversity of its representation in a number of contemporary novels of detective fiction published after 1968, many of which are grouped under the collective label of the *néo-polar*. The first section presents an overview of contemporary Belleville, then considers relevant historical facts that have some bearing on its representation in the *néo-polar* genre, with particular reference to its pluriethnic population and its multifaceted reputation. The second section compares the portrayal of the suburb in novels and short stories by four authors: Thierry Jonquet, Serge Quadruppani, Joseph Bialot and Daniel Pennac. Three important elements of the *néo-polar* genre will be highlighted in this comparison: the representation of physical space, characters and themes. The conclusion gives an explanation for the authors' differing representations of the suburb of Belleville in the latter part of the twentieth century.

In order to understand Belleville as it existed in the *néo-polar* era, it is necessary to outline various historical events which have contributed to its contemporary image. Following an overview of relevant geographical, topographical and population issues, we will consider Belleville's reputation over time as a centre of Dionysian pursuits, a hive of criminal activity, and a stronghold of sedition.

Belleville's proximity to Paris prior to its annexation to the French capital in 1860 has played an important role in its development from a seigniorial fief in the seventh century, to the choice of country residence for the Parisian bourgeois in the twelfth century, when the fountains of Paris sourced their water from the springs of Belleville, and the vines which flourished on the slopes of Belleville produced

---

[1] The safety rankings of all the Parisian *arrondissements* in 1995 list the 11th in first place, with 42 crimes per 1000 inhabitants, the 20th in fourth place with 49 crimes, the 19th in fifth place with 54 crimes, and the 10th in thirteenth place with 73 crimes. The 1st arrondissement is ranked in last position, with 239 crimes per 1,000 inhabitants. See Dominique Thiébaut, "La Revanche des prolos", *Le Nouvel Observateur*, n° 1586, 30 March-5 April 1995, p. 11.

much of the wine drunk by Parisians. Unfortunately, the huge population growth which took place throughout the nineteenth century[2] was not matched by improved living conditions for the new residents; housing was still a problem throughout most of the twentieth century, due to haphazard and illogical plans put into place by overzealous architects and politicians, which resulted in the destruction of a large sector of the suburb.

The population of Belleville has always been predominantly working class. Cheap housing and the promise of work in the area attracted many working-class Parisians forced from the capital by Haussmann's radical transformations during the nineteenth century. Industrialisation in the second half of the nineteenth century led to the disappearance of many small workshops in favour of factories; despite this Belleville managed to maintain its reputation as a working-class stronghold.

Whilst remaining predominantly working-class, Belleville's population has undergone major transformations which have shaped the suburb as it stands today, and encouraged commentary from many contemporary writers and sociologists. From being the most Parisian of suburbs at the end of the nineteenth century, Belleville found itself the recipient of various waves of immigrants throughout the twentieth century. At the beginning of the century, Ashkenazi Jews of Eastern Europe chose Belleville as a refuge from the pogroms taking place in their homelands; employment opportunities in the clothing and shoe industries already established in Belleville explained their choice of destination. World War I brought an influx of Armenian and central European refugees. The growing Jewish population was joined by Greeks, a second wave of Ashkenazi Jews, mostly German, between the world wars, and Spanish republicans fleeing Franco's regime. If the infamous Jewish roundup at the *Vél d'hiv* in Paris in 1942 decimated the Ashkenazi population of Belleville, Jewish numbers were boosted after World War II by the arrival in droves of Sephardic Jews from Tunisia; regular influxes continued until the late 1960s. The first Algerian wave also dates back to post-World War II; these

---

[2] Between 1835 and 1845, the population of Belleville grew from 8,000 to 30,000 residents. The number increased to 45,000 in 1953, to 100,000 in 1870. See Émmanuel Jacomin, "Histoire de Belleville" in Henri Veyrier (ed), *Belleville* (Paris: Henri Veyrier, 1988), p. 189, 202-203.

arrivals were joined by refugees from the war of Independence throughout the 1950s. The Moroccan influx was also related to its independence from Spain and France in 1956; Yugoslavian, Turkish and African immigration continued until 1974, when new immigration laws instituted by incoming president Valéry Giscard d'Estaing slowed the flow somewhat. Asian immigration took off slowly from 1975; initially predominantly Chinese, the new arrivals were no doubt attracted to Belleville by the cosmopolitan ambiance, and by the predominance of newly constructed and long overdue cheap housing. The Chinese were gradually joined by Cambodian, Laotian and Vietnamese; their choice of suburb was also influenced by the saturation of the predominantly Asian 13th *arrondissement* during the 1980s, and by employment opportunities in the clothing and restaurant industries in Belleville.

The end of the twentieth century has seen a final group of not necessarily foreign immigrants to the suburb, grouped by sociologist Patrick Simon under the title of *multiculturels*;[3] generally middle class, their choice to reside in Belleville is not only financially driven, but also ideological. Simon has also noted the appearance in the suburb of a smaller group he calls the *transplantés* whose arrival in Belleville seems more related to the availability there of rent-assisted accommodation, and who do not share the ideological beliefs or social practices of the *multiculturels*.[4]

If the composition of the population has undergone an extraordinary transformation throughout the twentieth century, from a predominantly Parisian working class suburb at the beginning of the century to a cultural melting pot at its end, the suburb has appeared to the outsider to remain the same in relation to its long-held and somewhat seedy reputation as a centre of Dionysian pursuits. In the eighteenth century, the cabarets and cafés of La Courtille, one of the territories of what was then the commune of Belleville,[5] were popular

---

[3] Patrick Simon, "L'Esprit des Lieux" in Françoise Morier (ed), *Belleville, Belleville, visages d'une planète* (Paris: Créaphis, 1994), pp. 428-457 (p. 446).
[4] Patrick Simon, "La Société partagée. Relations interethniques et interclasses dans un quartier en rénovation. Belleville, Paris XXᵉ", *Cahiers internationaux de sociologie,* 98 (1995): 161-190 (185).
[5] In 1720 the parish of Belleville became a commune, incorporating the territories of Savies, Poitronville, Mesnil Mautemps, La Courtille and the hamlets of Mauny and

amongst all social classes as a place of leisure, for both the Belleville residents and the many Parisians who went to take advantage of the cheaper produce; wine in La Courtille was not subject to Parisian taxes prior to the construction in the late 1780s of the *Mur des Fermiers généraux*, whose main aim was to make a tax payable on incoming goods. The festive ambiance in these venues inevitably attracted to the suburb a less desirable component of society— prostitutes, beggars and drunkards. Songs and literature of the time make reference to the pursuit of wine, women and song by revellers in Belleville; the *Descente de la Courtille* was a particularly noteworthy and debauched all-night affair which took place at the beginning of the nineteenth century to celebrate the end of Mardi gras.

Belleville's reputation as a place of revelry was matched by its renown as a centre of crime. In the middle of the fifteenth century, the gallows of Paris were transferred to a part of what is now Belleville called Montfaucon, where they remained until the eighteenth century, attracting crowds to witness murderers and criminals meet their end. The construction of the *Mur des Fermiers généraux* inspired widespread contraband at the end of the eighteenth century in order to avoid the Parisian wine tax. During the nineteenth century, the gypsum quarries of the Buttes Chaumont were well reputed as a site of suspicious activities; John Merriman's claim that the suburb housed "the very worst people of the capital and the most turbulent of workers from the *faubourgs*" was indeed true of nineteenth-century Belleville.[6] The prevalence of *les apaches* in Belleville at the turn of the twentieth century is well documented; Jacques Becker's 1952 film *Casque d'Or* depicts this *Belle Époque* period. During the twentieth century Belleville's notoriety as a slum continued, aided no doubt by the appalling housing conditions which were yet to be addressed during the first half of the century, and which attracted a significant proportion of desperate and poverty-stricken Parisians.

It is little wonder that Belleville's reputation as a suburb of ill-repute has long been accompanied by its notoriety as a haven of political unrest. The construction of the *Mur des Fermiers généraux* in

---

Les Bruyères. The administrative delimitation of boundaries which followed Belleville's upgrade to commune doubled its size.

[6] John Merriman, *The Margins of City Life* (New York: Oxford University Press, 1991), p. 203.

1784-1787 played a large part in the outbreak in Belleville of the French Revolution, as it stood as a reminder to the local population of royal arbitration and unfair distribution of wealth, in the same way as the *Prison de la Bastille* in Paris.[7] Increasingly dissatisfied with their situation, the locals participated in the Revolutions of July 1830, and February and June 1848. The annexation of Belleville to Paris in 1860 was the next major bone of contention for the Bellevillois, and this is seen in part as responsible for the outbreak of the Commune in 1870,[8] in which Belleville played a large part, standing as the last revolutionary bastion during the *semaine sanglante* of May 1871 which finally brought the Commune to an end.

Contemporary Belleville strongly reflects its heritage: a cultural melting pot whose notoriety as a centre of vice is closely related to the seditious reputation of its inhabitants. Its physical space is a mixture of old and new, of wastelands and condemned edifices, of aging apartment buildings tastefully renovated to maintain an atmosphere of a bygone era, and brand new blocks cheaply and hastily constructed during the 1970s, devoid of any aesthetic appeal. This is the Belleville chosen by a number of authors of the *néo-polar* genre as the backdrop for their novels and short stories, a backdrop whose representation varies, perhaps not surprisingly, given the variety of architecture, social strata and race within Belleville itself.

Before embarking on a comparison of the works in our corpus, it is necessary to broadly define the terms *noir, polar* and *néo-polar* as they relate to this field of inquiry. The term *noir* refers to an urban genre which developed in France after World War II, was originally heavily influenced by hard-boiled North American literature, and whose very realistic plot centred around a private detective able to confront considerable violence, resist corruption, and ultimately resolve the enigma, but whose investigation is not the centre of the novel. The *polar* refers to the French *noir* model which gradually took on its own identity, maintaining the urban décor of the American version, but particularly emphasising the real issues relevant to French society. The 1970s saw the advent of the *néo-polar* genre in French detective fiction, a political literature whose authors were influenced

---

[7] Jacomin, p. 153.
[8] Gérard Jacquemet, *Belleville au XIXᵉ siècle ; du faubourg à la ville* (Paris: École des Hautes Études en Sciences Sociales, 1984), p. 163.

by the uprisings of May 1968, denouncing what they perceived as the worst aspects of contemporary French society, such as racism, corruption and unemployment.[9]

It is initially on these grounds that Jonquet, Quadruppani, Bialot and Pennac are categorised in the *néo-polar* genre. They all offer strong criticisms through their work of the inequalities present in French society during the last two decades of the twentieth century; these criticisms are evoked in the themes present in the works of our corpus, which are in keeping with those of the *néo-polar*: unemployment, racism and corruption, both police and political. The four authors also maintain to some degree the tendencies of the genre by closely reproducing their perceived reality of the setting, in this case Belleville. Hence, the physical space is generally a hostile urban décor, and the action often takes place in inclement weather in dark and dilapidated surroundings. Finally, the characters are to some extent typical of the *noir* genre: private or police detective, dead or endangered victim, and one or more criminals who may present as overt assassins or corrupt officials. Our authors conform to the specific rules of the *néo-polar* genre rather than to those of its more general *noir* counterpart with the additional presence of marginalised characters; their inclusion thus fulfils an ideological function in their portrayal of the injustices of contemporary French society. The *néo-polar* is hence a mechanism for its author to express his own opinions, and to encourage the reader to question the society in which he lives. The political engagement of the characters thus takes the *néo-polar* to a level beyond that of simply denouncing the criminal and resolving the mystery.

Our study of how three important elements of the *néo-polar*: the physical space, the characters and the themes, are diversely represented in the works of our authors will lend further support to the plurality focus of our discussion.

Physical Space

Joseph Bialot's *Babel-ville* (1979) offers the classic hostile urban décor of the *néo-polar*: there is a strong association between danger

---

[9] Definitions are based on those outlined in "Le Roman policier de 1927 à nos jours", http://www.mauvaisgenres.com (accessed 20 February 2002).

and night, during which time the four murders are all committed. Two of them take place in the labyrinthine, snow-clad streets of Lower Belleville—the winter setting is in keeping with the genre—and the *Père Lachaise* cemetery is a particularly dangerous spot; Bialot appeals directly to his readers to avoid it at all costs, thus warning them of the impending danger for Nelly, who chooses the wrong path through the cemetery and becomes the last victim of the schizophrenic assassin:

> Si le hasard vous mène un jour par là et que votre humeur soit couleur du ciel de Toscane, si votre cœur conjugue le verbe aimer et que le rire fait des bulles dans votre tête, si chanter vous plaît et que danser vous chante, alors changez, changez vite de trottoir.[10]

The only safe havens in Bialot's Belleville are the cafés, where even the assassin is able to take momentary refuge. The cafés of Belleville also provide a safe haven for the unfortunate criminals in Serge Quadruppani's short story "La Montée de la Courtille",[11] but his portrayal of the "XXe authentiquement crasseux" is, like Bialot's, very bleak.[12] In *La Forcenée,* (1994) Quadruppani describes Belleville as a "quartier de masures et de buildings de pacotille";[13] furthermore, he outlines the architectural history of the suburb via references to renovation projects proposed in reality by the *Ville de Paris* at the time. The theme is initially raised by Quadruppani in *Rue de la Cloche,* where squatters protest against the "énorme opération immobilière dans l'Est de la capitale".[14] The reference here is to the ultimate destruction of old apartment buildings, to be replaced by new constructions whose rent proves so high that the apartments are inaccessible to their former residents.[15] He continues the theme in *La Forcenée*: "La moitié des appartements sont murés. La ville de Paris

---

[10] Joseph Bialot, *Babel-ville* (Paris: Gallimard, 1979), p. 147.

[11] Serge Quadruppani, "La Montée de la Courtille", in H. Dougier (ed), *Paris, rive noire* (Paris: Autrement, collection 'Romans d'une ville', 1996), pp. 35-70.

[12] Serge Quadruppani, *Rue de la Cloche* (Paris: Métailié, 1992), p. 15.

[13] Serge Quadruppani, *La Forcenée* (Paris: Métailié, 1994), p. 146.

[14] *Rue de la Cloche*, p. 36.

[15] *Rue de la Cloche*, p. 229, 252. Lemonier interprets this action as a specific reference by Quadruppani to one of Mitterrand's major architectural projects: the construction of a funeral pyramid under the Père Lachaise cemetery near the Rue de la Cloche. See Marc Lemonier, *Balades policières dans Paris* (Paris: Nouveau Monde, 2006), p. 174.

rachète en douceur et laisse le bâtiment à l'abandon. Quand il sera bien pourri, on prendra un arrêté de péril et on jettera les derniers locataires dehors".[16] In *Les Orpailleurs* (1993), Thierry Jonquet paints a similarly gloomy picture of the dilapidated state of buildings and of the dangerous streets.[17] In *Moloch,* (1998) he alludes to the new class of resident attracted to Belleville by the low cost of accommodation and by its multicultural ambiance—an allusion which testifies to the existence of Patrick Simon's *multiculturels* in the area.[18]

Bialot, Quadruppani and Jonquet concur on the representation of the physical space of Belleville: demoralising, decrepit and sinister, made all the more realistic to the reader by constant references to historical facts which link contemporary Belleville to its roots. Quadruppani takes us back to the Middle Ages in *La Forcenée* with unsavoury references to the thermal springs of Belleville being tainted with the blood of those who met their end at the gallows of Montfaucon: "Les eaux thermales de Belleville, c'était du jus de cadavre!",[19] and Bialot's protagonist is obsessed by memories of the Belleville of his childhood, by streets which have long since disappeared, by the Commune, and by the Nazi roundup during World War II which decimated the Ashkenazi Jewish population of Belleville.[20] The use of authentic street and café names in the works by these authors reinforces the realistic effect by clouding the division between reality and fiction. Quadruppani's description in the first novel of his trilogy, *Y* (1991), of the suburb as an asphalt jungle, "un des orifices du réel", fits perfectly with the archetypal *néo-polar* city: labyrinthine and inhumane, a contemporary city in crisis.[21]

Pennac's vision of the physical space of Belleville at the end of the twentieth century sets him apart from his contemporaries. As a long-term resident of the suburb, like Jonquet and Bialot, Pennac is unable to ignore the dilapidation of the buildings and the progressive disappearance of his Belleville of yesteryear; he describes the suburb

---

[16] *La Forcenée*, p. 165.
[17] Thierry Jonquet, *Les Orpailleurs* (Paris: Gallimard, 1993), p. 14 and 11 respectively.
[18] Thierry Jonquet, *Moloch* (Paris: Gallimard, 1998), p. 38 and 42 respectively.
[19] *La Forcenée*, p. 132-133.
[20] *Babel-ville*, p. 89-92, 56-57, 56 and, again, 56 respectively.
[21] Serge Quadruppani, *Y* (Paris: Métailié, 1991), p. 7. Quadruppani's trilogy includes *Y* (1991) *Rue de la Cloche* (1992) and *La Forcenée* (1994).

as "foutu",[22] likening the few original buildings still standing which have been spared the bulldozers' wrath, to stumps of teeth in a set of old dentures.[23] The character of Cissou, to whom we are introduced in *Monsieur Malaussène* (1995), chooses to keep alive the memories of Belleville in an extraordinary fashion: by tattooing on his body the streets of the suburb as they are removed or renovated beyond recognition. Despite the suburb's state of disrepair, Pennac displays an optimism for its future of the suburb which is missing from the texts of his counterparts; the protagonist of his Malaussène series,[24] Benjamin, remarks in *La Petite Marchande de prose*: "Belleville me paraissait moins amoché que d'habitude… c'est dire ! Oui, il me semblait que les nouveaux architectes avaient à cœur de respecter un peu le 'caractère' du quartier".[25]

Benjamin, in fact, is a man of the city; he thrives on the pollution in the air, enjoying nightly walks through Belleville with his canine companion Julius. There is a noteworthy absence of association between night and danger, in contrast to that found in the works of our other authors. For Julius the dog, the suburb is a veritable paradise; the epigraph for one of the sections of *La Fée carabine*, testifies to this: "La ville est l'aliment préféré des chiens".[26] On the one occasion in all four tomes of the Malaussène series, where Benjamin leaves his beloved Belleville and Paris for the first time in his life, he feels unsafe, describing the world outside the suburb as the "vide".[27] Unlike the Belleville described by his counterparts, there are few dangerous sectors within Pennac's Belleville, only safe havens: the apartment which he shares with his family, the couscous restaurant which the family frequents, the cinema *Zèbre*, whose struggle for survival emulates that which has taken place in reality in Belleville with the cinema *Berry-Zèbre*, and the streets themselves through which he

---

[22] Daniel Pennac, *Au Bonheur des ogres* (Paris: Gallimard, 1985), p. 109.

[23] Daniel Pennac, *La Fée carabine* (Paris: Gallimard, 1987), p. 44.

[24] The original Malaussène series spans ten years, and comprises four volumes: *Au Bonheur des ogres* (1985), *La Fée carabine* (1987), *La Petite Marchande de prose* (1989) and *Monsieur Malaussène* (1995). Additional volumes were published in 1996 (*Des Chrétiens et des Maures*) and 1999 (*Aux Fruits de la passion*).

[25] Daniel Pennac, *La Petite Marchande de prose* (Paris: Gallimard, 1989), p. 163.

[26] *La Fée carabine*, p. 11.

[27] Daniel Pennac, *Monsieur Malaussène* (Paris: Gallimard, 1995), p. 215.

walks at night with Julius, generally unnamed, thus emphasising the idea of a safe suburb regardless of time or place.

The inclusion of the street as one of Belleville's safe havens is an interesting choice by Pennac when studied in relation to the assertion made by Jean-Noël Blanc in a study on the physical space of the detective fiction novel, that once characters have a safe haven in the form of a home of their own, the street, a typically dangerous place, becomes a secure zone.[28] In contrast, the same streets become a crime scene for Bialot, and provide shelter for Quadruppani's menacing tramps. The other surprising inclusion in the list of safe havens in Pennac's Belleville is the *Père Lachaise* cemetery. We are introduced here to a technique common to the *noir* genre and often employed by Pennac: that of the reversal of stereotypes. If Bialot's *Père Lachaise* is a perilous locality, as evidenced by the murder committed there in *Babel-ville*, Pennac's characters find it on the contrary reassuring, actively seeking it out to soothe and stimulate. Pennac's Belleville is for the most part not a place of danger; most criminal activity takes place outside the suburb, and the offenders are generally not inhabitants of Belleville. The colours of the Belleville drawn by Pennac present a final contrast with his *néo-polar* counterparts in the representation of physical space: where the bleakness of the winter décor is underlined by the other authors, Pennac chooses to paint Belleville, for the most part, as warm and welcoming: "C'est étrange, Belleville ne croit pas au froid. […] même par moins quinze, Belleville ne perdait pas ses couleurs, Belleville jouait toujours à la Méditerranée".[29] The physical space of Pennac's Belleville differs greatly from that of his counterparts; albeit rundown, it seems to have maintained at least some of the charm of yesteryear, a charm that is missing from the descriptions given by Bialot, Quadruppani and Jonquet.

Characters

Differences between the types of characters included in the texts of all four authors are less obvious. Our examination of the characters in the chosen texts focuses on the marginalised and their connection to

---

[28] Jean-Noël Blanc, *Polarville* (Lyon: Presses universitaires de Lyon, 1991), p. 36.
[29] *La Fée carabine*, p. 212.

Belleville. Bernard, the schizophrenic assassin at the centre of Bialot's *Babel-ville*, has his own cabinet-making shop, emulating the working-class Belleville whose disappearance he laments. Quadruppani's squatters and criminals are marginalised like Bernard, victims of the social system in which they live; their attempts to bring about change, whether on a world scale or a local one set them apart, however, from the archetypal *néo-polar* victim.[30] Jonquet's homeless anti-hero in *Moloch* is also a victim of his circumstances, who unwillingly takes on the role of detective in order to see justice prevail. In an accurate reflection of the latest population influx of Simon's middle-class *multiculturels* in a newly renovated Belleville, Jonquet chooses the suburb as the place of residence for the investigating magistrate in *Moloch* and *Les Orpailleurs*; whilst viewing the renovations favourably, she laments the lack of soul in her apartment building, which she shares with "des cadres, des médecins, des avocats".[31]

Pennac's characters, too, are closely linked to the Belleville décor. The mix is typical of the *noir* genre, with the obligatory presence of corrupt police and officials, innocent victims and detectives, both willing and unwilling, to solve the case in question. Benjamin is the classic contemporary *noir* protagonist: an innocent scapegoat who is forced into action to absolve himself from guilt and protect his loved ones. The characters surrounding him reflect contemporary Belleville; marginalised like him, they also exemplify the role-reversal technique common to Pennac's work. Innocent old ladies are clandestinely provided with guns and taught to protect themselves (*La Fée carabine*), intimidating thugs roam the streets at night, paradoxically protecting the innocent instead of threatening them (*La Fée carabine*), the burly locksmith who by day reclaims belongings in lieu of overdue rent, returns the same items to their rightful owners by night (*Monsieur Malaussène*), and the drug addicts are old men being taken advantage of by corrupt officials (*La Fée carabine*). Belleville's cosmopolitan mix is represented in Pennac's characters: a depressive Vietnamese cross-dressing detective (*La Fée carabine*), an Algerian restaurant owner (*La Petite Marchande de prose*), a Serbian security guard (*Au Bonheur des ogres*), and a Senegalese translator of Chinese literature (*La Petite Marchande de*

---

[30] *Rue de la Cloche*, p. 116 and 105, respectively.
[31] *Moloch*, p. 128.

prose). In a manner perhaps reminiscent of two great detective fiction writers of the twentieth century, Léo Malet or Georges Simenon, the suburb itself becomes a character in Pennac's novels. Belleville is thus a nurturing presence for Benjamin and his family; it protects them from danger and provides comfort in times of need.

Themes

If the population of Pennac's Belleville reflects the true cultural mix of the suburb at the end of the twentieth century, multiculturalism is also one of the themes chosen by all four authors. The title of Bialot's novel, *Babel-ville,* is a primary indication of this, and the text alludes to the struggles experienced in reality by Bialot himself, and by the many others who emigrated to Belleville over the course of the twentieth century, thus giving a realistic portrayal of its demographic mix at the end of the 1970s when his novel was published.[32] Jonquet makes mention of the cosmopolitan flavour of the neighbourhood, but Quadruppani best illustrates the pluriethnicity of the suburb:

> Sur les étagères, entre les bouteilles, un appareil à cassettes balançait *Swieta wojna* (Guerre sainte), du groupe polonais Blitzkreig. A un bout du comptoir, un grand Réunionnais à queue de cheval discutait à voix très haute avec deux Croates, à côté d'un groupe chahuteur de basanés et de Visages pâles, un Vietnamien se concentrait sur un flipper décoré sur le thème d'un golf californien, deux Noirs jouaient sur un autre appareil évoquant une saga gaélique, un jeu électronique que personne ne touchait poussait de temps à autre des onomatopées nord-américaines, les pieds écrasaient les coquilles de pistache turques, des doigts trituraient des olives espagnoles et des cacahuètes africaines, la bière belge coulait.[33]

It is, in fact, the constant historical references which set apart Bialot, Jonquet and Quadruppani from their *néo-polar* contemporaries, whose themes relate more closely to the demise of contemporary French society. That is not to say that drugs, corruption, unemployment,

---

[32] Bialot makes reference above all to the Jewish population of Belleville: their origins and above all their fate during the German occupation of France in World War II (*Babel-ville*, p. 113-114). He was himself sent to Auschwitz in August 1944, an experience which no doubt qualifies his description of Belleville as a "vivier de la déportation, piège sans issue à partir de 42, [qui] va payer un prix terrifiant à la paranoïa brune et l'ombre d'Auschwitz pèse encore sur le quartier" (p. 145).

[33] *La Forcenée*, p. 78.

racism and delinquency do not rate a mention in their works; Quadruppani in particular emphasises the corruption that is rife in the architecture and real estate industry in all of his texts with a Belleville setting, drawing examples from real measures taken by the *Ville de Paris* during this *néo-polar* period, such as those we have already described, designed to force the working class residents of Belleville to the outer suburbs. Jonquet chooses to underline the themes of racism and delinquency, particularly in *La Vie de ma mère* (1994) with a Belleville youth's police statement of the part he played in a crime committed in the suburb. Bialot also takes up the issue of racism, describing "la crasse, la misère, les Arabes, les Noirs, les Juifs", who cohabit in a different way from the Bellevillois of French origin: "Les Français de Belleville ne vivent pas dans la rue et forment un groupe indigène cohérent qui fraie au minimum avec tous ces gens différents de peau, de langue ou de religion".[34] Bialot also tackles the theme of occultism, which is a fitting one for a novel in this *néo-polar* genre, but which is also noteworthy for its historical connections to the suburb. The intrigue in *Babel-ville* is based around the murder of a number of Belleville women who are all members of a feminist group modelled on the original nineteenth century philosophical religious Saint-Simonian sect whose followers vowed to end poverty and bring about a more egalitarian French society. If the existence of a contemporary feminine sect in the suburb is fictitious, there are obvious links to the Saint-Simonian socialist community, which was in reality housed for a number of years in early nineteenth-century Belleville.

If Pennac chooses to highlight some of the same themes as his contemporaries, such as police and political corruption, racism and the architectural demise of the suburb, he also focuses on specific issues in his novels, which are not immediately recognisable as typical *noir* themes: commercialisation, aging, literature, and cinema, for example. It is, however, his representation of Belleville itself which sets him apart from the other authors of our corpus. In *Babel-ville,* Bialot expresses a pessimism about the future of the suburb that is shared by Jonquet and Quadruppani: "Belleville replongea dans sa misère, une vague de paumés succéda à la vague précédente, et le quartier continua à s'effriter de sa lèpre crasseuse".[35] Hostile and repugnant,

---

[34] Thierry Jonquet, *La Vie de ma mère* (Paris: Gallimard, 1994), p. 113.
[35] *Babel-ville*, p. 205.

this Belleville incarnates the classical *néo-polar* city, by its geographical position on the outskirts of the French capital, as well as by its apparently well-merited criminal reputation. On the other hand, Pennac's Belleville, if run-down and lacking some of the charm of yesteryear, is nevertheless safe and welcoming, made so by the attitudes of its multicultural inhabitants, who coexist peacefully in a world of conflict, and whose successful integration is perhaps exemplified by the character of Loussa, Pennac's Senegalese translator of Chinese literature (*La Petite Marchande de prose*).

Pennac's nostalgia with regard to the suburb of Belleville is expressed through his characters in different ways throughout the series: Cissou's tattoos of Belleville lost are an indelible living memory (*Monsieur Malaussène*); Clara's photos immortalise a disappearing Belleville, whilst Barnabé prefers the shock value of illusion to render the suburb more permanent.[36] The focus is not all in the past, however. Through his characters' voices and actions, and through his representation of Belleville which is so different from that of his *néo-polar* colleagues, Pennac offers a universal, contemporary, prospective and optimistic view of a future suburb which fulfils the definition of utopia. His world is certainly not a perfect one, but his humanistic characters co-existing in harmony stand as the embodiment of an ideal society.

If Pennac's representation of Belleville at the end of the twentieth century as an unusually peaceful planet in a universe filled with conflict is based on his perception of the contemporary suburb in reality, he does not pretend, however, to describe the reality of contemporary Belleville, rather to evoke it through metaphor and allusion. Accused of idealising Belleville, he readily admits to this, but justifies his right to do so as a novelist. If we turn once again to Blanc, who is one of many to attest that a writer's personal experience influences his representation of reality, we can allow for the variety of representations of contemporary Belleville that have been presented.[37] There is no doubting Pennac's universal appeal; unlike the other authors we have looked at, he has been widely translated and successful in breaking into mainstream literature where Jonquet, Quadruppani and Bialot have remained firmly in the *néo-polar* genre.

---

[36] *Au Bonheur des ogres*, p. 54, and *Monsieur Malaussène*, p. 151-152, respectively.
[37] Blanc, p. 272.

In attempting to understand Pennac's Belleville, journalist Myriam Anderson describes what she calls *Pennacville* as "un Belleville rêvé, un Belleville avec un peu d'imagination en plus"; but, she reiterates, "l'imagination n'est pas le mensonge".[38] The reader is thus able to derive a complete picture of Pennac's view of the Belleville in which he was living at the time of writing the Malaussène saga. At the end of the third tome, whilst noting the increasing Asian influence in the suburb, Pennac's protagonist Benjamin remarks that "Belleville est la Géographie résignée à l'Histoire: la manufacture des nostalgies".[39] This statement effectively sums up his sentimental representation of Belleville as it exists in his own memory, with the lively and picturesque atmosphere of a bygone era.

---

[38] Myriam Anderson, "Insaisissable Belleville", *Paris*, October 1997.
[39] *La Petite Marchande de prose*, p. 401.

Concrete Criticism: Annotation and Transformation in Haussmannized Paris

Katherine Gantz

In the context of this larger discussion of social and cultural change in contemporary France, this essay proposes revisiting a moment in Parisian history that self-consciously identifies itself as *la Transformation.* It was Napoléon III's own push for the New, to generate change through civic, esthetic, and architectural innovation, and—radiating from the capital outward—to redefine French identity. Charging his prefect, Baron Georges-Eugène Haussmann, with the Herculean task of liberating Paris from its antiquated and claustrophobic medieval map, the emperor was of course rejecting one kind of stasis while engineering a new kind of visual and social fixity. With ever-shifting internal logic, *les Grands Travaux* (1853-1870) systematically displaced large quadrants of the city's populace, razed the infrastructure, and slowly respatialized Paris, ushering in a series of design and zoning changes that heralded a new age of homogeny made chic—an urban oasis for the growing bourgeoisie, constituting the emperor's power base. Returning, then, to the question of change in the present day, Haussmannized space becomes a curious case study: how might we examine the interplay between the relative immutability of Second-Empire Paris (its boulevards engineered to be as monumental and commanding as its statuary) and the increasingly dissimilar twenty-first-century residents who inhabit it? That is, to what degree did Haussmann succeed in arranging the physical elements of Paris in such a way as to lastingly impose a singular reading of the city, and more significantly, of its citizens?

In response to this question, I will thus look back to look forward, employing the literary construct of the nineteenth-century *flâneur* to suggest a more subversive perspective on present-day public space constructed during the Second Empire. As a kind of prototype of urban experientialism, the *flâneur* is a useful *point de départ* from which to encounter varied street-level discourses. I will argue that the content of these competing commentaries, calling into doubt the ostensibly cohesive image of Parisian identity imposed by *les Grands Travaux,* in turn generates a telling critique of the *flâneur* model. Undermining the presupposed skills of the elitist urban stroller is a city that, quite in advance of the *flâneur*'s arrival, is already speaking for itself, the crowd comprised of individuals insinuating their own narrative alongside Prefect Haussmann's masterwork.

This discussion examines the contemporary presence of what I will call 'urban annotations'—such phenomena as graffiti, stickers, amateur public art, posters and handbills. Ultimately, I will contend that these manifestations of unauthorized discourse, posted and exchanged in Haussmannized space, may be read as examples of a sophisticated and diversified integration of individual commentaries into the cityscape, too often visually depicted as the same unmarked and uninflected Parisian panorama, somehow unchanged since the nineteenth century. With the aid of original photographic images taken from present-day Paris, I propose that new attention be paid to the fine print, those forms of literally and metaphorically marginal writings that engage the urban stroller at ground level before a broad spectrum of discourse; as illustrated in the series of photographic images to follow, the urban annotations of today, juxtaposed (figuratively and literally) against the architecture of yesterday, expose social ironies and incoherences outside the parameters of the story Haussmann wished the newly transformed Paris to tell.

Introduction: Revisiting the 'New' Paris

From notions of *déconstruction* to de Certeau's *Marches dans la ville,* French critical thought boasts an extensive lexicon for representing the philosophical and structural intersections between the city and text. Occupying a particularly literal intersection is Haussmann studies, a discrete category of interdisciplinary scholarship. As the Parisian prefect hand-chosen by Louis-Napoléon to undertake the comprehensive urban rebuilding project, Haussmann relentlessly pursued the mission of France's Second Empire to redraft the crumbling Paris into a new form befitting the capital. In the winter of 1850, the decree from Louis-Napoléon (Emperor Napoléon III by the time rebuilding had begun in earnest in 1853) announced the commission of *la Transformation*, both practical and rhapsodic in its objectives: "Paris est le Cœur de la France; mettons tous nos efforts à améliorer le sort de ses habitants. Ouvrons de nouvelles rues, assainissons les quartiers populeux qui manquent d'air et de jour, et que la lumière bienfaisante du soleil pénètre partout dans nos murs".[1] Haussmann was charged with redesigning Paris in such a way as to be more competitive with other European capitals vying for commerce and tourism. Wider boulevards would facilitate a freer flow of trade in a city still hindered by labyrinthine medieval streets. Disencumbered traffic also meant a less publicized advantage for the state: a more immediate infusion of troops into the downtown should violence again seize insurrection-prone Paris.[2]

Perhaps most significantly, Napoléon III mandated a more visually commanding cityscape, one that would rival the charm of nearby London. In the hope of stemming the exodus of the wealthy bourgeoisie from the decaying city center, Haussmann implemented an unprecedented plan for luxury housing—a plan that would uproot hundreds of Parisians at a time during the construction phase, and effectively prohibit the return of those unable to afford the elevated rent upon its completion.[3] With both social and architectural refinements in mind, the rebuilding embraced a new style of

---

[1] Quoted in Pierre Pinon, "Les Conceptions urbaines au milieu du XIXe siècle", in Jean des Cars and Pierre Pinon (eds), *Paris-Haussmann: Le Pari d'Haussmann* (Paris: Picard Editeur, 1991), p. 52.

[2] While Patrice Higonnet contends that the threat of barricades was not a primary concern in Haussmann's redesign of narrow streets into expansive boulevards (*Paris: Capital of the World*, trans. by A. Goldhammer [Cambridge: Harvard University Press, 2002], p. 179), it is nonetheless true that Paris had seen no fewer than eight instances since 1827 in which its streets were barricaded by civilians against government troops (see David P. Jordan *Transforming Paris: The Life and Labors of Baron Haussmann* [Chicago: University of Chicago Press, 1995], p. 109).

[3] Jordan, p. 93.

cleanliness, uniformity, and monumentality, all scenographically arranged for greatest visual impact, graceful architecture lining double-wide boulevards, the eye moving effortlessly along the new expanses to a prominently displayed monument at a central vertex.[4] The chaos of medieval Paris disappeared over the course of *la Transformation*; promises for low-cost housing were never kept, and only the wealthiest Parisians were able to return to the newly constructed apartments along Haussmann's signature boulevards. With more uniformly affluent residents and businesses moving in, Paris took on its modern shape over those seventeen years of nearly constant demolition and construction. It is not surprising that the photographic record of Haussmannization chronicled this razing and rebuilding so completely. The Transformation of Paris brought such extraordinary change that parts of the cityscape and its inhabitants were rendered unrecognizable; upon completion, the terrain, the street names, even one's neighbors were all shockingly unfamiliar. Perhaps we may best understand the Second Empire's compulsive desire to collect companion 'before-and-after' images as an opportunity to visually acclimate—one may mourn or marvel over the photographic remains of medieval Paris before taking a breath and moving on, learning to accustom oneself to new cityscape. At its core (and as compellingly illustrated by such photographs), *la Transformation* was an unprecedented overhaul intended to radically modernize Paris. In this respect, history has judged Haussmann a success, as 'modernism' is now synonymous with his work. If progress was indeed a religion in the west during the nineteenth century, as Susan Buck-Morss writes, then the 'new' Paris rebuilt under the Second Empire was its Vatican City.[5]

    In 2003, when France marked the 150th anniversary of the launch of Napoléon III's lofty *Transformation de Paris*, the commemorative volumes displayed in the city's bookstores largely took the form of historical biography, chronicling Haussmann's rise to fame as the mastermind of the redesign of Paris, a defining act of what is today known as urban planning. Another prominent percentage of

---

[4] Patrice de Moncan and Claude Heurteux, *Le Paris d'Haussmann* (Rennes: Les Editions du Mécène, 2002), p. 31.
[5] Susan Buck-Morss, *The Dialectics of Seeing: Walter Benjamin and the Arcades Project* (Cambridge: MIT Press, 1999), p. 90.

Haussmann scholarship attempts to document and reanimate 'old' Paris before *la Transformation* in the form of photographic essays— some with serious critical commentary and others closer to what might be best categorized as coffee-table books. They are visually united, however, by their approach: glossy collections of old photographs evoke the specter of a city still medieval in its foundations and, to a significant degree, in its esthetic. Each photograph is typically matched with its companion image from immediately after *la Transformation*. It should be noted, however, that the nineteenth-century images of Haussmannized space were crafted by official photographer Charles Marville and other professionals in the employ of the Second Empire. In this regard, these comparative pre- and post-rebuilding views should be understood not so much as objective documentation of the *la Transformation* as carefully constructed visual evidence meant to persuade the viewer of successful civic improvement, with the same manipulative self-justification as the 'before and after' photos in fashion magazine make-overs.

This particular 'then and now' approach has persisted well into the twenty-first century as a favored method of depicting Second-Empire urban design.[6] Equally pervasive in contemporary photos of these sites is what can only be called the Haussmannian perspective, which privileges panoramic splendor and monumental scale, a symmetrically arranged architectural tableau unsullied by human presence. This visual conservatism belies the numerous adaptations of public space presently in play but rarely visible from those great distances; and yet, because it serves both a history and an esthetic that have come to define Second-Empire urban design, this singular perspective remains dominant. Haussmann was, in the language of Situationist theory, a gifted manipulator of *spectacle*, an arrangement of visual elements staged to impose a social relationship between the state and the individual,[7] all the while resisting alternative readings. Lest there be any question about his lasting ability to connect French

---

[6] For examples of this photographic esthetic, see Peter and Oriel Caine, *Paris Then and Now* (San Diego: Thunder Bay Press, 2003), and Leonard Pitt, *Walks Through Lost Paris: A Journey into the Heart of Historic Paris* (Berkeley: Counterpoint Press, 2006).
[7] Deron Albright, "Tales of the City: Applying Situationist Social Practice to the Analysis of the Urban Drama", *Criticism*, 45.1 (2003), 89-108 (92).

identity with public space, one need only consider a few of his most famous *spectacles*. For most of us who have visited Paris—and more significantly, even for those who have not—the casual mention of Paris immediately evokes sweeping boulevards and the wagon-wheel street design around the Arc de Triomphe, scenes that Haussmann designed a century and a half ago.

While many have seen those places first-hand, the instant visual recall of those images is largely due to the widespread availability of photographs, strikingly similar in their composition, accumulated in the media over the decades. The motivations of present-day photos of Haussmannized space differ radically from those of Marville's age. Their pairings no longer depict contrast but constancy; not progress, but persistence. Other than the addition of color, recent photographic images lend to the fantasy I hope to dispel, that of the 'museum-ification' of Paris. Here, the visual record rarely diverges from images of grand but lonely monuments, the empty and sanitized European capital carved in stone. If the great hope for Marville's documentation of the Transformation was to capture Paris in flux, moving into its next great age, then his work came with ironic after-effects, as the monumentalism of Haussmannization then captured in those early photographs actually fed into a new visual fixity, one unwilling to take note of the social changes unfurling in the cityscape.

Even while the textual component of Haussmann studies has generated sharp-edged critique of the cultural and civic after-effects of *la Transformation*, the photographic component has remained surprisingly conventional, preferring the esthetic of postcard-quality Paris to a more analytical reading of urban space. Haussmannian *spectacle* has allowed the Second Empire's prepackaged visual image to persist unchallenged from the close of the nineteenth century into the twenty-first. In nostalgic, carefully staged images from twenty-first-century Paris, there is no trace of the ways in which the post-modern individual finds expression from within the tightly conscribed cityscape.

Indeed, despite what such present-day depictions of the city suggest, recent visits to Haussmannized sites reveal numerous iterations of the urban individual, consciously writing him- or herself into the French master-narrative. Despite the Second Empire's well-documented desire to fabricate a sensibility predicated on the ideals of spatial uniformity, public cleanliness, and bourgeois conformity, there is ample discursive evidence that today's city-dwellers, wise to the power of visibility, have taken advantage of the snow-globe that is Haussmannized Paris, and have subverted and appropriated these *spectacles* for their own purposes. The question thus becomes how to reread Second-Empire Paris. Through whose eyes might we revisit Haussmannized sites without being immediately overwhelmed by Haussmannized *spectacle*? And is that city-text as lastingly cohesive as the Second Empire hoped it might be?

Writing the City: Reanimating the *Flâneur*

One cannot investigate the distinctively French intermesh of city and text without inevitably tangling with that fellow urbanist of the nineteenth century, the literary figure of the *flâneur*. To do so, I intend to walk a difficult line, at once proposing the *flâneur* as a sort of model for the pedestrian-based encounters with public space I describe in this study, while simultaneously problematizing his legacy in Haussmann studies.

A well-educated and voyeuristic urban stroller, the *flâneur* was motivated not by the bland pleasures of tidy bourgeois esthetics but instead by curiosity for the unseemly element never completely eradicated by Second-Empire design. Walter Benjamin saw the *flâneur* as Haussmann's antithesis, resisting the Second Empire's authoritarian impositions on Paris.[8] Here is where the significance of *flânerie* begins to refract under our contemporary prism: certainly the *flâneur*'s preference for the human over the monumental, his tolerance for the indecorous and the unbeautiful situates him in opposition to the larger goals of *la Transformation.* That said, his position of social privilege meant that he had the mobility to witness life in the opium dens and at the docks before returning to his life along *les Grands Boulevards,* among those classes eager to hear about his adventures. His was an uncontested perspective by virtue of his perceived ability to walk fearlessly into *la foule*, translating the practices of the urban masses into a new vernacularism made available to the privileged classes.

---

[8] Higonnet, p. 8.

Aptly evoked in this discussion of nineteenth-century public space, the much-theorized Baudelairean *flâneur* is the archetype of the genre. Chris Jenks defines him as the inquisitive urban meanderer endowed with an "infinite capacity to absorb the activities of the collective".[9] Even while seeking out the masses, however, the *flâneur* stands apart, defying assimilation, and instead remaining untouched and unchanged by the crowd. Baudelaire's definitive discussion on *la flânerie* appears in "Le Peintre de la vie moderne", in which he details the curious paradox of the nineteenth-century *flâneur*, at once among the people but never part of them:

> La foule est son domaine. […] Sa passion et sa profession, c'est *d'épouser la foule*. Pour le parfait flâneur, pour l'observateur passionné, c'est une immense jouissance que d'élire domicile dans le nombre, dans l'ondoyant, dans le mouvement, dans le fugitif et l'infini. […] [V]oir le monde, être au centre du monde et rester caché au monde, tels sont quelques-uns des moindres plaisirs de ces esprits indépendants, passionnés, impartiaux, que la langue ne peut que maladroitement définir. L'observateur est un *prince* qui jouit partout de son incognito.[10]

In this model, it is the work of the *flâneur* to watch, retreat, and report. In essence, he serves to provide a cultivated narration for his titillated readership to what are understood as the unarticulated and inarticulate actions, practices, and sights of Paris—to merge *le reportage* with *la poétique* in such a fashion as to reconfigure the city as text. But in this respect, instead of building a discursive and experiential bridge between the working class and the bourgeoisie, the nineteenth-century *flâneur*'s translation generates heavily biased commentary reinforcing class divisions and notions of cultural hierarchy. The resulting per-spective of Haussmannized Paris—singular, cohesive in its internal reckoning, and elitist—defies Benjamin and correlates the *flâneur* far more closely with the Empire than with its subversion.

With these contradictions thus acknowledged, I will moment-arily separate the product of *flânerie* (the singular reading) from its transformative practices. As a means of disrupting the visual

---

[9] Chris Jenks, "Watching your Step: The History and Practice of the *Flâneur*", in Chris Jenks (ed), *Visual Culture* (New York: Routledge, 1995), p. 146.

[10] Charles Baudelaire, *Oeuvres complètes* (Paris: Seuil, 1968), p. 552. For a translated version, see Charles Baudelaire, *"The Painter of Modern Life" and Other Essays*, translated and edited by Jonathan Mayne (London: Phaidon Press, 1964).

chokehold of Haussmannian *spectacle*, the next part of my essay calls the *flâneur* into dialogue with a series of photographic images collected from present-day Paris. My motivation is not to force an ill fit between a nineteenth-century analytic form and twenty-first-century images. To the contrary, there is a compelling logic to adopting the *flâneur*'s ground-level perspective as one already focused on the exploration of Second-Empire public space. A kind of pioneer of urban experientialism, the *flâneur* is defined by his mobility, his strolls through the city motivated by his own whims, and by the changing dynamics of the crowd. By refusing to passively consume the vistas and scenes arranged by *la Transformation*, the act of *flânerie* serves to short-circuit the Haussmannian advantage of scale. Much of the force behind the Second Empire's *spectacles* depends upon one's willingness to step back, to stand in place and simply behold a static scene, to ignore the visual details in the immediate vicinity and instead privilege the overwhelming view of monuments at a distance. Rejecting the esthetically mandated vantage points adopted by so much still photography since the Second Empire, the *flâneur*'s perspective insists that one move through these spaces, accommodating not only the fixed structural impositions of buildings, streets, and sidewalks, but the changing influences of crowds, traffic, and other circumstances resulting from human beings occupying a city. In the act of traversing Paris on foot, one encounters street-level discourses willfully and strategically exhibited in public space, thus calling into doubt the ostensibly unified rendering of Paris imposed by Haussmannization.

Conversely, these competing commentaries available for viewing in the city reveal critical weaknesses in the *flâneur* model. The photographic series to follow reveals a contemporary Paris that has no immediate call for the *flâneur*'s artful transformation of the chaotic city into a singular, comprehensible narrative; instead, Haussmann's city-text finds itself annotated, respatialized yet again through the presence of individuals insinuating their own commentary alongside the Second Empire's larger message. These 'urban annotations' (stickers, handbills, graffiti) stand in contrast to other commercial and regulated forms of discourse displayed in public space, like billboards and street signs, which carry the institutional sanction of the state. Ultimately, these manifestations of unauthorized discourse may be read as examples of a more willful and subversive integration of the increasingly plural urban self into public space than previous models of city-as-text have allowed. And quite in contrast with de Certeau's famous aerial view of the city in which he looks down upon "les caractères les plus hauts du globe," ("the biggest letters in the world"),[11] I propose that we opt instead to turn our attention to the fine print—those competing and overlapping forms of commentary from the city's margins that engage the urban stroller at ground level.

Scanning the Margins: Reading (and Rereading) Paris

To briefly address my methodology, all images to follow were taken by photographer Keith Herbert and me between the early summer of 2003 and the spring of 2008. Because a primary objective has been to disrupt the cycle of reproducing postcard-quality shots in one of the most undeniably picturesque cities in the world, the photographic element of this project has adhered to two guiding precepts. First, we could not stage the photos we took by 'arranging' passers-by, disrupting traffic, or cleaning up debris from the area. Second, in an effort to better approximate the visual experience of pedestrians in Paris, I devised a timed system in which we spent no more than one hour walking through and photographing each Haussmannized spot. Here I hope to draw a sharp contrast with previous work in Haussmann studies, so often defined by either the 'museum effect' of deserted streets or by the 'before and after' photo sets meant to encourage detailed inspection. The visual element of this project is predicated on the understanding that, by design, Haussmann anchored his monuments in the intersections of the city's busiest neighborhoods, making a comprehensive and esthetically flawless visual impression of these sites a practical impossibility for the average passerby.

A great percentage of unauthorized display in Haussmannized space pre-empts the voyeurism inherent in the *flânerie* model by willfully addressing the passerby. Far from serving as the discovered or accidental object of the *flâneur*'s gaze, it instead invites collaboration in the form of a one-to-one moment of engagement. The most prevalent manifestation is small-scale, unregulated commercial

---

[11] Michel de Certeau, *L'Invention du quotidien, I: Arts de faire* (Paris: Gallimard, 1990), p. 140.

advertising in the form of stencils, stickers, and flyers, requiring neither the budget of more expensive mainstream advertising nor the endorsement of institutional forces regulating commercial discourse. A collective examination of their aggregated messages at any given Haussmannized site reveals a number of assumptions about the interests and income of the presumed viewer.

Figure 8: Music ads

Compare, for example, the eye-catching, color graphic ads for music found in the student-centered place St-Michel (figure 8) with ads discreetly posted along l'avenue Bosquet, an otherwise pristine stretch of private schools and embassies in the seventh *arrondissement*. Understated, handwritten 'work wanted' notices by self-identified *femmes polonaises* share space alongside ads for piano teachers, dealers in antique bath fixtures, and—tucked into the doors and windshields of the cars lining the street—handbills for an oriental rug sale and for on-site computer repair (figure 9). Quite in opposition to Baudelairean *flânerie*, this urban moment of assessment implicates the passerby, no longer an untouched and anonymous observer. Even as la place St-Michel and l'avenue Bosquet continue to bear the strikingly uniform look of *la Transformation* (Haussmann's signature six-story apartment buildings of dressed stone façades, the double-wide boulevards, street-side *mobilier urbain*), a willingness to read between the lines of cultural conformity and affluence expose these annotations, present-day commentary from individuals who reveal a population in defiance of that uniformity.

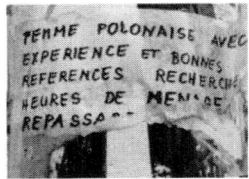
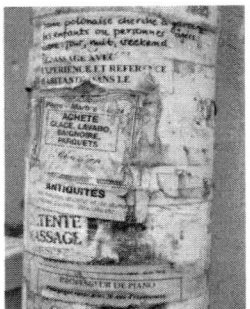

Figure 9: Work wanted

Another variant of annotation that directly addresses the city stroller is political material and propaganda. To an even greater degree than the ads, political subgroups reach out for potential allies in the crowd.

Figure 10: Street sign

Unlike the local prefecture's street-sign symbology of cleanliness and civic pride (figure 10) inscribed in the unconvincingly ventriloquized first person—"J'aime mon quartier, je ramasse"—individual causes and positionalities in conflict with the state tend to take the form of second-person appeals, relating to an absent or afflicted third person. Outside that formidable Parisian symbol of city/text interplay, the Gibert Jeune bookstore, another political message in sticker form calls for the "libération immédiate de Georges Abdallah" (figure 11).

Figure 11: Abdallah

In another radical transformation of the alienated nineteenth-century *flâneur*'s separation from the masses, the inclusion of an e-mail address on the sticker allows for this encounter between city and urban spectator to be transformed from one-sided appeal into the possibility of a two-way conversation, from monologue to dialogue.

As is the case with any master-text, commentary in the margins may be found at the right just as easily as from the left. The unification of appearance that the Empire had hoped to impose on its urban design was mirrored in its effects on the class structure of *fin-de-siècle* Paris. If the centrifugal force of *la Transformation* was intended to spin the undesirables to the periphery and to draw the moneyed classes to the sanitized center, what is visible today seems to be an extension of that theme. A year after the divisive 2002 French presidential elections, the downtown was still heavily saturated with posters and political images from le Front National, headed by ultra-conservative candidate, Jean-Marie Le Pen.

Figure 12: FNJ ads

Two such ads, both part of the Front National Jeunesse campaign, shared space on an empty storefront one block away from the crown jewel of *la Transformation*, Haussmann's beloved Opéra Garnier. In the first image, a blonde young woman smiles out from a poster beneath the slogan "Avec Le Pen". Coexisting with these overlapping bills were much smaller stickers the size of index cards, readable only from close proximity. The most prevalent of these stickers depicted a grotesque caricature of an Arab immigrant, circled and marked out in red.

Here again is discourse predicated on complicity: the city assesses the *flâneur*, concluding that the passerby along the affluent streets bordering the Opéra Garnier and les Galéries Lafayette will more likely share assumptions with the blonde woman, and not with the Arab caricature. The implicit and explicit symbolism in these ads—'for and against,' 'us and them'—is unmistakable, and the ideology that informs it is in many ways the direct inheritor of the Second Empire's mandatory relocations, which displaced the disenfranchised classes of the mid-nineteenth century to the shanty-town *terra incognita* at the city's periphery, later to become the troubled Paris suburbs. It should be noted as well that the message accompanying the caricature on the smaller sticker ("Contre le racisme... Halte à l'immigration!") hearkens back to Haussmann's project of subtly rezoning those 'undesirables' into concentrated *quartiers* on the outskirts of Paris, leaving the downtown for a rarefied, distilled bourgeois populace. The theme of 'infiltration' thus doubly defines these particular urban annotations: fueling France's contemporary epidemic of Islamophobia, the FNJ has devised a campaign against a segment of the population they believe to have so permeated the country as to have fundamentally threatened the nature of French society (the 'overabundance' of Arabs in France creating a plurality of cultures where there had once been linguistic, religious, and cultural singularity, and this plurality in turn corrupting the legibility of the Haussmannian city-text).

Equally significant is the insidiousness of their propaganda in public space, also relegated to a strategy of infiltration. The Second Empire made use of towering monuments to the state and its citizens in a largely uncontested effort to promote nationalism. Today, the considerable dissent about how one defines French identity may be measured by the ways in which the Front National saves its most vitriolic attacks for its smallest-size print ads, inserting them in unexpected ways in the visual field. Unlike Haussmann's monuments, these commentaries are not meant to draw the attention of every passerby at great distance, but only those who should happen upon them. Whether in agreement or not, those readers become participants in the exchange; as such, they are looped into the discourse in a way that cannot be affected by the overstated grandeur of statuary.

Another iteration of this unanticipated street-side commentary is urban discourse explicitly acknowledging the state's message. Whereas Baudelairean *flânerie* assumes a unidirectional flow of mediating power—that is, the observation *of* the crowd *for* the pleasure of the *flâneur* and his privileged readership—what stands in evidence in Haussmannized Paris of the twenty-first century is the presence of the city dweller publicly responding to the state. Occasionally, this takes the form of Situationist *détournements,* the playful diversion of meaning, as with the artistic disruption of a street sign designating a towing zone. The addition of a sticker reading "Jeff7" on the icon of a car being towed transforms the message in such a way as to absurdly personalize the abstract and to trivialize the autarchic.

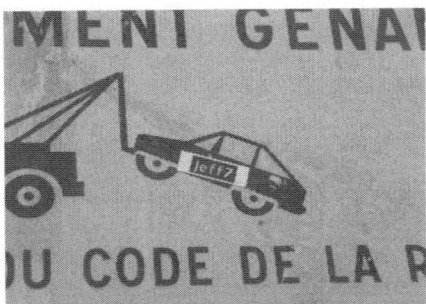

Figure 13: Tow zone

In other moments, urban annotations engage the state in more strident critique. Along the boulevard Raspail, one encounters the Haussmann-ian penchant for urban geometric zoning, in which the defining elements of nineteenth-century modern life were visually and symbol-ically aligned. Higonnet reminds us that "Haussmann's long per-spectives made it possible to take in an entire avenue at a glance, to decipher and organize the city's space. Not even the Internet is quicker".[12] The exclusive four-star Hôtel Lutetia on the boulevard Raspail shares an intersection with la Banque Hervet and la Banque de France, effectively narrating the story of the Second Empire's bourgeois paradise: high society and high finance, all within a leisurely block. What was never in the original picture, however, is the presence of disruptive new interlocutors who enter the city-text at eye-level, with angry commentary on both economic disparity and social injustice.[13]

Not only do these urban annotations often directly critique the specific and tacit messages of the state, but the positions chosen for their postings also reveal a sophisticated understanding of the manipulative power of Haussmannian *spectacle*. Analogous to the kind of spatial regulation of the masses implemented by the Great

---

[12] Higonnet, p. 172.

[13] This image of le boulevard Raspail was taken a few days before *jeudi noir*, the general strike that shut down Paris on 10 March 2005. It should be added that while my photos predate the Paris riots of summer 2005 and the extensive demonstrations throughout France in the Spring of 2006, these images nonetheless point to the link between subversive, interventionist discourse exhibited in public areas and actual physical resistance to the state being played out in public space.

Works is the discursive regulation of public space. City Hall in the thirteenth *arrondissement* displays explicit rules for what kinds of text may be displayed where. A number of panels go unused in the display case of *Affichage Associatif*. In like fashion, the space set aside for the public to post notices remains bleakly empty, and even that bears the state's stern textual/spatial prohibition—"Défense de dépasser les cadres". This apparent silence on the part of the residents of la place d'Italie is not to suggest that they have nothing to express.

Figure 14: Banque Hervet

On the contrary, they seem keenly aware that the vibrant yellow the state has employed to make its mailboxes more visible makes a far more eye-catching background for their commentary than the concrete wall of *la mairie*.

Figure 15: Mailbox

The placement of stickers and handbills very often takes advantage of the most conspicuous elements of what is already available at the site. The arrangement of these postings often mirrors or imitates the most visually striking elements of Second-Empire monuments. Such is the case at la place St-Michel; flyers a few feet away from the fountain mark off a vertical segment of the Metro entrance in such a way as to visually align with the fountain's marble columns. Similarly, the lamp-posts, park benches, and other carefully selected elements of Haussmann's *mobilier urbain* have become surfaces upon which Parisians adhere countless adhesive stickers—some giving visibility to political action groups and subcultures, others publicizing underground music events. In the middle of la place de l'Opéra, the architectural *chef d'œuvre* of the Second Empire, one cannot overlook the jarring cultural irony that occurs from the juxtaposition of the Opéra Garnier, the uncontested symbol of musical high art in Paris, with bumpersticker-sized ads for the upcoming show by mix artist DJ Queen P, featuring the hit, "Where my ladies at?"—not only in English, but in street English.

Figure 16: Columns

Figure 17: DJ Queen P

Perhaps most challenging to the perspective of the nineteenth-century *flâneur* are those forms of unauthorized discourse that undermine both his abilities and his *raison d'être*, the act of decoding the chaos of Paris into a comprehensible, unified vision. Today, Haussmannized space finds itself in a state of flux. Once within the dominion of the *flâneur*, Second-Empire Paris carries all the signs of the post-*euro* moment; in this age of globalization, even the most erudite urban stroller might find sets of signifiers outside his interpretive capacities—*visible* but not always *lisible*.

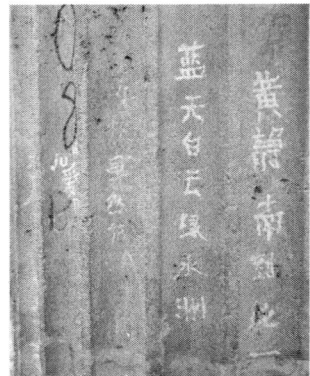 

Figure 18: Non-French graffiti

These are texts that presume a conscribed readership, resisting translation, exchanged in public space among subsets of the population, inscribed in the languages of France's increasingly diverse immigrant populations, of competing political ideologies, articulated through fragmenting and overlapping cultural identities. This is an exclusive discourse: it is neither directed at all passers by nor at the state's master-text; rather, it blithely speaks over them.

Amateur artistic expression in public space is similarly disruptive. Defined by a subjective urban esthetic in its production and exposed to a multitude of interpretations in its popular reception, street art obviates the *flâneur*'s mediating narrative. Certainly graffiti, the stylized fusion of word and image, is not unique to the present day. Its popularization through the latter half of the twentieth century as a declaration of the individual in city space takes on new meaning, however, when layered overtop nineteenth-century monuments de-signed to reify France's claim of cultural superiority. I am especially fascinated by the blurry line between traditional spray-painted 'tag' art and the increasingly visible *autocollant* or 'sticker' tag.

Figure 19: Tagging

Not only does this technological advance in the world of urban annotations offer the tag artist a smaller scale upon which to inscribe the city, but it also brings the option of enhanced graphics and mechanical reproducibility. Of course, the subversive history of tag art seems somewhat compromised by the commodification and relative ease of sticker tagging. As if responding to this criticism, a sly *détournement* of mainstream discourse appears in a hybrid genre of sticker tags, imprinting commercial, common-use stickers with original art: mundane, mass symbology rendered defiantly individualized.

Figure 20: Modified stickers

The sticker tag affords some stylistic advantages over the graffiti of old. Occasionally, the quality and the esthetic appeal of the *autocollant* graphics beckon to the passerby in ways that plain text cannot. Whether admired or dismissed, they are micro-works of artistic expression positioned in the public view so as to invite the interpretation of all: no world-weary urban dandies required.

Conclusion: Re-Transformations of Paris

Echoed by Rob Shields,[14] Jenks reminds us that "[t]he *flâneur*, though grounded in everyday life, is an analytic form, a narrative device, an attitude towards knowledge and its social context".[15] How, then, might that analytic form be reconfigured to accommodate the afore-mentioned challenges posed by the small print in this larger discussion of city and text? One might begin with what Mike Featherstone has described as *flânerie*'s particular dexterity with the estheticization of everyday life, a complex ideological negotiation as the Baudelairean urban wanderer finds himself moving into both the post-modern moment and the post-modern city. The key, Featherstone argues, will be the *flâneur*'s willingness to become "receptive to the sign".[16] I would go one step further, and argue that to theorize the *flâneur* of the present day is to once again reintegrate the powerful practices of *flânerie* with what has been its singular and overly authorized perspective. Those who move through Haussmannized Paris today must accept not only the challenges of a city that writes back, but also the frustrations of what must occasionally be an incomplete exchange of ideas. This series of photographs, unquestionably subjective in its rendering of the visual experience of moving through Second-Empire public space, is meant to address precisely those complexities. Part of Haussmann's enduring impact includes designing a city that remains lastingly spectacular, a vast backdrop for the symbols of patriotism and prosperity that Napoléon III saw fit to erect during his reign. To contextualize that within this larger dialogue of how we might evaluate sites of cultural change in France in the present day, then, what is extraordinary about Haussmannized space is that in the more than 150 years that it has defined Paris, there has been no sweeping

---

[14] For a discussion on the division between the figure and the function of the Baudelairean *flâneur*, see, for example, Rob Shields, "Fancy Footwork: Walter Benjamin's Note on Flânerie", in Keith Tester (ed), *The Flâneur*, (New York: Routledge, 1994), pp. 61-80.

[15] Jenks, p. 148.

[16] Quoted in Jenks, p. 153.

revolution of icons, no demolition of these monuments to make way for the next great age of urban design. Still, transformation is undeniably underway, occupying the empty spaces created within Haussmann's *places*. And in defiance of the stunning sameness of these sites, and the esthetic uniformity intended to carry trickle-down effects to their inhabitants, the change visible today is an impressive array of discursants engaging with the passerby, with the state, with each other. In short, the blankness of these margins is now overflowing with commentary.

It is apparent that the metaphor of the palimpsest would be unsuitable in its application to the varied examples of urban annotations in Haussmannized Paris. The city-text available for reading in the earliest days of the twenty-first century does not suggest the obscuring presence of new discourses layered atop the old. Instead, it reveals the force of the fine print, not eclipsing authorized discourse but simultaneously disrupting it and co-existing with it from between the lines. The insinuation of individual expression in public space continues to change our reading of city-as-text by functioning as margin notes, capitalizing on the positioning of the state's master-text as a way of heightening the visibility of competing and multiple discourses. The presumed uniformity of message imposed by *la Transformation de Paris* has ultimately failed; instead, that message has come to share space with these urban annotations from a diverse range of contributors, who in turn have a direct influence on all present-day interpreters of the Second Empire's text.

In very practical ways, the annotation of Paris has meant a new respatializing force; even as the physical cityscape has remained unchanged, the unforeseen and multiple ways in which present-day inhabitants make use of the sidewalks, the park benches, and the trashcans suggest a savvy shift in the visual paradigm, ignoring the fashion in which the oversized scale of Haussmann's monuments and long vanishing points once forced the eye skyward. Instead, these annotations privilege exchanges with the pedestrian at eye level, and consequently, they have drawn focus, claimed new spaces in the terrain as primary and meaningful. If the monumentalism and grandeur of Haussmann's *Grands Travaux* mandated a dominant reading of nineteenth-century Paris, then the experience of walking through those same streets today reveals an unwillingness to be tied to those interpretations—or perhaps more specifically, the unmistakable presence of the city's inhabitants alternately critiquing them or ignoring them, but always making use of those same spaces to offer up whatever message interests them most.

Finally, the practice of annotating Second-Empire public space exposes enormous innovation in the relationship between city and citizen: whereas Haussmann's *Grands Travaux* were ostensibly unidirectional, extending physical and psychological influence on the population, urban annotation boldly pushes back, reorganizing the experience of physical space. To articulate the mutual influence of Haussmann's 'new Paris' and its residents of the twenty-first century is to embrace Featherstone's directive that one be 'receptive to the sign'. The tremendous gravitas of Haussmannian *spectacle* still exists and is still readily consumed, but alongside it comes a host of new ideas in human scale, in a spectrum of media, and with messages that may or may not be intended for the average passerby—a defiant subversion of what was once the Empire's sole platform. Challenging the longstanding representation of Haussmannized Paris as a mono-lithic city projecting a monovocal message, this work reveals an urban population at work on the *re-Transformation* of Paris.

Hexagonal Variations

On a Postcolonial Dialogue de Sourds: Exotisme in Contemporary French Criticism

Vladimir Kapor

At a conference on the *Exotic in French Art and Literature since 1800* held at the University of Bristol in 2007,[1] the very mention of the newly-opened Musée du quai Branly sparked a most lively debate. Amongst the participants—affiliated exclusively to English-speaking academic institutions—the museum was perceived not only as a cultural puzzle, but also as a source of shock and disbelief. This reaction illustrates one instance of what I propose to name the postcolonial *dialogue de sourds* that French and English-speaking intelligentsia have engaged in over the last few decades. That contemporary France is struggling to negotiate its postcoloniality is a fact noted time and again among English-speaking postcolonial scholars.[2]

---

[1] University of Bristol, Centre for the Study of Visual and Literary Cultures in France. 8th Annual conference, March 3–4 2007, *Invitation au voyage: the Exotic in French Art and Literature since 1800.* This text, initially delivered as a paper at the ASFS conference at the University of Technology, Sydney, in July 2007, has benefited greatly from insightful feedback by Dr Amanda Macdonald.

[2] See, for example, Emil Apter, "French Colonial Studies and Postcolonial Theory", *Substance*, 24 (1995): 169-180; and John McLeod, "Contesting Contexts: Francophone Thought and Anglophone Postcolonialism", in Charles Forsdick and David Murphy (eds), *Francophone Postcolonial Studies* (London: Arnold, 2003), pp. 192-201.

Yet the opening of the Musée du quai Branly is emblematic of a rising interest in the study of otherness within contemporary French culture, suggesting that established modes of framing intercultural encounters do exist within the French cultural sphere, but may be incompatible with postcolonial theories dominant in the English-speaking world. The study of *exotisme* as a literary and cultural phenomenon in France has, for instance, enjoyed a marked revival in the last twenty-five years[3] and the creation of the quai Branly collection can be associated with this trend. As devalued and compromised as the concept of exoticism may be in the context of postcolonial studies, *l'exotisme* proves to be an increasingly attractive object of academic interest in France.

Regarding French critical discourse on literary exoticism, it should also be noted that with the exception of Tzvetan Todorov's *Nous et les autres,* translated as *On Human Diversity* in 1993, all approaches have demonstrably had very little impact beyond France. The aim of this article is therefore twofold: I shall strive to chart the main streams of the little-known French thought on the exotic while arguing that it is at least to an extent conditioned by the specific position contemporary France assumes vis-à-vis its colonial past. In limiting the scope of my argument chiefly to literary exoticism, I am consciously leaving out more than one idiosyncratic use of the term

---

[3] Tzvetan Todorov, *Nous et les autres. La Réflexion française sur la diversité humaine* (Paris: Editions du Seuil, 1989); Jean-Marc Moura, *L'Image du tiers monde dans le roman français contemporain* (Paris: PUF, 1992); *Lire l'exotisme* (Paris: Dunod, 1992); *La Littérature des lointains. Histoire de l'exotisme européen au XXe siècle* (Paris: Honoré Champion, 1998). In addition, 44 doctoral theses completed in French universities, all defended since 1986, mention exotisme among their subject key words, according to the Docthèse database. Exoticism has also been the main topic of a number of conferences since 1983: *Exotisme et création* (Lyon: Publications de l'Université Jean-Moulin-L'Hermès, 1985); *Exoticism in French Literature*, "French Literature Series", vol.13 (Columbia, SC: Department of Foreign Languages and Literatures, College of Humanities and Social Sciences, University of South Carolina, 1986); *Exotisme. Actes du colloque de Saint-Denis de la Réunion*, edited by Alain Buisine, Norbert Dodille and Claude Duchet, Cahiers CRLH-CIRAOI, n°5 (Paris: Diffusion Didier-Erudition, 1988); *Exotisme, een droom van afstand* (Antwerpen: Vlaamse Vereniging voor Algemene Literatuurwetenschap, ALW-cahier nr.11, 1991); *Crise fin-de-siècle et tentation de l'exotisme*, edited by. G. Ducrey and J-M. Moura (Lille: Presses Universitaires du Nord, 2002); La France et l'exotique, University of Birmingham, 22-23 March 2003; and finally the conference held at the University of Bristol in March 2007 referenced in note 2 above.

exotisme across the humanities and social sciences, not least those by Francis Affergan in *Exotisme et altérité,* Michel de Certeau in *L'Ecriture de l'histoire* and Jean Baudrillard in *La Transparence du mal : essai sur les phénomènes extrêmes.*[4]

Adopting the display techniques reminiscent of *cabinets de curiosités* which emphatically structure the quai Branly exhibits, I shall catalogue some of the discursive curiosities collected across this little-known corpus and sketch a concise history of the Anglo-French *dialogue de sourds* surrounding the concept of *exotisme/exoticism.*[5]

I. Exotic Oldspeak

Before engaging with contemporary thought, I wish to evoke early endeavors in the study of literary exoticism in France. Predating the era of massive decolonization, these instances of 'oldspeak' may seem completely obsolete and misplaced from a contemporary point of view, but supply standard scholarly references which many of today's French critics need to consider while elaborating fresh positions on the topic, even if only to refute them.

By all accounts, the oldest monograph on the topic appears to be *L'Exotisme. La littérature coloniale* by Louis Cario and Charles Régismanet published in 1911. The title is quite telling and sets the general tone of the work, which states its aim as follows: "Considérable est l'influence de l'exotisme sur notre littérature et cette influence s'est exercée dans tous les temps. Préciser cet apport extérieur aux sources nationales de la littérature française, tel est le but que nous nous sommes proposé".[6]

The conception of exoticism as an external contribution to national sources puts France in a typically colonial position of creditor

---

[4] Francis Affergan, *Exotisme et altérité* (Paris: PUF, 1987); Michel de Certeau, *L'Ecriture de l'histoire* (Paris: Gallimard, 1975); Jean Baudrillard, *La Transparence du mal: essai sur les phénomènes extrêmes* (Paris: Galilée, 1990).

[5] Charles Forsdick has already commented on the postcolonial use of the term 'exoticism' in "Travelling Concepts: Postcolonial Approaches to Exoticism", *Paragraph,* 24.3 (2001), 12-29; he also confronts the English usage of the term with the French one in "Revisiting Exoticism: From Colonialism to Postcolonialism", in Forsdick and Murphy, pp. 46-55.

[6] Louis Cario and Charles Régismanet, *L'Exotisme. La Littérature coloniale* (Paris: Mercure de France, 1911), p. 5.

or beneficiary. Throughout the review of exotic themes and motifs in French letters carried out by Cario and Régismanet, the distinction between exoticism and colonial literature, simply juxtaposed in the book's title, is all but clear: it appears to be envisioned as the difference between the superficial stance of a tourist and the thorough knowledge of a settler and thus relies on sociological as well as biographical criteria. In their concluding remarks, the authors acknowledge the wealth of exotic themes in French literature (i.e. the extent of credits accumulated), whilst deploring the lack of a French Kipling and encouraging authors thoroughly familiar with the colonial way of life to cultivate this new form of exoticism. The reasoning behind this exhortation curiously wobbles between a defense of national interests and prestige on the international literary scene, and a need to achieve a deeper anthropological insight into the culture of the colonized 'other', thus embedding this dialectics firmly within the paradigm of the colonialist enterprise.

While Cario and Régismanet's monograph is nowadays considered to be at best a collector's item and a curious artefact, the two volumes of Pierre Jourda's *L'Exotisme en France depuis Chateaubriand* remain a standard reference work of scholarly approaches to *exotisme*. In the first volume, published in 1938, the method is outlined in the following terms:

> Je laisse de côté *a priori* tout le côté scientifique de la question, ce qui a été, étape par étape, la connaissance géographique, politique, économique ou statistique de tel ou tel pays. Je néglige les progrès faits dans l'étude exacte de leurs conditions d'être, les travaux de science pure, les influences littéraires ou artistiques. Je ne m'occupe ni du cosmopolitisme grandissant après 1815, ni des littératures comparées. A tout cela je ferai parfois des allusions, mais fugitives. Là n'est pas mon objet. Je veux simplement me demander comment, depuis 1815, nos écrivains ont vu l'étranger, proche ou lointain.[7]

'Images', that is to say literary representations of foreign cultures are presented as independent of any political and economic con-siderations. In practice, this leaves the rehearsal of recurrent themes and motives relative to geographic locations analysed devoid of any attempt to explain how the selection of these features was shaped and informed by the ideological or political context of the time. The

---

[7] Pierre Jourda, *L'Exotisme dans la littérature française depuis Chateaubriand* (Paris: Boivin, 1938 and 1956).

second volume, written in 1939 but published only in 1956, covers the post-Romanticist period and contains a chapter on colonial exoticism, assessed as follows:

> L'exotisme colonial enrichit notre littérature de thèmes originaux, l'oriente dans des voies nouvelles : il ne supprime pas l'œuvre des grands voyageurs romantiques ou réalistes. Son apport psychologique, sa valeur documentaire sont sans prix. En est-il de même de sa portée littéraire ? Pas toujours.[8]

Economic tropes designating French literature as the beneficiary, as well as the merits of colonial exotic literature as described by Jourda, indicate clearly that the author does not challenge the dominant ideology (an attitude which would probably have been more congenial to the context of writing in 1939, than to the date of publication). The value of colonial exotic literature resides, according to Jourda, in its contribution to the knowledge of the colonized peoples, their ethnic psyches, their cultures, and the geo-political descriptions of the colonies. Jourda contests, however, the aesthetic, literary worth of this output, putting forth the same arguments as Cario and Régismanet and hankering after a French Kipling: "Le colonialisme est une forme de l'exotisme, plus exacte, peut-être que ne l'étaient les formes antérieures, mais qui n'a pas encore donné son chef-d'œuvre: un livre à la Kipling".[9]

Although obviously out-dated, Jourda's books are well documented and stand as one of the compulsory milestones in the study of exoticism in France. In addition, the aim and thematic structure of his work, contriving to chart the 'visions of foreign countries' delineated by French writers designate Jourda as a potential influential precursor of a current of comparative literary studies that has come to be known as *Imagologie*.

II. Imagologie

This approach first took shape in the 1950s, through the writings of Jean-Marie Carré and Marius-François Guyard[10] and subsequently

---

[8] Jourda, II, p. 217-218.
[9] Jourda, p. 222.
[10] Carré prefaced Guyard's controversial compendium, *La Littérature comparée* (Paris: PUF, 1951), which exposed the main postulates of imagology in the chapter "L'étranger tel qu'on le voit".

gave rise to a great critical debate, resulting in the rift between the
'French' and the 'American' comparatist schools.[11] This may explain
why imagology even in its more recent and thoroughly revised
version, never took root in the English speaking world, whereas
German and Dutch-speaking academia, on the other hand, have
accepted and eagerly pursued it since the 1960s. As early as 1953,
René Wellek cunningly perceived that the ideological background to
this inter-national conception of comparative literature was in fact 'the
warfare of cultural *prestige*', because nascent imagology, like the
early twentieth-century comparativist endeavour, relied on the
mechanist concepts of 'source' and 'influence', which are always one-
way vectors:

> Still, the basically patriotic motivation of many comparative literature studies
> in France, Germany, Italy, and so on, has led to a strange system of cultural
> bookkeeping, a desire to accumulate credits for one's nations or, more subtly,
> by proving that one's own nation has assimilated and 'understood' a foreign
> master more fully than any other.[12]

The kinship with the creditor-debtor tropes I have discerned in 'exotic
oldspeak' is plain to see. No representation of the other envisaged
within this framework can break free from the hierarchical insights
typical of cultural chauvinism, within colonial ideology or without it.

The foundations of *imagologie* in its present revised form, at
least in its French variant—as opposed to the Dutch and German
schools—have been laid by Daniel-Henri Pageaux. Since the 1980s,
Pageaux has been thoroughly reassessing the positions of the old

---

[11] In 1953, René Wellek famously discarded imagology as a form of 'literary
sociology', which distracted literary scholars from their true object of study, i.e. the
typology of what made literary texts special. This divide was subsequently
reformulated through the dichotomy of 'intrinsic' textual analysis and the 'extrinsic'
contextualization encompassing imagology, which led to the constitution of two
distinct 'schools' of comparative literature: the North-American (intrinsic) and the
European. See René Wellek, "The Concept of Comparative Literature", *Yearbook of
Comparative and General Literature*, 2 (1953): 1-5; "The Crisis in Comparative
Literature", in W. P. Friedrich (ed), *Proceedings of the Second International Congress
of Comparative Literature* (Chapel Hill: University of North Carolina, 1959), pp. 149-
159, later reprinted in *Concepts of Criticism* (New Haven: Yale UP, 1963), pp. 282-
295. The somewhat utopian cosmopolitism of Robert Etiemble's *Comparaison n'est
pas raison* (Paris: Gallimard, 1963) reflected on the 'crisis in comparative literature'
and announced a new turn of French comparativism.
[12] R. Wellek (1963), p. 289.

imagology, renaming his approach *imagerie culturelle* to start off with, and drawing on contemporary thought shaped by the 'structuralist revolution' of the 1960s and the work of philosophers such as Cornelius Castoriadis and Gilbert Durand. In his seminal article "Une perspective d'études en littérature comparée : l'imagerie culturelle", Pageaux qualifies this method as—in this order—structural, intercultural and historical.

Pageaux's main contribution to the field is arguably the emphasis he places on the ideological and political conditioning of the 'image', the collective representation of any foreign culture:

> Parce que l'image est représentation donc substitut en lieu et place d'autre chose, elle ne saurait avoir (à la différence de certaines images-icônes ou images poétiques) le caractère théoriquement polysémique qui est dévolu à toute composition artistique ou esthétique. En d'autres termes : à un moment historique donné et dans une culture donnée, il n'est pas possible de dire, d'écrire n'importe quoi sur l'Autre. Les textes imagologiques sont des textes en partie programmés, certains mêmes encodés et décodables plus ou moins immédiatement par le public lecteur, parce que les discours sur l'Autre ne sont pas en nombre illimité, mais en quantité repérable, sériable, pour reprendre le vocabulaire de l'historien.[13]

The method as described promises to work as a powerful tool for deconstructing the image-shaping power of colonial ideology. Exoticism is, moreover, explicitly enlisted among the favourite topics of imagological research: "L'orientalisme, cet Orient rêvé par l'Occident, ses expressions littéraires, artistiques et son idéologie ou son imaginaire, selon les cas, l'exotisme sont des questions où l'imagologie trouve d'importants thèmes de réflexion".[14] The choice of topics tackled by Pageaux and his disciples, (i.e. the choice of stereotypical representations analysed), by and large fails, however, to fulfil this promise, since imagological studies on ex-French colonies remain scarce. In addition, the method itself somewhat lacks impact, because its ground postulates remained scattered across articles and

---

[13] Daniel-Henri Pageaux, "De l'imagerie culturelle à l'imaginaire", in Pierre Brunel and Yves Chevrel (eds), *Précis de littérature comparée* (Paris: PUF, 1989), pp. 138-139.
[14] Daniel-Henri Pageaux, *La Littérature générale et comparée* (Paris: Armand Colin, 1994), p. 74.

isolated book chapters until being selectively regrouped in *Le Bûcher d'Hercule* in 1996.[15]

The one imagologist who has consistently pursued the exotic line of enquiry is Jean-Marc Moura. Moura's first book, *L'Image du tiers monde dans le roman français contemporain* remains quite faithful to the imagological tradition,[16] while choosing to focus on a typically postcolonial topic: the economically-grounded and controversial concept of the 'third world'. In his more recent work the link between the study of exoticism and post-colonial pursuit is even more explicit, as in *La Littérature des lointains* published in 1998.

In this vast study, exoticism is defined through a metaphor which appears to be a direct reversal of the external contribution trope found in Cario and Régismanet's or Jourda's books: "On l'entendra comme la totalité de la dette contractée par l'Europe littéraire à l'égard des autres cultures (idées, thèmes, formes, genres, mythes)".[17] The beneficiary has now come to be envisaged as a debtor: although the flow of symbolic, cultural merchandise does not change its vector, it is regarded not as a contribution to the national wealth, but rather as a debt to be payed off. The act of writing a book on exoticism in French or European literatures does not amount to an inventory of treasures or souvenirs amassed across foreign cultures, as the monographs of Cario and Régismanet and that by Pierre Jourda (no less so than the musée du quai Branly at that) might strike us nowadays, but rather as an homage paid to this debt. The book's main ambition is defined as a "history of European exoticism in the twentieth century", while the choice of corpus and angle of analysis are justified by designating the dominant ideology underpinning the period as the prime factor of coherence:

> L'appréhension de l'exotisme comme fait littéraire inscrit dans le régime général du savoir sur l'autre s'accomplit plus aisément au niveau européen à partir du moment où l'on envisage le fait majeur qui organise les relations de

---

[15] Daniel-Henri Pageaux, *Le Bûcher d'Hercule* (Paris: Honoré Champion, 1996).

[16] Jean-Marc Moura, *L'Image du tiers-monde dans le roman français contemporain* (Paris: PUF 1992).

[17] Jean-Marc Moura, *La Littérature des lointains* (Paris: Honoré Champion, 1998), p. 38.

l'Europe à l'égard des pays lointains : le passage d'un impérialisme colonial triomphant à une décolonisation quasiment complète.[18]

Moura reveals an in-depth knowledge of English-speaking postcolonial thought, and often assumes the role of cross-cultural mediator, acquainting French readership with a little-known foreign field of enquiry. However, focused on mapping recurrent themes, motives and figures across an enormously vast corpus in seven European languages, Moura's approach inevitably privileges comparative and general insights over close readings or case studies of the works analysed, not least the very original and inspired interpretations of such classics as Kipling's *Kim* and Conrad's *The Heart of Darkness*. In contemporary French criticism, Moura's work is demonstrably among the rare attempts to associate the study of literary exoticism with postcolonial enquiry; however, his historical and thematic approach, informed partially by the imagological method, admits some traditional and Romanticised categories, such as *exotisme de la nostalgie*, which may seem understated when set against hardcore postcolonial scholarship geared at demonstrating that the exotic was first and foremost a tool for constructing Western identity.

Concluding remarks to *La Littérature des lointains* designate the field of Francophone literature as a domain particularly favourable to postcolonial enquiry, and announce Moura's subsequent works, namely, *Littératures francophones et la théorie postcoloniale* published in 1999 and critically acclaimed in both the French and English-speaking realm.[19] Through a series of essays spanning African and Quebec French-speaking authors, Moura engages more directly with the critical paradigm promoted by English-speaking scholarly traditions in an overt effort to capitalize on the rich insights this blooming field affords and endow francophone letters with a reading model more apt to encapsulate its inherent traits.

---

[18] Moura (1998), p. 39.

[19] Jean-Marc Moura, *Littératures francophones et théorie postcoloniale* (Paris: PUF, 1999; second edition 2005; in 2007 the book was reprinted in PUF's 'Quadrige, Manuels' edition).

III. Relativism

The seminal work by Tzvetan Todorov, *Nous et les autres,* illustrates a different stance towards the exotic. Although using chiefly French materials (the subtitle of the book is *La Réflexion française sur la diversité humaine*), Todorov displays a cosmopolitan impartiality, which allows him to maintain a critical distance from the texts examined. Exoticism is envisaged as a form of relativism, alongside racialism and nationalism:

> Idéalement, l'exotisme est un relativisme au même titre que le nationalisme, mais de façon symétriquement opposée : dans les deux cas, ce qu'on valorise n'est pas un contenu stable, mais un pays et une culture définis exclusivement par leur rapport avec l'observateur. C'est le pays auquel j'appartiens qui détient les valeurs les plus hautes, quelles qu'elles soient, affirme le nationaliste ; non c'est un pays dont la seule caractéristique pertinente est qu'il ne soit pas le mien, dit celui qui professe l'exotisme. Il s'agit donc dans les deux cas d'un relativisme rattrapé à la dernière minute par un jugement de valeur (nous sommes mieux que les autres ; les autres sont mieux que nous), mais où la définition des entités comparées, 'nous' et 'les autres', reste, elle purement relative. Les attitudes relevant de l'exotisme seraient donc le premier exemple où l'autre est systématiquement préféré au même. Mais la manière dont on se trouve amené, dans l'abstrait, à définir l'exotisme, indique qu'il s'agit ici moins d'une valorisation de l'autre que d'une critique de soi, et moins de la description d'un réel que de la formulation d'un idéal.[20]

This usage implies that exoticism is itself a form of 'ideology', that of xenophilia, and hence clearly distinct from racialism, a term Todorov uses to designate theoretical thought on the concept of race, in opposition to the practice of 'racism'. A promoter of exoticism is, according to Todorov, an anti-nationalist, or an ethnic altruist, presupposing, however, that a clear-cut feeling of national belonging exists in the first place, before being rejected.

The most important consequence of this highly theoretical approach is the de-Eurocentration of exoticism. Whilst Moura maintains, following the postcolonial lead, that only Western Europe was capable of securing a similar ideological position in the period on which he focuses in *La Littérature des lointains*, Todorov leaves room for alternative non-Eurocentric forms of exoticism. His conception of

---

[20] Tzvetan Todorov, *Nous et les autres; La réflexion française sur la diversité humaine* (Paris: Seuil, 1989), p. 355.

exoticism as relativism has found its way into contemporary lexico-graphical definitions. *Le Trésor de la langue française* lists as the first meaning of the adjective *exotique*: "[En parlant de pers. ou de choses envisagées p. réf. au pays ou à la culture propres du locuteur] Qui est relatif, qui appartient à un pays étranger, généralement lointain ou peu connu". In addition, the relativist revision of exoticism may have contributed to the expansion of the already existing trend of 'exoticism in reverse', focusing chiefly on African perceptions of Europe.[21]

It should be observed that Todorov's relativism was informed by two chiefly French sources: eighteenth-century philosophers, not least Montesquieu and, more importantly for the study of exoticism, Victor Segalen, regarded as the founder of 'alterity'-oriented approaches to the exotic.[22] Segalen's *Essai sur l'exotisme* is a series of fragments towards a comprehensive study of the phenomenon, which were published posthumously in 1978. The approach takes its cue from the meaning of the prefix *exo-*: "Définition du préfixe *Exo* dans sa plus grande généralisation possible. Tout ce qui est en dehors de l'ensemble de nos faits de conscience actuels, quotidiens, tout ce qui n'est pas notre 'Tonalité mentale' coutumière".[23] In the foregoing definition, Segalen's idiosyncratic aesthetic of diversity couches exoticism in subjective perception without explicitly defining the boundaries of *nous*. A closer reading of his fragmentary text, reveals that it should be understood as an attack targeted at European (and particularly French) hegemony, the then dominant genre of travel-writing, as exemplified by Pierre Loti, twinned with an ominous vision of globalisation described in quaint jargon borrowed from thermodynamics.

---

[21] Cabakulu (M.C.C.), *L'Exotisme européen dans la littérature africaine de langue française 1926-1977. Les Blancs en Europe vus par les Africains*, PhD thesis, Paris XII, 1988; the special issue *L'Occident exotique* of *Histoire*, May 1983; Wolfgang Zimmer, "Voyages africains de recherche et de découverte à l'intérieur de l'Allemagne: l'exotisme à rebours", in L'Exotisme. *Actes du colloque de Saint-Denis de la Réunion*; Mildred Mortimer, *Journeys through the French African Novel* (Postmouth: Heinemann / London: James Curry, 1990); Romuald Fonkoua, "'Le voyage à l'envers'. Essai sur les discours des voyageurs nègres en France", in Romuald Fonkoua (ed), *Les Discours des voyages* (Paris: Karthala, 1998), pp. 117-145.

[22] On Segalen, see Charles Forsdick, *Victor Segalen and the Aesthetics of Diversity* (Oxford: Oxford University Press, 2000).

[23] Victor Segalen, *Essai sur l'exotisme* (Montepellier: Fata Morgana, 1978), p. 38.

In an attempt to frame the exotic, other French-speaking literary critics have tread the path of relativism, not least Bernard Mouralis, who included exoticism as one of the subversive instances of *contre-littérature* in his book of that title,[24] and Pierre Halen who defined exoticism as a "regard altérifiant".[25]

All the relativist approaches from the Enlightenment onwards are linked in their attempt to shatter customary euro-centric connotations attached to the concept of exoticism. Implicitly, this is tantamount to debunking imperialist ideology by annihilating the hierarchical power-structure upon which it builds. However, the relativist logic runs the risk of rendering the notion of exoticism inoperative within the framework of critical concepts, due to its broad definition. For what relativist approaches all struggle with is de-lineating the boundaries of the observing pole, the *nous* against which the exotic is defined. Are the bases of it national, as Todorov seems to imply; cultural, social and individual, as in Ségalen's aesthetic; or all of these, as Halen believes? The admission of the last possibility would require a comprehensive overhauling of the critical apparatus in use, and a reassessment of basic ontological and perceptive categories, and this is a limit very few thinkers would be willing to cross.

IV. Universalism: The Return of the Shifting *Nous*

All of the reviewed literary approaches to the exotic may admittedly be envisaged as a series of distinctive discursive positions, determined to an extent by canonic institutionalized practice within the field of literary studies and the rejection of 'cultural studies' as a valid epistemological and pedagogical paradigm within French academia. However, the link to power and the ideological freight in the following example cannot be denied, for it springs from its very source, so to speak, whilst striking a chord with the literary approaches previously examined. To round up this short survey of the contemporary French thought on the exotic, I wish to return to the

---

[24] Bernard Mouralis, *Les Contre-littératures* (Paris, PUF, 1975).
[25] Pierre Halen, "Pour en finir avec une phraséologie encombrante : la question de l'Autre et de l'exotisme dans l'approche critique des littératures coloniales et post-coloniales", in Jean-François Durand (ed), *Les Littératures coloniales. Afrique franco-phone: Découvertes*, Volume I, (Paris; Montréal: L'Harmattan, 1999), pp. 41-62.

controversial Musée du quai Branly and the presidential discourse that marked its opening.

In trying to examine what may cause uproar and make this museum shocking within the English-speaking setting informed by the postcolonial theory, I shall take as a starting point the short text by the former president Jacques Chirac published in the *Spectacle du monde* from November 2005.[26] Chirac personally endorsed the creation of this collection, and envisaged it as the dream come true of one of his close personal friends, the late Jacques Kerchache. The very title sets the note for the arguments to come—"Un témoignage du dialogue des cultures":

> Les voix des peuples autochtones sont essentielles à la polyphonie du monde pour permettre à la diversité humaine de s'exprimer pleinement. En instaurant un dialogue respectueux de nos différences avec les sociétés traditionnelles, nous contribuons aussi à renouer certains des fils déjà rompus de leurs traditions.[27]

While advocating tolerance of cultural difference, the act of naming the other, the exotic, gives rise to a remarkable amount of linguistic wobbling throughout the article: *sociétés traditionnelles, cultures extra-européennes, arts non-occidentaux.*

The political correctness of this enterprise is envisioned chiefly as a blow to the cultural hegemony of either France, or Europe, as hidden behind the shifting *nous*: by regrouping the items of the anthropological collections of the Musée de l'Homme and of those of the palais de la Porte-Dorée, and granting them the status of 'artefacts', the newly founded institution hopes to erase the dividing line between European and non-European cultural and artistic practices:

> Témoignage du refus d'une conception étriquée des savoirs et d'une prétendue hiérarchie des arts établie au détriment des productions artistiques des autres continents, il illustrera l'engagement de la France en faveur de la diversité culturelle. Il rappellera que notre histoire est étroitement liée à celle des pays

---

[26] I wish to thank Professor Richard Hobbs, of the University of Bristol, for pointing me to this text.

[27] Jacques Chirac, "Un Témoignage du dialogue des cultures", *Spectacle du Monde,* November 2005, p. 5.

d'origine de ces œuvres, avec lesquels il contribuera à instaurer un dialogue plus juste.[28]

The position of France as the promoter of cultural diversity is thus justified by tight historic links between it and the countries of origin of the artefacts gathered. Excluding the promise of a 'fairer' dialogue, any allusion to the nature of these links and the methods of acquisition of the said artefacts is absent from the present statement. Furthermore two features of the museum display seem to put into practice this discursive stance. Firstly, the organization of museum exhibits juxtaposes items from very dissimilar periods on account of their geographical origin, unashamedly underpinned by the anthropological topos of (primitive) 'cultures without history'—as opposed to civilized ones with. Secondly, the explanatory notes often remain silent about the mode of acquisition of the artefacts, hiding behind the inconclusive verb 'collected' and the aura of scientificity endowing the 'missions' dispatched by the *métropole* to remote parts of the globe. Chirac's text closes in what appears to be the best neo-Gaullian tradition: "A un an de l'ouverture, je forme le vœu qu'il donne aux jeunes générations des clés de lecture pour mieux comprendre l'universalité de notre patrimoine".[29] The ambiguous use of the possessive *notre* allows, however, for two possible readings: are we to understand that the already shifting first person of plural which stood for France and Europe alternatively is now extended so as to include the whole of mankind and interpret Chirac's claim as the universality of global heritage? Or is the *notre* simply referring to France, and falling back into the same tropes of exotic 'contributions' enriching French culture, which we detected in the very first works dealing with exoticism in French literature? The ending quote by Malraux—"La France n'est jamais plus grande que lorsqu'elle l'est pour tous" seems to privilege the second reading, along the traditional lines of French universalism.

In a recent article, Achille Mbembé has pinpointed precisely this lingering French ideology of universalism, a convenient fig leaf of political correctness, as one of the main obstacles to the development

---

[28] Chirac.
[29] Chirac.

of postcolonial thought in France, which would require an adherence to a more cosmopolitan worldview of democracy.[30]

Conclusion

French thought on the exotic is, as we have seen, diverse, without a neatly perceptible mainstream orientation. Whether the exotic is discussed under the guise of relativism, universalism or diversity, what most approaches reviewed do have in common is a certain lack of novelty. From the uncanny resemblances, and interchangeability of the economic tropes in Chirac's speech with those encountered in the works published at the height of the colonial era, to the relativism of the Enlightenment era philosophers extrapolated to its extreme consequences in the work of Todorov and others, to contemporary French *imagologie,* conceived as a reformed version of an approach based on the calculus of national credits and debts, whose deconstructive potential is yet to be proven, these discourses may appear as instances of history repeating itself. Bar a few notable exceptions, is the French newspeak on exoticism suggesting that the difference between the colonial and the post-colonial era is one of degree, rather than one of kind? Or is it the somewhat radical nature of the English-speaking postcolonial stance, conceiving the rift between the two periods as more than then a mere issue of posteriority, which conditions the perception of contemporary French discourse on the exotic as backwards and misplaced in the current global geo-political setting?

Rather than engaging in these amply debated considerations, I shall content myself with pointing to the root cause of this terminological split. What seems quite unacceptable about the French usage, from the point of view of postcolonial thought, is the seemingly nonchalant neutrality with which French scholars employ an obviously relational term, such as *exotisme,* reliant on the center-periphery semantics (exo- means 'outside') and worldview that postcolonial scholars have been striving to shatter. In a context increasingly informed by the latter view exoticism can hardly be regarded as anything more than a pejorative term, a negatively-tinted remainder of bygone practices rather than a neutral analytical tool.

---

[30] Achille Mbembé, "La République désoeuvrée", *L'Esprit* (2005), 159-174.

As it is, the contesting semantics of this specious terminological equivalent make it a very unpractical tool to use in an international context. Exoticism and *exotisme* remain for the moment tools of self-consolidation and differentiation between the two sides of the *dialogue de sourds,* rather than one unified vessel of communication. Calling for a more cosmopolitan perspective in this matter, Charles Forsdick noted in 2001 that there may be more than one way of interpreting what appears to be French insensitivity to the terminology used:

> French versions of exoticism do not necessarily indicate an insensitivity to the condition of postcoloniality itself, but suggest instead that there is a need to open up understandings of terms used in a postcolonial context and take account of (un)translatability of these terms travel between contexts.[31]

While similar initiatives for cross-cultural dialogue have remained sparse,[32] the *dialogue de sourds* continues. And the cultural warfare of national prestige, which underpinned the early study of exoticism is not a thing of the past, but has been given a new lease of life, escalating to a meta-reflexive level.

---

[31] Charles Forsdick (2001), p. 15.

[32] In an interview given to the online review *Africultures* in 2002, Jean-Marc Moura pleaded: "Il faudrait cesser de nous raidir contre la domination de l'anglais. Cela nous permettrait de percevoir les bienfaits de la critique postcoloniale. Nous commence-rions à la voir, non plus comme une machine anglo-saxonne qui va encore davantage dominer le monde critique francophone, mais comme un outil critique qui pourrait nous aider dans nos propres études francophones. La première cause est cela : la mé-fiance profonde des francophones à l'égard de l'anglophonie." Quoted in "La Critique postcoloniale, une étude de spécificités. Entretien avec Jean-Marc Moura", http://-www.africultures.com (accessed on 16 March 2008).

Postcolonial France: Immigration and the De-Centring of the Hexagon

Fiona Barclay

In a recent article, Charles Forsdick analyzes the unwillingness of the French academy to embrace theories of the postcolonial and links it to the extensive debates which have taken place regarding French colonial history and its memorial afterlives.[1] For Forsdick, the French reluctance to address the implications of the major population displacements of the twentieth century, from the First World War to the migration precipitated by decolonization, is indicative of the centralizing, universalizing logic of French republicanism. One consequence of this ideology has been the refusal of the demands of minority groups, whose desire for recognition of their specificities in terms of gender, sexual orientation or ethnicity has been rejected on the grounds of 'communitarianism', a disparaging label associated with the Anglo-Saxon model of integration. In contrast, the republican model sees French national identity as formed through the officially sanctioned processes driven by education, legislation, an insistence on secularism and, most recently, by direct government intervention in the form of Nicolas Sarkozy's creation in 2007 of a 'Ministère de

---

[1] Charles Forsdick, "Colonial History, Postcolonial Memory: Contemporary Perspectives", *Francophone Postcolonial Studies* 5.2 (2007), 101-118.

l'immigration, de l'intégration, de l'identité nationale et du codéveloppement'.

The French emphasis on republican thought has ensured that, despite the country's imperial history, research into questions of postcoloniality has been dominated by Anglophone scholars.[2] Their focus has often broadly been on the need to recover the voices and experience of formerly colonized peoples rather than emphasizing any reassessment of the implications of the postcolonial for the imperial centre. This is hardly surprising, given the desire to move beyond a dichotomy in which the imperial motherland is located at the centre of the power structure, with the former colonies as distant peripheral satellites. Within the discipline of French studies, the lack of enthusiasm for the postcolonial has meant that issues of colonial identity have largely been studied under the auspices of Francophone studies. One of the corollaries of the rise of Francophone studies has been the development of two, often quite separate, fields of enquiry, leading to ongoing debates around the relationship between the French and the Francophone, debates now evidenced in the revised titles of many university departments of 'French and Francophone Studies'. A second consequence of this division has been the restriction of investigations of (post)colonial identity to the geographical remit of *la Francophonie*, to the exclusion of metropolitan France. Accordingly, much of the work which has been directed towards understanding colonialism and its aftermath has overlooked its effects on the Hexagon.[3] Where research has been undertaken into contemporary

---

[2] As Forsdick points out, there are now signs that this is changing, beginning with the sesquicentenary of the abolition of slavery in 1998, and supported by the work of the Association pour la Connaissance de l'Histoire de l'Afrique Contemporaine (ACHAC), which includes *La Fracture coloniale* (2005), *Culture post-coloniale* (2006) and *La Colonisation française* (2007).
[3] Notable exceptions include the work of Charles Forsdick and David Murphy. See, for example, David Murphy and Alec G. Hargreaves (eds), "New Directions in Postcolonial Studies", special issue of *Journal of Postcolonial Writing*, 44.3 (2008); Charles Forsdick and David Murphy (eds), "France in a Postcolonial Europe: History, Memory, Identity", special issue of *Francophone Postcolonial Studies*, 5.2 (2007); and Charles Forsdick and David Murphy (eds), *Francophone Postcolonial Studies: A Critical Introduction* (London: Arnold, 2003).

France, it has tended to concentrate on the cultures of minority groups living within the *métropole*.[4]

While detailed attention to the cultures and identities of minority groups is clearly long overdue, to concentrate exclusively on them risks overlooking the extent to which the imperial centre is also fragmented and plural. Within postcolonialism, there has, at times, been the implicit suggestion that what is dominant must also be unified.[5] In practice, as Raymond Williams reminds us, the lived experience of hegemony can never be singular, because it is continually challenged by pressures that require it to be repeatedly renewed and modified.[6] Williams's work serves as a reminder that society and culture have always been plural, consisting of a series of competing discourses and counter-narratives which are selectively incorporated into a hegemonic tradition. The apparent unity of the hegemonic exemplifies the gap that exists between the 'hard' discourses of collective identity, which operate in certain public spheres, and which contribute to the assumption that the imperial centre is unified, and the 'soft' identities, which are acknowledged to be fluid and constructed. If, as scholars, we talk of a unified 'French identity', it is on the basis of a tacit suspension of disbelief, a state into which we agree to enter in order to participate in a politico-legal system that is not interested in the extent to which identities are provisional, and often contested.

Williams identifies various sources of challenge to the cultural dominant, pointing to the way in which hegemonic norms are altered by residual and emergent cultural elements, and affected by institutions and formations. The latter he identifies as being made up of conscious literary, artistic, philosophical or scientific movements.[7] While the role of writers and artists in analyzing systems of

---

[4] See, for example, Alec G. Hargreaves and Mark McKinney (eds), *Post-colonial Cultures in France* (London: Routledge, 1997).

[5] See, for example, Homi Bhabha's critique of Edward Said in "The Other Question: Difference, Discrimination and the Discourse of Colonialism", in Francis Barker, Peter Hulme, Margaret Iversen and Diana Loxley (eds), *Literature, Politics and Theory: Papers from the Essex Conference 1976–84* (London; New York: Methuen, 1986), pp. 210-229 (p. 158).

[6] Raymond Williams, *Marxism and Literature* (Oxford: Oxford University Press, 1977), p. 112.

[7] Williams, p. 119.

representation and identity processes at work in France's former colonies has long been recognized, less attention has been paid to the literature dealing with issues of postcoloniality, produced by Hexagonal writers. This chapter offers an intervention in this arena through the examination of a text by one such contemporary author, Dominique Bona. The work of these authors is all the more important because, although postcolonial theory is now receiving a tentative welcome in France, writers from white, metropolitan France have for some time been reflecting on the effects of decolonization and postcolonial immigration, and the contemporary transformations which consequently are being enacted within the Hexagon. Their work draws attention to the extent to which metropolitan identities are fragmented and fluid, their organizing principles subject to the evolution in social meanings and values, which Williams calls "structures of feeling".[8]

Tradition and Françoise Sagan's *Bonjour tristesse*

In her novel, *Malika*, Bona uses a two-fold strategy to explore the fragmented nature of hegemonic French culture.[9] On a structural level she draws on an earlier literary text to demonstrate that the plurality which characterizes French society in the 1990s has not changed in the last fifty years, although the subject of society's concerns has evolved. On a thematic level, she traces the way in which metro-politan culture is destabilized by reactions to immigration, in particular the phenomenon of postcolonial immigration, which John Ball has referred to as "the reinvasion of the centre".[10] To turn first to the question of structure, Williams's analysis of tradition is useful in understanding Bona's strategy in constructing a conception of French-ness which, while not typical, is a recognizable representation of twentieth-century Hexagonal culture.[11] The concept of tradition en-ables us to view culture as a process of connections whereby the present is legitimated through reference to a selective version of the

---

[8] Williams, p. 132.
[9] Dominique Bona, *Malika* (Paris: Mercure de France, 1992).
[10] John Clement Ball, *Imagining London: Postcolonial Fiction and the Transnational Metropolis* (Toronto: University of Toronto, 2004), p. 4.
[11] Williams, p. 115.

past. Moreover, since it is linked to the lived experience of families and other groups, the process of incorporation not only shapes the present, but indicates directions for the future.

Bona uses tradition on two levels in *Malika*. The first of these is through her intertextual reference to Françoise Sagan's debut novel, *Bonjour tristesse*, with which *Malika* shares significant plot characteristics.[12] Both novels are set on the Côte d'Azur, where a wealthy Parisian family has rented a luxurious, secluded villa for the summer. Their leisurely rhythm is interrupted by the arrival of a character from outside (Anne Larsen and the eponymous Malika, respectively), whose presence challenges the family's values. Conflict ensues, together with various sexual adventures, before the interloper chooses to leave. Both novels conclude with a fatal car crash. Although brief, this summary should be sufficient to indicate that, in *Malika*, Bona is borrowing the structure of the earlier novel. In doing so, she is establishing a point of connection in which a version of the past is used to ratify the present: she is not only drawing on the literary tradition established by Sagan's provocative modern classic, but is also using her reference to the earlier text as a shorthand means of communicating her interest in the same issues. Secondly, on a thematic level Bona, like Sagan, draws on the Parisian tradition of the summer holiday on the Côte d'Azur to signal the particular form of Frenchness upon which she is focusing. The annual move from Paris to the Mediterranean coast is a form of internal migration which reconstitutes the social network of bourgeois Parisians in the provinces, and so extends the centralizing pull of the capital to the extremity of the Hexagon. By participating in the tradition, Parisians declare their membership of a particular bourgeois and centralized cultural group; by setting her narrative in this location, Bona communicates her concern with the same form of French culture which appeared in Sagan's 1954 novel.

Given Bona's use of Sagan as a model for her text, a brief overview of the narrative of *Bonjour tristesse* is necessary. The teenage narrator, Cécile, tells of how her world is turned upside down when a new arrival, Anne Larsen, joins the holiday group. While Cécile's family structure is unconventional, her dead mother's place

---

[12] Françoise Sagan, *Bonjour tristesse* (Paris: Julliard, 1954).

being taken by a succession of her father's mistresses, Cécile is secure in her relationship with her father and happy with the carefree, hedonistic lifestyle which they lead. Anne's arrival affects the group on a number of levels. For Cécile, Anne is a threat to her in-dependence and a rival for her father's attention. On another level, Anne's status as an independent, divorced woman poses a challenge to Cécile's milieu, in which a woman's identity is constructed in relation to men, whether as daughter or mistress. Above all, with her sleek American convertible, Anne symbolizes the growing influence of American culture in years following 1945.[13] The car symbolized the move towards speed, industrialization, and with it the rise of a global capitalism dominated by America, which threatened the French rural idyll and exacerbated French anxieties about the loss of prestige associated with the end of empire. Seen as the exotic harbinger of consumerism, America was perceived ambivalently, as a source of threat and fascination which Bona reproduces by other means in *Malika*. The disruption to French culture emanating from beyond the Hexagon is therefore a source of anxiety neatly encapsulated by Anne's arrival.

Sagan is careful to nuance her representation so that the conflict created by Anne's arrival is not simply that of traditional bourgeois *mœurs* scandalized by newfangled American values. Although linked to the Americanization of French society, with her insistence on comportment Anne is emblematic of French chic, her presence characterized by an elegant but detached refinement. Cécile and her father, in contrast, represent a superficial lifestyle which privileges fun and beauty over intelligence. Moreover, Cécile herself has been read as a disruptive influence within French society, given the novel's portrayal of her carefree sexual relationship. As her feelings towards Anne oscillate between resentment and a longing for approval and affection, her new sexual freedom, embraced in defiance of Anne's strictures, enables her to develop a degree of autonomy: "[S]ans doute craignis-je moins son influence depuis que j'aimais réellement et physiquement Cyril. Cela m'avait libérée de beaucoup de peurs".[14] It

---

[13] For details, see Kristin Ross, *Fast Cars, Clean Bodies: Decolonization and the Re-Ordering of French Culture* (Cambridge, MA; London: Massachusetts Institute of Technology Press, 1995).

[14] Sagan, p. 132.

empowers her to manipulate her boyfriend, Cyril, to free herself from Anne's influence, and to drop Cyril when her manipulations are no longer necessary. Cécile's emerging sexuality is therefore a second manifestation of the cultural plurality which Bona also references in her novel. Although the influence of American culture is replaced by postcolonial immigration, the exotic ambivalence associated with extra-national cultures and feminine sexuality remains a potent focus of French anxiety. In *Malika*, these two aspects are combined in a single figure: the immigrant who represents the movement of the peripheries to the imperial centre.

The Nature and Effects of Disruption: Exoticism in *Malika*

Set in a St. Tropez villa, where a wealthy Parisian couple are on holiday with family and friends, Bona's novel opens on a world of contemporary bourgeois norms. The tradition of the Parisian summer holiday enables Bona to indicate the aspirations of her characters, whose public display of wealth is intended as a class indicator. The bourgeois love-affair with American sophistication continues, although Anne's convertible is now replaced by dinner-party conversation peppered with English terms and references to the delights of Florida. In a few pages, therefore, Bona swiftly constructs a Hexagon-centred world, whilst at the same time signalling that she shares Sagan's concern with cultural analysis. Ironically, given the importance of bourgeois values, the disruption which shakes the carefully orchestrated world comes from within, in the form of the family au pair. In contrast to Sagan's nuanced world, Bona makes a clear cultural distinction between the white French characters, and Malika. From the outset, she is presented as a solitary figure whose presence splits the reality of the villa and gives the reader access to "un autre monde".[15] In spatial terms this other world is located to the rear of the house: an unseen domestic sphere of cooking and child-care. But there is also a metaphysical dimension to Malika's difference: early textual references to a lost world which she alone can see, and which she carries within her, convey overtones of mystery and primitivism, and endow her with a sense of the exotic. This insistence

---

[15] Bona, p. 23.

on the exotic proves fundamental to the cultural disruption which she causes.

As Kateryna Longley observes, exoticism is a politically and sexually charged form of othering which endows the exotic with "a peculiarly alluring flavour, with suggestions of strange beauty, enticing difference and, most of all, the potential to be conquered and claimed".[16] It draws on the Orientalist tradition, in which the difference of the Arab woman was perceived as a novelty and valorized to the extent that it conformed to Western expectations of beauty, sensuality and submissiveness. The exotic is associated with a certain ambivalence: the mystery of the Arab woman attracts and fascinates the Western onlooker but, in a parallel with French attitudes towards America, there is a fear of her power and difference. Historically, as Victor Segalen has noted, the exotic has often been associated, even conflated, with the colonial, but the ambivalence of the exotic undermines the notion that power is located solely in the hands of the colonizer.[17] According to Longley, the exotic wields its own slippery power, resisting Western attempts at totalizing discourses and escaping the categorization produced by other Orientalist representations:

> The exotic [is] elusive and ungraspable, more slippery and less stably positioned than the 'oriental' and more capable of sliding away or striking back. The exotic is the sting in the tail of orientalism because it is the alluring and potentially entrapping aspect of otherness [...] Language and discourse always invent as much as 'record' their 'object' and the idea of 'containment' is a fiction.[18]

Longley's suggestion here is that the power of the exotic is potentially available to the exoticized subject, allowing her to escape or retaliate because she exceeds the orientalist discourses habitually used to refer to her. Because it is subversive in nature the power largely remains unseen, but it is hinted at in the references to the 'other world' to which Malika belongs.

---

[16] Kateryna Olijnyk Longley, "Fabricating Otherness: Demidenko and Exoticism", in Isabel Santaolalla (ed), *'New' Exoticisms: Changing Patterns in the Construction of Otherness*. Postmodern Studies, 29 (Amsterdam: Rodopi, 2000), pp. 21-39 (p. 23).
[17] Victor Segalen, *Essai sur l'exotisme: une esthétique du divers* (Montpellier: Fata Morgana, 1978), p. 81.
[18] Longley, p. 28-29.

Because Malika occupies the domestic sphere of the villa, the extent of her otherness is not immediately remarked upon by the Paul-Martin circle. Her arrival to serve dinner one night is striking, silencing the murmur of conversation:

> La jeune fille rayonnait. Avec ses cheveux noirs très courts, ses dents de nacre, elle exprimait une merveilleuse jeunesse. Elle ne s'estompait pas comme Marie-Hélène l'eût souhaité, telle une figurante dans le décor. Au contraire. Elle avait l'éclat d'une star. De la soubrette, elle n'avait que le costume: une robe noire et un tablier blanc. La robe, à décolleté bateau, arrivait à mi-cuisses. Benoît Darman savourait du regard les jambes et les bras satinés, doux comme une peau d'abricot. Le tablier blanc avec le volant épinglé sur la poitrine à moitié visible ressemblait à un accessoire d'opérette. La jeune fille semblait jouer, être quelqu'un d'autre. Quelqu'un que personne ne connaissait, bien différent du rôle incertain et secondaire de servante qu'on lui attribuait. Quand elle se penchait, un curieux bijou en or, qui représentait une main, se détachait de ses seins ronds et se balançait au-dessus de l'hôte auquel elle présentait le plat.
> La jeune fille fit en balançant des hanches le tour de la table, vivement, sans s'attarder, mais en se laissant contempler, sous tous les angles. Elle disparut. On fut bien incapable de reprendre la conversation là où on l'avait laissée.[19]

Malika here is engaged in the performance of exoticism which calls into question the social context around her. Ostensibly focused on Malika and her silent and conscious use of what she knows to be her greatest asset—her body—the incident acts as a catalyst which disturbs the equilibrium of the group and prompts them to re-evaluate their self-image and that of their companions. The girl's appearance induces a process of de-centring whereby the attention moves from a unified focus on the Centre, to a fragmented vision in which the Centre is seen only in relation to and as a reflection of the North African Other. The moment is a turning point in the novel; it establishes the social hierarchy between characters, confirming that, despite the differences in status, Malika dictates the responses of the other characters.

Constructions of the Exotic

Malika's presence clearly destabilizes those around her, but the precise form in which her exotic power manifests itself is worthy of

---

[19] Bona, p. 36-37.

analysis. The passage introduces the two elements primarily respons-ible: her sexuality and her metaphysical beliefs, represented at the dinner table by the hand of Fatima pendant. Both are linked in the eyes of the French onlookers to her country of origin, and both play a key role in the novel, driving the narrative as it builds to the final, fatal climax. What is left deliberately vague is the source of Malika's exotic power. The exotic is constructed through the attributes of feminine sexuality and religious belief, but whether Malika's power resides in the perception of the French characters who are perturbed by her difference, or whether she indeed possesses an intensity which she can deploy at will remains ambiguous. An understanding of the causes of the de-centring that takes place in the novel therefore relies on analysis of the way in which the character of Malika is presented.

Throughout the novel, Malika's beauty and presence arrest the attention of all those around her. Instinctively, the French guests attribute this to her ethnic origins: "D'où pouvait-elle venir? Quel était son passé? De quel exotisme tirait-elle son étrange et fascinante beauté? Depuis le passage de l'inconnue, chacun demeurait sous l'emprise de son érotisme".[20] Her ethnicity is perceived as the source of her sexual attraction, and, therefore, of the disturbance which she creates in the St. Tropez holiday party. The women are threatened by her youth and dark beauty, finding their evening dress wanting when compared to the impossibly perfect skin and bare feet of the serving girl. The men respond to her eroticism in predictable ways, reproducing colonial attitudes of obsessive sexual desire in which Malika becomes a post-Flaubertian version of Kuchuk Hanem. While she appears to offer a convenient taste of the Orient for consumption in France, those men who pursue her as a prize to be taken find that consummation, rather than satiating their desire, only makes it more urgent.

Initially, in giving herself sexually, Malika appears to be subject to the traditional exploitation of the colonial woman, but she con-founds the tradition of the passive odalisque by exerting her own control over her male admirers/exploiters. By remaining consistently aloof, she maintains the distance necessary to her exotic aura, which, because it is dependent on the novelty of perceived difference, would

---

[20] Bona, p. 38.

be diminished by familiarity. Cultivating her independence as a free spirit, she is prone to leave without warning, as her lovers quickly discover. Each man learns to negotiate his apparent powerlessness in the face of the emasculation threatened by Malika's appropriation of her own subjectivity. Her elusiveness adds to her fascination since her actions seem dictated by some unseen higher power. The power of her sexuality is therefore linked to the other disturbing aspect of her presence—her religious belief—for in leaving her lovers, Malika is responding to her sense of individual destiny.

Malika's religious belief is complex, drawing on a web of influences. She comes from a Muslim village where her family, with the exception of her Berber grandmother, follow Islamic principles. Rejecting the practices of Islam as the imposition of conformity, Malika is drawn to the magic and pagan rites of her grandmother, from whom she learns to pray to the stars and how to attract the protection of the *marabout*. While Malika is dismissive of the outward signs of Islam, she accepts its emphasis on fatalism and believes fervently in her own destiny—the Arabic *mekhtoub*—as set out by the stars. Her unique perspective manifests itself through references to the hidden 'other world', while her unswerving belief in what she sees as a deeper, more authentic, pagan faith enables her to endure exploitation by others in the knowledge that she is following the path set out for her. The hand of Fatima, which she wears around her neck, symbolizes the sometimes sinister air of magic that surrounds her, and which disconcerts others, who refer to her as "Esmeralda" or "l'ensorceleuse" who casts a spell over the men around her.[21] Malika is thus set apart even from those closest to her, including her sisters, who believe that she can bring misfortune to those who wrong her. Bona emphasizes Malika's sense of otherworldliness by having her story narrated by a character known as 'la voyante'. Despite a career which demands a familiarity with the magical, the fortune-teller confesses that she has never before encountered a presence like Malika's.

Through repeated references to the growing sense of unease, and the suspicion that Malika has cast a spell on the group, Bona encourages the reader to take at face value the disruptive potential of Malika's exoticism. However, in parallel with the sexual fantasies and

---

[21] Bona, p. 181, 194.

suspicions of magic to which she gives rise, the narrative contains traces which indicate alternative causes of the disruption. The response of David, her French employer, demonstrates most clearly the link between Malika's sexual presence and her ethnic origins, for in addition to exciting David's sexual fantasies, her presence brings back painful, repressed memories of his *pied noir* childhood. These memories, like "des esprits malins, sournois, qui venaient troubler sa paix",[22] are compounded by his son Jérémie's use of the Arabic term '*sidi* papa', which disturbs David because it recalls the unhappiness of another era and provides evidence that, far from being lost, this era is alive and influencing the next generation. His wife, Marie-Hélène, shares his reaction when she stumbles across her two young children making an offering of stones collected on the beach, as part of a mystical rite led by Malika. Through specific examples, Bona thus depicts the doubts and anxiety of the *Français de souche* when faced with the presence of North African immigrants and their culture in metropolitan France. She represents the vestiges of colonial attitudes amongst a privileged section of mainstream French society which has turned its back on its past relationship with North Africa, repressing the memories of its time there and refusing to acknowledge the legacy of decolonization. However, paradoxically, it may be that the refusal of the white middle-classes to come to terms with their past is responsible for attributing power to Malika. The perceptions of Malika are so coloured by colonial stereotyping that it is difficult for the French characters to move beyond them, to see her in a new light as a young immigrant girl who speaks little French.

The Exotic: Alternative Sources of Power

The persistence of colonial thought contributes towards the possibility that the disturbance that accompanies Malika may not be the result of any power immanent in her. On one level, Malika appears to wield the power of the elusive and exotic object referred to by Longley. She achieves a degree of recognition through a photographic career as a model but is dismissive of its material rewards. She prefers to maintain her freedom on her own terms, accepting the attentions of her

---

[22] Bona, p. 43.

lovers but liable to disappear without warning. Having followed her destiny to France, she chooses to remain distanced from the French society within which she finds herself. However, the conclusion that, as an Arab immigrant, Malika possesses the ability to de-centre French society through her presence is less than convincing. As an un-stable, subjective category, the exotic is dependent on the perspective of the spectator; as Longley says, because it is always an attribute given to someone else, exoticism, like orientalism, is a way of seeing which sustains the myth of the cultural centrality, and therefore the superiority, of the viewer.[23] On closer examination, Malika's exotic power can be seen as having been constructed by Bona to fit con-temporary Western expectations of the Oriental woman, and provide a modern odalisque suitable for consumption by a Western audience. The consequent de-centring of white French culture which takes place in the novel is therefore less the result of any power inherent in Malika than of the traces of Western discourse and prejudice made evident through the reactions of other characters.

Various aspects contribute to the construction of the exotic, beginning with the choice of a female protagonist. Femininity and female sexuality have traditionally featured strongly in literary and artistic representations since, as feminists have noted, Woman occupies a position as "the prime representative of difference".[24] As we have seen, Malika enjoys an idealized Oriental beauty and, with her bare feet and haughty demeanour, her appearance communicates a pride and disdain reminiscent of the portrayals of defiant Algerian women forcibly unveiled by French soldiers during the Algerian War. She inhabits an ambivalent space with regard to the white French characters, finely balanced between the domestic banality of the villa, the social world of its guests and an exotic and undefined meta-physical 'other world', while as a girl barely past adolescence, she occupies the liminal space between child and adult. Since the exotic is a representation of difference translated for the spectator, her inter-stitial position crucially allows her difference to be comprehensible to her French onlookers.

---

[23] Longley, p. 23.
[24] Valérie Orlando, *Nomadic Voices of Exile: Feminine Identity in Francophone Literature of the Maghreb* (Athens: Ohio University Press, 1999), p. 17.

The aloofness that so attracts Malika's lovers is another instance of the ambivalence of the exotic. Despite being the novel's
protagonist, she remains silent throughout the novel, and is accorded
no direct or even reported speech. This could be attributed to her lack
of French, since the narrator tells us that she learns the language with
difficulty some time after her arrival in the country. However, it
reinforces the assumption that, because the exotic cannot speak for
itself, it must be spoken for. Moreover, Bona uses Malika's silence to
emphasize her mystery. According to the clairvoyant, whose first-
person narrative retells her story, the other characters are kept at a
distance from Malika, who deliberately maintains her enigmatic
persona in her relationships with others by restricting their access to
different aspects of her life:

> Personne parmi ceux qui ont croisé sa route—sauf moi peut-être qui tente de
> rassembler nos souvenirs éparpillés—n'a connu Malika dans son unité. On
> croyait la connaître et pourtant elle nous échappait toujours, ne donnant
> chaque fois qu'une part d'elle-même, une pièce plus ou moins originale du
> puzzle de sa vie.[25]

The fragmented nature of this reported story, based on Malika's
recollections of her childhood, recounted years after her arrival in
France and supplemented by the findings of the narrator's own
investigations, introduces layers of unreliability into the narrative and
effectively distances reader from subject.

The distance and mystery created by Malika's self-conscious
reticence plays a major role in leading other characters to perceive her
as exotic and different. Segalen argues that individualism is an
essential component of the exotic: "L'exotisme n'est donc pas cet état
kaléidoscopique du touriste et du médiocre spectateur, mais la réaction
vive et curieuse au choc d'une individualité forte contre une
objectivité dont elle perçoit et déguste la distance".[26] With a swipe at
the tourist collective, Segalen emphasizes the need for individualism
on the part of the observer. Bona's novel, however, suggests that the
difference which sets Malika apart is linked to her individuality,
indicating that this element also has an important role to play in the
construction of the exoticized subject. The rise of individualism in the

---

[25] Bona, p. 214.
[26] Segalen, p. 25.

exotic can arguably be traced to the development of modernity. As Zygmunt Bauman maintains, the erosion of community and family structures that characterized earlier periods has produced an atomized society which emphasizes the discrete unit. Contemporary society is characterized by fluidity, with individuals working to create their own identity in locations which owe more to the demands of the labour market than to their place of birth or family residence so that, as Bauman argues, "to speak of individualization and of modernity is to speak of one and the same social condition".[27] With Westerners now more attuned to individual rather than collective identity and difference, contemporary exoticism has evolved such that the status of the exotic is less attributable to a mass of undifferentiated groups or communities. A representation of the objective differences between North African and French society might emphasize the importance of the extended family or the nomadic tribe. In contrast, Bona is careful to insist on a separation between Malika, and her family and neighbours, who regard her as different and set apart. In doing so, she demonstrates that, although a contributory factor, ethnicity alone is not sufficient to render a subject exotic.

Religion, and more precisely, Malika's personal faith in her destiny, offers another means of exotic differentiation. While the exact form of her belief is strange to the French characters around her, the idea of an individual religion is appealing because the notion that religion, or the metaphysical, is something which belongs to the private sphere is a peculiarly Western view. In contrast, Bona's representation of Islam conforms to the contemporary media construction of it as a religion incommensurate with French secular norms;[28] it is shown in a negative light as a cultural imposition which refuses any division between public and private. Malika's rejection of the dominant North African religion in favour of Berber religious practice—which can be seen as 'the Other of the (Islamic) Other'—can be read as another move towards social disruption, as an attempt to counter the hegemony of Arabization imposed by North African governments and to reclaim the diversity of pre-colonial Maghrébine culture. However, given that Berbers generally follow Islam, the

---

[27] Zygmunt Bauman, *Liquid Modernity* (Cambridge: Polity, 2000), p. 32.
[28] Paul Silverstein, *Algeria in France: Transpolitics, Race, and Nation* (Bloomington: Indiana University Press, 2004), p. 58.

reference to the grandmother's pagan beliefs can be seen as an instance of French imperialist nostalgia for an authentic primitive culture, a phenomenon which has become increasingly important to contemporary constructions of exoticism.[29] It also reinforces the colonial stereotype of the Berber as being ethnically closer to the French, and therefore potentially more assimilable than the Arab, downplaying the threat presented by Malika while maintaining her enticing sense of difference.

Malika's belief thus becomes a site of liminality, distancing her from the putative 'clash of civilizations' and bringing her closer to a style of religion which, although alien to French culture in content, conforms to Western tastes in terms of form.[30] Despite ongoing debates about the place of religion in public life, Western forms of religion remain overwhelmingly confined to the private sphere, with restricted public influence. The character of Malika conforms to this tendency, offering a brand of personal fate which forms part of what bell hooks has criticized as the 'spice' of the Other, whilst not conflicting with the secular norms of modernity.[31] Although often mysterious to the West, with its emphasis on the collective worldwide *umma* Islam is not a religion of individualism, and so resists the tendency towards exoticism.

Analysis of the various aspects of the character of Malika, such as gender, physical appearance, age, individual solitude and personal religion, indicates that she conforms to modern Western expectations of exoticism. This effectively undermines the claim that she appears to 'exceed' the norms and conventions of French society, and appropriates the power which her exoticism makes available. Instead, the power that she apparently wields, for example, to leave without warning, simply shows her to be operating according to the ideals of Bauman's liquid modernity, allowing the flow of power to move unhindered by ties of family or other commitments. In light of this, Malika can be read simply as an exoticized version of the

---

[29] For analysis of 'imperialist nostalgia', see Renato Rosaldo, *Culture and Truth: The Remaking of Social Analysis* (Boston, MA: Beacon, 1989), p. 69-70.

[30] Samuel P. Huntington, *The Clash of Civilizations and the Remaking of World Order* (London: Touchstone, 1998).

[31] bell hooks, "Eating the Other: Desire and Resistance", in *Black Looks: Race and Representation* (Boston, MA: South End, 1992), pp. 21-39.

conventional *Bildungsroman* liberal subject. The disruption that accompanies her is less the result of any inherent power than a consequence of the exoticizing expectations and colonial attitudes of the French characters and, potentially, the implied French reader, which are projected onto her.

Consequences of Disruption

Nonetheless, regardless of its source, Malika's presence effectively disturbs and de-centres the white French society that surrounds her. The overall effect on the group is the impression of a gathering metaphorical storm which grows nearer as the summer progresses, and which transforms into a physical thunderstorm in the dénouement. In *Bonjour tristesse*, the dénouement is triggered by Cécile's manipulations: like a Racinian tragedy, once set in motion her plans for Cyril and Elsa gain a momentum which inevitably leads to a climax. The ambiguity around Anne's fatal car crash, which may have been suicide or accident, problematizes the question of control. Cécile succeeds in her apparent aim of forcing Anne to leave; she repels the intruder who threatens her independence and way of life. The extent to which Anne decides the manner of her leaving is left open, however. The question of whether she truly posed a threat to Cécile's world is left similarly vague; Cécile realizes at the moment of Anne's departure that her fight was not against a pitiless force but against another human being with whose hopes she can empathize. Happily for Cécile, the disturbance to her way of life appears to be temporary. But as postcolonial theorists have shown, the effects of cultural interaction cannot be reversed; once a new cultural element has been introduced it may be incorporated, but a return to the status quo is impossible. While the final climax is succeeded by Cécile's assertion that "[l]a vie recommença comme avant",[32] the closing paragraphs of the narrative, with their famous reference to the 'tristesse' of the title, indicate that the margins of her daily life remain marked by traces of what has taken place. Order is restored, with the proviso that the imagined unity of cultural experience, always illusory, has been exposed once more.

---

[32] Sagan, p. 153.

While Sagan sowed the seeds of her dénouement in the actions of her heroine, Bona's climax builds through the growing sense of unease. However, in parallel to the impression of impending disaster, each of the French characters becomes drawn towards elements outside their everyday life. The practical de-centring of their lives also appears to be indirectly linked to the au pair, but, in contrast, it manifests itself positively in a new sense of creativity. It inspires a complete volte-face from the architect, Benoît Darmon, who abandons the clean lines of glass and steel, which have been his trademark design, to conceive his new collection in a decadent, oriental style that will bring him commercial success and critical renown. His change in direction thoroughly unsettles Benoît's hostess and design client, Marie-Hélène, for whom it represents an artistic betrayal. None-theless, Marie-Hélène also finds herself drawn to explore her own artistic leanings, and embarks on painting and sculpture, which en-ables her to develop her individual creativity outside the roles of design manager, wife, hostess and mother which have defined her previously. Malika thus brings associations that are both threatening and empowering: at the conclusion of the novel, each of the French characters is energized to enter a new and constructive phase of their lives.

The positive consequences of Malika's stay raise the question of whether the sense of threat occasioned by her disruptive presence is justified, a point underlined by the way in which events are brought to a head. The catalyst for the dénouement is in fact unrelated to Malika: it is borrowed straight from Sagan, in the form of a car crash which kills one of the minor characters, a woman called Élizabeth who barely features in the narrative. Her death forces each character to re-assess their situation. It also coincides with Malika's unannounced departure from the villa. Unlike Anne, she is fully in control of the moment and manner of her leaving, an event which, because it passes unnoticed, has little bearing on the other characters. Instead, the narrative concludes in the manner of Sagan's, projecting forward into the future of each French character. The summer is revealed to have been a turning point, in which each has learnt "une certaine forme de vérité" which moves them on to the next stage of their lives.[33] Unlike

---

[33] Bona, p. 336.

the conclusion of Sagan's narrative, there is no suggestion of a lingering sadness: despite the threatening atmosphere, the summer has been overwhelmingly an empowering experience.

The positive conclusion of Bona's novel, in contrast to the ambivalence of Cécile's narrative, calls for a reassessment of the disruption which Malika's presence occasions. As an Arab immigrant, she is expected to remain in the background, but instead her beauty and sexuality makes her the focus of the holiday group. Her ethnicity brings with it unresolved memories of French colonialism and the persistent residue of Orientalist thought. While the French characters experience her presence as a threat and disruption to their social structure, analysis indicates that the power attributed to the girl by these attitudes is less an inherent quality that she possesses than the result of colonial stereotypes, which, when projected onto her, influence the behaviour of those around her. Ultimately, the threat associated with the ambivalence of the exotic and linked to the 're-invasion of the centre' is revealed to be empty. The de-centring which takes place is therefore revelatory more of contemporary French social mores than of any perceived power latent in a young immigrant girl.

Taken together, Sagan and Bona's novels demonstrate that the challenge to hegemonic culture which is periodically posed by extra-national movements often creates only a temporary disruption before being recuperated into the dominant narrative, leaving only traces. In this process, however, such moments of cultural disruption serve to expose the plural nature of the apparently dominant and turn the critical gaze upon French culture, calling for a reassessment of French values, norms and attitudes towards otherness. By drawing on *Bonjour tristesse* as intertext, Bona constructs a powerful representation of bourgeois society and, thus, represents the de-centring effects of immigration whilst refusing to bow to contemporary anxieties about the consequences for French culture. In doing so, she illustrates the ability of the novelist to engage, albeit in a literary rather than a theoretical mode, with the issues of postcoloniality present in the Hexagon, which—to date—have been neglected by French scholars working in other fields.

Erasmus, Exchange Value and Euronormativity in Cédric Klapisch's *L'Auberge espagnole* and *Les Poupées russes*

Enda McCaffrey and Murray Pratt

The aim of this chapter is to examine the diverse attempts at allegorical flight from French national identity to a transnational but ultimately problematic otherness in Cédric Klapisch's *L'Auberge espagnole* (2002) and *Les Poupées russes* (2005). [1] Whilst manifestly extolling the virtues of European integration and the socio-cultural values associated with the university Erasmus exchange programme, both films simultaneously reinforce conventional representations of French national identity in the form of republican universalism, symbolic masculine heteronormativity and French exceptionalism. As a consequence of this dichotomy, the much-lauded Erasmus vision is perceived to be weakened, exposed in its complicity with prescribed constructions of nationhood and often circumscribed by expressions of Euronormativity. We propose to situate this thesis within a structure that is defined by a number of major oppositions: universalism versus pluralism, tradition versus progress, republican versus democratic, the 'French' versus the 'European' (global), 'high' versus 'low' culture,

---

[1] Cédric Klapisch, *L'Auberge espagnole* (Bac Films, 2002); *Les Poupées russes* (Lunar Films, 2005).

'*dirigiste*' versus neo-liberalist, 'grandeur' versus decline, inclusion versus exclusion. These oppositions will underpin our analysis of the dichotomy at the centre of the two films, particularly with respect to representations of national identity and sexuality, and alternative representations formed respectively in the 'European' hub that is Barcelona and in the geographical 'margins' of Europe, exemplified by London and Saint Petersburg.

Since the 1980s, France, which prided itself on its ability to regulate its own affairs, has had to recognise the new reality of increasing economic globalisation and European integration, and has been faced with the political, social and cultural consequences of this process ever since. In part, this has meant a continuation of the question of American cultural imperialism which has characterised the entire post-war period, as well as the more recent implications of the Maastricht Treaty for French exceptionalism. It is against this backdrop of socio-economic and cultural change that *L'Auberge espagnole* and *Les Poupées russes* locate a France struggling to come to terms with its role in a rapidly changing European union with new attitudes to citizenship, globalisation, sexual difference and alterity. To this degree, both films are a timely reflection on France in the post-PaCS and post-parity eras, casting a wide net over issues of single-hood, coupledom, sexuality, memory, language, identity and cultural exchange. French identity in *L'Auberge espagnole* is seemingly 'liberated' from its myopic exceptionalism only to embrace a sham and bounded Europeanness which turns out to be an ulterior manifestation of doctored nationhood itself; the very idea of cultural exchange is valourised on one level only to be undermined on another. This dichotomy is shored up in *Les Poupées russes* with Klapisch 'locating' otherness in the 'island' of England (or London to be exact) where Xavier (played by Romain Duris), the principal character in both films, and the personification and allegorical representation of 'perfect' French republicanism, is free to flirt with an eccentric and quirky version of otherness only to end up conforming to a bare-chested, beer-swilling English stereotype. In other words, abstract French republicanism in Xavier is afforded the opportunity to inter-face with a new and different Anglo-Saxon version of multi-culturalism (the idea of "getting real" according to Wendy [Kelly Reilly]). But the reality it embraces not only mirrors its French counterpart in aspects of national and sexual behaviour but actually becomes infected with more sinister forms of aggression, machismo and threatening normativity.

Erasmus and Exchange Value: *L'Auberge espagnole*

L'Auberge espagnole, Cédric Klapisch's multilingual paean to the year abroad, is a movie that takes Xavier, a common or garden French business student, uproots him from all that he refuses to hold dear (the still grim campus of Nanterre, the girlfriend whom he models on the central character of a quite unreconstructed children's book entitled *Martine à la ferme*, his hippy mother, and all "leur merde"), and plonks him in trendy, downtown Barcelona, ostensibly for a year of "Erasmus". Exchange study, or what the denizens of EU-land have come to term Erasmus in a homage to the original wandering scholar, is promoted across European universities as a central plank of student internationalisation. In addition to promoting language acquisition, a key objective of the well-funded and promoted project for the European Union is its role in the construction of a Europe of 'common cultural values', mutual understanding and intercommunication. While the notion of a common European language remains too thorny to tackle headlong, recent European Union initiatives make it clear that the proto-nation-building moment requires a quest for common ground, an attachment to broadly European values, in order to construct a committed and Euro-identified citizenship. Through the circulation and exchange of young minds, and perhaps more importantly, if Klapisch's film is to be taken literally, bodies, Erasmus creates links across the continent, that produce, even reproduce, a new Europopulace with potentially stronger allegiances to the neo-federal entity than to their national locales.

Socialising then, together with an engagement with the local and an openness to change and difference might be considered as central to the success of an exchange year, and the sense of camaraderie and mutual support and cooperation which Klapisch's household show would, on the surface at least, seem to reinforce this notion. Not only does Xavier explore Barcelona and become adopted by his local bar, he also participates in the multinational community of the household. *L'Auberge espagnole*, like Klapisch's earlier Paris-based film *Chacun cherche son chat* (1996), delights in assembling heteroclite characters who find common ground in Ealingesque quests, in this case firstly to fend off the threat of eviction from their rambling abode, and then, in the climax of the Erasmus year, the extraordinary lengths to which they go to save Wendy's relationship. Giving the impression of a precision-planned operation, Klapisch uses split screens and dramatic cuts to her boyfriend's journey from the airport to convey the synchronicity and commitment of the house-mates' actions in covering up for her affair. This episode ironises the high dramatic tension as Wendy's relationship with the serious (and seriously same-nationality) Alistair (Iddo Goldberg) must be saved at all costs: all conspire to prevent him discovering her in bed with the American guitarist with whom she is having "just fucking sex". The commando sequence descends into farce—a homage to Shakespeare and his major technical innovation, the bed trick—as Wendy's brother hops into bed with the American at the last moment. Wendy's face is saved, in large part thanks to the multinational task force that diverted Alistair, although at the expense of her brother's reputation.

On one level, a level perhaps close to the centre of Rubin's charmed circle of sexuality,[2] this chapter establishes a dichotomy in the film between, on the one hand, the marital, the national, the stable and the familiar, and on the other, the temporary, the transcultural, the fleeting and the unknown or unknowable. The role of the Eurochums, despite, or perhaps because of, their adherence to the second of these camps, is to shore up the fixed heterocentre of the established homo-national relationship. In the process, the sexuality of Wendy's brother, William (Kevin Bishop), a character already positioned as 'trouble-fête' and jester, is compromised, sacrificed, as he is humourously outed as at the very least 'bi-curious' to Alistair. William's late arrival in the household has marked him as an outsider to the Eurogroup, and his tendency towards xenophobia disrupts the harmony of their community. Not only does his OTT screen persona include such traditional Englishman-in-Spain behaviour as vomiting, urinating at random and mooning, he also caricatures and belittles the housemates and their nationalities through recourse to reductionist stock jokes. Notably, he alienates the only Spanish girl in the household, by stereotyping Spaniards based on one encounter, and annoys the

---

[2] Gayle S. Rubin, "Thinking Sex: Notes for a Radical Theory of Sexuality", in Carole S. Vance (ed), *Pleasure and Danger: Exploring Female Sexuality* (Hammersmith and New York: Harper Collins, 1989), pp. 267-319.

German representative by a predictable descent into comedy Nazism. It is clear that the film would like to set William up, in a series of scenes with different characters, as distinctly un-Erasmic in his approach to Eurobonding and use William's tendency to racism as a kind of inoculation, against which the Erasmus team might emerge as some pan-national, Eurotolerant new order. And, to some extent, their extensive bonding and familial proximity suggest affinities which transcend national borders and set up a model for European harmony. Yet, as with all good comedies, the malcontent is eventually accommodated within the *polis*, and William, for all his faults, and largely through his uncanny ability to impersonate houseflies, becomes a valued member of the community.

However, an alternative reading of the film, nodding irreverently towards Baudrillard's theorization of "use value" as an alibi for "exchange value",[3] suggests that its system for signifying and valorising shared Europeanness functions as a sham and terroristic organization of the film's motivations and ambivalences. For, as Baudrillard reveals, "[w]hatever it denies and represses, it will attempt to exorcise and integrate into its own operation [....] [T]he sign attempts to mislead: it permits itself to appear as totality, to efface the traces of its abstract transcendence, and parades itself as the reality principle of meaning".[4] To the extent that Euroacculturation and linguistic competence can be considered as the use values of the Erasmus scheme, their abstract and arbitrary utility, Baudrillard might posit that they "do not constitute a qualitative, incommensurable, concrete reality exterior to political economy, but rather a system that is itself induced by the [exchange value] system and which functions according to the same logic".[5]

The 'exchange value' of student exchange then, calculated for Xavier as its commodity price in the labour market, determines the forms taken by Erasmus as use-full experience, effectively undermining and replicating the ostensible motivation for studying abroad

---

[3] Jean Baudrillard, "For a Critique of the Political Economy of the Sign", in Mark Poster (ed), tr. by Jacques Mourrain and others, *Jean Baudrillard: Selected Writings* (Palo Alto: Stanford University Press, 1988), pp. 57-97, originally published as Jean Baudrillard, *Pour une Critique de l'économie politique du signe* (Paris: Gallimard, 1972).
[4] Baudrillard, p. 92.
[5] Baudrillard, p. 86.

at another level. As suggested by the priorities set for Wendy's best interests in the boyfriend stakes, or ostensibly gainsaid by the integration of William, the system's other, within its diegetic universe, the systemic signification is the same: the film's narrative might be better thought of as promoting, not the abstract value of pan-European cultural difference *per se*, but rather the exchange value of this commodity within monadic, nationally and, in what emerges (in a further conjuring act) as the dominant narrative strand, hetero-normatively circumscribed contexts. According to this interpretation, exchange is best thought of (and musically and cinematically suggested) as fugue, idyll, "just fucking Erasmus": ultimately it becomes Europlay itself, quite detached from any local anchorage and with little bearing other than on the national outcomes according to which it is truly valued. The place of Otherness in the film is heavily controlled, sidelining first the non-European and the overly-local in the Catalonian-debate scene where a random Gambian (who plays no further part in the proceedings until the farewell party) takes on the task of defending the specificity of the local language. Moreover, if university experience is erased from the film, so too is the very rationale for mobility, another city, another country—effectively Barcelona and Spain, which find themselves squeezed into neatly-packaged 'travel show'-shaped chunks, as Xavier's visits to the city highlights. Indeed, the *lingua franca* of the household is almost predominantly English ("because we want life to be cool together") and it is far from evident, within the diegesis of the film, exactly how, or when, Xavier acquires his near perfect "espagnol" by the end of his stay.

Euronormativity: An Alternative Nationhood

Euronormativity, rather than an earth-shattering exposure to difference and otherness, is of value to the extent that it informs national priorities, and *L'Auberge espagnole*, rather than a melting-pot, offers up to its domestic audience a concealed narrative more concerned with French national priorities, especially heteronormative masculinity, than with Euroexposure. The race to save Wendy's real relationship conforms to a momentum within the film towards sameness and knowability, reducing otherness to the transience and thrill of a bungee jump. Hetero-experimentation with the other opens a franchise for the Wendy's of this world to taste a quasi-Hocquenghemian, or perhaps post-Houllebecquian, liberty before settling down to a life of same-same in terms of national coupling. Crucially, this momentum is fuelled by a hypervalidation of national and heteronorms in the key areas of language and nationhood, memory and nationhood, and most notably in the narrative crisis experienced by Xavier, particularly in his encounters with women.

Underpinning this movement towards Euronormativity is the continual struggle between nationhood, as expressed in French republicanism, and resistance to traditional forms of it, as expressed in certain characters' differing levels of engagement with what we have thus far characterised as Erasmus "exchange values". On the whole, Xavier adopts a positive attitude to his new life in Barcelona, but Klapisch also deploys several visual aides to demonstrate that the transition is not all plain sailing. Throughout the film, memories of France (visual, vocal and imaginary) and expressions of a 'hard to shake off' French national identity permeate Xavier's immersion in European culture. Right from the outset, the ghost of France haunts his every step; no sooner has he landed at the airport in Spain but he is befriended by two French ex-pats with whom he goes on to establish a close bond. His first night in Barcelona is spent with a French friend of his mother's, reinforcing the never-ending ultramontaine con-nection. Phone calls from his 'formal' girlfriend Martine (Audrey Tautou) and his mum (Martine Demaret), including a visit from the former (and a subsequent whistle-stop 24-hour return visit to Paris to see his mother), all serve to remind him of his French roots, and in the words of one of the many aptly chosen songs in the film "In this great future, you can't forget your past".[6] It would not be folly to suggest that Xavier would happily forgo these romantic and filial obligations to nationhood and the past, but part of the complexity of allegiance to nationhood here is that he is unable to do so, at least not at this point in his journey, and it is not until he is back permanently in France at the end and reinserted as a 'fonctionnaire' that he has the courage and realisation to abandon France altogether. Klapisch touches on an important point here about the transformative power of displacement in the context of nationhood, namely that Xavier's confrontation with

---

[6] Vincent Ford (with Bob Marley), "No Woman No Cry" (Kwark Publishing, Ryko-musik Ltd.).

otherness is not a sham or a cosmetic exercise in Euro relations but an experience that leaves him fundamentally changed, so much so that he takes decisive action to change career, albeit at the end. Equally significantly, Klapisch draws a key distinction between Xavier's understandable puerile obligations to nationhood/past, and the more sinister expressions of nationhood from 'wiser' citizens who have upped sticks and relocated to Spain but who continue to export unsavoury versions of Frenchness.

Anne-Sophie (Judith Godrèche) and her husband Jean-Michel (Xavier De Guillebon) are the embodiment of a Euronormativity that expounds the negative side of French national self-interest abroad. On the surface, they are the perfect transnational couple; affluent, professional, educated and keen to experience other cultures. There is also an endearingly human side to the way they help Xavier acclimatise to life in Barcelona by offering him a sofa to sleep on and a 'partner' in Sophie with whom to visit the city. At closer inspection however, we see that behind the Eurogloss there is a genetic exceptionalism/isolationalism that manifests itself in their gastronomic idiosyncracies, Gallic chauvinism, racism, Jean-Michel's rabid misogyny and heterosexual self-assurance. Geographically, they are in Barcelona: mentally they inhabit France. As a couple, they are symbolic of a conservative universalist republicanism that has resisted and continues to resist social and cultural change in France, and by exporting this version of republicanism to a progressive and traditionally Eurofriendly Spain, Klapisch sets up a framework in which Xavier's respective allegiances to nationhood and Erasmus exchange value are thrown into sharp relief. At the centre of this framework is the role of the French couple, and specifically Jean-Michel in his capacity as a neurologist. Early in their encounter, Jean-Michel explains to Xavier the nature of his neurological work with the aid of a dissected model brain. After a trauma to the brain, inflicted either by injury or by emotional/cultural collision where the right lobe is damaged, Jean-Michel claims that "verbal memory is impaired". As a consequence, "an unconscious trauma can allow a person to retain his first language (i.e. mother tongue) whereas a second language is erased" [our parentheses]. The implications of this instruction are not readily apparent to Xavier, but in the wider context of his cultural displacement, his labouring Spanish and the short-term comfort he derives from the example of French heteronormative coupledom before him, it is clear that Klapisch means to highlight Xavier's dilemma as a potential ambassador for an exclusive French republicanism on the one hand and as a Europhile on the other.

However, it is equally clear that Klapisch is also suspicious of the way in which Jean-Michel invokes a neurological/scientific discourse to rationalise, reinforce and inscribe the primordiality of the French language within an exclusively republican and universalist construction of French national identity (not that Jean-Michel and Anne Sophie are the personification of a 'race pure' themselves, given that over the dinner table they make much of having met in a *pizzeria* speaking Italian, a further testament to how in fact their Frenchness is itself mediated positively by outside influences). The idea, however, of a first language versus a second acquired language (where the mother tongue is the voice of prejudicial exclusivity and the second language is the Spanish of tolerance in the *auberge*) is brought home to bear in two telling ways. When paged late one evening, Jean-Michel is requested by the hospital to attend to an emergency. He replies affirmatively in very polite Spanish, only to let his own truly xenophobic feelings be known in French when he hangs up the phone; his real prejudicial temperament surfaces in his maternal tongue, giving a lie to all his pretensions to European assimilation. Similarly, all the housemates agree to try to speak Spanish together but in moments of crisis (when William for example disrupts the harmony of the *auberge* by sending up Germany with references to goose stepping and Hitler), individuals, notably Wendy, revert instinctively to their native tongue in deference to a waning allegiance to bullish Britishness and a vain sense of duty to sibling/family love, both of which could be construed as the fading emblems of nationhood which the authenticity of exchange value continually undermines. Klapisch is particularly sensitive to these linguistic fluctuations as differentiating expressions of nationhood alliance within the Eurozone; the mother tongue becomes synonymous with fear, exclusion and resistance to the language of negotiation, community and camaraderie associated with second language acquisition.

The same rationale that we have applied to language is used by the neurosurgeon Jean-Michel in defence of memory. As with the mother tongue, memory is described as an expression of permanence in the same way that France is a constant in the minds of Xavier, Anne-Sophie and Jean-Michel. Even as a 'surrogate' family soaking

up the sunshine on a day trip to the gay resort of Sitges, they point in
the direction of France from the beach asking poignantly "Where is
France?" In the same instinctive way, France is Xavier's essentialist
benchmark for heteronormativity, bureaucracy, regulation and architectural conservatism, in spite of his continual exposure to lesbianism,
sexual difference and the symbolic implications of buzzing flies and
chaotic fridge-interiors, in a subversive re-casting of the nature/culture
binary. Even the surrealism of Gaudi and the architectural
postmodernity of the *Sagrada Familia* fail to compete with the tow of
nostalgia towards France. And in the twin contexts of neurology and
nationhood, cultural curiosity for the present and wider social change
form part of what Jean-Michel characterises as "amnesia"; in other
words, Erasmus exchange, second language acquisition, con-
structionism, urban mix, pluralism and contingency (the new lexicon
of the Eurozone if you will) all seem eminently forgettable when
measured against the gravitas of memory anchored in France. Of
course, it could be argued that these reflexes to memory and the past
are expressions of a republican sense of nationhood and that Klapisch
distances himself sufficiently from them by exposing his characters,
notably Xavier, to the positive aspects of transnationality, difference
and alterity. But for all the film's Europhile and otherly aspirations,
the irony is that these aspirations are themselves restricted by the same
republican imprimatur. The climactic episode towards the end of film
when all the housemates converge from different parts of Barcelona to
save Wendy's relationship with Alistair demonstrates on a simplistic
level the importance of friendship in a moment of crisis. But when
friendship is deployed to shore up hypocritical heternormativity, and
when the preservation of heteronormativity is at the expense of
homosexuality (to the extent that William forfeits his heterosexuality
and pretends to be gay in order to protect his sister's heterosexual
promiscuity), we get a sense of how this episode, for a French viewing
public, and in all its technicality and conspiratorial intrigue, testifies to
the insipid collusion between Euronomativity and heteronormativity.

     While Wendy experiments, albeit safely, with her American in
Barcelona, and Isabelle (Cécile de France), the Belgian lesbian, gets
all fired up by her Flamenco teacher, Xavier's taste of the other is
remarkably tame, an unthreatening relationship with Anne-Sophie, the
very French, "vousvoying" (overly polite), "vieux jeu" (old-fashioned), and entirely "coincée" (uptight) wife of Jean-Michel. Rather than

embracing the difference of a Spanish *señorita*, far less wanting to kiss a *matador*, the extent of his experimentation with difference is to try it on a bit with an entirely charmless French girl. Admittedly, she is married, and perhaps the thrill of adultery is as close as Xavier (or the French heteroman) should get to non-normative sex. In two scenes framing the arrival of Wendy's English boyfriend, Xavier's fling reaches crisis point as his relationship is discovered by Jean-Michel, Anne-Sophie's husband. First, Xavier's hallucinated encounters with the historical character of Erasmus (Jacques Royer) oblige him to seek out Jean-Michel in his professional capacity. While being brain-scanned, Xavier dream-sequences an eroticised Anne-Sophie as part of that "bordel" in his head he has to clean up, mashed up with images of him losing his mother tongue. Post Wendy's relief, the film returns Xavier to reality where he learns that while the scanner isn't so technically advanced as to allow Jean-Michel to read his thoughts, Anne-Sophie had indeed confided all to her husband the previous night and he is forbidden to see her again. Having already been ditch-ed by his Parisian farm-girl Martine, Xavier is effectively brought to a point where he is excluded from the film's heteronomy (heterosexual economy) and left only with the consolation that Isabelle, the Belgian lesbian on the verge of as seriously French stardom as that enjoyed by Duris and Tautou themselves, regrets that he hadn't been born a girl.

For Isabelle's role in the film, while pivotal to Xavier's crisis, is actually entirely dependent on her ability to serve, service, fine-tune, his potential as a heteromale. Earlier in the film, his success in en-rapturing Anne-Sophie is achieved thanks to a metonymic chain of learning linking him back to Isabelle's flamenco teacher (Paulina Gálvez), as the Belgian steamily recreates her own seduction, in the process reversing the traditional male-female positions of Latin lore, although also maintaining, and on one level, re-establishing a correct gender balance in that the participants are suitably gendered male and female. This scene serves as Isabelle's 'raison d'être' in the movie. Largely absent from the rest of the proceedings, she is reduced to a plot device central in exoticising and eroticising Xavier, as he comes not to encounter but to incarnate the other, effectively playing the part of the Spanish and the lesbian and presenting as the forbidden fruit of the other to Anne-Sophie. In a further sleight-of-hand, rather than the subject of the film, Xavier ultimately functions as its exotic/erotic object, marked beyond use or redemption by the values of exchange which he comes, however unrealistically, to embody for a French audience. Far from clearing up his head-"bordel", Xavier's privileged sense of national, gendered, heterosexuality is ambivalently both confirmed and disrupted by his experiences in Barcelona.[7]

If *L'Auberge espagnole* constructs a norming momentum towards national and sexual conformity, the story-value that brings the conventional to life derives from its ability to pressgang othernesses into their service, distilling difference to a homeopathic essence which must be measured just so. Exposure to Europe is the spice that

---

[7] As confirmed by Klapisch's earlier film, *Chacun cherche son chat*, for all Xavier's interEuro transsexualisation, these are tales for good national heterocitizens, who, after the film is over, and after their own fugues—be they holidays, exchange years, or flings with danger—will happily go on in real life to file some things in red folders, others in blue folders, and yet others in yellow folders, and whose cats will come home to roost. In a nutshell, the earlier film sees Chloé (Garance Clavel) go on holiday, confiding her cat to a wonderful old Parisian lady (played by a reality-cast neighbour of Klapisch with the wonderfully apposite name of Renée Le Calm), who does that kind of thing (cat-guarding). Chloé comes home to discover that the cat is lost, and with the help of a random and diverse team-spirited search-team drawn from across the previously divided community, goes on to turn the neighbourhood upside down as they scour the *quartier*-in-transformation for the unfortunate cat, Gris-gris (Arapimou). Chloé's real life is left in suspense (she neglects herself at work) and in the process of exploring the streets and the apartments of the neighbourhood from all sorts of unusual angles, a new and stronger set of values and social harmony emerge. Chloé's most important journey however is not the one-second clip of her splashing in the Med that represents her holiday, but the process of self-discovery she undergoes in searching, not only for the cat, but also in scanning the grey-grey of relationality for her Platonic other hetero half. In the process, she fixates on a dreadlocked stranger, played by Romain Duris, later to play none other than Xavier himself, in an "Oh, he's gorgeous" moment near the start of the film. When she eventually gets up close and personal however, his exoticism turns out to be skin deep and scrapes easily off leaving him with a self-obsessed, and therefore in filmworld terms obviously undesirable, personality. Other red herrings include Djamel (Zinedine Soualem), the North African village idiot (too homely), a medley of menacing seducers encountered in a nightmare night out, including a woman Chloé thinks she can trust but who turns out to be a lesbian and after her too, and her gay flat mate, with whom she cuddles up a bit too much in her post-traumatic desolation. As the cat comes out from behind the cooker where it was stuck the whole time, Chloé comes to see the background very standard French figure of Bel Canto (Joël Brisse) for the man he really is, and a whole new perspective opens out. For Djamel (and, one would suspect, the gay flat mate and random lesbian, "la vie est mal faite") but for the community, or perhaps better put the extended family of the now revalued *quartier* in song, "Ça c'est Paris". It's not so much that the cat is away—it just gets misplaced for long enough for us cinema-going community-minded heteromice to get a perspective, if not necessarily a life.

confirms national identity and allegiances. Flirting with the foreign is a fling that brings you back to the happy (or, as Anne-Sophie's experiences prove, not so happy) couple. The film's failed endings, Xavier's unfulfilling reunion with Martine and his rejection of the world of work in order to word-process a book title (for he never gets further than the title as far as we can see), indicate the danger, although perhaps also the heady requirement if art is to happen, of overdosing on the other and ending up outside the heteroloop. On many levels, and to a heteronormed viewership, Klapisch's film, and Xavier's travel diary, represent heady, heartening and wholly thrillsome escapes from conformity. Framed for a Eurocurious yet nationally preoccupied French audience, the youthful flings and flights of fancy, the "bordel" in the head that goes with you regardless, tracks that take off somewhere more Moorish and Almodovaresque *montages*; all contrast with the rigidity and monotony of the office and the system, the irrelevance of the paternal, the eventual grown-up fixity of the heterocouple to come, that other "bordel" that never goes away. While Xavier, ending the film on the runway of life as an author, might think he has become "Tout l'Europe, un vrai bordel" ("All Europe, a real mess"), the reality of the film's value is considerably less grandiose, and more domestically palatable. He has, after all, spied his own mysterious female stranger at his leaving party, who will visit him in Paris after the titles roll. This is the value and the way of Erasmus, EU style: not a new departure but a recuperable year somewhere else that teaches you, if nothing else, that there may be more airlines than *Air France*, but that it is never wise to stray too far from the national and heteronormative, except in a cinema, and this is a film that lingers with a beatific smile as you pass the next generation of Euroexplorers in Montmartre and ask, as inanely as Xavier does, "Erasmus?"

Les Poupées russes

Les Poupées russes, released in 2005, reprises Klapisch's more popular *L'Auberge espagnole*.[8] Whereas the pretext for the 2002

---

[8] According to a search conducted on http://lumiere.obs.coe.int/web/search/index.php on 10 April 2009, *L'Auberge espagnole* has enjoyed over 4.6 million European admissions compared to just over 3.6 for *Les Poupées russes*.

experiences was an Erasmus exchange in Barcelona, the later film moves between Paris, London and Saint Petersburg, as Xavier's temporary jobs as a ghost autobiographer and scriptwriter subject him to "les aléas de la mondialisation". We have argued above that *L'Auberge espagnole* can be understood as a cathartic exercise in incarnating the eroto-exotic, a filmic fugue whereby Xavier skirts that bit too close to losing his Francosexual roots and being hopelessly othered, drifting free from a nationally determined hetero-economy and risking his rightful place beside Parisian farm-girl Martine, appropriately cast in both films as Audrey Tautou. However, the all-European household and extra-hexagonal year of 2002, while framed as exchange, revalue his national and sexual identities in ways that can neither be directly cashed in to French social currency on his return, or fully converted by Xavier into a Eurolifestyle free from constant translations back to the Franc. This section suggests an extension and update of this analysis to take account of the 2005 sequel's portrayal of Xavier's further heteroadventures in an expanded Euroland, with a particular focus on the Anglo-French axis connecting him to what the film holds out as the redemptive hope of his eventual maturation into one half of a responsible new *trans-Manche* couple. We argue that Klapisch's evocations of England and Russia in *Les Poupées russes* have the potential (like Barcelona) to offer up opportunities for individual self-transformation but more often than not reduce both countries and cultures to clichéd capital city dioramas. Rather than a transnational cinema that displaces, rejuxtaposes nationalised experiences and beliefs such as found, for example, in other films from the same decade like *Babel*,[9] Klapisch's European diptych reconfirms national belonging, exoticises to varying degrees, and ultimately 'orientalises' France's closest others in an extensive movement of cultural appropriation. It is the same dichotomy that frames *L'Auberge espagnole,* but transposed to new Euromargins. Paradoxically, as we shall see, it is Wendy (Reilly again), the embodiment of Englishness and otherness, who ends up pointing the way to a possible 'othering' of the problematic Frenchness that has shadowed Xavier throughout both films.

---

[9] Alejandro González Iñárritu, *Babel* (Paramount Pictures, 2006).

The film is marketed, and to a large extent markets itself, as a Casanovaesque quest by Xavier to find the 'perfect' woman. The phrase repeats across the dialogue, and is actualised around his discovery of a street in Saint Petersburg said to embody perfect dimensions, a street Xavier later returns to in his imagination as the perfect set for his perfect woman. The front cover of the original French DVD distributed by Christal Films borrows from Klapisch's screen collage technique, itself owing much to David Hockney's photographic experiments of the 1980s, to portray Duris surrounded by the film's "sept femmes", as if to suggest the limitless choices and availabilities on offer to Xavier. Effectively however, when the frills are set aside, we are left with a more classic love story, a typical choice between his long term friend, Wendy, originally considered as more of a sister than a potential partner, and the glamour, perfection but ultimate unattainability represented by Celia Shelburn (Lucy Gordon), globetrotting supermodel with the capacity to change every-thing in one night, make dreams come true, and transmogrify a *mobilette* into a handsome steed ... but equally to ditch Xavier in a Moscow nightclub for a limo-load of cosmo-acquaintances and the promise of a better party. By deserting Wendy for Celia at the romantic crux of the film, Xavier is fully aware that he is making the wrong choice but "lets the train move on" anyway, and faces the threat of the credits rolling with him seven down, none to go.

The bare bones plot of *Les Poupées russes*, then, collapses, in some ways, into the hackneyed TV-movie script that Wendy and Xavier are co-writing, with its soapy dialogue and over-dramatisation of infidelity echoed in their shared leitmotif "I love you, and I have always loved you", and the key decision to visit Celia in Moscow. However, Klapisch's Eurocinema is first and foremost a busy and noisy continent, perhaps a messy one, and is characterized, as much in its structuration as in its diegesis by a concern to keep its options open. Outcomes are held out as constantly available, rather than signed and sealed, and this is integral to understanding both Xavier's familiar "Oui, Non, Oui" approach to answering a question about whether he has a girlfriend with "Je n'en ai pas, j'en ai plein", and to the false starts, proliferating screens, and refusal to settle in one set that provide *Les Poupeés russes* with a feel of having it both ways. Sliding across the surface of the conventional love story then is a multiple assemblage of more or less successful intimate moments for

Xavier, a fantasized and infinitely substitutional chain of conquests that both sexes up the cinematography and at the same time feeds back into the plot, revealing him as incapable of growing up, bewildered by the modern day version of the fairy tale where princes and princesses, in stark contrast with the unexpected persistence shown by William (again Bishop) in learning Russian to pursue, woo and win his balletic love at first sight.

Returning to its generative matrix, the Eurostar toilet where Xavier is now trying to type, as the film does at pivotal points in a bid to voice written order over its visual chaos, a key conceit emerges that echoes the defining phrase of *L'Auberge espagnole*: "Toute l'Europe, un vrai bordel". In the sequel, Xavier still writes, but now he has a mission, to "ranger le vrac de la vie" or put more crudely, contextualized by the location of writing, and announced by the film's first spoken word "merde", to sort out his shit. And while dresses in *Les Poupées russes* really only come in pink, Xavier's shit comes in several colours. Work is shit because it's boring; and Klapisch's scene-switching techniques gloss over or collapse the discussions and decisions that nonetheless structure Xavier's trajectories as corporate gobbledygook. Family is potentially shit because it gets in the way of a good time, as detailed in the impatience with which Xavier deals with his mother's phone calls. Interestingly however, this contrasts markedly with the time he makes for indulging his elderly grandfather, crossing roads slowly with him and disguising Isabelle as a heterosexual for his predilection. Perhaps ultimately, and here we enter the shallows of Xavier's troubled psyche, most of the shit in Europe is caused by women. His mother's phone call screen-splits off to his left, Martine's simultaneous call and to his right, and a harridan of a landlady appears at the door; this early sequence encapsulates the traps of domesticity that being a man in a heterocouple entail, and that the 'almost 30' Xavier, just like his '20-something' counterpart, is desperate to flee at all costs. Domesticity is of course home, and for Duris, Klapisch, Tatou, and the intended viewers, that is also France. And thus the promise of playing away, be it the charms of seducing a woman outside the couple or travel overseas, comes into effect.

However, as Pratt proposed with Mireille Rosello in their introductory essays to a special issue of *Culture, Theory, Critique* on creolizing Europe,[10] otherness in the New Federation is often bounded and circumscribed, a version of alterity packaged as digestible, a reconfirmation of ideological rectitude rather than, as Fanon intends with his coinage of "creolization", a confrontation that leaves those that meet fundamentally changed. Thus the unexplained exits screen left of Martine and Kassia (Aïssa Maïga) within the first half of the film. In the former case, it is a combination of the over-domestic with her surprising conversion to altermondialism, and its implicit critique of Xavier's cosmochoices that positions Martine as simulatenously too close to home, and too far removed from his perfect sphere, and he leaves her as a speck on the corner of the Parisian balcony of his story. Kassia, played by Malian actor Aïssa Maïga, provides Klapisch (and Xavier) with the proof that Paris is a fully integrated, multi-ethnic space, where it can simply happen that, to quote Maïga in relation to a later 2007 role she takes alongside Duris, "Lui est blanc, elle est noire, mais ce n'est pas traité du tout sur le mode 'problèmes des couples mixtes'. Ce sont juste deux êtres qui s'aiment et qui ont beaucoup de difficultés".[11] Yeah. Right. This of course explains Klapisch's would-be comic inversion of gender positions and heights in their scenes together and the fact that it is Kassia, completely through a narrative quirk of course, who is at the receiving end of Xavier's most appallingly misogynistic diatribe against all women, for which he rightfully receives a punch in the face from an outraged lesbian.

"Que serait le monde sans les filles?"

While women may be the source of all Xavier's problems, there is also an argument that they (and in particular Wendy) point to his salvation. As the slogan on Kassia's tee-shirt vividly ("Que serait le monde sans les filles?") suggests, Xavier's world is one where he is not only preoccupied with the search for the right woman, but women (including, ironically, lesbians) are the only sex capable of validating

---

[10] Murray Pratt, "On Being Optimistically European" and Mireille Rosello "We … Europe", *Culture, Theory and Critique*, Special Issue: "Creolisation: Towards a non-Eurocentric Europe", eds. Murray Pratt and Mireille Rosello, 48.1 (2007), 11-24 and 1-9, respectively.

[11] Aïssa Maïga, "Mes désirs sont impérieux", Interview by Valérie Robert, *Version Femina*, (magazine of *Sud Ouest Dimanche*), 284.9 September 2007, p. 36.

his heterosexual existence. His encounters with women are the exclusive projections of his heteromale ego and without them his life is meaningless. As overstated as this may seem, it is a philosophy that determines Xavier's behaviour throughout most of the film, but particularly in the early stages set in Paris. The capital, and by extension republican France, is a foil for Xavier's heteromale persona; a largely feminised space (there are no male counterparts to cramp his style), Paris is his natural and exclusive sexual playground, allowing him to rule the roost, flirt and tease, and believe he can bed any woman who looks twice at him. Gay women (but surprisingly no gay men) conform to the 'female first, sexuality second' mindset, enshrining them within the straight jacket of a symbolic universal equality that has come to 'respect' them as 'women', but little else. Indeed, this straight man's paradise bestows on Xavier superdelusional qualities, to the extent that his parting invitation to Kassia as he leaves *Kookaï* is: "I'd call if I were you". Whether genetically programmed, or desperate to find his perfect match, Xavier has landed back in Paris after his Erasmus year abroad only to find an atomised world of hyper-individualism, interchangeable partners, dykes acting like dudes, and unfulfilled casuality. On the one hand, it is a Paris that appears to sit easily with Xavier's Gallic republican nature, liberated as he is from other pedestrian responsibilities to indulge his more pressing charm offensives. But on another level, the scale of his task to find a perfect match is complicated by the discovery of a republic in crisis: Xavier's Paris reveals a France in transition, from conservative republic to democratic multiculturalism, from Hippopotamus monogamy to sexual particularism, from *Martine à la ferme* to Disney-led *Prince and Princess* revisionism, from the nurturing and exclusive effects of topiary to the unfettered expansion of individualism. And so while Xavier's priority is to travel Europe in search of the perfect female partner (a journey where on a personal level he has to balance the normalising effects of his heteromale Gallic genes, family expectations and normative aspirations, against the temptations of feminine charm that bedevil his every step), his journey also reflects a parallel journey of a nation in search of reconciliation between its old traditions and new obligations, between its 'perfect' and 'imperfect' hexagonal variations.

In the context of a sequel to *L'Auberge espagnole* and the experiences gleaned from transnationality in Barcelona, it would not be amiss to suggest that *Les Poupées russes*, at least in its Parisian settings, does not advance the case for Xavier's positive "exchange value", let alone his shabby treatment of women. If anything, it is William, Wendy's xenophobic brother, who emerges transformed by his meeting with a Russian ballerina (Евгеня Образтсова, [Evgenia Obraztsova]), and for whom otherness represents a pathway to love, marriage and fluent second language acquisition. Viewed in another way, William's unlikely route to romantic self-fulfilment (which the film recounts in flashback to Xavier over the course of a full evening) highlights the 'imperfections' of Xavier's brush with alterity in Barcelona. But at the same time, it also offers up the possibility of a second chance for Xavier should the opportunity arise, which of course it does in London and Wendy. Having convinced his employers that he cannot only speak but write perfect English, he is sent to London to research material for a new soap opera. Long subject to cultural protectionism, attitudes to the English language in many sectors of everyday French life are gradually thawing, in particular among the generation X of Klapisch's filmgoers and the corporate sectors that lie behind his (and his characters') fugues of fancy. Xavier's familiarity with the language, his ease of access to the heart of London, extends his imaginary to a kind of secondFrance, one where romantic possibilities can encompass both the exotic and the familiar, where the daily *merde* can be conjugated as 'same same but different' enough for him to add some marmalade to his eggs and bacon, as he appears to be doing in a pivotal breakfast scene where Wendy performs a similar slightly-failed transnational appropriation via a bad croissant choice. The English language, and the journey, led by the hand of a lover through the streets of London, for Xavier, become appropriable, at reach, perhaps colonisable and ultimately as unthreatening as a reconstituted Irish pub on a French city boulevard.

Klapisch's Eurofrance is both connected to its near continental context and separate, his characters both drawn to difference and opportunity, and petrified of losing their national distinction; obliged to acknowledge that *l'exception française* is perhaps little more than a collective delusion of a nation that, perish the thought, on a broader stage, is revealed as a community of common interest. In particular the linguistic and cultural difference, or perhaps the "différend" to draw on Jean-François Lyotard's strong concept of mutual in-commensuability,[12] both bring former "huis clos" into communication with each other, and reinforce at a second level the norms and codes that anchor each society within systems of radical incomprehension vis à vis each other. London offers the possibility of an alternative to Paris in that it allows Xavier to shake off his heteromale hump and Gallic arrogance (as well as the trappings of *bateaux-mouches* and *Notre Dame* that have framed his idealistic and romantic pinings) and get down to "real life". London is the site of a possible resolution, the place where art (his fictional world and soap opera writing with Wendy) and reality (his loneliness and her domestic plight) converge to shape love in a different direction, one which is more serious, gritty, Pinteresque, Londonesque. But it takes several trips back and forth between London and Paris—a psychological rite of passage if you will—(during which time he rediscovers the delights of the model Celia and invokes the wrath of Wendy's "I just don't get you") before reality finally dawns on him. Klapisch's focus on his subsequent arrivals at Waterloo testifies to the change in Xavier's state of mind as he becomes more Anglicised. In the first episode, he is met by Wendy who acts as his guide through the West End. He even has the consolation of a virtual image of Isabelle (de France again) greeting him on the digital screen as she discusses the financial markets over the global airwaves for Bloomberg. The second arrival however is entirely different. What appears as a direct retake of the first episode soon materialises into a poignant sequence of events as Xavier, a post-modern Stephen Daedalus, shorn of past, nation, identity and memory, makes his way alone through the streets of London to Wendy's flat.

Wendy, of course, is the linchpin in Xavier's transnational tour. She was his best friend among the housemates in *L'Auberge espagnole*. She is now the one who has made the effort to sit Xavier down and have him piece together his past experiences into a coherent narrative. And at the heart of this process, as alluded to above, is getting Xavier to adapt to "real life": when asked by Wendy to reflect on his past, Xavier recalls a scene of himself and a former girlfriend, Neus (Irene Montalá), running nude through the streets of Paris. Nudity, coupled with the urbanity of London and its pub culture,

---

[12] Jean-François Lyotard, *Le Différend* (Paris: Editions de Minuit, Collection "Critique", 1983).

booming rap music and a kiss on an island in the middle of a pedestrian crossing, all serve to ground Xavier in the bare essentials of life. He even begins to assume a certain (albeit comic) bulldog spirit by resorting to violent language to defend Wendy from her ex (Gary Love): "I can speak English now, *man*" (our italics) followed immediately by "Don't fucking come back", all pronounced in the most perfect French accent. However, as light-hearted as this may seem, we would argue that there is a serious edge to these comic vign-ettes, specifically the comic representations of Xavier's appropriation of Englishness. Nudity, it could be argued, is taken too far as he sits bare-chested in the garden swilling lager. Similarly, the British love for curry is taken too far as he contemplates a full English breakfast 'Asian style'. These appropriations jar with authentic cultural and national sensitivities, undermine the serious nature of Xavier's under-standing of exchange value and all in all question the transition to the adult and the real initiated by Wendy. Could it be that London is a Barcelona revisited in that, despite his efforts to integrate and open himself to change, Xavier merely puts his Gallic heteromale persona on hold for a year and in the meantime keeps on playing the Erasmus game or, as in the case of London, takes shallow satisfaction in acting out how he thinks Englishmen traditionally behave? In both instances, the engagement with otherness is problematic, induced perhaps, on one level, by Xavier's wider misunderstanding of his own national make-up and, on another level, by a lack of forward planning about his foreign trips. One is minded in this respect of Georges Perec's *Les Choses* and the two student protagonists Sylvie and Jérôme who abandon France for Tunisia in an attempt to escape the 1960s "société de consommation". They depart in haste, *Pléiade inter alia* in suit-case, and establish a little corner of France in the hot, desert streets of Sfax. Unable to adapt, missing their home comforts and reverting to xenophobia, their minds turn back nostalgically to France. Perec underlines the point that "les *vrais* départs se préparent longtemps à l'avance. Celui-ci fut manqué. Il ressemblait à une fuite".[13] One implication we can draw from this is that Barcelona, London and St Petersburg were never designed in the first place to be life-changing journeys for Xavier: they were, if anything, trips generated by a

---

[13] Georges Perec, *Les Choses: Une histoire des années soixante* (Paris: René Juillard, 1965), p. 122.

compulsory year abroad, or by force of circumstance. But a more compelling implication of the analogy with Perec is that a basic prerequisite to positive engagement with alterity is the understanding of what you are leaving behind and why you are leaving. Xavier's attitude was wrong on all counts, including unresolved issues with family, girlfriend and national institutions. His departures were destined to end in failure.

As suggested earlier, Xavier's personal journey is also the parallel journey of a French republic at a crossroads between a 'perfect' abstract republic where everyone is equal regardless of difference, and a more 'imperfect' pragmatic republic where everyone is equal and difference is acknowledged. Paradoxically however, it is not Xavier returning to France from overseas who takes up the challenge to bridge the republican divide (as we might have expected), but rather a foreign English woman whose otherness from afar manages to not only rationalise the perfect and imperfect motivations confounding Xavier but manages to reconcile them and then forgive him his *homo duplex* condition. In the instinctive knowledge that Xavier is about to take the train to Moscow to meet Celia and thus betray her, Wendy stands her ground triumphantly on the platform, unbowed and as much in love with her betrayal as before. Wendy decrypts Xavier's Frenchness so much so that it is Frenchness that is unexpectedly and indirectly 'othered' from afar: it is not the domestic that is indirectly transformed by Xavier's failed engagement with otherness but rather Wendy's otherness directly transforming the domestic. Wendy is "real life". It is her tolerance, patience and *Englishness* that undoes Xavier and potentially France. So much for a trite slogan on a tee-shirt!

Conclusion

And so it is that Xavier is drawn away, to an 'away' which he finds, like Keats's naughty boy,[14] to be much of a muchness, to be England. England represents an only slightly wider European context, while incarnating and inhabiting a desire for rootedness, homeliness, a way of being French, not in the world but in France in perpetuity, that makes

---

[14] John Keats, "A Song About Myself" (1816).

for a cinema that both looks around, looks different (a bit like the world seen through Attention Deficit Disorder) and looks elsewhere (to Almódovar, to take the most obvious example), yet that clings for dear life to the classical *topos*, the "film à trois" of French cinema. If 'home' and 'away' are terms that recall the road movie, then *L'Auberge espagnole* and *Les Poupées russes* are perhaps movies that time and again, pack their bags, get as far as the crossroads then turn back before even having time to stand in their shoes and wonder. 'Elsewhere', in Klapisch's universe, like the stereotypes that tag to mentions of other countries in France and the linguistic policing that occurs across the nation on a daily basis, is a process of reductionism, exploitation and missed opportunity. If England and the English language occupy privileged places in the Klapischian multiverse through their proximity, and much more importantly their potential for an alternative and 'real' multiculturalism personified for instance in Wendy, they remain nonetheless very French versions of the Anglo, staged, occupied uncomfortably, ultimately appropriated. None of which is particularly worrying *per se*, but when spliced alongside the film's rampantly misogynistic logic (noticeable in Xavier's persistent recourse to thinking of women in terms of dresses, and his pseudo-comic discomfort when talked into wearing one) and its fantasy of heterosexual coupling, they raise concerns about the extent to which the films serve to do little more than reinforce, perhaps defend, a pervasive masculinist French mythology according to which a meaningful heterosexual relationship is both required and detested.

Contributors' Biographies

Fiona Barclay is Lecturer in Francophone Postcolonial Studies at the University of Stirling. Her research focuses on the ways in which France's colonial history in North Africa influences conceptions of contemporary French culture and society. She has published on the function of exoticism and the foreign in French representations of North Africa, and is working on a monograph which focuses on literary representations of France as a postcolonial space.

Martine Fernandes is Associate Professor of French at the University of South Florida St Petersburg. She is *agrégée* with a doctorate from UC Berkeley and the Sorbonne-Paris IV. Her main research interests are contemporary French and Francophone novels, first novels, and immigrant literature. She is the author of *Les Ecrivaines francophones en liberté* (L'Harmattan, 2007). Her interest in Portuguese immigrant writing and culture in France stems not only from her being the daughter of Portuguese immigrants in France, but also from her desire to question current visions of immigration in France and uncover understudied cultural productions.

Katherine Gantz is Associate Professor of French at St. Mary's College of Maryland. Her publications include work in the areas of nineteenth-century Decadent fiction, French cultural studies and American pop culture, as well as in the developing field of French queer theory. Her current project is a discussion of present-day uses of public space in Paris originally designed during the Second Empire.

Angela Giovanangeli is a lecturer in French studies at the University of Technology, Sydney, Australia. Her research interests are in the area of French regionalisation, European interregional cooperation and French language policies.

Kiran Grewal has worked as a lawyer in the areas of immigration, human rights and international criminal law. She is currently a lecturer in the

Department of Sociology and Social Policy at the University of Sydney, where her research spans international feminist theory and activism, gender and nationalism, and diaspora and postcolonial theory.

Sam Haigh is Associate Professor in the Department of French Studies at the University of Warwick. Until recently, she worked on the Francophone Caribbean and has written and edited numerous articles, books and journals on the subject. Her current research is on contemporary French representations of disability in photography, fiction, philosophy and politics.

Joe Hardwick lectures in French cinema, literature and cultural studies at the University of Queensland. He was guest editor for a special edition of the *Australian Journal of French Studies* on French cinema in the new millennium in 2008 and was curator of the French new New Wave retrospective at the Australian Cinémathèque in Brisbane in 2007. He is currently preparing a monograph on wandering protagonists in *le jeune cinéma français*.

Rada Ivekovic is Professor of Sociology at Université Jean Monnet, Saint Etienne, and Programme Director at the Collège International de Philosophie in Paris. Her research interests span comparative philosophy, anthropology, politics and gender studies, and she collaborates extensively with research networks in Europe and Asia. Rada's publications include *Le Sexe de la nation* (Scheer, 2003) and is the author, editor and co-editor of an extensive series of texts considering globalisation and the ideas of nation, language and identity, with a focus on the partition of reason and a commitment to combating inequality and discrimination.

Hélène Jaccomard is Professor of French at the University of Western Australia. Her research revolves around the theory and practice of contemporary autobiographies and fiction written in French. The corpora she studies are informed by issues of discrimination due to health and sexual practices (AIDS/HIV testimonials by women) or dual nationalities (including descendants of Arabic migrants in France and French writers with foreign origins). She is currently working on a monograph on Yasmina Reza's plays.

Brigitte Jandey lectures in the Department of International Studies at Macquarie University, Sydney. She teaches language, literature and French for Business with a focus on intercultural relationships. Her research background is in French literature, in particular women pioneering in French literature, genetic textual analysis and autofiction. In recent years, she has also researched student attrition in first year language studies, and the making of French identity.

Vladimir Kapor is Lecturer in French at the University of Manchester. Prior to this position, he lectured at the University of Western Australia, University of Cyprus and University Lille-3 and held a post-doctoral research fellowship at the University of Melbourne. He is author of two monographs, *Pour une poétique de l'écriture exotique* (L'Harmattan, 2007) and *Local Colour: A*

Travelling Concept (Peter Lang, 2009), and numerous articles on eighteenth- and nineteenth-century French literature, which have appeared in journals such as *Word and Image*, *Eighteenth-Century Studies*, *Nineteenth-Century French Studies* and *Poétique*.

Jean-Marc Kehrès is an assistant professor of French at Trinity College, Hartford, Connecticut, and specializes in eighteenth-century literature and culture. He is the author of *Sade et la rhétorique de l'exemplarité* (Champion, 2001) and his publications include articles on Sade, Marivaux and the press of the Revolution. His current book project focuses on epistolarity in the press of the Ancien régime.

Enda McCaffrey is Reader in French at Nottingham Trent University, UK. He is the author of a number of books including *The Gay Republic: Sexuality, Citizenship and Subversion in France* (Ashgate, 2005), and more recently *The Return of Religion in France: From Democratisation to Postmetaphysics* (Palgrave, 2009). He has been working on debates in the philosophy of religion and French cultural studies.

Ben McCann is Senior Lecturer in French Studies at the University of Adelaide. He has published widely on French cinema, and is the co-editor of *The Cinema of Michael Haneke* (Wallflower, 2010). He is currently completing a book on set design in 1930s French cinema.

Monique Monville-Burston is professor of French Linguistics in the Department of French Studies and Modern Languages, at the University of Cyprus. Her current research interests in general and French linguistics include discourse analysis, in particular journalistic discourse, discourse and sociolinguistics ("youth" language and its representations in cartoons, films and the press), and the history of linguistics. In the area of applied linguistics she works on the acquisition of French as a second language (in particular the acquisition of grammar and discourse).

Martin O'Shaughnessy is Professor of Film at Nottingham Trent University. He is the author of *Jean Renoir* (Manchester University, 2000), *The New Face of Political Cinema* (Berghahn, 2007) and *La Grande Illusion* (I. B. Tauris, 2009). He co-edited *Cinéma et engagement* (L'Harmattan, 2005) with Graeme Hayes. He is particularly interested in cinema and the political.

Murray Pratt is Dean of the School of Arts and Humanities and Professor of French and International Studies at Nottingham Trent University. His publications include articles, chapters and edited and co-edited volumes on autobiography, identities and self-representation in comics, contemporary literature and film; and on European and French cultural identities and belonging.

Chris Reynolds is a Senior Lecturer of French and European Studies at Nottingham Trent University. His research work includes a number of articles in the following areas: the French and European Events of 1968, contemporary social protest movements in France and Europe, and French regionalisation.

Francesco Ricatti has a PhD from the University of Sydney. He is Cassamarca Lecturer in Italian at the University of the Sunshine Coast. He has published numerous articles on the relation between body, emotions and popular culture in Italian and transnational contexts. (For more information about the author, including a list of publication, please visit http://drfric.-wordpress.com/about/.) Currently he is investigating the role played by the football team AS Roma in Roman contemporary history and society. He is also working on a new comparative project on football and identity in migratory contexts.

Alistair Rolls is Senior Lecturer in French at the University of Newcastle (NSW, Australia). His research interests include Boris Vian, Existentialism and French detective fiction. His recent books include *French and American Noir: Dark Crossings* (Palgrave Macmillan, 2009), which he co-authored with Deborah Walker, and an edited collection *Mostly French: French (in) Detective Fiction* (Peter Lang, 2009).

Lawrence R. Schehr is Professor of French at the University of Illinois. His work focuses on nineteenth-, twentieth-, and twenty-first-century literature. In 2009, he published *Subversions of Realism* (Fordham UP) and *French Post-Modern Masculinities* (Liverpool UP), and co-edited an issue of *Yale French Studies, Turns to the Right?*

Carolyn Stott is a lecturer in French Studies at the University of Sydney, Australia. Her research interests include detective fiction and the roman noir, immigration, race and identity, and the city of Paris—its history, sociology and literature. She is currently writing a book on the representation of the Parisian suburb of Belleville in literature and popular culture.

Russell West-Pavlov is Professor of Postcolonial Literatures at the Free University of Berlin, Germany. His most recent book publications are *Spaces of Fiction / Fictions of Space: Postcolonial Place and LiteraryDeiXis* (Palgrave Macmillan, 2010) and *North-South / East-West: Global Entanglements in Post-Imperial Writing in French and German* (Trier: WVT, 2010).

Index